"Sonny" Hoffman

Speech

ANDREW THOMAS WEAVER
CHAIRMAN OF THE DEPARTMENT OF SPEECH, UNIVERSITY OF WISCONSIN

GLADYS LOUISE BORCHERS
ASSOCIATE PROFESSOR OF SPEECH, UNIVERSITY OF WISCONSIN
DIRECTOR OF SPEECH TRAINING, WISCONSIN HIGH SCHOOL

HARCOURT, BRACE AND COMPANY

New York · Chicago

COPYRIGHT, 1946, BY
HARCOURT, BRACE AND COMPANY, INC.

All rights reserved. No part of this book may be reproduced in any form, by mimeograph or any other means, without permission in writing from the publisher.

[c · 11 · 46]

PRINTED IN THE UNITED STATES OF AMERICA

Preface

IN ITS APPROACH to the problems of speech training, this new textbook is definitely functional. Principles and practice are organized around the four major objectives formulated by a national committee of representative educators: (1) self-realization, (2) happy social relationships, (3) good citizenship, and (4) economic efficiency. We have accepted these goals as the controlling criteria of all educational processes and have endeavored to present the various forms of speech as indispensable correlates of them. We believe that without considerable competence in speech it is impossible to attain a satisfactory degree of self-development, to make adequate social adjustments, to discharge the full responsibilities of citizenship, and to fit oneself effectively into the economic order.

It should be noted that these four fundamental aims of education are not mutually exclusive. Indeed, there is so much overlapping among them that it is difficult to decide under which to classify specific phases of speech. For example, shall we treat visible action and voice mainly as means of self-realization, social adjustment, civic living, or earning a livelihood? Obviously action and voice are vital in each of these. However we have decided to consider all fundamental skills in the management of action, voice, language, and meaning in Part I, on the premise that, before we can deal properly with speech problems involving other persons, we must learn these basic techniques of making the best and the most of ourselves. Needless to say, after we have achieved a working measure of self-cultivation, we shall find that the give and take of social, civic, and business contacts will stimulate our personal powers into still further growth which should continue as long as we live.

We have earnestly tried to make the exercise projects with which the book is replete as definite and concrete as possible. We have included none which we have not tried in the fires of actual classroom experience. Our purpose has been to provide pupil and teacher with such explicit directions for the practical application of principles that, through daily practice, specific speech skills may flower from the soil of knowledge. There are many more of these drills than will be assigned in any single course. This fact will permit teachers to enjoy considerable latitude of choice and will allow for differences in emphases and points of view.

The reader who turns the pages of this book for the first time may be impressed with the number of drawings and photographs which it contains. We have included these illustrations not merely to make the book more interesting, although we hope that they may accomplish this good result; they are designed to dramatize and clarify our treatment of principles and techniques. They are closely integrated with the text and are to be studied as carefully as the printed pages. We regret that there is no way by which sound motion-pictures can be put into textbooks. Speech is as volatile and fluid as life itself and static pictures fail to suggest its living and dynamic essence.

We have planned the book for use in the senior high school. It is so organized that it may be adapted easily to a wide variety of circumstances and conditions. It offers sufficient material for a two-year course but it readily may be telescoped into a one-year or even a one-semester course. A single-semester course can be based upon the Preview and Part I. Such a course can be extended to a full year by adding Part II. Specialized courses in Public Speaking, Discussion, Interpretation, Debating, Play Production, and Radio Broadcasting can be taught from this text by combining the materials on fundamentals with those on the particular activities to be stressed. In schools where speech training is an integral part of other courses — science, social studies, mathematics, English, music or art — or where each teacher, without regard for traditional subject-matter boundaries, seeks to contribute what he can to the vital experiences of the student, this book offers the fundamental and specialized materials which will be required.

Whatever the shortcomings of our work may be, they do not spring from inexperience. This volume is the mature fruit of many years of teaching and of much deep reflection. We hope that it may find a useful place among the texts available to teachers in the field of speech.

Madison, Wisconsin

Andrew Thomas Weaver
Gladys Louise Borchers

Contents

A PREVIEW   1

    Successful Living Requires Four Goals   1
    Analyzing Our Speech   5

Part One   SELF-REALIZATION THROUGH SPEECH

CHAPTER ONE   **AN INVENTORY OF OUR SPEECH**   13

    The Basic Elements   13
    Learning to Speak   16
    The Importance of Satisfactory Speech   18
    The Qualities of Good Speech   20

CHAPTER TWO   **VISIBLE ACTION**   30

    Reasons for Acquiring Mastery of the Whole Body   31
    General Principles of Visible Action   35
    Posture — Movement — Gesture   38
    Gaining Skill in Body Control   45

CHAPTER THREE   **VOICE**   53

    How the Voice Works   54
    General Rules for Improving the Voice   62
    Poor Voices and What to do About Them   63
    Useful Qualities of Voice   68
    The Voice and Meaning   71
    The Problem of Vocal Interestingness   81

CHAPTER FOUR   **PRONUNCIATION**   97

    Letters and Sounds   97
    Dialects   101
    The Elements of Spoken Language   102

What Is the Dictionary?	103
How to Use the Dictionary	104
Words in Connected Speech	108

CHAPTER FIVE **LANGUAGE AND MEANING** 119

Building a Vocabulary	120
Methods of Defining Words	123
Meanings and Context	126
Kinds of Meaning	128
Oral and Written Styles Have Characteristics in Common	130
Good Oral Style Differs from Good Written Style	135
Sources of Differences Between Spoken and Written Language	138
Differences Between Spoken and Written Language	141

CHAPTER SIX **CREATIVE LISTENING** 163

Creative Listening Is Active Listening	165
Creative Listening Is Selective Listening	166
Two Kinds of Speeches	169
How to Take Notes	170

Part Two SPEECH IN HUMAN RELATIONSHIP

CHAPTER SEVEN **KEYS TO THE MIND** 179

Getting and Holding Attention	181
Attention and Perception	187

CHAPTER EIGHT **CONVERSATION** 196

The General Test of Good Conversation	197
Ten Considerations in Improving Conversation	198

CHAPTER NINE **CLASSROOM SPEAKING** 224

Practice Good Speech in all Classes	227
Common Weaknesses in Classroom Speaking	229

CONTENTS

CHAPTER TEN STORYTELLING — 237

- Aims in Storytelling — 237
- The History of Storytelling — 241
- Choosing the Story — 243
- Preparing the Story — 248
- Telling the Story — 250

CHAPTER ELEVEN INTERPRETATIVE READING — 255

- Purpose and Nature of Interpretation — 255
- Understanding the Written Code — 257
- Giving the Meaning to Others — 265
- Interpretation and Impersonation — 274

CHAPTER TWELVE DRAMATICS — 318

- Informal Play Production — 321
- Formal Play Production — 325
- The Principles of Acting — 330
- Staging a Play — 338

CHAPTER THIRTEEN PUBLIC SPEAKING — 346

- Steps in Preparing a Speech — 346
- Types of Speeches — 364
- Methods of Delivering Speeches — 368

Part Three SPEECH IN CIVIC LIVING

CHAPTER FOURTEEN DISCUSSION — 391

- The Purposes of Discussion — 393
- Types of Discussion — 396

CHAPTER FIFTEEN DEBATING — 401

- Debate as a Method of Determining Policies — 401
- The Proposition for Debate — 406

Contest Debating	408
New Types of Debate	417

CHAPTER SIXTEEN **PARLIAMENTARY PROCEDURE** 420

Organizing a Group	422
Conducting Business	425
Duties of Members	427
Condensed Working Code	432
Constitution and Minutes of a School Society	437

CHAPTER SEVENTEEN **RADIO SPEAKING** 443

Why Radio Speaking is Different	444
Script Writing	451

Part Four SPEECH IN BUSINESS

CHAPTER EIGHTEEN **TELEPHONING** 457

Improving Telephone Technique	458
Telephone Etiquette	461

CHAPTER NINETEEN **INTERVIEWS AND CONFERENCES** 474

The Interview	474
The Conference	483

CHAPTER TWENTY **DICTATING LETTERS** 491

Planning the Letter	492
The " Seven C Qualities " of a Good Business Letter	494
Dictating Distinctly	499

CHAPTER TWENTY-ONE **BUYING AND SELLING** 504

Successful Buying	504
Successful Selling	508
How to Make and Receive Complaints	515

CONTENTS

CHAPTER TWENTY-TWO BUSINESS SPEECHES	520
Conference Speaking	521
Promotional Speaking	522
Expository Business Speaking	524
Goodwill Speeches	526

Part Five AFTER HIGH SCHOOL

CHAPTER TWENTY-THREE SPEECH AND GOING TO COLLEGE	533
CHAPTER TWENTY-FOUR SPEECH AND LIFE VOCATIONS	542
Selecting the Job	543
Applying for the Job	547
On the Job	548
Better Living Through Better Speaking	550

A Preview

WE ARE GOING to make our own careers in the world. Our parents, our teachers, and our friends are not going to work them out for us. They will help us to get started, they will encourage us along the way, but in the final analysis, we are the ones who will make of our lives successes or failures. Success is 90 per cent a matter of beginning right; some persons find that out too late. They dream about what might have happened if they had started earlier, if they had been better informed at the beginning, or if they had had better luck. Most happy and successful people agree that, in large measure, everyone is the master of his own fate. They believe that we can do pretty much what we want to do. They discount luck; they attach more importance to careful foresight, skillful planning, good management, and hard work.

SUCCESSFUL LIVING REQUIRES FOUR GOALS

A national educational committee made up of parents and teachers has said that in order to live satisfactorily, an individual needs to attain four goals. He must discover and develop his own potentialities; he must learn to get along with others in his home and in his community; he must be able to do his part in governing the democracy in which he lives; and he must earn a satisfactory living.

One of the principal factors in making the most of ourselves, in getting along with others, in contributing to government, and in earning a living, is the ability to speak effectively. Emerson said: " A man cannot speak but he judges himself. With his will, or against his will, he draws his portrait to the eye of his companions by every word. Every opinion reacts on him who utters it."

Goal One: Self-realization. We have all experienced the feeling of inadequacy and insecurity resulting from participation in conversations when we stumble and mumble instead of speaking clearly and interestingly. We have all felt the lack of confidence accompanying recitations which our classmates were unable to hear and understand. Some of us know how it feels to learn that our voices have been labeled unpleasant or inexpressive. Some of us have been criticized for disagreeable facial expressions when talking with others. Some of us have monotonous or antagonistic visible mannerisms. Some of us are at a loss to know how to use the right words and sentences. Some of us are handicapped as listeners because we are prejudiced or uninformed. If we have never had these experiences, we are rare persons indeed. Most people have them occasionally; some, frequently; and others, constantly. One major purpose of the course which we are now taking is to reduce the number of times we are made unhappy by ineffectiveness in speech.

The first step in becoming our best selves is to discover our strong and our weak points. When we have clear pictures of our needs, we can lay out an intelligent program for improvement. For most of us, an exploratory venture in which we set out to discover ourselves will turn out to be a rediscovery of our capabilities in speech. The chances are that with effort and direction we shall find ourselves more able than we have believed.

Goal Two: Human relationships. The importance of speech in human relationships has always been recognized. Four thousand years ago Ptah Hotep, an Egyptian, wrote a manual of rules for effective living. He gave it to his son because he wanted him to be successful and happy. "Make thyself a craftsman in speech," he said, "for thereby thou shalt gain the upper hand. The tongue of a man is his weapon, and speech is mightier than fighting." Cicero expressed the same idea: "For it is by this one gift that we are most distinguished from brute animals, that we converse together, and can express our thoughts by speech." Robert Louis Stevenson wrote: ". . . it is in talk alone that we can learn our period and ourselves. In short, the first duty of a man is to speak; that is his chief business in this world; and talk, which is the harmonious speech of two or more, is by far the most accessible of pleasures. It costs nothing in money; it is all profit; it completes our education, founds and fosters our friendships, and can be enjoyed at any age and in almost any state of health."

In an interesting fable, Kipling stressed the importance and power of speech as a way of getting on with others. He told of a man who came to a strange land where no one had ever used speech. This man taught the citizens how to talk, and everyone, recognizing the power of speech, called the teacher a miracle man. The king, observing the influence of speech among his people, felt that it was dangerous to have in his land a man more powerful than the ruler. He therefore put the miracle man to death. But lo, the real miracle was the talk rather than the man; and since the teacher had taught well, the talk remained, and the power of the king was not so great as the power of the oral communication which his subjects had mastered.

Speech is a way of living with others. Woodrow Wilson called it "a meeting of minds." There is no worse situation for most of us than to be isolated. One of the most dreadful forms of punishment is solitary confinement, putting a prisoner off by himself and denying him all human companionship. If this treatment is long-continued, insanity is almost certain to result. The lower animals are content with merely physical companionship; for them the presence of others of their kind is all that is necessary. But man wants more; he wants mental and spiritual comradeship, and he attains it principally through speech.

It is extremely important for us to make the right impression in our face-to-face relationships; to know how to get and hold attention in all speech situations; to communicate effectively with our families at home; to get along with our friends at school; to be able to say what we wish to say in class; to stir up rich and detailed meanings when reading aloud; to make characters in plays live as real people; and to express our views and convictions effectively in public.

Goal Three: Civic responsibility. Participation in government is the third essential factor in successful living. Democratic government is conducted by people who speak. If an American accepts his full responsibility of citizenship, he must be prepared to discuss vital questions and to hold public office. The duties of citizenship, however, begin in the home and in the school. Most schools have some form of self-government; if we are good citizens, we participate in it. Discussions with our friends in our homes or while walking to and from school; discussions in club meetings and assemblies, or over the radio; and discussions with representatives from other schools — all these are helpful in reaching the successful solution of school problems. We may be members of, and hold offices in, one or more clubs where a knowledge of parliamentary law is a necessity; or there may be propositions up for adoption or rejection which require an understanding of, and skill in, debate.

Our responsibilities as high-school citizens are not so different from our parents' responsibilities as American citizens. Even before we are old enough to vote, we well may discuss local, state, and national questions with our parents and friends. In the classroom, in the neighborhood store, on the bus, in our fathers' offices, and in our homes we participate in discussions of current events. A citizen of a democracy must help to solve the problems of the community, the state, the nation, and the world of which he is a part. This duty may involve merely discussion and voting, but it also may lead to holding office. When selected for leadership, the true American citizen should be prepared to accept and discharge his full responsibilities.

If we study the characteristics of our school leaders, we will discover that good voice quality, expressive and communicative action, mastery of the English language, acceptable social attitudes, and something worth while to say have helped to make these people the leaders they are. Most men and women in high offices all over the world know how to say effectively what they want to say.

Goal Four: Economic efficiency. Economic efficiency has been set up as the fourth goal of all education. The average person considers his job, selects his job, applies for his job, and holds his job,

SUCCESSFUL LIVING REQUIRES FOUR GOALS

through speech. Let us note that there is not one of the following for whom speech is unimportant: doctors, lawyers, teachers, secretaries, homemakers, farmers, engineers, journalists, clerical workers, ministers, nurses, merchants, salesmen, business executives, maids, bus drivers, railroad conductors, clerks, actors, public entertainers, diplomats, politicians, unskilled laborers, designers, bankers, airplane pilots, miners. In the United States today there are more than twenty thousand different ways of earning a living, and effective speech is useful in every one!

Not only is it desirable for us to get and hold jobs that bring us a good income; it is important also that we invest that income wisely. In buying and selling, the need for speech is obvious. It might be interesting to try purchasing a quart of milk at the corner grocery store without using speech; buying a new fall or spring outfit without saying a word to the clerk; or opening an account at the bank in complete silence. Without oral communication, it is almost as difficult to spend our incomes as it is to earn them. Telephoning, making appointments, holding interviews and conferences, dictating letters, and delivering formal speeches are all involved in winning success in business. Education for economic efficiency requires speech training.

ANALYZING OUR SPEECH

It is not possible to accomplish at once all of the purposes of education. We must attack our problems one at a time. Since it is our own speech that we intend to improve, it is important at the very outset to take an inventory to find out what habits of speech we wish to retain and what habits we wish to replace with better ones.

In deciding just what kind of speakers we will make of ourselves, we must realize that a good voice which we admire in someone else may not be a good voice for one of us. The best pitch, volume, quality, and rate are determined by the size and shape of one's vocal resonators and the structure of one's body. Since no two persons have exactly the same bodily structure, it follows that no two voices can or should be exactly alike.

The same principle of individual differences must be followed in attempting to improve our visible actions in speech. We must learn how we can make our own actions most effective. The way another person moves and acts may not be at all appropriate for us; our height, build, and weight are not the same as his. Moreover, language and subject matter, like action and voice, will be satisfactory only when they grow out of our own personal experiences.

No one of these four elements — voice, visible action, language, and thought — can be neglected; each should be perfected to fit us and no one else. As we proceed with our training in speech, we should each become less like other people and more like our own best selves.

To make our purposes in speech training clear, let us examine some typical high-school students to see wherein they succeed or fail as speakers.

Although Ralph Weeks is not perfect in the other three elements of speech, his principal weaknesses are in visible action. His voice is clear and expressive, he usually pronounces his words correctly, he finds phrases and sentences to say what he wants to say, and his subject matter is worth while. But unfortunately, in spite of these good qualities people avoid him when he talks. If he stands before an audience, he moves about constantly in ways that have no proper relation to the thoughts and feelings he is expressing. He buttons and unbuttons his coat, toys with objects near at hand, and thus says with his actions that he is very ill at ease. In conferences, interviews, and conversations he shows similar unfortunate habits. He slides down in his chair, crosses one leg over the other and then reverses the process, pulls at his tie, and adjusts and readjusts his coat or sweater. His facial expression is equally annoying. He grins with embarrassment, he squints, he bites his lips, and he raises and lowers his eyebrows when such changes emphasize his discomfort rather than the ideas he is trying to communicate. The quickest way for an individual like Ralph Weeks to improve his speech is to improve his bodily action. In Chapter Two are specific suggestions from which Ralph or any student like him can lay out a remedial program.

Unlike Ralph Weeks, Ruth Arnold is not handicapped by poor visible action. Her facial expression is appropriate, and she can use her visible action effectively to emphasize important ideas. Since she has read widely and lived interestingly, others are eager to hear what she says. Her command of language enables her to express her ideas exactly.

Ruth's main weakness lies in her voice. It is nasal, high-pitched, and lacking in force. Perhaps Ruth realizes that her voice has an unpleasant quality, and that is why she speaks very softly. True, this practice conceals the other weaknesses, but it also conceals the worth-while meanings which Ruth wishes to communicate to her listeners. Ruth's speech problem, then, is primarily one of voice improvement. She will be able to make the most of her abilities in visible action, language, and thought by substituting a good voice for her poor one. She will discover the elements of her remedial program in Chapter Three.

William Holman's main trouble seems to be with the pronunciation of words. When he speaks or reads aloud, he either pronounces the words incorrectly or hesitates so long before saying them that he gives the impression of being unfamiliar with them. William is especially careless about final consonants. In words ending in *ing* only the sound of *n* is heard; in *wouldn't* both the *d* and the *t* are dropped; *git* is substituted for *get; jist* for *just;* and *yuh* for *you*. It is difficult to get the general trend of what William is saying because of the impression of carelessness he always makes. In laying out his plan for improvement, he should take advantage of his fine, well-controlled body, his pleasant voice quality, his interesting experiences, and then concentrate on learning how to pronounce his words.

Frank Martini, like William Holman, should turn to Chapter Four for advice on his first steps in speech improvement, although his difficulty stems from a different source. Frank was born in Italy and speaks with a marked foreign accent. In addition to typical Italian sound substitutions, he has a speech rhythm which is clearly not American. Because he has lived in both Europe and America, he possesses exceptionally interesting subject matter for public speeches as well as for conversation. He controls his body well, has a pleasant voice quality, and speaks English fluently. His speech will be acceptable when he pronounces his words without a trace of dialect.

Shirley Cooper has more skill in some of the elements of speech than any other student in high school. She has acted in several plays, and her audiences have been enthusiastic about the way she makes them feel and understand the characters she portrays. She always remembers her lines, and uses inflections of voice which bring out the finer details of the meaning. She is so skillful with pantomime that an audience forgets she is Shirley Cooper and thinks of her only as the character she is playing. Shirley also knows how to interpret literature aloud. Seldom is one of her listeners inattentive. In short, Shirley is successful in speech when she does not have to depend upon her own words and sentences. When she does, her language is not clear, it is not precise, and it does not sound well. Therefore she can improve her speech most by concentrating on the elements of language which are considered in Chapter Five.

Richard Fairchild has little worth-while subject matter about which to speak. This is unfortunate, since the other elements of his speech are satisfactory. A well-controlled body, an expressive voice, cultured diction, and well-constructed sentences give him the ability to speak well, but he sorely needs more interesting ideas to communicate. Frequently his listeners walk out on him with such comments as " superficial," " empty," " hot air," " stupid." Richard will profit from a careful study of the sections on meaning in Chapter Five. Also he will want to do everything else that he can to acquire worth-while and interesting things to say.

Helen Smith gives the impression of being inconsiderate of others in conversation. She talks so much more than she listens, and she interrupts others so often, that her schoolmates avoid her. She might well begin her program of self-realization by concentrating on Chapter Six.

The importance of individual analyses. An examination of these seven high-school students shows the importance of individual analysis. It demonstrates the folly of prescribing the same remedial program for all. It indicates that one person may have marked skill in the very element of speech in which another suffers from a disabling deficiency. It suggests the need for an examination of each individual's speech at the very beginning of this course in order that he may concentrate his time and effort where they will do him the most good. It opens the way to accomplishing the first aim of education — " Self-realization through Speech," discussed in Part One of this book. This in turn lays a foundation for success in Parts Two, Three, and Four, which follow: "Speech in Human Relationships," "Speech in Civic Living," and "Speech in Business."

Tests of Comprehension and Application

1 Make a careful study of your own speaking ability. What are your conclusions? Write out your impressions in detail. Read your description of yourself to your best friend and profit by his comments. Get the reactions of other members of your class. See whether they agree on your strong and weak points. Write out your final appraisal and conclusions. Now, knowing what you want to change and what you want to keep, you have started your speech-training program.
2 What are the four elements of speech? In which lies your greatest strength? In which lies your greatest weakness?
3 Select students in class who are skillful in each of the following: (a) the use of visible action, (b) the use of voice, (c) the use of language, (d) the use of worth-while subject matter.
4 Select students in class who are weak in each of the elements mentioned in Exercise 3.
5 Write a paper on "Good Listeners Are in Demand."

Part One

SELF–REALIZATION THROUGH SPEECH

THE BASIC OBJECTIVE *of the educational process is to develop the latent powers of the individual. A man's first duty is to make the best of himself. Such self-realization is prerequisite to efficiency and to happiness in living, and no man can become his best self unless he perfects his speech.*

1   An Inventory of Our Speech

2   Visible Action

3   Voice

4   Pronunciation

5   Language and Meaning

6   Creative Listening

CHAPTER ONE *An Inventory of Our Speech*

AT THE OPENING of each new year, the merchant takes inventory; he checks over his stock in trade and makes a careful list of items on hand. Perhaps as we begin this course it may be profitable for us to take stock of our speech in order to determine for ourselves at what points it is satisfactory and at what points it is disappointing. We may well remember President Lincoln's words spoken in quite another connection: " If we could first know where we are, and whither we are tending, we could better judge what to do and how to do it."

THE BASIC ELEMENTS

At the outset it is well for us to understand clearly that in normal speech there is a fusing of four basic elements: (1) visible bodily action, (2) voice, (3) language, and (4) mental processes. If we would know what our speech really is like, we should consider it carefully from each of these four essential angles.

Visible bodily action. When we are speaking, we reach other people through their eyes as well as through their ears. Tennyson tells us that " things seen are mightier than things heard." This is true because the visible element is older than the other elements; man used visible signs for purposes of communication before he had developed voice and language. Therefore what we say in the form of visible action may outweigh what we say in words and voice. Thus meaningful visible action may become one of our greatest assets in speech and one of our most fundamental sources of power over others.

Voice. Next in developmental order after visible action comes voice. We affect other people by the vocal sounds we make — quite apart from the words we utter. This element of voice includes: tones, inflections, rhythms, stress, timing, and all of the variants which make up the "tune" to which our spoken words are set. We should understand clearly that voice colors and determines language meanings; by voicing a sentence in different ways we can give it a variety of meanings. Through skillful use of voice we can indicate the special sense in which we are using our words and reveal the attitudes and purposes which lie behind the language itself.

Language. In Chapter Five of this book we shall present a detailed statement of the speaker's major problems in the field of language. It may suffice to say here that the words, phrases, and sentences which we use to make our meanings effective in the thinking and feeling of others must be selected judiciously and competently if our speech is to measure up to what we want it to be.

Mental activity. Finally, we must take into account the element of mental activity, without which our speech becomes as sounding brass or a tinkling cymbal. Our visible actions, our voices, and our language must serve our purposes, our attitudes, our ideas, our desires, and our feelings. Without proper organization of our mental processes we can never reach a high level of efficiency in speech. There can be no substitute for having something really worth while to say. When two speakers are equal in visible action, voice, and language, but one is superior in mentality, we must concede an enormous advantage to him.

All elements are important. If we can completely master any one of these four elements of speech, we shall get along fairly well with other people. If we can handle two of them in an outstanding manner, we shall have unusual social influence. If we have three of them at our service, we shall be well on the road to distinction.

The best plan for most of us is to make an honest effort to improve all of these necessary elements of good speech. It is a mistake to rely upon any one of them exclusively — or almost so. We can do better than we are doing now in all these elements if we will only try, and no program of self-improvement will bring us greater returns for our investment than will the time we spend in trying. One trouble with speech is that we take it for granted; we assume that we are doing about as well as we can, and let it go at that.

However, education is a struggle to move up from the imperfect and the unsatisfactory to the perfect and the satisfactory. The old adage "The good is often the enemy of the better" applies in full strength to speech training. Frequently those who are rather above the average in speaking ability make the least effort to improve; and yet when they do undertake a program of self-betterment, they grow more rapidly than do those not so well equipped by nature. So it will pay all of us to look into the complicated habits which make up our speech. By taking our speech habits apart and putting them back together again, we shall learn how they work. Also we shall discover the effectiveness of our speech habits. Undoubtedly, we shall find out some very startling things about ourselves.

We have already had thousands of lessons in speech. Since the day we uttered our first word we have been exposed to a great variety of influences, which have made our speech what it is at this moment. Imitation has played an important role in our learning, so much so that family resemblances in speech are quite as marked as family resemblances in physical features. Now, as we start afresh, we may well remember the sergeant who after drilling the awkward squad for some time with little effect, grew exasperated and said, "I wish you fellows would just step out here in front and take a look at yourselves!" The teacher will do the best she can to help us in this difficult process of hearing and seeing ourselves as others hear and see us. Our classmates also will be able to give us valuable assistance — if we can learn to take their criticisms without too many hurt feelings.

People often neglect opportunities for speech improvement in their earlier days; then, when they have grown up and have found that their poor speech habits are damaging their lives, they set about the long-delayed and arduous task of bettering themselves. Such people usually find that late learning is costly in time, effort, and embarrassment. Our speech class will offer us opportunities to get some indispensable practice, guided by competent, kindly, and constructive criticism. Furthermore, in the classroom failures do not hurt so much as they will later in our lives. After all, the amount of gain we are going to make in the class must be directly proportional to the intelligent and sustained effort we are willing to invest.

LEARNING TO SPEAK

Perhaps as we approach the task of relearning some of our speech habits, it may be helpful to consider how they were acquired in the first place. If a baby were perfectly satisfied all of the time, if he had everything that he wanted, he would never learn to speak. The mother who always hovers over the baby, feeding him, moving him, picking him up, and giving him things to play with, may easily overdo such solicitous care to the point where the child is deprived of any real incentive for developing normal speech. Why should such a child learn to speak? Why should he take the trouble to develop all the complex habits involved in speech when he is getting along well enough without them?

But, fortunately, most babies are not perfectly comfortable and satisfied all the time. They thresh about with their arms and legs, and they utter vocal sounds. These visible activities and voiced sounds have little or no communicative value at first, but as soon as the mother learns to interpret them as signs of specific wants, we have the beginnings of speech. It does not take a baby long to learn that certain movements and sounds cause specific responses on the part of his mother! However, as the child grows older and reaches the point at which he can control his muscles more precisely, the mother rightly insists that her child learn to use the specific sounds and the visible actions upon which human beings have agreed long before the child was born. Thus in this all-important matter of communication the baby learns to conform to the social order about him. We all know boys and girls who show in their speech the evidence of bad training; they use " baby talk " even though they are old enough to know better. People who have been encouraged to carry babyish habits of any kind on into manhood and womanhood may be fearfully handicapped.

Language is acquired. Once the child has learned that if he wants things he must ask for them in the code upon which society has agreed and not in his own special baby lingo, his method of acquiring speech consists almost wholly in imitating the voiced sounds and the visible actions which others use. Naturally enough, the child employs the particular language of those with whom he grows up. The Chinese child learns one language; the Norwegian child, another; and the American, still another. Each language is a special conventional code agreed upon by the people who live together in one area of the earth's surface — at least by those who have lived together in one area at some time in their history. You may remember Mark Twain's story of the American tourist who wrote: " Even the young children over here in Paris talk French fluently."

If we are going to get along with our fellow human beings, we need to learn all we can as to ways and means of indicating to them what we think and feel; and we must also learn to infer from their visible actions, voice, and language what they are thinking and feeling. Thus learning to speak really means learning to make and to interpret the outward signs through which human beings reveal to others their attitudes, thoughts, and desires. The most difficult problem in learning to speak is to control all our muscles in such a way as to say one thing at a time and not several different and conflicting things.

Speech a two-sided activity. We have often heard that it takes two to make a quarrel. It also takes at least two to make speech: the speaker, and the one to whom he speaks. Although we generally refer to " the party of the second part " as the listener, he is more than a listener; he is also an observer. The one on the receiving end of the speech process normally receives through both his eyes and his ears. In satisfactory speech the speaker is always vividly aware of the fact that he is speaking to someone in particular, not just talking to hear himself talk. If we are ever tempted to talk merely for the purpose of clearing up our own cloudy notions, we ought not to inflict what we are saying on anyone else; we should go off by ourselves and not bother other people. We may say fairly that speech is good directly in proportion to the strength of the inner urge to make what one is saying effective upon the thinking and the feeling of someone else.

THE IMPORTANCE OF SATISFACTORY SPEECH

In 1944 General Sir Bernard Law Montgomery said: " I have never once issued a written order to my subordinate generals about operations. Command must be personal and it must be verbal; otherwise it will have no success, because it is wrapped up in the human factor.

" I often have at the back of my mind a passage from the New Testament: ' Except ye utter by the tongue words easy to be understood, how shall it be known what is spoken? ' That is a very valuable thing to remember.

" How can a soldier know what is wanted unless you tell him clearly and personally? "

The failure of people to get along satisfactorily with others is caused by the inability to speak well more often than by any other reason. It is not so much a lack of intelligence that brings unhappiness to us as it is a lack of capacity to adapt ourselves to our social surroundings. Speech is the most useful instrument that man has yet devised for establishing and maintaining satisfactory relations with others. Speech has done more to advance culture and civilization than have all the other inventions of man put together. In this book we are interested in all forms of speaking: conversation, informal discussion, interpretative reading, public address, debating, storytelling, dramatics, and radio speaking. We are more concerned about our speech in informal everyday situations than we are about speech in more formal performances on the public platform. Successful public speaking is a great accomplishment, but efficient private speech is much more important for most of us. We cannot hope to get what we want out of life unless we develop the ability to speak effectively.

The old proverb "Speech is silvern; silence is golden" does not mean that people should always prefer to remain silent. It is well enough to be silent when silence is more appropriate than speech and more likely to adapt us satisfactorily to other people, but it is a tragic experience to find ourselves face to face with opportunities to do something worth while and to fail because of inability to talk effectively. There will be innumerable times in our lives when we must speak if we are to amount to anything. The issue will not be to speak or to remain silent, but rather to speak poorly or to speak well.

Speech is not only an important means of communication; it is also an essential factor in thinking. Let us examine this proposition for a moment. The poet Shelley in *Prometheus Unbound* says, " He gave man speech and speech created thought." John B. Watson, one of the foremost of modern psychologists, tells us that thinking is just talking to ourselves. He says: " The feeling entertained by so many that they can think, or even reason, without language is an illusion." On the same point, Sir Richard Paget writes: " The perfecting and improving of human speech and language are essential to the perfecting and improving of the human powers of thought."

This point of view makes it tremendously important that we should work hard and persistently to bring our speech and language up to the highest possible level of efficiency. Man would cease to have his peculiar advantages over other animals if he were to lose his speech. This is why he is well described as " the speaking animal." Any high degree of mental life without speech is a complete paradox; speech skill and mental competence develop together.

Speech and personality are inextricably interwoven. Is it not true that most of our impressions of personalities come from what people say, and how they say it? Let us consider someone whom we know well. Try to leave out all the impressions his speech has made upon us, the words he uses, and the tones and the actions which accompany the words, and we shall find that little remains of his personality. One of our most entertaining radio programs has made a real, living personality out of a ventriloquist's dummy. How has Charlie McCarthy come to be a person? Is it not by " his " characteristic speech patterns? His language and his modes of utterance make Charlie seem so real that some of us actually forget that " he " is carried around in Mr. Bergen's suitcase. To go from the ridiculous to the sublime, do not Lincoln's letters and speeches reconstruct for anyone who will read them a great and living personality? Think how much more vividly we should appreciate his personality could we actually hear and see him as he appeared at Gettysburg.

It follows that if we would acquire positive, pleasing, well-rounded personalities, we should train ourselves to use the speech which characterizes the kind of a person we would like to become. Nobody ever built a refined and cultured personality out of the speech of the gutter, or out of the cramped and starved vocabulary of slang phrases. Slang is all right when it is more vital, expressive, and appropriate than other words; but when it is used to the exclusion of all other language forms, its repercussions upon the personal character of the addict are serious indeed. An education which does not reflect itself in competent, discriminating, and refined speech somehow has failed to accomplish its purpose. The spectacle of a girl at commencement attired in cap and gown, holding her diploma in her hand, and shouting cheap slang phrases to a friend may be grotesque enough to be laughable, but if that type of speech represents the girl's only stock in trade, it is also tragic enough for tears.

THE QUALITIES OF GOOD SPEECH

What tests can we apply to decide when speech is really good and when it is ineffective? Remembering that the ultimate purpose of all speech is to influence someone at the receiving end of the process, we may answer in general terms: *The speaker who in the shortest time can induce those whom he addresses to do willingly what he wants them to do is the best speaker.* Now let us examine this general principle in some of its implications.

Purposefulness. Satisfactory speech grows out of a definite purpose on the part of the speaker and is dominated by that purpose. No one can hope to speak effectively without first settling in his own mind just what he wants to accomplish. Before speaking, we always should ask ourselves: What do I want the person or persons whom I address to understand, to believe, or to do? Too many speakers are aimless. We should remember that a gun is effective not because of the noise it makes or because of the smoke that pours out of its muzzle, but rather because of the precision with which it is aimed. Many speakers hit nothing because they aim at nothing.

What would we think of a man who packed his grip, rushed to the railway station, and took the first train that came along without inquiring where it was going? Yet that is no more foolish than to speak without a purpose; in fact, it might not be so bad, for the aimless traveler probably would not be using up the time and energy of other people without repaying them. Like any other sensible person, the speaker should decide where he wants to go before he starts.

If we are directing someone how to go from one city to another, our purpose should be to convey the necessary information as clearly and easily as possible. If we are talking about the best time we have ever had, our purpose should be to give others all the enjoyment possible. If we are explaining why we have failed to do what was expected of us, our purpose should be to justify our behavior. If we are soliciting a subscription for a magazine, our purpose should be to get the prospect's name on the dotted line. In every instance the speaker's purpose can be accomplished only when those to whom he speaks are induced to respond in the appropriate way. The first requirement of successful speaking, therefore, is for the speaker to make up his mind clearly just what he wants to do.

Visibility and audibility. Some of us as children recited the little jingle

> "Children's speech should always be
> Plain to hear and clear to see."

This applies to adult speech also. The speaker's visible action should be seen and his voice should be heard without straining the eyes and ears of the persons to whom he speaks. We must guard against one error in applying this principle. Sometimes when a child has "spoken a piece," he feels that he has done well because his fond relatives tell him that they have heard every word perfectly. Of course that may be true and still he may not have been worth hearing. However, we need to remember that our chance of getting what we want from other people is pretty poor if they have difficulty in seeing and hearing our speaking. We all have talked over the telephone when only

CONVERSATION AT SEA. *For obvious reasons ships in convoy within a danger zone do not use their radios. This man is talking with someone aboard another ship by means of a visible code. At the same time he is communicating with someone on his own ship via " mike " and sound helmet. What problems are involved in translating visible signals into spoken words and vice versa? (International News)*

about half of what we said reached the person at the other end of the wire and even less than half of what he said reached us. It is difficult to imagine anything much less satisfactory than that kind of conversation. The situation is made worse by the fact that we cannot see each other when we are talking over the telephone. When we each can get the visible signals the other is making, we may be able to piece out the fragments which we cannot hear.

When our signals are indistinct, our speech is likely to fail in achieving its purpose. To a ship which is trying to pass safely through waters infested by enemy submarines, low visibility is a great advantage; but if a ship has been sunk and the survivors in a lifeboat or on a raft are sending signals of distress, visibility is an asset, not a liability. A silencer may make a gun more effective by making it hard to locate; but if a man is lost in a forest and is firing a gun to notify his friends of his predicament, the silencer makes the gun useless. Similarly, a movement too slight to be seen and a tone too weak to be heard are useless as speech signals.

Interestingness. Finally, satisfactory speaking must get and hold attention. So long as a speaker can hold attention, he has a chance to accomplish almost anything. But the moment he loses attention, his actual speaking is at an end, no matter how long he may go on making motions and sounds. If we are in the midst of a telephone conversation and find that the connection has been broken, do we go right on talking, or do we see to it that the connection is restored before we proceed? Just so, whenever a speaker finds the connection broken, he should re-establish it before he continues. Many speakers seem to assume that this law of attention does not apply to them. They speak with a minimum of effort on their part and trust that their hearers will make whatever effort is necessary to get their meaning. Where there is no attention there will be no agreement, no subscriptions, no influence.

Liveliness is almost synonymous with interestingness. When anything is uninteresting, we say that it is " dead." The speaker who wants to hold attention must " come alive," and look alive. If he moves nothing but the muscles in his neck and jaw, there is no very good reason for people to watch him. Once they cease looking, it is not likely that they will give attention to what he is saying. The baby early learns to use its lung power in order to get attention. We have to do the same thing in speaking. We attract attention by the use of vocal force.

People pay attention to what they like and refuse attention to what they dislike. Therefore we can be interesting by being tactful and considerate of others. The speaker who interests us is usually one who seems to understand our feelings and who is sympathetic.

Variety is the keynote of interestingness; perhaps that is why it is called the spice of life. The ultimate compliment which a speaker can receive is such a remark as "We could not think of anything except what you were saying from the time you began until you finished. There wasn't a dull moment." Dull moments come from monotonous vocalization, monotonous visible action, monotonous language, and monotonous thinking. If we would succeed, we should beware of falling into routine habits in our speaking.

Tests of Comprehension and Application

MASTER THE FACTS

1 How do deaf-mutes speak? In what ways is their speech like the speech of normal persons and in what ways different?
2 Discuss the comparative advantages of voice and visible action in speech. If you could have just one of the two, which would you prefer, and why?
3 Do animals speak? Give some specific illustrations to support your answer. What can you learn about human speech from a study of animal communication? Do animals understand human speech? Again illustrate.
4 Show how your interests differ from the interests of someone else in the class, and explain why this difference might be important to anyone who talks to you and to him.
5 How many different kinds of variety can you think of? How many of them can a speaker use?

PRACTICE TO IMPROVE

6 Make a speech to the class, using only pantomime.
7 Can you communicate with the class using voice without words? Try repeating the alphabet or numerals in vocal patterns which will stir up meanings in the minds of your classmates.
8 Give the class a detailed description of the speech habits of some child who is very backward in learning to talk.
9 Have you ever been told that your speech is like that of some other member of your immediate family? Is your voice ever confused with the voice of this person when you answer the telephone? Are you aware of special verbal patterns which seem more or less

peculiar to your family? Do you use expressions which have special meanings within your family circle but which are not fully understood by others? Illustrate.

TEST YOUR PROGRESS

10 Describe some conversationalist or public speaker whom you have recently heard, explaining his weak and strong points in terms of the tests which have been discussed in this chapter.

A SPEECH TEST

11 Consider each of the following questions carefully and write down answers honestly and fairly, *Yes* or *No*. When you are not sure which answer is correct, consult your fellow students or your teacher. The latter should be an especially reliable and helpful critic.
1. Do I make and maintain direct eye contact with others?
2. Am I usually poised?
3. Am I lively and animated?
4. Are my movements and gestures relevant to my meanings?
5. Do my gestures precede the utterance of the words with which they belong?
6. Is my visible action free from distracting mannerisms?
7. Do I complete the gestures which I begin?
8. Does my physical attitude suggest a desire to communicate?
9. Is my visible action drawn on a sufficiently large scale to be seen easily?
10. Are my gestures unnoticed *as gestures?*
11. Do I use gestures whenever they will help?
12. Does my facial expression reinforce my words?
13. Do I mark transitions in the meaning with appropriate visible action?
14. Do I appear free physically?
15. Are my hands and fingers vitally a part of what I am saying?
16. Am I using my whole body?
17. Do my hand and arm gestures start near the center of my body and move outward?

(*Yes* answers to the preceding questions indicate strength in the

MIRROR STUDY OF VISIBLE ACTION. *This high-school girl is making excellent use of the mirror in analyzing her own techniques of visible action. Frequently all that the speech student sees in the mirror is a speech student looking into a mirror! Nevertheless, the mirror rightly employed can be a real aid to the young speaker.* (Keystone View)

use of visible actions. *No* answers indicate weakness. Pay attention especially to your *No* answers. What can you do to make *Yes* answers correct?)

18. Do I avoid eye contact with other people?
19. Are my hands kept out of my speaking by playing with notes, pencils, keys?

20. Do my eyes follow the movements of my hands?
21. Is my face a " dead pan "?
22. Do I lean on the stand, or slouch?
23. Do I start to speak before getting " set "?
24. Do I give an impression of working hard?
25. Do I get my hands between my face and the eyes of those whom I am addressing?
26. Are my arms glued tightly to my sides?
27. Are my movements jerky and abrupt?
28. Do I teeter up onto my toes or rock back onto my heels?
29. Do I sway from side to side?
30. Are my arms rigid in gestures?
31. Do I tug at my coat lapels, coat buttons, belt?
32. Do I overwork one gesture (the index finger, for example)?
33. Are my gestures vague and indefinite?

(*Yes* answers to questions 18–33 inclusive indicate weakness in the use of visible action. *No* answers are desirable. What can you do to make a unanimous *No* vote justifiable?)

34. Do I talk loud enough to be heard easily?
35. Do I use pauses where they will heighten effectiveness?
36. Do I pronounce my words correctly?
37. Do I speak in phrases and sentences rather than in single words?
38. Is my voice free of unpleasant nasality?
39. Do I begin my sentences smoothly and easily?
40. Do I speak in a key or pitch which permits my voice to rise and fall easily?
41. Do I sustain tones to the end of sentences?
42. Do I have sufficient breath?
43. Does my voice vary with my moods and feelings?
44. Do I give each syllable its proper value?
45. Do I emphasize important words and phrases?

(*Yes* answers to questions 34–45 inclusive indicate successful use of voice. *No* answers indicate weaknesses in use of voice. What can you do to justify *Yes* answers throughout?)

46. Do I strain the ears of my listeners?
47. Do I speak in a singsong pattern?

48. Do I speak at a uniform tempo?
49. Do I speak in a monotone?
50. Do I talk through my teeth?
51. Do I overstress words and syllables?
52. Do I slur consonant combinations?
53. Do I drawl when a drawl does not fit the sense?
54. Do I clip my sounds when clipping is inappropriate?
55. Does my voice fade out at the ends of words, phrases, and sentences?
56. Do I overdo my articulation?
57. Do I swallow the ends of words?
58. Do I insert " uh's " and " ah's " between words?
59. Do I use weak and indefinite inflections at the end of statements?

(*Yes* answers to questions 46–59 inclusive indicate weakness in the use of voice. *No* answers suggest strength. What can you do to make all answers *No*?)

60. Is it impossible to distinguish my spoken language from the language of a formal essay?
61. Do I use vague words and expressions?
62. Do I overwork such words as " just," " why," and " and "?
63. Is my language slangy?
64. Do I use long sentences most of the time?
65. Do I use rambling sentences?
66. Do I used mixed figures?
67. Do I use trite expressions?
68. Do I use flowery language when my thought is direct and simple?
69. Do I use involved and complicated sentences?

(*Yes* answers to questions 60–69 inclusive indicate weakness in language. *No* answers are good. Consider what you can do to improve the situations in which you now feel obliged to answer *Yes*.)

70. Is my oral language readily distinguishable from written language?
71. Do I use variety in sentence structure and length?
72. Does my language sound smooth and pleasant?

COMPREHENSION AND APPLICATION TESTS

73. Do I use a large number of personal pronouns, especially "you," "we," "your," and "our"?
74. Are my sentences instantly clear in their meaning?
75. Is my vocabulary understood by those to whom I speak?
76. Do I begin and end what I have to say with strong, impressive sentences?
77. Is there a proper degree of formality in my phrasings?

(The successful speaker should be able to answer questions 70–77 *Yes*. The poor speaker may have to answer some of them *No*. What can you do to make your answers affirmative?)

78. Is my information accurate and adequate?
79. Do I know and consider the attitudes of my hearers?
80. Are my transitions made clearly?
81. Do I figure out in advance just what response I want?
82. Are my ideas put together in an orderly and logical pattern?
83. Do I connect what I am saying with my hearer's interests?
84. Do I capture the attention of my hearer?
85. Do I treat opposing opinions tactfully?
86. Do I clarify my own ideas before I talk?
87. Do I repeat my most important ideas?
88. Do I use stories, anecdotes, illustrations, and examples?
89. Do I try to prove what I assert?
90. Do I make clear to my hearer just what I want him to think, feel, or do?
91. Do I adapt what I am saying to the reactions of my hearers as I go along?
92. Do I keep my temper in trying circumstances?
93. Do I use humor effectively?
94. Do I establish common ground with other people readily?

(Questions 78–94 should be answered *Yes*. *No* answers indicate something amiss in the mental activity from which speech comes. What can you do to overcome the difficulties revealed in your *No* answers?)

95. Do I make many personal references to my own experiences in an egocentric way?
96. Am I short on facts to support my assertions?

97. Do I generally belittle the views of those who disagree with me?
98. Do I "panic" myself without amusing my hearers?
99. Do I use a great deal of sarcasm?
100. Do I drag in irrelevant and controversial issues?
101. Do I make vague and ambiguous statements?
102. Do I fail to define my terms?
103. Do I explain more than is necessary?
104. Do I fail to prepare my material carefully in advance?
105. Do I assume that whatever interests me always will interest others?
106. Do I allow one emotional mood to dominate everything I say?
107. Do I fail to note the responses and attitudes of others?
108. Do I try to cover more than I can in the available time?

(Questions 95–108 should be answered *No*. *Yes* answers betray weaknesses in mental backgrounds of speech. What can you do to change the *Yes* answers in your list?)

A perfect score on the test above would be 108; there are 108 questions which, if answered satisfactorily, would total up to that score. Why not figure out your score on the test? If you are above 80, you are probably already an unusually effective speaker. If you are above 70, you are probably a good speaker. From 50 to 70 would give you a ranking of fair. Below 50 is unsatisfactory. Perhaps you would like to make some amendments to the test. If so, what would they be? After you have checked yourself on the questionnaire, you may want to get your rating from someone else to see whether or not others agree with your own estimates of your performance.

CHAPTER TWO *Visible Action*

LET US ASSUME that some philanthropist has come to our community to invite one boy and one girl to represent the high school at an international conference of secondary-school students to be held in some foreign country. All of the expenses are to be paid by the wealthy man, who intends to select the individuals himself, according to criteria which he has laid down. The first consideration is that the student representatives shall have attractive personalities. The man believes that one of the most important elements of personality is physical appearance, and he plans to eliminate undesirable candidates first by applying the test for that element. Let us assume further that this man is assigned a room in our high school where he will sit in judgment and through which all students will pass. Every high-school boy and girl will enter from one side of the room, pause a moment in front of the judge, and leave the room without uttering a word. If in doing this the student makes a poor impression, he will not be considered further.

Doubtless the man will judge the physical appearance of high-school students in much the same way in which we judge the physical appearance of any person. Very likely he will criticize students most for failing to take advantage of elements of visible behavior over which they have control. He will give credit to boys or girls who are able to make capital of strong points and overcome weaknesses.

There are eight visible elements in personality, and the normal individual can gain control over six of them. Which of the following are susceptible to training and control?

| size | neatness | movement | facial expression |
| clothes | posture | features | mannerisms |

REASONS FOR ACQUIRING MASTERY OF THE WHOLE BODY

There are three principal reasons why a general mastery of the whole body is necessary in learning to speak effectively. They concern: (1) voice control, (2) efficient thinking, and (3) visible speech signals.

Without a controlled body a controlled voice is impossible. Skill in the use of the voice comes only as a result of general muscular control. Voice is produced by exactly the same sort of activity that we use in moving our arms and legs; that is, by the contraction and relaxation of muscles. Since no muscle anywhere in the body can be contracted or relaxed without affecting to some extent every other muscle, great and small, any strain or tension in any muscle of the body is sure to affect the muscles of the vocal apparatus and thus change the character of the voice. Anatomists tell us that there are more than five hundred muscles which have to act together smoothly and properly before we can utter articulate speech sounds. These muscles are so interconnected with the other muscle systems of the body that they cannot be satisfactorily trained separately. To train the voice, therefore, we must " tune up " the whole body.

When we are greatly surprised, frightened, or excited in any way, we are likely to find ourselves partially tongue-tied or even voiceless altogether. During wars, when soldiers are in frightful, nerve-racking situations, their speech is often the first muscular process to be disturbed. Stuttering and even complete loss of voice are among the first symptoms of shell shock. This is to be expected, because under strain the most delicate and complex types of control break down first. Many of these men with aphonia (loss of voice) retain the control of their larger muscles. They walk and make visible signals with their hands and arms. They even write. Yet they cannot make sounds with their voices at all.

Efficiency in thinking depends on the control of muscles. Thinking in speech can be carried on effectively only when a general mastery of the whole body has been achieved. We must learn to think with the whole body and, more important still, we must be able to think with the whole body when speaking. When we are angry, we are angry all over. When we are sad, we are sad all over. Do you remember the old dog Rover who " when he died, died all over "? He could not help it; he was made that way. So are we. We should get over the notion that we do our thinking solely with our brains. We do it with our whole bodies, with *all* there is of us.

The reason for the failure of many persons in speech is not that they are incapable of thinking; the trouble is that they cannot think and speak at the same time. Why? Because speaking puts kinks and twists, strains and tensions, into the muscles which they must use in effective thinking, and so renders these muscles incapable of doing the work of thinking. The most fundamental part of speech training

REASONS FOR ACQUIRING BODY MASTERY

THEODORE ROOSEVELT IN ACTION. *It is apparent from this photograph that the speaker is tremendously energized throughout his body. The facial muscles, the hands, and the arms all suggest " the strenuous life " which " T. R." lived and urged upon his countrymen. An excellent demonstration of " acting all in one piece." (Culver Service)*

is learning to master the body so that we can have all of it at our disposal for thinking when we speak.

What happens to us when we have thought a matter out clearly by ourselves and yet cannot tell the class or the teacher what we think? What happens when we commit to memory a dozen lines of poetry and then cannot stand up before a group of people and repeat the words aloud? We have all noticed the difference between thinking when we are alone and thinking while we are trying to speak with others. The trouble is that when we are attempting to tell others something, our muscles get tied into knots, and our " thinkers " are out of commission. Mark Twain used to tell about a steamboat on the Mississippi which had a very small boiler and a very large whistle. Whenever the whistle blew, the engine stopped. That is exactly what happens to some of us when we try to talk. The effort to speak involves so much strain that there are no muscles left free with which to think. Therefore, since it is plain that both voice and thinking are dependent on a mastery of the whole body, it is evident that what we should develop first is general muscular efficiency.

The visible signals of speech are made with the whole body. Without control of bodily movements there can be no control of the speech signals which people read with their eyes — the signals that can be understood most easily. Let us turn now to the question of using the body in making speech signals. Everything that people see us do means something to them. Our bodies, whether we control them or not, inevitably tell things to those who look at us. The question is: Do our bodies say what we want them to say? The way others feel about us is often determined by what they see us do, even though they may not know why they feel the way they do. When we say, " I do not like So-and-so," we usually do not know just why. But in all probability we have heard him say something or have seen him do something which has turned us against him.

Some years ago in Elberfeld, Germany, there were several trained horses that seemed more intelligent than many human beings. By pointing out letters with their forefeet, thus spelling out words, they could answer many questions. They could multiply, add, subtract, divide, compute cube and square roots, and do other very marvelous " stunts." They amazed all who saw them. Many scientists came to investigate. Finally it was discovered that when a screen was placed between the horses and the man who had trained them, the animals were no longer able to do these remarkable things. The trainer had been making very delicate visible signals with his muscles, indicating to the horses the answers to the problems which they supposedly were solving. The horses had learned to watch his actions and interpret his almost invisible movements. Is it not to be expected that a human being can detect and interpret movements as fine as those which can be seen and understood by a horse? It is often from these subtle, almost unnoticed postures and gestures of the speaker that we get our deepest impressions of his character. What is called " mind reading " is usually muscle reading.

For reasons already explained, when we talk with people we watch them intently. We get meanings from what they do. The signs which they make with their arms, hands, and heads give us more emphatic evidence of their meaning than does their language. Each of us has tried to fool a friend by telling him a " wrong story " and then has been disappointed to find that he has not been fooled at all. From watching us as we told the story, he decided that we were playing a joke on him. In such circumstances one generally says, " I couldn't keep my face straight "; the facial expression gave away the falseness of the story that voice and language were telling.

GENERAL PRINCIPLES OF VISIBLE ACTION

There are five general principles which we may use as guideposts on the road to the control of our bodies for speech: (1) animation, (2) co-ordination, (3) power, (4) seeming naturalness, and (5) appropriateness.

Animation. In developing effective visible action the primary essential is to have the body wide-awake all over. What would we think of an automobile driver who tried to make a speed record with only one-half of the cylinders in the motor working? Suppose the car had eight cylinders and only four were " hitting." What about the other four cylinders? They would be just so much dead weight for the active parts of the motor to pull around. The first thing to do is to tune up the motor and see that every cylinder is working perfectly and that there is nothing useless or broken in the engine.

Just so with anyone who is to speak. He should have no cylinders out of commission. From the soles of his feet to the top of his head, he should be wide-awake, alert, alive, and active. It is hard to talk with others satisfactorily when using all one's resources; one cannot afford to try with less. Too many speakers are dead from the neck down; and some, except for a little activity in the muscles of the throat, jaw, and tongue, are almost dead from the neck up! Their arms and legs are either useless or a positive hindrance to them. Their bodies do little more than support their heads. Frequently not even their facial muscles are in the game.

Animation need not manifest itself in a whirl of outward, visible motion. At its best, it is an inner activity. It is a general readiness to act. We all know the difference between being half-asleep and being wide-awake. The man who is half-asleep cannot talk, he can only mumble. Only the man who is wide-awake can speak earnestly and with vigor. No one can be very much in earnest and not have his feeling affect him all over. We say that people who are enthusiastic about things " go in for them heart and soul." It would be more accurate to say that they go in for them with their whole bodies. The more deeply we feel, the more active we become all over. This is true whether the activity is seen by others or hidden from the eye. Nature made us to work as a unit. So long as we can work easily and as a unit, we do not feel embarrassed.

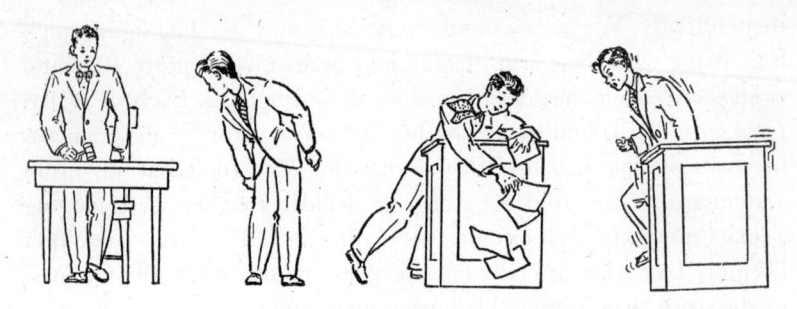

Co-ordination. A second important principle is smoothness in the working together of the parts of the body. Visible action should be smooth, not jerky. To return to the analogy of the automobile: we want a smooth-running engine — what the automobile manufacturers advertise as " smooth power." When the automobile first came into use, it was equipped with a one-cylinder engine that jerked the car along in a series of fits and starts; this was quite a different affair from the sixes and eights of today. Bodily activity needs smoothness even more than does an automobile.

Power. Next we want power. Not only should our automobile have a dependable, smooth-running motor, but it should have power with which to take us up the hills as well as along the level stretches. Just so the speaker should be active all over, all the time. He must make his observers feel that he has the power to do whatever is required. It is effective to give the impression of reserve.

Seeming naturalness. The fourth principle of effective action is seeming naturalness. The speaker must look natural to his audience.

To seem natural requires control, and is a very different matter from doing what one is in the habit of doing regardless of its effect on those with whom he is communicating. This principle requires that the comfort of the audience be regarded as more important than that of the speaker. It demands that when we talk, we do whatever is necessary to give our listeners an impression of naturalness.

The chief trouble with most student speakers is embarrassment. They are shy, overawed, even afraid, and as a result they begin to do almost everything except what they want to do. In their excitement they sometimes " go to pieces "; they tremble, shuffle about, pull at their clothes, and do what they would rather not do. When criticized, they often say that it is natural for them to behave that way before an audience. This statement may be true, but the speaker must learn to substitute for his natural behavior action and movement which make the desired impression on the audience. In the beginning the speaker may have to be unnatural in order to appear natural.

There is only one way to achieve seeming naturalness, and that is to practice diligently. We must ignore many discomforts at first for the sake of the ease which will result when controlled behavior has become a habit. Those of us who play games know this. To place a ball in the corner of the tennis court, to sink a ten-foot putt on the golf green, to make a neat flying tackle, to cut the corner of the plate when the count stands " 3 and 2 " — all such skilled performances are possible only when there has been a great deal of hard preliminary practice. But if we have practiced enough, we do not suffer embarrassment " in the clutch." Such practice makes perfect.

All of the preceding discussion is an attempt to put meaning into the advice " Be natural," so often urged on those who are learning to speak. "Be natural," if it means anything helpful, means "Do not let the task of speaking make you lose control of your muscles." No matter how nervous or frightened we may be in conversation or on the platform, if we *learn to control our muscles*, we can make them say what we want them to say.

Appropriateness. To animation, co-ordination, power, seeming naturalness, should be added appropriateness. Our postures should not tell those to whom we speak that we are flippant when we mean to be serious, impolite when we want to be considerate, half-asleep when we should be wide-awake, uncomfortable when we should be at ease, nervous when we should be poised, informal when we should be formal, antagonistic when we should be friendly, and uncertain when we should be clear and definite. Our actions always should fit the ideas which we wish to communicate.

POSTURE

The five principles of effectiveness in visible action are applied to and exemplified in: (1) posture (the physical position and attitude of the speaker); (2) movement (changes in physical position and attitude); and (3) gesture (meaningful visible activity of the shoulders, arms, hands, legs, feet, head and face). The first thing that observers usually notice about a speaker is his posture. In general it should be a proper combination of ease and strength. It should tell the audience that the speaker has a proper mental attitude toward himself, his subject, and the occasion.

One of the most common faults in posture is slouchiness. We relax too much when we stand and sit. Such a posture tells those who observe us that we are slipshod and indifferent at times when we do not intend to create such an impression.

Too much tension is quite as bad as too little. The speaker's posture usually should be erect but not rigid and stiff; it should not be the attitude of military "attention," but rather of "parade rest." Often when we consciously try to obey the command "Stand erect," we try to stretch upward as if preparing to fly. This seems the very essence of unnaturalness and always appears awkward. Our "stance" in speaking should be just what it is in all situations when we are on our best behavior and desire to be polite and courteous to others. We should not press our elbows tightly against our sides; we should let our arms hang comfortably relaxed when we are not using them in gesture.

The speaker's weight should be more on one foot than on the other, generally on the one which is placed forward, closer to the audience. The head should rest easily upon the neck, the neck upon the shoulders, the shoulders upon the trunk, the trunk upon the hips, the hips upon the legs, and the legs upon the feet. It may be helpful to imagine an elastic band extending from the soles of the feet to the crown of the head and to stand so that it will be stretched slightly.

MOVEMENT

One of the surest signs of embarrassment is to stand as if the feet were glued to the floor. Speakers who have ideas to present and are anxious to do the job effectively shift weight and move about in order to make their message clear and to reveal how they feel about what they are saying.

Movement is to speaking what paragraphing and punctuation are to the printed page. The speaker cannot very well say, " Comma here," " Now a semicolon," or " That's a period "; but often he can get similar meanings across by shifting his weight from one foot to the other or by moving from one position to another. When a speaker stands stock-still all the time, he gives much the impression that a printed page would give if it were devoid of paragraphs, commas, and periods.

A certain amount of movement is desirable and helpful in nearly all circumstances. It is a way of holding attention and of telling those to whom we speak that we are alive, alert, and interested in what we are saying. When a rabbit or a fox wishes to escape attention, it " freezes " — stands perfectly still in its tracks. In this way it avoids communicating messages to its enemy. What do we think when a speaker strikes a rigid posture and reduces movement to a minimum? Are we not likely to feel that he is uncomfortable, afraid, or embarrassed? Normal boys and girls are seldom motionless. When they speak on the playground, they are on the move; and when speaking elsewhere, they should show just as much life as they do on the playground. We cannot solve the problem of movement by standing still.

Movements are of three general kinds: (1) forward or backward, (2) to right or left, and (3) turning.

Often added meaning is given to what we are saying if now and then we step forward or backward. Such steps may fit the changes in thought, the transition points, in what we are saying. A single step forward may go nicely with a " therefore," " besides," " and moreover," " in addition to this," " above all," and kindred connective words. A step backward may say " yet," " still," " despite this," " granting that."

Side-stepping is sometimes valuable — side-stepping literally, not figuratively. It is a good variant from forward and backward stepping. It serves the same general purposes. It is also subject to the same abuses. The side step, or shifting of weight from one foot to the other, may go well with " in the meantime," " next," " as for that," " to be sure," and " nevertheless."

One of the best ways of testing our bodily control is to find out whether we can turn easily on a vertical axis from our feet to our heads. It is one of the simplest things in the world to do when we are not frightened. The stiffness so common in high-school speakers is almost wholly the result of inability to turn on the ankles, at the knee, and at the hips. It is very important to be able to turn with all muscles and joints freely co-ordinating. This simply cannot be done with a stiff body.

Rules of Bodily Punctuation

1. Keep the weight on one foot at a time, on ball or heel.
2. Do not remain too long in one position.
3. Change position as thought changes. Usually: forward for vigor, or something new; backward for relaxation, concessions, repetitions; sidewise for transitions.
4. Do not sway back and forth aimlessly; every change should be purposeful.

5. Do not cross the feet in stepping sidewise; step sidewise leading off with the foot that is already toward the direction in which you are going.

6. Do not double-hitch in order to step; just go as if you wanted to get somewhere sensibly and purposively.

7. Do not let your feet seem glued to the floor; keep them free and ready to go.

How much movement should the speaker use? The answer is easy — just enough! But how much is enough? The answer depends on the factors that make up the speech situation — the people who look and listen, the place, the time, and what the speaker is saying. There must be just enough movement for the particular person speaking to stir up the right meaning in the particular individuals whom he is addressing. Chapter Seven explains the principle of *empathy*, which is fundamental in deciding how much movement to use in any particular situation. It helps a speaker to understand why audiences lose intended meanings when a speaker moves about aimlessly.

GESTURE

Almost any activity of the instruments of gesture may at some time be effective, and, just as in the case of movement, not only gesture, but the absence of gesture, is likely to stir up meanings. Hands, arms, head, and face, moving or motionless, mean something all the time. No speaker can dodge the problem of gesture any more than he can dodge the problems of posture and movement. There are some rather definite conventional restrictions on gesture — certain general principles of effectiveness, widely accepted, to be neglected at the speaker's own risk. Let us now consider some of these general principles.

Every gesture should be of the whole body. Gesture is not something to be added to speech; it is an integral part of speech, and should be trained into the total activity of the whole body. In gesture, no joint or muscle liveth unto itself alone. All our gestures are affected by what the basic muscles do — those of back, trunk, arms, legs, and neck. These muscles are mastered earliest in infancy, and their habits are most deeply fixed. The activity of these muscles is most easily understood as speech signs, and such activity makes or mars the effect produced by the more delicate muscles of the hands and face. Very often the cause of awkwardness at the wrist or the elbow may be found at the ankle, the knee, or the hip. The stiff hand and finger positions of boys and girls when they are speaking formally are almost always the results of tensions in the larger muscles of the body. A gesture is seldom effective unless it originates in and is an integral part of a general attitude or activity of the body.

Gestures should be appropriate to the meaning. This is the one rule of gesture which has no exceptions; gestures should always serve the meaning rather than call attention to themselves. Obviously, if gestures are to be appropriate to the meaning, it is erroneous to say that they should always be graceful. If an awkward gesture best expresses the meaning, then an awkward gesture should be used. When members of an audience commend a speaker because of his graceful gestures, we may suspect that the gestures were not appropriate. But when an audience forgets what a speaker did and remembers only what he said, and that clearly and distinctly, then his gestures probably have been appropriate. Graceful gestures should be used more often than awkward ones simply because ease and strength of movement normally fit our thoughts and feelings better than do jerky, angular, abrupt actions.

Gestures should precede utterance. Gesture as physical activity develops before voice and language. Men almost always speak first by posture, movement, and gesture; and after that by words. If we watch others, we can see how this works. When we reverse this order, we get comic effects. If we say, " The child was *so* tall," indicating " *so* tall " by gesture after we have spoken the words, the effect is funny because we have broken the law that gesture should come before vocal utterance.

Gestures should suggest reserve power. No matter how vigorous a gesture may be, it should leave the impression that the speaker could be more emphatic if occasion demanded. When gestures lack reserve, they are likely to call attention to themselves and to carry wrong meanings. A speaker should always appear to be in control of his gestures. Hamlet says to the players, ". . . for in the very torrent, tempest, and, as I may say, whirlwind of your passion, you must acquire and beget a temperance, that may give it smoothness." By "temperance" Hamlet means what we call reserve.

Parts of the body in gesture. Since gesture is the visible activity of arms, hands, head and face, shoulders, legs, and feet, it is worth while for us to consider each of these instruments.

The arms are important in gesture. They move in two general planes: up and down, and sidewise. Sidewise, they move from the center of the trunk outward. All arm gestures should involve the whole arm. The impulse should start from the shoulder and bring into action the whole arm clear out to the finger tips. The principle of reserve applies to arm gestures as to others. The arms should rarely be extended to the limit, but should rather leave the suggestion that if there were something more significant or extensive, the arms could say more.

The hands are important in gesture. Excepting only the face, the hands are the most delicately expressive part of the body. The signs which can be made with the hands are practically innumerable; yet the meanings of certain hand positions are very definite and almost universally understood.

The head and face are important in gesture. In some ways the head is the best of all the instruments of gesture. An armless speaker could be very effective in speaking if he knew how to use his head — literally as well as figuratively! The head and face are the center of attention for those who look at the speaker. What the head and face do cannot possibly escape notice. Therefore we should let the head and face give no meanings which we do not want them to give. If our words suggest pleasure, we should smile; if they are solemn, our faces should be sober. In learning to control our faces as instruments of gesture, it is a good plan to study the faces of others closely.

The eyes are important in gesture. They are extremely expressive agents of communication. To give the impression that we are dealing directly and straightforwardly with people, we must look at them. When we stand before audiences, we should not gaze at the ceiling, fix our eyes on the floor, or glance nervously about the room or out the window. If we do, we will give a fundamental impression of indirectness, uncommunicativeness, and lack of self-confidence which may destroy everything that we want to say. A good rule is to try, at some time during a speech, to give to every person in the audience the feeling that we are talking directly to him. This will make it necessary for us to look right at each person. The same principle holds good in conversation; we should learn to look the persons with whom we are talking straight in the eyes. Failure to do this makes it very much more difficult for us to accomplish our purposes. Talking without looking at those to whom we speak is very likely to lapse into mere meditating out loud.

Shoulders are important in gesture. We can all use our shoulders to express "No, not if I'm expelled from school," and "All right, if that's the way you feel about it, go ahead." In the first, the body is usually tense and drawn to its full height with the shoulders back and up; in the second, there is usually a general relaxation with a quick shrug or movement of the shoulders up and down. Persons show eagerness, discouragement, relief, enthusiasm, anger, restlessness, carelessness, and hatred with shoulder gestures. In interpreting literary material, we meet numerous situations in which the action of the shoulders is one of the important means of revealing meanings.

Legs and feet are also important in gesture. No one is able to show clear definite meanings with his body without making his legs and feet say what the rest of his body is saying. When Aunt Polly was insisting on co-operation from Tom Sawyer, it is easy to imagine that her feet helped to make her intentions clear. Determination to proceed along a certain course cannot be communicated without tense and firm leg and foot positions. The principles considered under a study of movement can be carried out only if the speaker understands the importance of the legs and feet in stirring up meanings.

Types of gesture. There are three general types of gesture, classified according to the general purposes for which they may be used: (1) emphatic, (2) descriptive, and (3) suggestive.

Emphatic gestures, such as slapping the hands together, shaking the head, stamping the foot, are made for the purpose of drawing special attention to what is being said. The characteristic thing about emphatic gestures is the vigor of their execution. These gestures are interpreted to mean that the speaker is very much in earnest about what he is saying, or that he is very eager to have the attention of those to whom he is speaking.

Descriptive gestures are used for the purpose of making clear the size, shape, or location of physical objects and their relations to each other. If we are describing a box, we indicate with our hands what its dimensions are. When we place our hands out before us, palms downward, to show a person's height, we are making a descriptive gesture. When we say, " There were three windows and a door," we may use descriptive gestures to indicate relative positions.

Suggestive gestures symbolize ideas and feelings. These gestures reveal the speaker's emotional attitudes toward what he is saying. In a sense, they resemble descriptive gestures, but there is one important difference: Descriptive gestures picture objects and relations which may be seen with the physical eye; suggestive gestures make their appeal to the imagination. Examples of suggestive gestures are:

" The whole world " — both arms up and extended, the body turning on the center axis from one side to the other

" We rushed forward " — a hand and arm sweeping out ahead, a forward step

" Every inch a king " — rising to fullest possible stature, hands clenched at sides

" The storm swept everything before it " — turning the whole body, arm and hand sweeping to extreme right or left

These suggestive gestures often say what we cannot possibly put into words. How much meaning can be conveyed by a facial expression, a shrug of the shoulders, a movement of the hand! A study of screen artists shows how wonderful is this art of suggestion through gesture.

GAINING SKILL IN BODY CONTROL

We must not make the mistake of assuming that the authors of this textbook would direct the speaker's conscious attention to posture, movement, and gesture in actually speaking before an audience. We should no more think about our tongues, lips, arms, and faces when speaking than we should think of our fingers when playing the piano. The movements of muscles in speech should be habitual, carried on unconsciously. But in improving our speech we must learn consciously, just as we must learn consciously if we are to improve our piano playing. Suppose we want to improve our game of golf after we have been playing golf for some time and fairly well. Our golf habits are more or less fixed. We hire an expert to help us. He shows us that we have not been holding our clubs properly and that our stance is not what it should be. He requires us to give *conscious attention* to some of these matters. We discover that at first when we pay conscious attention to how we hold the clubs and to how we place our feet, we cannot play as well as we have played before.

Conscious learning of new habits is always a slow and tedious process. Some of us may be like the girl who began to take singing lessons. A friend asked how she was getting on and she replied: "Oh, I've quit taking lessons. I found that it would take me a year to learn to sing as well as I thought I could when I began."

In order to improve, we must learn to see and hear ourselves and to criticize ourselves constructively. An old rhyme tells of the centipede that was running along the road one day when someone inquired, "Pray, which leg comes after which?" When the poor creature began trying to figure out the answer, it could no longer run at all, "and lay distracted in the ditch, considering how to run." The point of the story for us is that if the centipede had wanted to improve its running, it would have had to keep right on figuring until it got out of the ditch and began moving differently from the way in which it had moved before. At first it probably would not have been able to run so rapidly; but as the new method became more and more automatic, it might have proved more efficient than the old one.

The problem which teacher and pupils must now undertake is, broadly speaking, that of improving this muscular control, deepening it, and making it more effective. Whatever training is undertaken should involve the whole body, for we actually speak with the whole body — not merely with the throat, vocal cords, and mouth. Speech is a means of communication through a code made up of signs which can be seen, heard, and interpreted. Practically every part of the body is useful in speech, and to use less than all of it is to fall short of the highest effectiveness.

A good way to gain skill in bodily action is by pantomiming. In pantomime we are usually pretending to be somebody else. We are trying to make people see a character. Certain rules must be followed if pantomime is to be effective. Some people try to pantomime, using just the hands and arms, but without success. The following elements are all necessary:

1. Proper posture, or " stance "
2. Proper walk
3. Proper use of hands and arms
4. Proper use of face and head
5. Proper use of trunk and shoulders
6. Proper use of legs and feet

Pantomime is good for more than entertainment and training actors. It is useful also in helping to understand certain types of literature. After having taken part in a Shakespearean play, we may have discovered that we have gained a much better understanding of the characters and situations. One of the good ways to study literature is to act like the people we are reading about.

This use of the entire body to portray characters is a most interesting and valuable method of learning to bring our bodies under control. When we have mastered these techniques, we will be better able to stir up meanings in all speech situations.

Tests of Comprehension and Application

MASTER THE FACTS

1 Make a scrapbook on action. Show originality in developing it as a guide for training in bodily action. Include snapshots or pictures from magazines to illustrate what you have written.

2 Which of the following items are unimportant in judging a person? Justify your decision.

Dirty hands
Uncombed hair
Dirty fingernails
Wrinkled dress
Soiled shirt

Torn blouse
Run-over heels
Crooked stocking seams
Food stains on necktie
Frayed cuffs

Holes in stockings
Inexpensive material in clothes
Expensive material in clothes
Evening clothes at school
Poor color combinations
Continual playing with pencil, handkerchief, or other articles
Always smiling
Never smiling
Never standing still
Rising on toes instead of standing still
Being taller than others of the same age
Being shorter than others of the same age
Having blue eyes if you prefer brown
Having brown eyes if you prefer blue
Small or large ears
Small or large eyes
Light or dark complexion
Large or small mouth
Moving all of the time
Stumbling when walking
Uneven teeth
Weighing more than others of the same age
Weighing less than others of the same age
Awkward movements
Smacking lips audibly
Straight hair
Curly hair
Dirty face
Chewing gum
Soiled handkerchief
Round shoulders
Kicking a door shut
Sitting slumped over
Mud on shoes
Being rude to others
Scowling all the time
Slouching
Dragging feet while walking
Unbrushed teeth
Chewing a toothpick
Wearing a poorly tied necktie
Biting fingernails
Keeping mouth open continually
Putting feet on desks or furniture
Never looking directly at the person with whom one is communicating
Holding head down continually
Yawning
Making a clicking sound with tongue against teeth
Walking with stiff jerky movements
Others which you would add . . .

3 Stand before the class, illustrate possible standing postures, and describe the difference in the "feel" of the different postures. Do you feel comfortable when your audience feels uncomfortable? vice versa? Can you explain?

4 Choose a partner and work out the following assignment: Illustrate possible sitting and standing postures for polite conversation, showing what each may mean and to what kind of conversation it would be adapted. Then take chairs before the class and demonstrate your findings.

5 Watch an effective public speaker. Write a report on his use of movement.

6 Watch a moving picture of a person giving a public address. Report on his use of movement.

7 Explain to the class why speakers are advised not to do the following as they speak.

 a Play with pencils   d Wave notes aimlessly
 b Fuss with clothes   e Get notes mixed up
 c Twirl coat buttons   f Fidget

8 Explain why it is usually well not to move about very much when beginning to speak.

9 Watch the gestures of movie stars. What can you learn from them?

10 Select someone who, in your estimation, gestures effectively. Study his techniques.

11 Collect pictures showing individuals who are violating one or more of the general principles of effective visible action.

12 Have someone take one set of pictures of you as you violate the principles of effective action and another set as you live up to them. Show the pictures to the class, explaining why the action in one set is superior.

13 Attend church and observe the visible action of the clergyman. Write a paper explaining how he lived up to or violated the five principles.

14 Attend a movie and write a description of the use of the five principles by the actors in the play.

15 Plan an assignment for the class which will test their knowledge of the five principles of effective action.

PRACTICE TO IMPROVE

16 Practice before your mirror to make your face flexible and expressive. Turn away from the mirror; get your face set to express

some definite meaning; then turn to the mirror and observe your expression, making every effort to maintain it while you observe it. Cultivate an expressive face; people do not like to deal with a stolid mask.

17 Assume a speaking stance; then say these sentences:
   a On the other hand, I ask you to consider this.
   b Let us look into his argument.
   c Where did that noise come from?
   d You say it is right; I say it is wrong.
   e One was weak, the other was strong.
   f If this be treason, make the most of it.
   g I ask the House, I ask the galleries, why?
   h Yet this is far from the whole truth.
   i Consider this new point: We are not prepared to fight.
   j I reject such ignominious proposals!

18 Imagine yourself doing each of the following and then get the right bodily set to express what you think and feel:
   a Accusing someone   d Refusing a petition
   b Defying a mob   e Insisting that you are right
   c Pleading for something f Telling how it happened

19 Give a pantomimic characterization of the following types of persons:
   a Lively, energetic, alert
   b Dull, apathetic, slow
   c Self-conscious, diffident, embarrassed
   d Self-assertive, confident, composed
   e Proud, haughty, egotistic

Add to this list, bringing in pantomimic character sketches of interesting types which you have observed.

20 From a story you have read, select a description of a character — his walk, actions, general appearance, and so on — and read the passage to the class, playing the part as described.

21 Prepare a speech on some subject that is very important to you. Deliver it before the class, using appropriate movement.

22 Assume the sensible stance for saying the following sentences. Act all in one piece, weight mostly on one foot. Make every part of the body help in telling the same story.

COMPREHENSION AND APPLICATION TESTS 51

  a Can you see that plane up there?
  b I will not budge an inch!
  c I cannot quite reach it.
  d This is the proper stance for:

A drive from the tee	Waiting on table
Pitching horseshoes	Military attention
Scooping a grounder	Shooting a free throw
Serving a tennis ball	Opening a debate
Acting as bridesmaid	Addressing a chairman

  e Go, and stay away as long as you like.
  f Oh, what was that?
  g Come to me, come!
  h Why, how do you do!
  i Miss Fair, may I introduce Mr. True?
  j I rise to a point of order.
  k Is this a dagger I see before me?

23 Tell a story to the class without words. Plan to show where the action takes place in the first part, lead up to a climax in the second part, and show the climax in the third part. Do not tell your friends specifically what you plan to do. Your performance will deserve a superior rating if the audience is not confused on a single detail. Practice at home before members of your family, in order to be sure that your body does what you want it to do.

24 Come out before the class and say all you can of the following in the visible code, without using any language. Later, repeat using pantomime and voice together. These performances will be interesting or dull, depending on your skill and originality.

  a I will have absolutely nothing to do with it!
  b Well — after all, I am in doubt about it.
  c Take care! Don't do that again.
  d Be quiet back there!
  e Do you really mean that?
  f Aha! Not that time.
  g That does not concern me in the least.
  h Your offer pleases me greatly.
  i If I could only do something!
  j Here I am! What do you want with me?

k I am to blame; I confess it.
l Stay away from me!
m Don't tell me! I don't want to hear a word of it!
n That is perfectly disgusting to me!
o I am not afraid!
p What shall I do?
q That is a malicious lie!
r Did he go out that door, or that one?
s Run, quick!
t Don't do it! Wait a minute, please!
u Heaven be thanked for that!
v I have nothing to apologize for. I can face any man with a clear conscience.
w I feel friendly toward you!
x I am confident that I can do it.

TEST YOUR PROGRESS

25 Write a description of yourself. Include ratings for neatness, taste in clothes, mannerisms, posture, facial expression, movement walking, poise, features, and size. File this in a safe place at home or with your teacher so that you can compare it with a description written at the end of this course. If there is marked improvement, you have profited by your training.

26 Take moving pictures of each member of the class sitting, standing, walking, talking. Save them to compare with others taken at the end of the semester. Keep the backgrounds and dress exactly the same for both sets of pictures. Join the films for the first and second pictures of each person, sometimes with the picture taken at the beginning of the semester first, and sometimes with the picture taken at the end of the semester first. Show the films and have students decide which students have improved their visible action.

27 Ask members of your family to tell you ways in which you impress them favorably and ways in which you impress them unfavorably.

28 Ask members of your class to help you to discover your good and bad points in the use of your visible action.

29 Get an honest picture of yourself. If you discover that you have

physical elements of personality over which you have control and which react against you, now is the time to change them. It is a generally accepted truth that young people can train their bodies more easily than old people can. Every day that you wait helps to set your bad habits and make change more difficult.

30 Work out as many different useful standing postures as you can and present them to the class for analysis and criticism. Ask the other students to tell what meanings they get from the different postures, for what occasions they would be appropriate, and how they can be made more effective. Do they say that you are improving?

31 Work out different sitting postures and carry out the activity in the same way that you did in Exercise 3. In which are you more successful? Why?

32 Notice your use of movement in conversation. How does it compare with that of the persons with whom you converse?

33 Study a moving picture of your gestures. Discuss your strong and weak points.

34 Observe the members of your class as they talk to you in conversation, recite in class, and read or speak before an audience. Notice how each one uses his body. Does his body seem wide-awake, animated? Do all parts work together to express the ideas he wishes to express? Do you feel that he has the power to express deep and important meanings? Does he appear to communicate easily, with seeming naturalness? Does the action of his body fit what he is saying?

CHAPTER THREE *Voice*

IT IS DIFFICULT to overemphasize the importance of a good speaking voice. Although we are not always conscious of the fact, we are constantly being influenced one way or another by the voices we hear. Actions which we can see deeply affect our judgment of a person, but his voice also makes a considerable contribution to the total impression which we call personality.

Perhaps we have discovered how hard it is to learn from a teacher with a poor voice, or how unwilling we are to buy from a salesman who squeaks or squawks or growls. Some people are so unpleasant to listen to that almost nobody wants to converse with them. The public speaker whose voice is distressing starts with an almost hopeless handicap. Now and then we find a speaker who has such interesting ideas, such effective or vivid language, that we listen to him despite his bad voice; but, for the most part, speakers with poor voices do not get a favorable hearing.

The voice supplements the words used; it even determines the meanings of the words. The voice reveals the attitudes of the speaker; it makes known to the audience whether he actually means what he says, how keenly he feels about it, and what he wants them to feel and do. The speaker who has full command of his voice has definite control over the meanings he wishes his audience to get; he can say more nearly just what he means than can the person whose command of his voice is more limited. Many people are silent in public because they realize that their voices do not sound well. Often enough a man with excellent ideas and superior knowledge keeps still in a public meeting and lets others do the talking, even when he knows he has much more to contribute than they have. And it works both ways, for the man who knows that his voice is good sometimes does more talking than his experience and knowledge justify! Moreover, a poor voice gives out quickly, while a good voice keeps going comfortably for a long time. Many men avoid occupations like preaching, law, teaching, and salesmanship because they know that their voices tire too easily.

Therefore in training ourselves to get along with other people it is important to find out whether or not our voices help or hinder us. Are others attracted by us because the vocal sounds they hear are pleasant and communicative, or are they repelled because our voices are raucous and unexpressive?

HOW THE VOICE WORKS

Many of us have been curious to know exactly what voice is and how it operates. The voice comes from a machine which, like other machines, can be explained and understood. A knowledge of how the voice works may help us to cultivate better voices.

Some people make the mistake of supposing that they are doomed to use through all their lives the voices they are using now; that nature made their voices as they are and that nothing can be done to improve them; and that it is just good or bad luck if their voices are pleasant or unpleasant. Thus they go through life paying little or no attention to how their voices sound or how others react to them.

BERGEN AND McCARTHY. *How can we account for the popularity of a ventriloquist in radio? Why do we feel that Charlie is a real personality? Is Charlie more, or less, real in the movies than he is in radio? Why? (Culver Service)*

YOUNG READER AND MICROPHONE. *This little girl is reading a story into a microphone which is attached to the recording device shown in the picture on the opposite page. The two children behind the reader seem much interested in something. What is it? They are awaiting their turn to make records. Is the reader holding the book properly? (Library of Congress)*

This point of view is decidedly wrong. Voices can be studied and mended just as radios and phonographs can be; the vocal machine works according to definite laws which can be understood and applied. There is no good reason why a boy with a squawky growl or a girl with a squeaky whimper should grow to adulthood with such handicaps; they can learn how to speak more agreeably.

One of the chief difficulties we encounter in attempting to improve our voices is that we do not hear ourselves as others hear us. When our voices are reproduced by a dictaphone, a phonograph, or an electric recorder, we are likely to exclaim, " Is that the way I

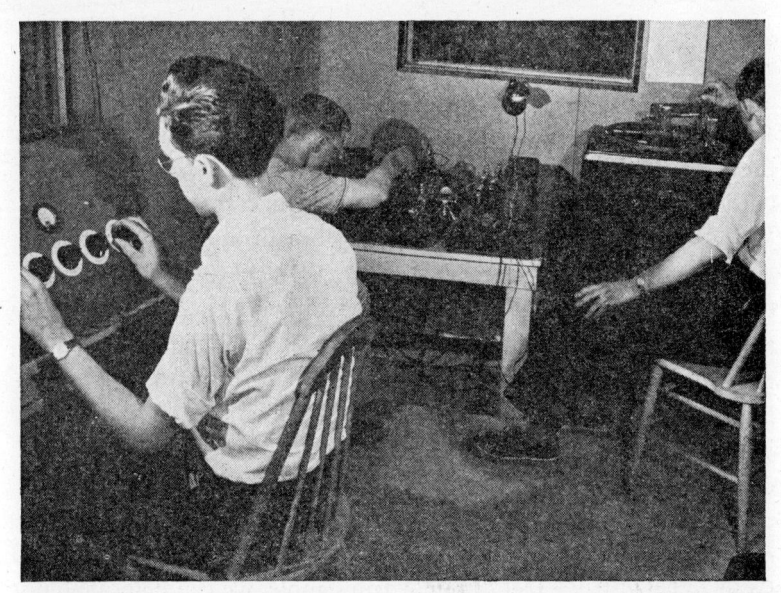

RECORDING VOICES. *Making a disk record of the little girl's reading (see picture on opposite page). There are a number of rather complex operations involved in the recording process, and all of them must be handled competently if voice is to be reproduced accurately. A student will find it exceedingly helpful to hear his own voice and study his own vocal habits. (Library of Congress)*

sound? " And much to our surprise and possibly to our chagrin, our friends hasten to assure us that it is. We have lived with these voices of ours for so long, have got so used to them, and have so consistently ignored or accepted them, that our ears have not told us the truth. Furthermore, our hearing of our own voices is greatly affected by the fact that the sound waves within our throats, mouths, and noses are transmitted directly to our inner ears by bone conduction. Our ears may say that our voices are perfectly all right, and what our friends say, or very carefully keep from saying — in our presence — may be quite different. So let us see how the voice works, and what can be done to teach our ears to tell us more nearly the truth, so that we may be able to improve the vocal sounds with which we meet the world.

Every musical tone depends on two factors: (1) a vibrating body and (2) a source of energy which sets the vibrator going. Usually a third factor, resonance, is added, to amplify and enrich the tone and to make it loud enough to be heard at a distance. We remember how in the summer we have pulled a blade of grass, and pressing it between our thumbs, have blown a blast like that of a fish horn. Voice is made in much the same way: breath blown past vibrating elements produces a tone which varies: (1) according to the length, tautness, and thickness of the bodies which vibrate; (2) according to the force we put back of the blast of breath; and (3) according to the size and shape of the cavities into which the vibrations are released. The nature of the surfaces against which the vibrations strike within the resonator also determines what sort of tones will be produced.

The vocal vibrator. In the vocal mechanism the vibrator consists of a pair of fibro-muscular folds stretched across the larynx from front to back. If we feel of our Adam's apple, we can determine just where these vocal folds are. They are from three-quarters of an inch to seven-eighths of an inch in length from front to back. In breathing they alternately close and open to allow the breath to pass through freely. The space between the vocal folds is called the glottis. When we speak, the folds are brought tightly together. The result of this action is to form a sort of dam for the outgoing breath, and when it is forced against the folds, they vibrate. By the action of a number of small, delicate muscles in and around the larynx, these folds may be made taut or slack. As they are tensed, they vibrate more and more rapidly, and the pitch of the voice rises; as they are relaxed, they vibrate more and more slowly, and the pitch falls. The essential point to remember is that by the operation of this vibrator mechanism we control the pitch of the voice. All pitch changes in the voice have meanings, so it is necessary to control the vibrator whenever we speak.

The vocal generator. But the vocal folds cannot vibrate unless something forces them to do so. Some source of energy is needed, and in voice production this is breathing. As we increase the pressure of the breath against the vocal folds, they vibrate with a wider " swing," and a louder tone is the result. A stronger blast of breath, by increasing the tension of the folds, also produces a tone of higher pitch unless the speaker has learned to relax the folds as he increases the breath pressure. We all have observed that when we talk louder, we generally use a higher pitch.

Breath control is extremely important in the production of voice. Those of us who have studied singing know how much time must be spent in developing right habits of breathing. These habits are no less vital in speaking. A firm, steady stream of breath is required to keep the voice from wavering and to give it strength. This sort of breathing is achieved better by the use of the longer, stronger muscles of the lower chest and the abdomen than by the use of the shorter, comparatively weaker muscles of the upper chest.

We may not be able to identify all the elements of good breathing at the first trial, and perhaps not at the second. Certainly we will not have mastered respiration in so short a time. But so important is correct breathing in the production and sustaining of good speaking tones that it is well worth the effort to keep at it until we have established proper habitual control, the point at which we need no longer think about it at all. But the rule is: Practice, *practice*, PRACTICE!

The vocal resonators. If we sing into an empty barrel, the sound is different from what it would be were we to sing into a cistern, a box, or any other cavity. This fact leads us to a discussion of resonating cavities and what they have to do with voice. The hollow spaces in the throat and head are of tremendous importance in the production of good voices. The tones started by the vocal folds are greatly affected by the shape and the size of these cavities. They resonate, or amplify, the voice. It is the presence or absence of appropriate resonance which makes our voices pleasant or unpleasant, rich or thin, capable of standing wear or likely to roughen up and give out quickly. No doubt many of you have seen the instrument called the marimbaphone. It consists of a series of wooden bars which are accurately tuned to the musical scale. Under each bar is a metal tube. The long wooden bars have long tubes, and the short bars, short tubes. These tubes act as resonators for the tones which the bars give out when they are struck. A short tube would not resonate the tone from a long bar, and a long tube would not resonate the tone from a short bar. The principle is this: Every pitch is best amplified, or resonated, by a resonator of a certain size.

The different vowels are produced principally by different sizes of the mouth-cavity resonator. Note the movement of the tongue, jaw, and lips in changing from $\overline{oo}$ to *ee*. For $\overline{oo}$ the back of the tongue is raised high; for *ee* the front (not the tip) is high. Take the following series of vowels: *ah, ă, ĕ, ā, ee, ĭ*.[1] Note how from a flat position at the floor of the mouth the front of the tongue gradually rises until it reaches the highest point in the vowel *ĭ*. Now take this series: *ah, aw, oh, $\overline{oo}$*. Observe in this case that it is the back of the tongue that rises, reaching the highest point in $\overline{oo}$. What you are actually doing, of course, is changing the size and the shape of the resonator.

An interesting experiment may be performed by comparing these vowels and their tongue positions with whistled tones. If we whistle the highest tone we can (not through the teeth, however), and then say *ĭ*, we notice the similarity in the two positions of the tongue. If we whistle the lowest tone we can, and without changing the position of the tongue, sound whatever vowel comes most easily, what is it? This simple experiment demonstrates that these changes in tongue and lip positions change the resonance, and so make different vowels. It is clear, then, that there is a close connection between different pitches and different vowels.

When we hear a musical tone from a violin, a clarinet, a cornet, or a voice, we are hearing not one single tone, but a number of tones all blended together. This is because the vibrators operate in a very complicated manner to produce a complex tone, consisting in reality of a number of different tones called "partials." The proper function of the resonator is to select from this complex those particular partials which will blend most pleasantly and give the richest, fullest effect. That is why a Stradivarius violin is better than a cigar box with a finger board attached to it, and why a free, open throat with good resonators is better in voice production than one which is tight and stiff and which has small, ineffective resonance cavities. Different musical instruments vary in the particular partials which they resonate best. This fact makes it possible for us to distinguish

[1] In Chapter Four we shall use a more accurate method of representing vowel sounds. Rough approximations will be sufficient here.

between the tones of the cornet and those of the flute, or between those of the violin and those of the oboe. Voices differ in the same way; in some the low partials are amplified; in others, the higher ones; and in still others there is a good balance between the high and the low. No two voices have exactly the same combination of partials. For this reason, we are able to distinguish the voices of people we know, even over the telephone.

Some voices are of poor quality because mouth cavities of the wrong size and shape are used for the vowels. Some voices consist mainly of a growl which suggests that the speaker is angry or surly. Others have a deep hollow tone which sounds as if the speaker were telling ghost stories all the time. Still others are thin and weak, giving the impression of physical exhaustion.

There is another type of resonance by which tones may be amplified. It is illustrated in the piano. The vibration of the piano strings is communicated to the sounding board, which because of its large area sets a large volume of air into vigorous motion and thus increases the strength of the tone. This is surface resonance. Set a vibrating tuning fork down on the top of a table, and note how the sound is strengthened. In the violin, while the volume of air within the body acts as a true resonator, the vibrations from the strings are communicated through the bridge to the wood, producing surface resonance also. In the vocal mechanism there are a number of surfaces which probably respond in this manner. The hard palate, the bony structures of the head, the teeth, and the chest wall may act as surface resonators.

A study of charts and models from the department of science showing the exact formation of the human vocal apparatus will help to make plain what has been discussed in the text. If such helps are not available, it will be well to visit a meat-packing plant and secure the lungs, trachea, and larynx of a sheep or a pig. We can observe the spongy lungs which hold the air, the tubes through which the air travels in and out, the narrow slit between the vocal folds where the vocal vibrations are begun, and the cartilages of which the voice box is built. If we are very careful, we may be able to dissect out some of the delicate muscles which control the larynx in voice production.

GENERAL RULES FOR IMPROVING THE VOICE

The people who have the worst voices frequently are ignorant of how they sound. All of us must learn to "listen in" on ourselves. We ought to experiment with our own vocal instruments until we get the best possible tone. Then we should study how we got it, listen for it so that we can recognize it when we hear it again, and keep everlastingly at it until we can produce at will the quality we want. Then we should continue until the production of that best, richest, fullest tone becomes a habit — until we no longer have to think how we do it. Probably the best control of resonance is to be gained through our own ears, aided and guided by someone who can hear and judge our voices and give us expert advice.

We will do well to read aloud passages from good literature just for the sake of studying the sound of our own voices. Thus we may find out whether our voices are loud or soft, rough or smooth, high or low. It is best to work in pairs and tell each other what we hear. Attention to voice makes us aware of how we and others actually sound.

Wake up the speech muscles. The commonest kind of bad voice comes from lazy and sleepy speech machines — jaw, lips, tongue, and throat. Let us liven them up and have better voices.

1. Be sure that the jaw is not set like a steel trap.
2. Take off the smile and the grin, especially the grin of embarrassment.
3. Make the whole throat and mouth cavity free and flexible, especially on low tones.
4. Be sure to make a long enough face in saying: *all, more, our, go, growl, Rome, home, rule, bald, drawn, beauty, truth, boom, brown.*

The unpleasant effect of many voices is the result of making vowel sounds in the wrong way. This goes back to the matter of hearing oneself inaccurately. People use wrong vowel sounds because they do not listen to their own voices carefully. If they heard accurately, they would speak better. Some vowels are made easily and others with difficulty. In order to make correct vowel sounds there must be much freedom and even looseness of the jaw.

RULES FOR IMPROVING THE VOICE 63

These words can be pronounced easily with the face unlengthened:

beam	say	triple	brilliant
sit	what	immense	cherished
ouch	tears	creation	happy
yes	fair	indifferent	gently
free	yet	capture	wasted
light	hand	unquestionably	wilderness
can	red	extricate	tenacious
will	been	daylight	antagonist
eat	great	indict	mistake
labor	thrilled	sacrifice	salvation
ought	life	silently	surrender
cramp	death	courage	intelligent
corn	indistinct	gift	sweet

But the vowel sounds in the foregoing words are not the sounds we like most to hear. Those who sing know that such sounds are hard to sing satisfactorily. The vowel sounds that please us most are:

a as in *father*   *a* as in *fate*   *ou* as in *our*   *oi* as in *soil*
a as in *past*   *i* as in *fine*   *oo* as in *soon*   *oo* as in *book*
a as in *all*   *o* as in *home*

These sounds can be very agreeable or they can be very disagreeable. The secret of making them pleasant lies in freeing the jaw enough to use a face longer than when we say *cat, sit, met,* etc.

Pronounce *cat,* then *cot,* then *caught,* then *coat,* then *coot.* Notice that if we say them correctly, we have to keep freeing our jaw and lengthening our face more and more as we go through the list. If we do not, each successive word will get more and more rough, tight, and even " squawky." Vowel sounds can be made carelessly or they can be made carefully.

POOR VOICES AND WHAT TO DO ABOUT THEM

There are some distinctive types of poor voices which are due to specific causes, and which may be remedied in more or less specific ways.

Nasal twang. This is a whiny sort of voice with an unpleasant twang. It is caused by the passage of the tone through the nasal cavities. We have three sounds in our speech which should be nasalized:

m, n, ng. One wrong use of nasal resonance is to give it to *every* sound. This mistake produces what is called a " nosy " voice.

To test the presence of such nasality, stop up the nasal cavities by pinching the sides of the nostrils together. Speak a sentence having no nasals at all, such as:

1. A little boy ate a bite of bread.
2. As a flower of the field he perisheth.
3. Do you hear? Take it away!

If nasality is not present, the tone will sound the same whether the nostrils are closed or not. If a difference in tone is discernible, it

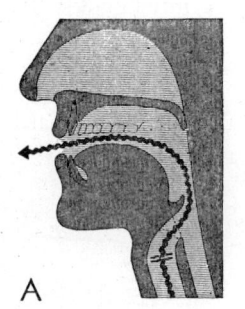

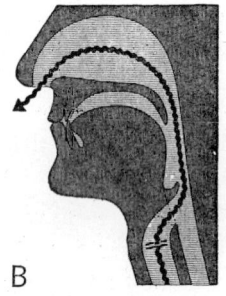

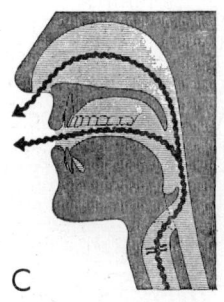

RESONANCE IN THE MOUTH AND NOSE. *(A) The black, wavy, arrow-tipped line shows the course of the vocalized breath stream in the production of vowels and consonants which are not nasalized. Note that the soft palate is held tight against the back wall of the pharynx, thus preventing the use of the nasal chambers as resonators. If the soft palate is held in this position on true nasal sounds,* m, n, *and* ng, *negative nasality will result. (B) The arrow-tipped line indicates the course of the vocalized breath stream in the production of the true nasal sounds,* m, n, *and* ng. *Here there is full employment of the nasal chambers as resonators. Note that the soft palate hangs relaxed and the lips are tightly closed. (C) This diagram shows the conditions which produce positive nasality — the use of nasal resonance on non-nasal sounds. The soft palate hangs relaxed and the lips are open. Part of the breath stream is resonated in the mouth and part in the nose. All sounds have a nasal twang. (From Marshall and Brish's* Understanding Yourself and Your World, *copyright, 1944, by Harcourt, Brace and Company)*

WHAT TO DO ABOUT POOR VOICES

indicates the presence of improper nasal resonance. If there is but a very slight difference, it is not enough to worry about; but if there is marked change, the following exercises should be practiced.

Determine first of all whether the nasal passages are in a healthy condition. Often some inflammation, or a growth, may prevent proper closure of the passage by the soft palate. Bear in mind that good voice production depends on the normal use of a normal mechanism. If the nasal passages are in good condition, the trouble will be found in the improper functioning of the soft palate. Diligent drill on specific exercises should remedy the difficulty.

Practice first on the simple vowel sounds, trying to get the same tone with the nostrils pinched shut as with them open. Vowels most likely to be nasalized are *ah, aw, ā,* although none escapes altogether. Sound the different vowels continuously, squeezing the nostrils shut and releasing them alternately. Repeat until this can be done without changing the tone.

Using a mirror, look back into the throat and note the movements and positions of the soft palate during nasal and clear tones. With practice we can control the soft palate at will to regulate the nasality of tones.

We have been discussing " positive nasality." There is an opposite defect of voice called " negative nasality " which arises from the presence of obstructions in the nasal passages and results in the failure or inability to use nasal resonance where it is needed. Anyone who has observed the effect of a bad head cold knows what we mean by negative nasality. One whose nose is stopped up says, " Do, I cad't cub " instead of " No, I can't come," or " I was sigig ' Roabig id the gloabig ' " instead of " I was singing ' Roaming in the Gloaming.' " If this difficulty is temporary because of a cold, it is not serious. If the nasal passages are permanently closed by adenoids or other pathological conditions, medical attention may be required.

Breathiness. Then there is a sort of " feather-edge " voice; the tone sounds " fuzzy." It lacks the clean-cut tonality that the voice should have. This difficulty is due to allowing the breath to pass out between the vocal cords without being set into vibration. The remedy is to practice getting what the singer calls a sharp attack. We should start a vowel sound with a staccato tone, gradually increasing the time the vowel is held until we can prolong the sound with a sharp edge. Let us not leave any breath unvocalized.

Hollowness. This sort of voice sounds as if it were " placed " way back in the throat. The pharynx seems too large in proportion to the mouth. People whose voices are habitually hollow nearly always lack sharp articulation. They should follow Hamlet's advice to the players: " Speak the speech *trippingly on the tongue.*" Let them liven up jaws, lips, and tongue and " bring the tone forward in the mouth."

The forward consonants particularly, such as s, d, t, p, b, v, f, should be made with extra precision. Taking care of these consonants will inevitably assist in shaping the vowels properly.

Another invaluable aid in " getting the tone forward " is the imagination. Imagining the tone out in front of the face undoubtedly helps in the development of " forward resonance." Three devices based on this principle have been employed with considerable success by many students of voice:

1. Thinking of the tone as filling a big round ball directly in front of the face. Closing the eyes and sounding the vowels while calling up this particular image, trying to fill this big sphere with tone.

2. Thinking of the tone as a missile which is being hurled with considerable force. Drawing back the arm and saying " Ha! " at the same time letting the arm go as if delivering a baseball to a waiting batter. Trying the other vowels, with other consonants. This exercise may also be used in developing strength of tone.

3. " Bouncing " the tone off the wall on the opposite side of the

room. Thinking of casting it against the wall with some force, and trying to imagine its rebounding. Combining this device and the preceding.

Shrillness. This fault is due usually to tightness of the throat. Enough has been said on this subject to indicate the procedure for the elimination of this quality from the voice. Work to bring out the full effect of the vowels that need a long face — *aw, $\overline{oo}$, ah*. Cultivate back and low resonance. Learn to relax the throat and the jaw. Keep the face long. Correct the breathing so that regulation of the breath stream is from the lower chest and the abdominal muscles rather than from the throat muscles. People with shrill voices are likely to be tense all over. They should learn to relax and to release the tensions which bind them so tightly.

Thinness. It is possible to overwork the "forward tones" to the exclusion of others, with the result that a thin, weak, "ladylike" voice is produced. A feminine voice may be a thing of beauty, but an effeminate voice is a misfortune. Loosen up the back of the throat; enlarge the pharynx by relaxing the muscles about the base of the tongue. Cultivate the open throat, the loose jaw, and relaxed neck muscles.

In all of this, the ear is our most valuable guide. Without its aid we cannot develop proper vocal tones. So we should listen carefully, criticize ourselves, and get criticisms from others, including our instructor. By adding the evidence of hearing to that of the muscle "feel," we will be able to make far better progress than by either alone.

Poor articulation and enunciation. Because the vowels determine the general quality of the voice, careful, accurate, definite production of the vowels is important; they are the tones that give life, ring, and fullness to voice. Clean-cut, incisive articulation of the consonants is necessary because they shape the words and make them intelligible, and because to a marked degree they influence the resonance of the vowels. The voicing of consonants undoubtedly affects the quality of the adjacent vowels. So watch both vowels and consonants. Vowels make speech heard; consonants make it understood. There may be good singers whose words it is difficult to understand, but there are no good speakers like that.

USEFUL QUALITIES OF VOICE

Just as there are certain types of poor voices, so there are other types of voices which are valuable to the speaker and which should be cultivated and used when occasion demands. Let us discuss eight useful qualities of voice.

The quality of the voice is to a great degree an individual matter. Each of us has a peculiar quality which makes our voice different

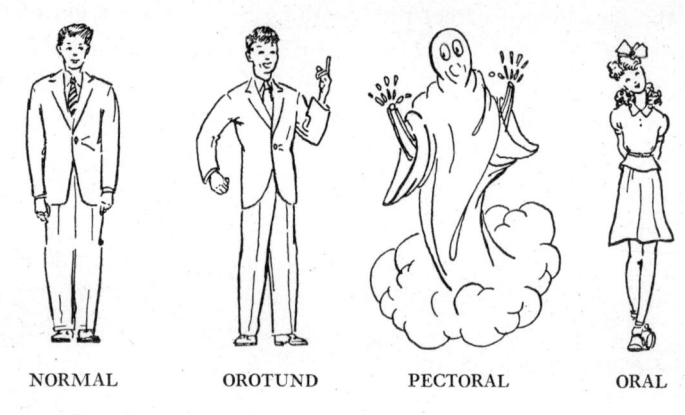

NORMAL	OROTUND	PECTORAL	ORAL

from that of anyone else. Essentially this same quality goes through life with us regardless of the amount of training we receive. Many of the faults can be eliminated, but the characteristic quality will still be distinguishable. Our close friends will always be able to recognize our vocal quality.

Normal quality. This quality is the voice which is used in ordinary, casual speaking; it is the everyday voice that we use when we are under no special emotional stress. It should be understood that the normal quality does not mean necessarily the voice we have always used. The normal is our ordinary voice when we make vowels accurately by fitting the pitch of the tones to the resonance cavities. The normal is the quality ordinarily to be used in conversation.

Orotund quality. For speaking before large audiences, and in certain emotional situations, we need a voice " bigger " than the normal. Consequently we bring into play lips, tongue, soft palate, and jaw, manipulating them so as to amplify the whole gamut of partials composing the vocal tones. The voice has what may be called depth.

USEFUL QUALITIES OF VOICE 69

It is full, round, and open; it rolls out. In producing this orotund quality it is especially necessary that the breath be controlled from the lower chest and the abdomen, to provide adequate support for the tones. The throat is open and relaxed. Articulation and enunciation are clear and well defined. The orotund well may be thought of as a magnified normal quality. It is used in expressing moods of expansiveness, or high emotional fervor, and in formal oratory. It should not be used in casual utterance, in informal discussion, in

NASAL   ASPIRATE   FALSETTO   GUTTURAL

conversation, or in other situations not calling for much emotional response. It is the public speaker's best voice.

Pectoral quality. This is the deep, hollow, sepulchral tone in which we tell stories of horror, weirdness, and deep mystery. It is produced by " drawing the tone back into the pharynx," relaxing the throat, and reducing the action of the lips and tongue. Perhaps the chest also helps to amplify the lower partials. The name " pectoral " means " from the chest."

Oral quality. There is a thin, feeble vocal quality which seems to be expressive of weakness, effeminacy, boredom, ennui, and sometimes irritability. It is usually described as being produced by excessive mouth resonance (hence the name " oral "), but it is probable that it comes chiefly from a pharynx somewhat tensed and reduced in size. It may be used to suggest extreme age, illness, childishness, gaiety, and similar states and conditions.

Nasal quality. This quality has already been discussed. Its legitimate use has been suggested, as well as its abuse. What we should note here is that the employment of the nasal quality may be perfectly appropriate in impersonation and acting. Both positive and negative nasality may be useful in such situations, and the trained speaker should be competent to produce them at will.

Aspirate quality. There are few people who do not make some use of the aspirate — the breathy or whispered quality. Strictly considered, it is not a quality of the voice at all, for vocal tone is not used; in producing it the folds do not vibrate. The pure aspirate has so little carrying power that it can scarcely be used effectively outside a private conversation. In public speaking, however, in reading, and in acting, it is often combined with vibrations from the vocal folds to produce the "stage whisper." The aspirate may be combined with any other quality, the effect being usually to intensify the particular emotional state represented and to give it extreme emphasis.

Falsetto quality. The characteristic of the falsetto is its high, piercing pitch. It is shrill and disagreeable to the ear. It is very thin, since it contains but few partials to which the resonators can be tuned; hence resonance is denied to all save a small number of lower partials. No one but an actor portraying a certain type of character in an exceedingly tense emotional situation would be able to make appropriate use of the falsetto. In real life, the quality is suggestive of nervous tension or hysteria.

Guttural quality. This is a throaty, doglike growl which suggests that the speaker is angry, or at least in an unpleasant mood. It is the kind of voice we associate with violent emotions. The root of the tongue is pulled back so as to interfere with the openness of the tone passage. Except for purposes of mimicry, either in plays or in real-life situations, the guttural quality should be shunned. When it is present in the ordinary speech of an individual, it is a handicap which he should seek to remove by relaxing the throat and centering the muscular activity in the lower chest and the abdomen instead of at the base of the tongue and in the throat.

How can we know just when we are to use each of these qualities of voice? The only answer is that we cannot, and need not, know. Voices do not fall easily into the sharply defined categories we have described. We are constantly changing from one quality to another as we change our attitudes toward what we are saying. There are many variants and combinations of the eight qualities. No harm will be done if on occasion we use a quality which we are unable to classify definitely, provided the quality is appropriate to the particular occasion.

It frequently happens that the quality of the voice changes during the utterance of a single sentence. Our moods are constantly changing, and it is to give full expression to these moods that we change our voices. This is particularly true in reading; in the representation of different characters it is necessary to fit the voice to each in turn. Occasionally a few lines may be given in a deep, hollow pectoral tone, followed by others in the normal tone, and then by others in the full round orotund. But each quality of the voice must be appropriate; it must fit the mood, the character, and the situation.

THE VOICE AND MEANING

Say this sentence aloud: " Yes, indeed, they will be delighted to see you." We know all the words, and we can pronounce every one without a miss. But as we read it, what does it mean? Has it *only one* meaning? Look it over and see how many meanings can be read into it. According to the tone of voice that is used in uttering it or the emphasis put on certain words, it can mean any of the following:

1. Beyond doubt they will be glad to see you. (Positively)
2. I think they will greet you cordially, but I will promise nothing beyond that. (Use a dull and almost tired voice)
3. Whatever anyone else feels, they — the ones I have been talking about — will give you a genuinely cordial reception. (Place emphasis on the word *they*)
4. Despite your denial, I insist that they are sure to greet you cordially. (Place emphasis on *insist*)
5. You thought they would be bored to see you. Oh, no, they will be delighted. (Use a slide down, up, and then down, as on *delighted*)
6. No, they may not care to hear you, but they will be pleased at what they see. (Emphasize *see*)
7. I am not at all sure how they feel about seeing others, but as to

seeing you, there is no question; they will be delighted. (Emphasize *you*)

8. They are hoping they will never see you again, and will be disgusted if you appear in their sight. (Use an ironical tone all the way through the sentence)

9. Oh, yes, you are most surely right; they will be very glad to see you. (Put downward slides on *indeed*. This implies that the " you " person of this sentence understands that he will be welcome and the person uttering the sentence confirms the opinion most heartily)

10. I am not so sure they care to see you as much as you think they do. (Upward slide on every syllable; very skeptical all through)

Now we have ten legitimate meanings in one simple sentence. Others could be given. Every sentence likewise is capable of many meanings. So simple a statement as " I am here " can have at least ten meanings. Say " I am here " aloud to express these ten meanings:

1. I have come.
2. Though it's hard to believe it.
3. Thank Heaven!
4. No matter who else has come, *I* have arrived.
5. Despite your denial, *here I am;* see for yourself.
6. No, I am not where you say I am, *I am* right *here*.
7. All right, this is I; make the worst of it; punish me as you will.
8. Well, what are you going to do about it? I am the man you are looking for.
9. Let them deny it to the end of time, *here I am;* look at me.
10. Yes, I have come back; oh, take pity on me!

If this is possible with a sentence of three words, what are the possibilities in long sentences with involved constructions and words of many syllables and meanings?

Take the sentence: " Life is a narrow vale between the cold and barren peak of two eternities." What does it mean? Is it a definition of life? If it is, it is unconvincing. Then it must be something other than a definition. If so, what is it? Well, very evidently it is a figure of speech, and it means something deeper than its literal significance. It seems to mean: " Life is short, very much hemmed in, and rather a sad place at best." Speak it to give it this meaning and it will not sound like a definition.

Let us consider the same point from another angle and say aloud: "How sweet the moonbeam sleeps upon this bank!" Suppose some man with a rough, gruff voice reads that statement all on one pitch, — what does he really say to a listener? Well, he just about says: "What a bore it is to have to talk about moonbeams!" We have heard boys — and girls too — read poetry just that way.

Take another sentence to be said aloud: "Sir, leave this room at once." A frail girl afraid to call her soul her own is saying it. She is apologetic, weak-voiced, shy. What she succeeds in saying is, in reality, "Maybe it would be nice of you if you would be so kind as to go; just maybe."

Any way we take it, we find that what is written on the printed page can have all sorts of meanings when spoken. Even though we use words according to their dictionary meanings and pronunciations, still people do not seem to get what we have on our minds, for the reason that we do not really *say* what we *mean*.

Utter this aloud:

"If a well were sunk at our feet in the midst of the city of Norwich, the diggers would very soon find themselves at work in that white substance, almost too soft to be called rock, with which we are all familiar as 'chalk.'"

What is the most important test of our speaking? In this instance it is surely the matter of making clear what we are talking about. The best test would be this: Can our listener repeat after us the substance of what we have said? Did he get our idea? Has he grasped the facts in the statement? If we quiz him as to what it was about, and he says, "Well, some men were digging and found a rock called chalk," evidently there are some facts he did not get. If he replies, "Wells in Norwich are filled with chalk," again he misses the factual part of our meaning. Yet people make answers just as inaccurate after hearing sentences like that read aloud. So, evidently, if listeners get only a part of what is said, there is something wrong with the reading or the speaking.

But the facts are not enough; there is something else. Read this statement aloud:

"Sydney Smith says of Lord John Russell's five feet in stature that when Russell went down to Yorkshire after the Reform Bill had passed, the stalwart hunters of Yorkshire exclaimed, 'What! that little shrimp, he carry the Reform Bill through!' 'No, no,' said Smith, 'he used to be a large man, but he worked so hard on the bill that it shrunk him!'"

What are we going to do if somebody asks us to report on the facts in this statement? Are we going to say that hard work actually shrank a large man down to five feet? Can a person telling this story tell it "straight," with a perfectly matter-of-fact manner? Obviously not. Then what must he do? Well, he must give it the right expression, say it expressively, put the right feeling into it. In other words, he must show how he feels about what he is saying.

No matter what we say, the way we say it shows how we feel. We cannot even say "Two plus two are four" without letting a listener know what we think of the matter. Most people would utter that as if they didn't care much, revealing an attitude of indifference, boredom, or casual unconcern. But men have been known to be much excited about that same sentence, insisting with heat that "two plus two are four"; meaning that "it must be, always has been, always must be so, and if any man doubts it he is a fool." By the way we utter any sentence we show how we feel about it.

Say this aloud:

>Under the wide and starry sky,
>Dig the grave and let me lie.
>Glad did I live and gladly die,
>   And I laid me down with a will.

If we speak this so that the listener understands only what we are talking about, we cause him to miss the chief point of the whole stanza. The reading must show how we feel about it. If we read this with the wrong attitude, it sounds more or less foolish — but if we read it so as to show a proper frame of mind, then it is rich and meaningful.

Take an even more striking example: If the following be uttered in a matter-of-fact way, like telling about digging wells and finding chalk, we get almost nonsense; but if it is said in such a way as to make the speaker's attitude clear, then we get a passage of the world's greatest literature:

What should I say to you? Should I not say,
"Hath a dog money? Is it possible
A cur can lend three thousand ducats?" or
Shall I bend low, and in a bondman's key,
With 'bated breath, and whispering humbleness
Say this, —
"Fair sir, you spit on me on Wednesday last;
You spurned me such a day; another time
You called me dog; and for these courtesies
I'll lend you thus much moneys"?

Or this, where William Tell is addressing his beloved mountains:

Ye crags and peaks, I'm with you once again!
I hold to you the hands you first beheld
To show they still are free!

Thus if we wish to talk well and interestingly, there are two problems we have to face: (1) showing how we feel and (2) making clear what we are talking about.

Of these which is the more important? Neither; they are equally important. What people want to know about us first is what mood we are in; whether we are in earnest or joking, angry or happy, uplifted or depressed, interested or bored, awake or half-asleep, merely going through the motions of speaking or speaking as if we mean it, just reciting something or really telling what is on our minds. The instant we break into speech they can tell what mood we are in. Accordingly we take up the matter of attitude first.

Here we go back to what we have already said about qualities of voice; it is in the revelation of attitude that kinds of voice are most important. A rough voice means one attitude, a soft voice another, a loud voice something quite different.

To help listeners in understanding meaning, there must be, in addition to the vocal indicators of the speaker's general attitude, something that makes clear what it is all about. The sentences must have not only feeling, but also sense; the listener must catch not only an attitude, but also ideas.

Emphasis may be defined as the attempt to bring out the sense by calling special attention to the more important ideas. Without emphasis there is no sense; for unless there is a proper subordination of the unimportant and a playing up of the important, there is no emphasis and no logical meaning. To study emphasis we must break the sentence up into its parts; we now must consider phrases and individual words.

Emphasis falls most often on the more important parts of speech, the most important of all being the nouns and the verbs. Nouns and verbs carry the burden of the meaning; they are the backbone of the sense. So they must have their share of emphasis. Next to nouns and verbs, come adjectives and adverbs. Then come pronouns, conjunctions, and prepositions. Interjections are in a class by themselves; they are always important, never subordinate, for they represent a whole sentence.

In saying this sentence aloud how do we emphasize it? "To speak intelligently one must speak with variety." How is the sense of this brought out? What does the voice do to make this sentence meaningful? What words are made to seem more important than others? We can all readily see that there are three words given special treatment: *speak*, *intelligently*, and *variety*. How is this done?

We shall find on close inspection that this emphasizing of these three words and subordinating of the other five is done in three ways: (1) by making the voice go up and down the scale, (2) by changing the length of time it takes to say a word, and (3) by the difference in the degree of strength used on the various words.

Voice the following sentence emphasizing the italicized words: "*Speak* the *speech*, I pray you, as I *pronounced* it to you, *trip*pingly on the *tongue;* but if you *mouth* it, as many of your *players do,* I had as lief the *town crier spake* my *lines*."

Can we make out what our voices do by way of emphasizing words? Can we hear our voices go up and down? Can we catch them holding certain words and syllables longer than others? Can we hear the louder tone we use on some syllables than on others? This sort of exercise will prove a great aid to our knowledge of whether we are speaking well or poorly. Use these sentences:

1. Did you ever notice what life and power the Holy Scriptures have when well read?

2. So long as we love we serve; so long as we are loved by others I would almost say we are indispensable; and no man is useless who has a friend.

3. My boy, the first thing you want to learn — if you haven't learned it already — is to tell the truth. The pure, sweet, refreshing, wholesome truth. For one thing, it will save you so much trouble. Oh, heaps of trouble. And a terrible strain on your memory. Sometimes — and when I say sometimes I mean a great many times — it is hard to tell the truth the first time. But when you have told it, there is an end of it. You have won the victory; the fight is over. Next time you tell the truth you can tell it without thinking. You won't have to stop and think what you said yesterday. You won't have to stop and look round and see who is there before you begin telling it. And you won't have to invent a lot of new lies to reinforce the old one.

4. Of all the qualities which great books and especially the Bible have, few are more remarkable than their power of bringing out the unity of dissociated and apparently contradictory ideas.

5. But this I confess unto you, that after the way which they call heresy, so worship I the God of my fathers, believing all things which are written in the law and the prophets.

6. There is a time in every man's education when he arrives at the conviction that envy is ignorance; that imitation is suicide; that he must take himself for better, for worse, as his portion; that though the wide universe is full of good, no kernel of nourishing corn can come to him but through his toil bestowed on that plot of ground which is given him to till.

7. The class that has hitherto ruled in this country has failed miserably. It revels in power and wealth, whilst at its feet, a terrible peril for the future, lies the multitude which it has neglected. If a class has failed, let us try the nation.

8. Marley was dead, to begin with. There was no doubt whatever about that. The register of his burial was signed by the clergyman, the clerk, the undertaker, and the chief mourner. Scrooge signed it. And Scrooge's name was good upon 'Change, for anything he chose to put his hand to.

9. They marched through ten towns.

10. The war is over.

11. Whatever may be the sentiments of the rulers, the people can be trusted to do what is right.

12. He was patient amidst tribulation, wise amidst popular folly, and courageous when men around him were faltering.

13. It seems I see before me far-stretching billows of full-ripened grain, and everywhere broad, smiling fields give promise of a happy harvest time. Even as I look the reapers come, each swing of their glinting scythe blades leaves behind long swathes of new-cut grain; and — yes, I hear the upswelling strains of the joyous song of the harvest home.

14. One afternoon, as Hilda entered St. Peter's in somber mood, its interior beamed upon her with all the effect of a new creation. It seemed an embodiment of whatever the imagination could conceive, or the heart desire, as a magnificent, comprehensive, majestic symbol of religious faith.

Growls, shouts, cries, squeals, cooings, snarls, gurglings — such sounds always show attitudes. When they are used in saying words and sentences, then attitude is made clear and unmistakable. The following verses well illustrate the principle.

TONE OF VOICE

It is not so much what you say,
    As the manner in which you say it;
It is not so much the language you use,
    As the tones in which you convey it.

"Come here!" I sharply said,
    And the baby cowered and wept;
"Come here!" I cooed and he looked and smiled,
    And straight to my lap he crept.

The words may be mild and fair,
    And the tones may pierce like a dart;
The words may be soft as the summer air,
    And the tones may break the heart.

For *words* but come from the mind,
   And grow by study and art;
But the *tones* leap forth from the inner self,
   And reveal the state of the heart.

Whether you know it or not —
   Whether you mean or care,
Gentleness, kindness, love and hate,
   Envy and anger are there.

Then would you quarrels avoid,
   And in peace and love rejoice,
Keep anger not only out of your words,
   But keep it out of your voice.
                — Sarah Edwards Henshaw

But we cannot say all that we want to say by mere cooing and snarling; to carry on talk we must use words. And it is in the adding of words to these elemental tones that so many people speak poorly and read worse. They do not make the words and the tones fit together. Boys often use the language of politeness — their "pleases" and "thank yous" — with about the same tone of voice that they use on the football field when they say, "Here, what do you mean by letting that man get around your end! Nail him! Hit him hard!" The two elements, words and tone, do not harmonize.

By this time we should know what, in general, is wrong with our own voices and with the voices of our associates. Why not strike a bargain? We can offer to help them to improve if they in turn will help us; it is much easier to grow in skill if someone else tests our progress. We should choose the exercises which will remedy our own peculiar troubles. We should work on them at home and then demonstrate our improvement during the class hours.

The more we get an understanding of how we give our sense to others, the more clearly we will realize that the secret of success in sounding sensible when we talk or read lies in using plenty of *variety:* variety of changes up and down, variety in the length of time we take to pronounce our words, and variety in the amount of vocal strength we use on the accented syllables and the important words. To use plenty of variety and to get the changes in the right places — there is the whole secret of how to sound sensible when we read and talk.

We should be able to make our voices do what we want them to do. In our ordinary speaking and reading, of course we do not watch constantly how we are saying what we say; certain meanings and attitudes " naturally " call for certain types of emphasis. But when we are studying to read a selection, ideas that someone else has set down on paper, ideas which we are attempting to interpret, that is the time when such control over the voice is a positive necessity. We should listen to our voices and study them carefully; experiment with them freely and put them through all manner of paces, to see how completely we can master the various changes that are needed in reading.

We have seen that the most common kind of emphasis comes from changes in pitch; the next most common comes from changes in time. A sure way of attracting attention to a word is to take a longer time than usual in saying it. In this sentence, note the emphasis on the word that is held: " You have the wro-o-n-g number." Again, " He has the stre-eng-th of a lion." " I will ma-ake them do it." Work out proper patterns of timing on the following:

1. The storm increased with the night. The sea was lashed into tremendous confusion. There was a fearful, sullen sound of rushing waves and broken surges. Deep called unto deep. At times the black column of clouds overhead seemed rent asunder by flashes of lightning which quivered along the foaming billows and made the succeeding darkness doubly terrible.

2. He faced his audience with a tranquil mien, and a beaming aspect that was never dimmed. He spoke, and in the measured cadence of his quiet voice there was intense feeling, but no declamation, no passionate appeal, no superficial and feigned emotion. It was simple colloquy — a gentleman conversing. Unconsciously and surely the ear and heart were charmed. How was it done? Ah, how did Mozart do it? How Raphael? The secret of the rose's sweetness, of the bird's ecstasy, of the sunset's glory — that is the secret of genius and eloquence. — George William Curtis speaking of Wendell Phillips

Most young people when they read charge ahead full tilt, take out just time enough to gasp for breath, then rush ahead again full speed. It is a very common and maddening fault. Nobody gets the full meaning out of such reading. True, the reader gets all the words in, but words are not speech; there must be meaning, sense. And sense is not conveyed without pauses.

An important use of the pause is for phrasing. Sense is dependent on the relation of parts of the sentence to each other. Phrasing is a matter of getting the pauses in the places where they help most to bring out the sense.

THE PROBLEM OF VOCAL INTERESTINGNESS

What makes listeners become restless after some persons have talked for about three minutes? The answer is simply stated: lack of variety. By this time we can appreciate that there are an amazingly large number of things we can do with our voices if we have trained them.

With so much to draw from, why will speakers continue to talk on and on using only a handful of what ought to be a bushel? Monotony of one kind or another — in thinking, language, voice, or action — is what causes so many people to shrink at the thought of going to a public meeting, and is what makes so many people little less than bores in conversation. And in interpreting literature vocally, variety is the great secret of success, and the lack of it is the cause of much failure.

In preparing to read aloud, survey the whole selection. Know what moods it contains. Change moods to suit the thought and also change voice to suit the moods. Be sure not to keep to one tone too long.

Shift posture when reading. If we allow ourselves to stand still in one position, we will be sure to become monotonous in voice, unless we are rare and almost miraculous exceptions. If we keep our bodies in varied attitudes and movements, our voices will tend to have variety also.

Use flexible voice. Many people become boresome when speaking because they lazily allow themselves to use only a part of the vocal machinery. They try to get along on changes in force only, or changes in time only, or changes in pitch only. Such partial variety will not work. The effective speaker uses all his vocal machinery, and modulates his vocalization constantly.

Think variety. When we find ourselves launched on a speech of some length, we should keep the needs of variety on our minds, even worry about it a little. We should keep alive an undercurrent of determination not to get into a rut; be bound to use all we have: slides, steps, pauses, long sounds, short sounds, loud and quiet tones, varied qualities — all the marvelous variety of which the human voice is capable.

Tests of Comprehension and Application

IMPROVE YOUR BREATHING

Get ready for some rapid classroom drill! Each of the activities on the following pages is designed for a special purpose and furnishes valuable materials for study. Work on the exercises at home, so that you will not stumble when your turn comes in class. The suggestions at the beginning of each set of activities are guides to the proper method of approach.

Can you figure out exactly what is happening in your body when you are attempting the following?

1 Determine first of all whether you can use all the muscles of inhalation. Work until you can feel the expansion of girth just below the breastbone. Remember that the muscles about the abdomen are not tensed in inhalation; what hardness may be felt is due to the outward pressure of the viscera as the diaphragm presses downward on them. One of the best ways of observing your method of breathing is to watch the muscular action as you are lying on your back. Do not work for the expansion of the abdomen alone; correct breathing requires that there should be a steady expansion of both thorax and abdomen; that is, of the entire torso. At first make it a voluntary action, so that you can accomplish it at will, and then keep on until correct breathing becomes automatic.

2 Work for control of exhalation. Learn to control the outgo of breath by varying the action of the muscles of exhalation in the lower chest and around the waist rather than by tightening the muscles of

the throat. Draw a full breath, purse the lips, and blow the breath out slowly by a steady pressure of the abdominal muscles. See how evenly you can blow against a thin strip of paper held edgewise about two inches in front of your lips.

3 Exhale slowly, sounding the vowel *ah* or *oh*. Listen for any wavering in the strength of the tone and try to eliminate it, not by trying to regulate the stream of breath at the throat, but by steadying the abdominal muscles. *Keep your throat relaxed.* Produce various vowel sounds in this manner; center your attention on the steadiness and the smoothness of the tone. Practice with different degrees of force.

4 Prefix to the vowel sounds *ah, ee, oh, ow, aw,* the consonants *h, b, p, d, t, k, f, v, wh, j, g, l*. Put plenty of energy into the consonants as well as into the vowels. There should be a sharp punch, a sudden contraction of the abdominal muscles as they tighten to force the breath out. To get the feel of this impulse, take a good full breath, and holding the hand just below the breastbone, expel the air in a series of short puffs. Note the action beneath your hands. Do not close the glottis; whisper the same sounds.

IMPROVE YOUR PRONUNCIATION

5 Read the following sentences as effectively as you can.
   a The groans of the dying tore at his heart.
   b What bring ye home to Rome?
   c Wind among the roses, blow no more.
   d Think no more of home.
   e Gather ye rosebuds while ye may.
   f Come, my Corinne, come, let's go a-Maying.
   g Give me liberty, or give me death!
   h Great in life, he was surpassingly great in death.
   i God intended all men to be free and equal.
   j It is easy to be patriotic in piping times of peace.
   k My Lords, I am charged with being an emissary of France!
   l Ask me no more whither doth haste
      The nightingale when May is past.
   m Why so pale and wan, fond lover?
      Prithee, why so pale?
   n I see the smile of contempt which curls your lips.

o Happy scenes! I shall never see you more!
p Hope springs eternal in the human breast.
q Of all the girls that are so smart
   There's none like pretty Sally!
r Rome and Carthage! behold them drawing near for the struggle that is to shake the world!
s Bereft of patriotism, the heart of a nation will be cold and cramped and sordid.
t True it is, generally speaking, that "murder will out."
u I am monarch of all I survey,
   My right there is none to dispute.
v To him who in the love of Nature holds
   Communion with her visible forms, she speaks.

6 Pronounce these words with the face lengthened; be sure to keep loose and free the hinge that works the jaw.

fore	honor	unflinching	brotherhood
power	whom	humanity	memorial
found	right	devotion	knowledge
one	fought	unspoiled	manhood
down	spot	exalted	compromise
home	time	predominant	trodden
come	fight	extraordinary	abroad
all	might	heroic	powerful
bow	god	instrument	incorporate
know	our	embody	responsible
roam	do	conscience	harmonious
awe	groan	humble	hollow
dream	institution	journey	rolling

7 Practice the following sentences for full alacrity of face, throat, tongue, jaw, and lips. Be sure to make the face long.
   a Smile, O voluptuous, cool-breathed earth.
   b Had Napoleon copied the example of Washington, he would have been the idol of all later generations in France.
   c There lies the port; the vessel puffs her sail.
   d She was a Phantom of delight
      When first she gleamed upon my sight.
   e My mind seems to have become a kind of machine for grinding general laws out of large collections of facts.

COMPREHENSION AND APPLICATION TESTS 85

f Peace! and no longer from its brazen portals
   The blast of war's great organ shakes the land.
g The cynic is one who never sees a good quality in a man, and never fails to see a bad one.
h   Let me play the fool:
   With mirth and laughter let old wrinkles come.
i Dreams are notable means of discovering our own inclinations.
j O! that this too too solid flesh would melt,
   Thaw and resolve itself into a dew.
k Oh, when will the St. Louis of nations arise!
l The old order changeth, yielding place to the new.
m Much have I traveled in the realms of gold,
   And many goodly states and kingdoms seen.
n Signor Antonio, many a time and oft
   In the Rialto you have rated me
   About my moneys and my usances.
o Most people dislike vanity in others, whatever share of it they have themselves.
p   Love is not love
   Which alters when it alteration finds.
q Good and evil, we know, in the field of this world grow up together almost inseparably.
r Come back, come back, across the flying foam,
   We hear faint far-off voices call us home.
s Wherefore rejoice? What conquests brings he home?
   What tributaries follow him to Rome
   To grace in captive bonds his chariot wheels?
t Here I have a pilot's thumb,
   Wrecked as homeward he did come.
u Think thou and act: tomorrow thou shalt die.
v The dog is the only living being that has found and recognizes an indubitable, tangible, unexceptional, and definite God.
w Mont Blanc is the monarch of mountains.
x The gray-eyed morn smiles on the frowning night.
y O Romeo, Romeo! wherefore art thou Romeo?

WORK FOR VARIETY IN QUALITY

8 Speak the following passage with a full voice (orotund tone).

a
>The day is cold, and dark, and dreary;
>It rains, and the wind is never weary;
>The vine still clings to the moldering wall,
>But at every gust the dead leaves fall,
>   And the day is dark and dreary.
>   — Henry Wadsworth Longfellow

To appreciate the need of getting the right tone to show how you feel, just read it in a light, happy tone (oral tone); it will not mean what you want it to mean.

Now read this passage with a light, happy tone:

b
>O the South and the Sun!
>How each loved the other one —
>Full of fancy, full of folly,
>Full of jollity and fun!
>How they romped and ran about,
>Like two boys when school is out,
>With glowing face and lisping lip,
>Low laugh and lifted shout!
>   — Edwards

9 Speak the following in a serious, earnest, purposeful tone of voice (strong orotund).

Minority! If a man stand up for the right, though the right be on the scaffold, while the wrong sits in the seat of government; if he stands for the right, though he eat, with the right and truth, a wretched crust; if he walks with obloquy and scorn in the by-lanes and streets, while falsehood and wrong ruffle it in silken attire — let him remember that wherever the right and truth are, there are always troops of tall ministering angels gathering around him, and God Himself stands within the dim future and keeps watch over His own!

WORK FOR VARIETY IN FORCE

10 Note how much strength of voice has to do with the meaning of the following. Read in a gentle voice.

> We watched her breathing thro' the night,
>   Her breathing soft and low,
> As in her breast the wave of life
>   Kept ebbing to and fro.
>
> So silently we seemed to speak,
>   So slowly moved about,
> As we had lent her half our powers
>   To eke her living out.
>
> — Thomas Hood

11 Give the following passage a medium degree of strength.

Roll back the tide of eighteen hundred years. At the foot of vine-clad Vesuvius stands a royal city. The stately Roman walks its lordly streets or banquets in the palaces of its splendors. The bustle of busied thousands is there; you may hear it along the thronged quays; it rises from the amphitheater and the forum. It is the home of luxury, of gaiety, and of joy. It is a careless, a dreaming, a devoted city.

12 Speak the following passage in a strong, loud voice. Note that it is supposed to be the address of the commanding officer of the American forces at the Battle of Bunker Hill. His men are hesitating, and he directs their attention to the British troops ready to attack them.

> Stand! the ground's your own, my braves!
> Will ye give it up to slaves?
> Will ye look for greener graves?
>   Hope ye mercy still?
> What's the mercy despots feel?
> Hear it in yon battle peal!
>   Ask it ye who will!
>
> — John Pierpont

13 Speak the next passage with both loud and quiet tones, aiming to get each into its proper place.

> Ye crags and peaks, I'm with you once again!
> I hold to you the hands you first beheld,
> To show they still are free. Methinks I hear
> A spirit in your echoes answer me,
> And bid your tenant welcome home again!
> — James Sheridan Knowles

14 In the following, change strength of voice as often as necessary — which is rather often.

But the right is more precious than peace, and we shall fight for the things that we have always carried nearest our hearts — for democracy, for the right of those who submit to authority to have a voice in their own governments, for the rights and liberties of small nations, for the universal dominion of right by such a concert of free peoples as shall bring peace and safety to all nations and make the world itself at last free.

To such a task we dedicate our lives and fortunes, everything that we are and everything that we have, with the pride of those who know that the day has come when America is privileged to spend her blood and her might for the principles that gave her birth and happiness and the peace which she has treasured. God helping her, she can do no other.
— Woodrow Wilson

15 Utter the following with a shout.
  a Forward, the light brigade!
     Charge for the guns!
  b Hurrah! hurrah! a single field hath turned the chance of war;
     Hurrah! hurrah! for Ivry and King Henry of Navarre!
  c " Make way for liberty! " he cried.
  d Down with the tyrant! Down with him!
  e We have won! Victory! Victory! Victory!
  f Ship ahoy! Ship ahoy!
  g All aboard! All aboard!

COMPREHENSION AND APPLICATION TESTS

16 Engage in the following ten-minute practice daily; preferably in the morning.

> Two minutes of deep breathing
> Two minutes of reading on a low level of pitch
> Two minutes of shouting
> Four minutes of reading aloud from literature

WORK FOR VARIETY IN RATE

17 Speak the following passages at a prevailingly slow rate.

a
>   The night hath a thousand eyes,
>   And the day but one;
>   Yet the light of the whole world dies
>   With the dying sun.
>
>   The mind hath a thousand eyes
>   And the heart but one;
>   Yet the light of a whole life dies
>   When love is done.
>   — Francis William Bourdillon

b
>   He knew to bide his time,
>   And can his fame abide,
>   Still patient in his simple faith sublime,
>   Till the wise years decide.
>   Great captains, with their guns and drums,
>   Disturb our judgment for the hour,
>   But at last silence comes;
>   These all are gone, and, standing like a tower,
>   Our children shall behold his fame.
>   The kindly-earnest, brave, foreseeing man,
>   Sagacious, patient, dreading praise, not blame,
>   New birth of our new soil, the first American.
>   — James Russell Lowell on Lincoln

18 The following passages call for a *rapid rate*.

>   A voice by the cedar tree
>   In the meadow under the Hall!

She is singing an air that is known to me,
A passionate ballad gallant and gay,
A martial song like a trumpet's call!
Singing alone in the morning of life,
In the happy morning of life and of May.
— Alfred, Lord Tennyson

b   A hurry of hoofs in a village street,
A shape in the moonlight, a bulk in the dark,
And beneath, from the pebbles, in passing, a spark
Struck out by a steed flying fearless and fleet:
That was all! And yet, through the gloom and the light,
The fate of a nation was riding that night;
And the spark struck out by that steed, in his flight,
Kindled the land into flame with its heat.
— Henry Wadsworth Longfellow

c   If ye are beasts, then stand there like fat oxen waiting for the butcher's knife; if ye are men, follow me! Strike down yon guard, gain the mountain passes, and then do bloody work as did your sires at old Thermopylae! Is Sparta dead? Is the old Grecian spirit frozen in your veins, that you do crouch and cower like a belabored hound beneath his master's lash?
— Elijah Kellogg

19   The following passages need a *changing rate*.

a   And there was mounting in hot haste: the steed,
The mustering squadron, and the clattering car,
Went pouring forward with impetuous speed.
And swiftly forming in the ranks of war;
And the deep thunder peal on peal afar;
And near, the beat of the alarming drum
Roused up the soldier ere the morning star;
While thronged the citizens with terror dumb,
Or whispering, with white lips — " The foe! They come! they come! "
— Lord Byron

b No royal governor sits in yon stately capitol; no hostile fleet for many a year has vexed the waters of our coast; nor is any army but our own ever likely to tread our soil. Not such are the enemies of today. They do not come proudly stepping to the drumbeat, with bayonets flashing in the morning sun. But wherever party spirit shall strain the ancient guarantees of freedom, or bigotry and ignorance shall lay their hands upon education, or the arrogance of caste shall strike at equal rights, or corruption shall poison the very springs of national life, there, minute men of liberty, are your Lexington Green and Concord Bridge!
— George William Curtis

c Are you asking, "How can I know my aptitude?" I answer. Stand off and watch yourself. A blacksmith watched himself and found that he had a quick eye for color. Soon he was earning double wages by sharpening drills for quarrymen. A clerk watched himself. He found he had a delicate sense of touch in woolen goods, and soon he was making his fortune as a buyer of woolens. A surgeon watched himself. He found he had a peculiarly sensitive finger. Soon he became an expert in diagnosis through the sense of touch. These were not accidents. Many a person has a sense of color, of touch, of proportion, of time, yet will always be "bound in shallows and miseries," because he never discovers and uses his peculiar gift. If Helen Keller, deaf, dumb, and blind, could discover herself, why not everyone?

IMPROVE YOUR CONTROL OF PITCH

20 A good speaking voice is always moving up and down the scale. And in this process of sliding up and down many voices go wrong. Try the following experiment.
  a Say the *ah* sound as in *father*.
  b Give it a downward slide; that is, say it as if you were answering the question "What sound is it you are missing?" and saying, "Why, it is *ah*." Say that sensibly and you have a downward slide.
  c Notice that while making this downward *ah* in order to keep the sound as good all the time as it is when you start, it is well to keep

lengthening the face and the mouth. Lengthening the face makes the sound clearer and purer.

21 Practice the following to help yourself realize how well — or how poorly — you use slides in bringing out the meaning. Most people use too narrow a range of pitch in reading: be sure to go high enough and low enough to sound interested and interesting.

    a You see me, Lord Bassanio, where I stand,
Such as I am.

    b Whoso would be a man must be a nonconformist. Nothing is at last sacred but your own mind.

    c I thought ten thousand swords must have leaped from their scabbards to avenge even a look that must have threatened her.

    d As music and splendor
Survive not the lamp and the lute,
The heart's echoes render
No song when the spirit is mute.

    e Suppose it were told any of you by a physician whose word you could not but trust, that you had not more than seven days to live.

    f O, what a rogue and peasant slave am I!

    g The present age is a critical one and interesting to live in.

    h Know, Caesar doth not wrong, nor without cause
Will he be satisfied.

    i The quality of mercy is not strained,
It droppeth as the gentle rain from heaven
Upon the place beneath.

    j You cannot, my lords, you cannot conquer America.

    k If ye are beasts, then stand there like fat oxen waiting for the butcher's knife.

    l Fire from every rock and tree, from door and window, from hearthstone chamber!

    m Kentish Sir Byng stood for his King,
Bidding the crop-headed Parliament swing.

    n I sprang to the stirrup, and Joris, and he;
I galloped, Dirck galloped, we galloped all three.

    o Muskeeters are a game bug, but they won't bite at a hook.

p   What a piece of work is man! how noble in reason! how infinite in faculty!

q   How sweet it were, hearing the downward stream,
    With half-shut eyes ever to seem
    Falling asleep in a half-dream.

r   Half-choked with rage, King Robert fiercely said,
    " Open, 'tis I, the King! Art thou afraid? "

s   A little while ago I stood by the grave of the old Napoleon, a magnificent tomb of gilt and gold, fit almost for a dead deity.

t   Lead, kindly Light, amid the encircling gloom,
    Lead Thou me on!

u   Suddenly, as they stood together in an open place, the bell struck twelve, and Scrooge was alone. He saw the Ghost no more.

v   All! I know not what ye call all; but if I fought not with fifty of them, I am a bunch of radish.

w   What are these,
    So withered and so wild in their attire,
    That look not like the inhabitants o' the earth,
    And yet are on't?

x   There is, first, the literature of knowledge, and, secondly, the literature of power.

WORK FOR THE RIGHT PITCH

22   Finally, for showing our general attitude about what we say, there is the device of talking in high pitch or in low pitch or on a level somewhere between high and low. Pitch level is a sign the listener can detect easily and can understand at once. When we hear a person using a shrill, high voice, we know that he is agitated; if he is not, then we mistake his meaning. If, again, he is speaking in a deep, low tone, we think of him as in an entirely different mood. High voice for excitement, anger, lightheartedness, great weakness; low voice for solemnity, august dignity, awed fear, deep meditation. The voice on the middle level tells us that the speaker or reader is rather calm, and going his regular, even way.

An effective speaker has control of the pitch of his voice. He has variety of pitch to help him in expressing any meaning he wishes to convey. The middle pitch from which his voice goes up and down is the one best suited to his particular vocal mechanism. For every individual there is a best pitch level at which he can speak with more power and control than at any other level, and it is variety around this as a center that should be cultivated.

In order to discover your optimum pitch, stop your ears with your fingers and hum up and down the scale. You will find that the loudness of your voice inside your head varies as the pitch changes. When you hit your best pitch level, you will get a maximum of sound with a minimum of effort.

23 Speak the following passages on appropriate levels of pitch.

a   Sail forth into the sea, O ship!
    Through wind and wave, right onward steer!
    The moistened eye, the trembling lip,
    Are not the signs of doubt or fear. . . .

    Thou, too, sail on, O Ship of State!
    Sail on, O UNION, strong and great!
    Humanity with all its fears,
    With all its hopes of future years,
    Is hanging breathless on thy fate!
    — Henry Wadsworth Longfellow

b   Oh, young Lochinvar is come out of the west,
    Through all the wide Border his steed was the best;
    And save his good broadsword, he weapons had none,
    He rode all unarmed, and he rode all alone.
    So faithful in love, and so dauntless in war,
    There never was knight like the young Lochinvar.
    — Sir Walter Scott

c   Gone to be married! gone to swear a peace!
    False blood to false blood joined! gone to be friends!
    Shall Lewis have Blanch, and Blanch those provinces?
    It is not so; thou hast misspoke, misheard;
    Be well advised, tell o'er thy tale again:
    It cannot be; thou dost but say 'tis so.
    — William Shakespeare

d   Go ring the bells and fire the guns,
         And fling the starry banners out;
         Shout " Freedom! " till your lisping ones
           Give back the cradle shout.
                          — John Greenleaf Whittier

e What a piece of work is man! How noble in reason! how infinite in faculties! in form, in moving, how express and admirable! in action how like an angel! in apprehension how like a god! the beauty of the world! the paragon of animals!
                          — William Shakespeare

f   It is a beauteous evening, calm and free,
         The holy time is quiet as a Nun
         Breathless with adoration; the broad sun
         Is sinking down in its tranquillity;
         The gentleness of heaven broods o'er the Sea:
                          — William Wordsworth

g During the whole of a dull, dark, and soundless day in the autumn of the year, when the clouds hung oppressively low in the heavens, I had been passing alone, on horseback, through a singularly dreary tract of country; and at length found myself, as the shades of the evening drew on, within view of the melancholy House of Usher.
                          — Edgar Allan Poe

h And the Raven, never flitting, still is sitting, still is sitting,
     On the pallid bust of Pallas just above my chamber door;
     And his eyes have all the seeming of a demon's that is dreaming,
     And the lamplight o'er him streaming throws his shadow on the floor;
     And my soul from out that shadow that lies floating on the floor
           Shall be lifted — nevermore!
                          — Edgar Allan Poe

i   We look before and after,
      And pine for what is not;
      Our sincerest laughter
      With some pain is fraught;
   Our sweetest songs are those that tell of saddest thought.
                              — Percy Bysshe Shelley

j *Marcellus.* Peace! break thee off; look, where it comes again!
Bernardo. In the same figure, like the king that's dead.
Marcellus. Thou art a scholar; speak to it, Horatio.
Bernardo. Looks it not like the king? Mark it, Horatio.
Horatio. Most like; it harrows me with fear and wonder.

k Oh! But he was a tight-fisted hand at the grindstone, Scrooge! a squeezing, wrenching, grasping, scraping, clutching, covetous old sinner! Hard and sharp as flint, from whom no steel had ever struck out generous fire; secret, and self-contained, and solitary as an oyster. The cold within him froze his old features, nipped his pointed nose, shriveled his cheek, stiffened his gait, made his eyes red, his thin lips blue; and spoke out shrewdly in his grating voice.
                              — Charles Dickens

l Such were, before the war, these three beautiful little towns of Flanders by the sea. The sea loved them. She swept toward them with a murmur of waves; the tremendous booming song of her equinoctial winds was their lullaby. Their towers gazed out over the sand hills to where the great ships were passing in the open sea. They dominated a fertile land rescued long ago by our Flemish ancestors from the very waves themselves. Fine roads, bordered with willows, lead from Ypres to Dixmude, from Dixmude to Nieuport. The three towns asked only to live at peace in the sunshine. But they have been chosen to endure the noise and the terror of great guns.
                              — Emile Verhaeren

CHAPTER FOUR *Pronunciation*

PRONUNCIATION is the correct utterance of speech sounds; it consists in giving to each sound its proper value and quality in its verbal setting, or context.

Pronunciation is a sure test of education and culture. In no way do we reflect the social backgrounds from which we come more than by our pronunciation. It is a paradox for anyone who has had the advantage of high-school training to go about mispronouncing simple common words. Yet how frequently do mispronunciations assail our ears. It seems strange that people who are careful about their apparel and their manners may be slovenly in their speech. And the worst of the matter is that our pronunciation is far more intimately related to our personality than are most of our other habits. The observance of proprieties and niceties in speech is vital in determining our social standing and our entire effectiveness in dealing with other people. By learning to pronounce our language we assure those about us that we are sensitive to social standards and that we have orderly and disciplined minds.

LETTERS AND SOUNDS

One of the first problems in pronunciation is to differentiate between letters and sounds. In English there are over sixty distinct sounds; Webster gives sixty-four. Since all of these sounds have to be represented by twenty-six letters, our alphabet is badly overworked. This fact accounts for many difficulties in pronouncing our language.

We write in letters, but we speak in sounds. In writing and in printing, the best we can do is to use letters to suggest the sounds which we intend. Of course, the letters which we see on a page of type are cues to the sounds for which they stand. The trouble is that each letter necessarily is used for so many different sounds that often in a particular instance it is impossible to decide just which of several sounds it is intended to represent. A perfect system of spelling would be one in which each sound had one invariable letter-sign; and each letter, one invariable sound-value.

"As a matter of fact," says one authority, "owing to various historical reasons, our English spelling has lost touch with our pronunciation. It does not amount to a divorce, nor even to a judicial separation; but, like too many married couples, these two have simply drifted apart; and nothing but a radical spelling reform can bring them together again into the state of holy wedlock." [1]

The rhymes used by poets indicate the pronunciations which were current when the poems were written. Spelling once was more definitely related to sound than it is now. For example, Shakespeare wrote: *theefe, beleefe,* and *greefe.* Milton used: *gon, don, spreds, els, sed,* and *bin.*

The letter *a* is now used to represent at least nine different sounds, which may be noted in the following words:

f*a*te	*a*m	*a*sk
pref*a*ce	fin*a*l	sof*a*
c*a*re	*a*rm	m*a*ny

The letter *e* is used to represent at least six different sounds, and so on through the entire list.

As we have already indicated, to make matters more confusing, the same sound may be indicated by different letters and different combinations of letters. For example, the sound of *I* (the pronoun) can be *spelled* in at least twenty different ways. Consider the following:

I	*ei*der	*eye*	*ai*sle	*aye*
m*y*	s*igh*	g*ui*de	*ay*	r*ye*

These samples should be enough to make the point that if we insist upon considering letters and sounds as identical, we shall find ourselves completely confused. We may sympathize with Lord Cromer in his amusing little poem:

> When the English tongue we speak,
>   Why is *break* not rhymed with *freak*?
> Will you tell me why it's true
>   We say *sew,* but likewise *Jew*?
> *Beard* sounds not the same as *heard;*

---

[1] Henry Martin, *Letters and Sounds,* Oxford University Press, p. ix.

>   *Cord* is different from *word;*
>   *Cow* is cow, but *low* is low;
>   *Shoe* is never rhymed with *foe;*
>   And since *pay* is rhymed with *say*,
>   Why not *paid* with *said*, I pray?
>
>   And, in short, it seems to me
>   Sounds and letters disagree.[1]

There is no easy way out of all this confusion. There are some rules that will be helpful, but in the last analysis there is no substitute for knowing the individual words and the ways in which letters are used in them. As we shall see later, whenever in doubt about pronunciation, the best procedure is to follow the dictionary.

Some time ago Daniel Jones, a distinguished authority on phonetics at the University of London, suggested a ludicrous spelling of *fish* — *ghoti*. How is this possible? Well, use: the *gh* as in *cough;* the *o* as in *women;* and the *ti* as in *nation* — and we have it!

A high-school student once undertook to figure out the number of ways in which the word *circus* might be spelled. He observed that the sound represented by the first *c* is written in a great variety of ways. He noted seven of these different spellings:

*s*ee	hi*ss*	*sch*ism	*p*sychology
*c*ent	*sc*issors	waltz	

The second sound in the word *circus*, represented by *ir*, he found could be spelled in at least seven ways also:

f*ur*	h*er*	*colo*nel	b*urr*
f*ir*	w*or*d	m*yrr*h	

For the third sound, represented by the second *c*, he listed the following:

*c*ave	s*ch*ool	*qu*ay
*k*ill	bu*cc*aneer	

For the sound represented by the *u* he discovered:

radi*u*m	bloss*o*m	zeal*ou*s

By computing possible permutations and combinations, he concluded that the word *circus* could be spelled in no less than forty

[1] Quoted in *Ibid.*, pp. 33–34.

thousand different ways. One interesting example would be *psyrrhquousch*, which at least suggests the part of the circus where the freaks are on display!

Working on a similar basis, we arrive at an interesting spelling *gheauphtheighttough*. Can you make that out? Suppose that the *gh* has the same sound as it does in *hiccough*, the *eau* as in *beau*, the *phth* as in *phthisis*, the *eigh* as in *eight*, the *tt* as in *putt*, and the final *ough* as in *though*. You probably eat *gheauphtheighttough* everyday of your life — and without choking on it either! We often think that the makers of the English language were pretty hard on us in the way of spelling, but they did not begin to live up to their opportunities. Think of what they might have done if they had really let themselves go!

One of the best ways to learn pronunciation is to become ear-minded instead of eye-minded — to hear speech sounds as produced by people about us instead of trying to visualize the spelling which might be used to represent the sounds on the printed page. We must become sound-conscious and use our ears to detect small distinctions between similar sounds; rough approximations will not do. We must be painstakingly accurate. Many mispronunciations are simply the result of auditory inattentiveness. Strange as it may seem, many of us grow up without hearing the differences between correct and incorrect speech sounds. The sort of ear training which is needed can be provided by listening attentively to phonograph records of good speech and to the excellent models provided by the better radio programs.

When we hear divergent pronunciations, we should make haste to find out which is correct. Of course, we may find that two or three different pronunciations of a word are all right, although usually one is more acceptable than the others. Whatever else we do, we should not continue in ignorance on such an important matter as the pronunciation of our own language. We should seize every opportunity for association with careful and informed speakers and try to copy their pronunciations.

DIALECTS

As we listen to the speech of cultured people from different parts of the United States, we quickly become aware of the fact that there are different regional pronunciations. We wonder whether some of these are not wrong, and of course our perplexity raises the question: What standard shall we accept? The answer is that there is no one

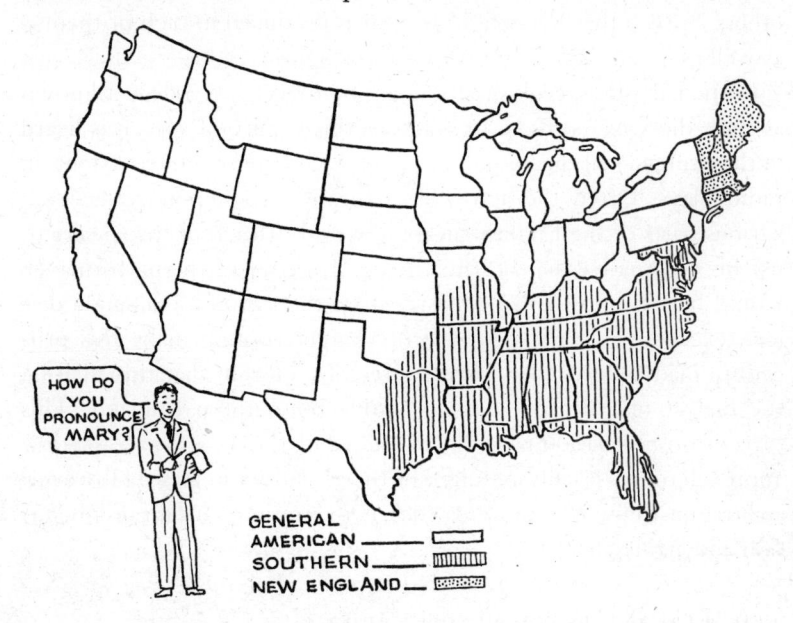

standard of pronunciation in this country — or in any other country, for that matter.

There are three major American dialects: (1) that of a comparatively small area along the Atlantic seaboard, north of New York; (2) that of the section south of a rather vague line running westward from Virginia, north of most of Kentucky, and thence slanting off to the southwest, including most of Texas; and (3) that of the rest of the United States. Of course there are minor differences of pronunciation within these three general regions. The Eastern dialect is used by about 15,000,000 people; the Southern, by about 25,000,000; and the Western, by about 90,000,000. Differences among these dialects are marked enough usually to make it possible for us to tell from which of the regions an individual comes. But fortunately they are not great enough to make it very difficult for Americans to understand each other. A native of Alabama experiences relatively little trouble in making himself understood in either Boston or Seattle. An Iowan gets along all right in Mobile or in Montpelier. A fisherman from Cape Cod speaks intelligibly in Atlanta or in Fargo. There is little or no point in rating any of these dialects as better than the others. Speech that is a delight to hear is produced in each of them — as well as much that is anything but a delight!

Certain artistic speech situations are best served by a dialect known as stage diction. As the term suggests, this variety of speech is heard in the professional theater and, to a somewhat more limited extent, in radio plays. Often the actors in a theater production come from various parts of the English-speaking world. If each of them were to use his own native dialect, the artistic character of the performance would be seriously damaged. Therefore the actors use a single dialect, except where the demands of characterization make this procedure inadvisable. It has been decreed by custom that this shall be the dialect of cultured speakers native to southern England. This type of pronunciation is taught in dramatic schools, and at least some approach to it is usually required of those who act in plays. However, an attempt to use it in our everyday conversation is a sign of affectation and artificiality.

THE ELEMENTS OF SPOKEN LANGUAGE

The production of acceptable speech sounds is dependent upon our utterance of: (1) vowels, (2) consonants, and (3) diphthongs.

Vowels. The term " vowel " is derived from the Latin *vox,* meaning " voice." A vowel, therefore, is a voiced sound; it possesses, or consists of, vibrations which come from the vocal folds. A vowel is a relatively free and unobstructed musical tone. It is a mistake to think that there are just five vowels in the English language, or even seven, as we do when we say " *a, e, i, o, u* (and sometimes *w* and *y*)." These are vowel letters, which are used to represent all of the twenty-six or twenty-seven vowel sounds in the English language.

Front vowels are so called because the forward part of the tongue, the lips, and the teeth are especially important in forming them correctly. These are the broad *a* as in *car*, the short *a* as in *fat*, the short *e* as in *met*, the long *a* as in *hate*, the short *i* as in *hit*, and the long *e* as in *me*.

Back vowels are so designated because the back of the tongue is especially important in forming them correctly. They are the short *o* as in *lot*, the *au* as in *fraud*, the long *o* as in *sole*, the short *u* as in *but*, the long *oo* as in *roof*, the short *oo* as in *good*.

Diphthongs. The word " diphthong " is derived from the Greek word *diphthongos*, formed from *di* meaning " twice," and *phthongos*, meaning " voice." A diphthong, then, is made up of two vowels so joined, or coupled, as to form one speech sound. For example, *ou* in *out* is a diphthong. Sometimes the diphthong is represented by a single letter, as *i* in *mice*, or *u* as in *human*. We should observe that not all doubled vowel letters stand for diphthongs. The *ea, ei, ie*, and so on are single vowel sounds represented by two letters.

Consonants. The term " consonant " comes from the Latin *consonare*, meaning literally " to sound with." A consonant is never sounded alone in speech, but always with a vowel or a diphthong. The vowels carry the power and the beauty of speech, the consonants make it clear and intelligible. A great many people who can produce vowel sounds pleasingly are lip-lazy and tongue-lazy in their utterance of consonants. Frequently we get the tune which such speakers are producing but it is hard to be sure of the words.

WHAT IS THE DICTIONARY?

A dictionary is a list of words with their meanings, spellings, derivations, and pronunciations. The word " dictionary " is derived from the Latin *dictio*, which means " word." It is frequently said that the dictionary is the authority on pronunciation. It would be more accurate to say that the dictionary is an authoritative record of pronunciation. One dictionary puts the matter this way: " It should be borne in mind that the pronunciations finally chosen as representing the best usage were selected only after scrupulously collecting all the published material available together with the results of careful investigations by the editor extending over many years. Disputed pronunciations were submitted to scholars, public speakers, actors, and specialists and a decision was reached only after a careful study of all this gathered information."[1] The preface of another dictionary states: "The pronunciations contained in this dictionary are not theoretical. They represent actual speech — the speech of cultivated users of English, *speaking formally with a view to being completely understood by their hearers.*"[2] Pronunciations, then, are determined not by the opinions of dictionary makers as to what *ought to be,* but rather by their knowledge of what *is.* Usage among educated and cultured people determines pronunciation.

We must rid ourselves of the misconception that the dictionary arbitrarily decrees pronunciation and imposes its decisions upon us whether we are willing or not. Whenever the editors of a dictionary are preparing a new edition, they make a careful canvass of usage throughout the area in which the book is to be sold, and include all pronunciations which are then in general vogue among informed and cultured persons.

Speech is dynamic and alive. Like all other living things, it is changing constantly. It is the business of the dictionary to tell us what the state of affairs is in pronunciation at a particular time by making available to us the best judgments of society. When in doubt about a pronunciation, it is better to consult the dictionary than to ask any one individual, because the dictionary contains the opinions of a large number of competent individuals.

HOW TO USE THE DICTIONARY

How may we find in the dictionary the answers to our questions on pronunciation? First of all, we should study carefully the guide to pronunciation which appears in the forepart of the dictionary; we should learn the code the dictionary uses to explain its meanings. The most important parts of this code are: (1) syllabication, (2) accentuation, (3) diacritical marking, and (4) respelling.

Syllabication. A syllable is "an elementary sound or combina-

---

[1] *Webster's Collegiate Dictionary,* G. & C. Merriam Company, p. iv.
[2] *Webster's New International Dictionary,* 2d ed., G. & C. Merriam Company, 1935, p. xii.

tion of sounds, uttered with a single effort or impulse of the voice and constituting a word or a part of a word." The syllable is of prime importance in pronunciation, for if we are to utter multiple speech sounds correctly, we must be able to analyze them into their elements — the syllables — and then put them back together into proper spoken patterns.

Many words are single syllables — monosyllables. We can pronounce these without difficulty if we know the vowels and consonants which they contain. Words of two or more syllables — polysyllables — present more serious problems in pronunciation, since we have to determine not only the vowel and consonant values, but also the relative importance of the several syllables. The first step in pronouncing a polysyllabic word is to break it up into its syllables. The old rule "Divide and conquer" is especially useful in dealing with this problem of syllabication. When we tackle the pronunciation of a long and complicated series of sounds in a polysyllabic word, it is best to take it sound unit by sound unit. When we are sure that we have these on the tip of our tongue, we then can put them together neatly into the over-all pattern; this is what we mean by articulation — joining together. Fundamentally, the pronunciation of a polysyllabic word is not essentially different from the speaking of a series of monosyllabic words.

"But," says someone, "if I take a long word apart, I shall have a tendency to talk in syllables instead of in words and phrases, and that will be worse than leaving out an occasional syllable." It should be conceded that there is something to be said for this point of view. Nevertheless, we should remember that we are here recommending ways and means of learning how to pronounce words. In this process it may be necessary in order to achieve final mastery to adopt an analytical approach even at the risk of seeming a bit artificial. There is no gainsaying the fact that many of us try to articulate syllables without first having acquired the necessary control over the several elements to be articulated.

The dictionary clearly indicates the syllabication of all polysyllabic words. In it you find not *monopoly* but *mo·nop'o·ly;* not *polysyllabic* but *pol'y·syl·lab'ic;* not *magnanimous* but *mag·nan'i·mous;* not *sociological* but *so'ci·o·log'i·cal;* not *sacrilegious* but *sac'ri·le' gious*. Each of the syllabic divisions is followed by a centered period except where an accent mark or a hyphen occurs. Our first step, then, in finding out how any word is pronounced is to look up the syllabication. How many syllables are there, and what are they? This is not the whole story of pronunciation, but it is an excellent beginning.

Accentuation. Accent is to the several syllables of a word almost exactly what emphasis is to the words in a sentence. When we have divided a word into syllables, we must then reassemble it, and we must do this with such a variation in vocal stress as to throw certain syllables sharply into relief and to pass more lightly over others.

One of the principal problems in learning to speak a foreign language is getting the correct accentuation. We say, " He speaks English with a foreign accent," meaning that he stresses the wrong syllables. He says, *em·phas′is* and *vo·ca·bu′la·ry*. (It will be noted that wrong accentuation often spoils syllabication, for these two words should be *em′pha·sis* and *vo·cab′u·la·ry*.) Of course, in speaking a tongue not native to us, we make a lot of other mistakes, particularly in vowel and consonant values. But one of the most characteristic marks of such speech is wrong accentuation.

Again, in the matter of accentuation, our friend the dictionary stands ready to guide us. It informs us that *address* is pronounced with the accent on the second syllable, not on the first; that *ally* is *al·ly′*; that *research* is *re·search′;* that *despicable* is *des′pi·ca·ble;* that *incomparable* is *in·com′pa·ra·ble;* and that *formidable* is *for′mi·da·ble*.

We should be sure that every syllable, even though it is unaccented, is produced distinctly enough to be recognized as made up of the right sounds; we should not slip over obscure syllables so lightly that they cannot be heard clearly. Remember that by definition a syllable is an elementary unit of speech. A syllable which cannot be heard just is not a unit of anything!

Diacritical marking. The dictionary indicates vowel and consonant values by a code of diacritical marks — signs attached to the letters or combinations of letters to indicate that they represent particular sounds as distinguished from other sounds for which the letters or combinations also stand. For example, *ā* stands for the *a* in *ale*, while *â* stands for the *a* in *care*, *ō* for the *o* in *old*, and *ŏ* for the *o* in *odd*.

It will be understood, then, that letters plus diacritical marks are more specific and accurate symbols of sounds than are unmarked letters.

It is unfortunate that different dictionaries use different diacritical marks. However, since they do, the most sensible procedure is to learn as many of the systems as we can, beginning with and mastering first the code of that particular dictionary which is most accessible to us. Instead of doing this, most of us offer the lazy alibi " I cannot learn them all, therefore I shall have to get along without knowing any of them." If we can familiarize ourselves with the markings used by *Webster's New International Dictionary* and those used by Funk & Wagnall's *New Standard Dictionary*, we shall be well on our way to developing a satisfactory technique for solving our pronunciation problems.

All systems of writing speech sounds depend upon *key words*. The difficulty is that people who speak different dialects necessarily interpret sounds in terms of their own pronunciations of the key words. Therefore it comes to pass that a user of the dictionary in New Orleans may get from it one pronunciation and another user in New York may get a very different one. However, all that we need to do is to be sure that we pronounce the key words the way the educated and cultured people of our own locality do. Then we may safely interpret the dictionary symbols accordingly.

Respelling. Having established the pronunciation of key words, and having learned the significance of the various diacritical marks, we now need to understand a bit more fully just how the dictionary uses these devices to give us information on matters of pronunciation. The technique is really very simple; it is not unlike that used in indicating to an Englishman how a German word is pronounced — we respell it, using the English letters which come nearest to suggesting the German sounds. Just so, the dictionary respells words using letters plus diacritical marks for the letters alone. To illustrate, take the word *sunrise*. We find that Webster's dictionary respells this *sŭn′rīz′*. By reference to the table of key words, we see that the *ŭ* with the diacritical mark is the vowel in *up*, that *ī* is the diphthong in *ice*, and *z* the initial consonant in *zone*. We should now have no difficulty in giving to each of the several sounds its proper quality and value. Finally, we observe that there are two accent signs, the heavier one indicating that the principal stress is on the first syllable, the lighter one that there is a secondary stress on the second syllable.

In many polysyllabic words the accent shifts with the meaning; we say *un·friend'ly* except when we want to contrast it with *friend'ly*, when we say *un'friend·ly*. We say *in·sane'* except when we are balancing it against *sane;* then we pronounce it *in'sane*.

Different parts of speech, spelled the same, differ in their accentuation. Verbs usually are accented on the second syllable, nouns and adjectives, on the first. Examples of words with such variable accentuation are *accent, abstract, contract, discharge, discount, import, object,* and *progress*.

WORDS IN CONNECTED SPEECH

As we listen to people conversing in a language we do not understand, we have great difficulty in determining where separate words begin and end; they seem to run together in phrases and sentences without any breaks between them. Our English speech sounds just like that to foreigners. We do not speak in syllables or in separate words, but in larger units. It is to be noted that the pronunciations we find in the dictionary are those which should be used on isolated words. We need to understand very clearly that words in combination are pronounced differently from words standing alone. The final sound of the preceding word and the initial sound of the succeeding word have an influence on the sounds of the word in between. As we are finishing the utterance of one syllable, we are already beginning the utterance of the next, and as we are completing one word, we are already starting the next word. This telescoping process, called *assimilation*, is at a maximum in informal conversation and at a minimum in formal public address. To put the matter in another way, we may say that words given their full dictionary pronunciation are called *strong forms;* those which are not pronounced so completely are called *weak forms*. Our everyday talk with our friends properly abounds in weak forms. Our speech over the telephone employs many more strong forms. There is always a tendency to carry the use of weak forms to such an extreme as to produce the effect of carelessness and even unintelligibility. The only safe rule is: Use the proper mixture of strong and weak forms which will make speech seem pleasingly natural without damaging its intelligibility. On the public platform and on formal occasions, strong forms are mainly employed.

The codes used in *Webster's New International Dictionary* and Funk & Wagnall's *New Standard Dictionary* are indicated in the following tables:

WEBSTER'S SYMBOLS

ā, as in fāte, āle
ȧ, as in chȧ·ot'ic, vȧ·ca'tion
â, as in câre, pâr'ent
ă, as in făt, ăm
ȧ, as in ȧc·count, in'fȧnt
ä, as in ärm, fär
ȧ, as in ȧsk, dȧnce
ȧ, as in so'fȧ, i·de'ȧ
b, as in baby, bob
ch, as in chair, much
d, as in day, do
dū, as in ver'dūre, grand'eur
ē, as in ēve, mēte
ẽ, as in hẽre, fẽar
ė, as in ė·vent', crė·ate'
ĕ, as in ĕnd, mĕt
ẽ, as in si'lẽnt, nov'ẽl
ē, as in ma'kēr, cin'dēr
f, as in feel, fill
g, as in go, begin
gz, for x, as in ex·ist', ex·act'
h, as in hat, hot
hw, for wh, as in what, why
ī, as in īce, sīght
ĭ, as in ĭll, hab'ĭt
ĭ, as in char'ĭ·ty, pos'sĭ·ble
j, as in joke, gem, soldier
k, as in keep; also for qu, as in conquer; for hard ch, as in epoch; for hard c, as in cube; for ck, as in pack; for que, as in pique

ḵ, for ch, as in German ich, loch
ks, for x, as in vex, perplex
kw, for qu, as in queen, quit
l, as in late, lull, holly
m, as in man, hum, hammer
n, as in no, man, sign
ɴ, as in French, bon, ensemble
ng, as in sing, sing'er; also for ngue, as in tongue; also for n before the sound of k or hard g, as in bank, lin'ger
ō, as in ōld, nōte, he'rō
ȯ, as in ȯbey', a·nat'ȯ·my
ô, as in ôrb, law, caught
ŏ, as in ŏdd, nŏt
ŏ, as in sŏft, lŏss, dŏg
ŏ, as in cŏn·nect', ŏc·cur'
oi, as in oil, noisy
o͞o, as in fo͞od, rude, rumor
o͝o, as in fo͝ot, go͝od, pull
ou, as in out, thou
p, as in pen, pop
r, as in red, rod; also for rh, as in rhomboid
s, as in so, this; also for soft c, as in cell; for sc, as in scene; for ss as in hiss
sh, as in she, ship; also for ch, as in machine; for ce as in ocean; for ci as in social; for sci as in conscious; for s as in sure; for se as in nauseous; for si, as in

pension; for ss, as in issue; for ssi, as in passion; for ti, as in nation

t, as in time; also for ed, as in baked; for th, as in Thomas

th, as in then, this, breathe

th, as in thin, worth

tū, as in natūre, pictūre

ū, as in cūbe, pūre, dū'ty

û, as in û·nite', mû·si'cian

û, as in ûrn, her, fir

ŭ, as in ŭp, stŭd'y, ŭn'der

ŭ, as in cir'cŭs, de'mon, nation

ü, for German ü, as in grün; for French u, as in mē·nü'

v, as in van, vile; also for f, as in of

w, as in want; also for u, as in persuade; for o, as in choir

y, as in yet; also for i, as in union

z, as in zone; also for soft s, as in is, wise, figs; for x as in Xenophon

zh, for z, as in azure; also for zi, as in glazier; for s, as in usual; for si, as in vision; for g, as in rouge

', as in pär'd'n, eat'n, ev'l

FUNK AND WAGNALLS' CODE

Key 1	Key 2	
ā	ä	as in art, father
a	ă	as in at, man
ā	â, ê	as in air, fare, pear, heir, there
e	ĕ	as in get, says, leopard, said, dead, bury, added
ē	ā, ẹ	as in prey, wait, fame, great, neighbors
i	ĭ, y̆	as in hit, cyst
ī	ē, ï, ÿ	as in police, mete, greet, sea
o	o	as in obey, window
ō	ō	as in go, blow, soul, goat, beau
ɵ	ŏ, ạ	as in odd, what
ɵ̄	ô, ą	as in or, all, haul, walk
u	ụ, ọ, o͝o	as in full, push, could, stood
ū	ụ, ọ, ō͞o	as in rule, true, food, who, lose
ᴜ	ŭ, ȯ	as in but, son
ᴜ̄	û, ē, ī, ȳ	as in burn, earn, whirl, myrrh
ai	ī, ȳ	as in aisle, pine, sign, type, height
au	ou, ow	as in sauerkraut, out, now
iu	ū	as in duration, futility
iū	ū	as in feud, tube, beauty
ɵi	ŏi, ŏy	as in oil, boy
k	k, c	as in kin, cat, back, ache, pique, quit
g	ḡ	as in go, egg, ghost, guard
ŋ	ṇ, ng	as in sing, ringing
th	th	as in thin, faith
th	th	as in this, with, rather
s	s, ç	as in so, house, cent, scene, psychology
z	z, ṣ	as in zest, buzz, was

WORDS IN CONNECTED SPEECH

Key 1	Key 2	
ĉh	ch	as in *ch*in, wat*ch*
j	j, ġ, dġ	as in *j*et, *g*in, ju*dg*e, pi*g*eon
ṣh	sh, çh	as in *sh*ip, i*ss*ue, na*t*ion, o*c*ean, func*t*ion, ma*ch*ine
ʒ	zh	as in a*z*ure, vi*s*ion
ᴀ	ȧ	as in *a*sk, d*a*nce
ə =	⁀a, e, o, u	as in sof*a*, fin*a*l, *a*bout, myst*e*ry (always unstressed)
ɪ =	⌣a, e, i, y	as in hab*i*t, sen*a*te, men*a*ce, aver*a*ge, privil*e*ge, vall*e*y, Sund*a*y (always unstressed)
H	H	as in Scotch lo*ch*
ṅ	ṅ	as in bo*n* (French)
ü	ü	as in L*ü*beck (German), D*u*mas (French)

COMMON MISPRONUNCIATIONS
(Webster's code)

1. Dropping the final *g* in *ng*:
   spēk′ĭn for spēk′ĭng (speaking)   gō′ĭn for gō′ĭng
2. Doubling the final *g* in *ng*:
   spēk′ĭng·g for spēk′ĭng (speaking)   gō′ĭng·g for gō′ĭng
3. Failing to distinguish between single *g* and double *g*:
   lĭng′ēr for lĭng′gēr   lŏng′ēr for lŏng′gēr
   sĭng′gēr for sĭng′ēr   brĭng′gĭng·g for brĭng′ĭng
4. Sounding a silent *c* as hard *c*:
   skĕp′tēr for sĕp′tēr (scepter)
   skĭn′tĭ·lāt for sĭn′tĭ·lāt (scintillate)
5. Using hard *ch* for soft *ch* — or for mute *ch*:
   chāz for shāz (chaise)   skĭsm for sĭzm (schism)
6. Substituting *s* for soft *z*:
   ēs for ēz (ease)   kŏn·fūs′ for kŏn·fūz′ (confuse)
   rōs for rōz (rose)   dė·sīn′ for dė·zīn′ (design)
7. Substituting soft *z* for *s*:
   ăb·zûrd′ for ăb·sûrd′   dė·crēz′ for dė·crēs′ (decrease)
   ăb·zôrb′ for ăb·sôrb′   lēz for lēs (lease)
8. Confusing *sh* and *zh*:
   plĕsh′ēr for plĕzh′ēr (pleasure)
   mĕsh′ēr for mĕzh′er (measure)
   lē′shēr for lēzh′ēr (leisure)
   dė·lū′shŭn for dė·lū′zhŭn (delusion)
   vûr′zhŭn for vûr′shŭn (version)

9. Confusing voiced and voiceless *th*:
   trōoth for *trōoth* (truth)   *path* for *path*
   mŏth for *mŏth*   *sōoth* for *sōoth* (soothe)
   hĕth'ēr for *hĕth'ēr* (heather)   *wĕth'ēr* for *wĕth'ēr* (weather)
   thŭth'er for *thŭth'ēr*

10. Substituting *w* for *hw*:
    wŏt for *hwŏt* (what)   *wĭch* for *hwĭch* (which)
    wĕn for *hwĕn* (when)

11. Substituting *t* for *th*:
    tĭk for *thĭk* (thick)   *hĕlt* for *hĕlth* (health)
    dĕt for *dĕth* (death)

12. Pronouncing mute consonants:
    lămb for *lăm*   *ŏf'tĕn* for *ŏf"n*
    lĭmb for *lĭm*   *krĭst'măs* for *krĭs'măs* (Christmas)
    plŭm'ber for *plŭm'er*   *ĕ·pĭs't'l* for *ĕ·pĭs"l* (epistle)
    flĕgm for *flĕm* (phlegm)   *swōrd* for *sōrd*
    kŭp'bōrd for *kŭb'ērd* (cupboard) *fōlk* for *fōk*
    shĕp'hērd for *shĕp'ērd*   *vĭc'tŭ·ălz* for *vĭt"lz* (victuals)
    ĕgz·hĭb'ĭt for *ĕg·zĭb'ĭt* (exhibit) *fōr'hĕd* for *fŏr'ĕd* (forehead)
    făs'tĕn for *făs"n*   *äl'mŭnd* for *ä'mŭnd* (almond)

13. Failing to pronounce difficult consonant combinations:
    rĕs or *rĕst* for *rĕsts*   *pōs* for *pōsts*
    hōlz for *hōldz* (holds)   *ĕ·fĕks'* for *ĕ·fĕkts'* (effects)
    mŭnz for *mŭnthz* (months)   *slĕp* for *slĕpt*

14. Substituting *d* for *t*:
    răd"l for *răt"l* (rattle)   *sĕd"l* for *sĕt"l* (settle)
    lĭd"l for *lĭt"l* (little)   *sŭd"l* for *sŭt"l* (subtle)

15. Substituting *ĭ* or *ĕ* for *ŭ*:
    jĭst or *jĕst* for *jŭst*   *jĕj* for *jŭj* (judge)
    stŭd'ĭ or *stĕd'ĭ* for *stŭd'ĭ* (study)   *brĕsh* for *brŭsh*

16. Substituting *ōō* for *ū*:
    dōō'tĭ for *dū'tĭ* (duty)   *sōō* for *sū* (sue)
    flōōt for *flūt* (flute)

17. Substituting *j* for *zh*:
    mĭ·räj' for *mĭ·räzh* (mirage)   *gȧ·räj* for *gȧ·räzh* (garage)

18. Substituting *ō* for *ä*:
    lōrk for *lärk*   *pōrt* for *pärt*
    bōrn for *bärn*   *dōrk* for *därk*
    kōr for *kär* (car)

19. Substituting *ŏ* for *ô*:
    lŏg for *lôg*   *lŏst* for *lôst*

20. Pronouncing according to spelling:
    sā'ĕth for *sĕth* (saith)
    sāz for *sĕz* (says)
    sād for *sĕd* (said)
    sûr'kū·ĭt for *sûr'kĭt* (circuit)
    rē'spīt or *rĕs'pīt* for *rĕs'pĭt* (respite)
    brēch'ĕz for *brĭch'ĕz* (breeches)
    hĭk'kôf for *hĭk'ŭp* (hiccough)

21. Omitting or shortening syllables:
    b'lōōn for *bȧ·lōōn'* (balloon)
    p'lēs for *pȯ·lēs'* (police)
    gŭv'mŭnt or *gŭv''r·mŭnt* for *gŭv'ērn·mĕnt* (government)
    prŏb'lĭ for *prŏb'ȧ·blĭ* (probably)
    jĕn'ērl·ĭ for *jĕn'ēr·ȧl·ĭ* (generally)

22. Using long vowels before doubled consonants:
    ō·kā'zhŭn for *ŏ·kā'zhŭn* (occasion)
    ō·fĕns' for *ŏ·fĕns'* (offense)
    ē·fĕkt' for *ĕ·fĕkt'* (effect)
    dī·sĕct' for *dĭ·sĕkt'* (dissect)
    ō'pō·nĕnt for *ŏ·pō'nĕnt* (opponent)

23. Accenting wrong syllables:
    ĭm·pō'tĕnt for *ĭm'pȯ·tĕnt*
    ĭn·kŏm·pâr'ȧ·b'l for *ĭn·kŏm'pȧ·rȧ·b'l* (incomparable)
    hŏs·pĭt'ȧ·b'l for *hŏs'pĭt·ȧ·b'l* (hospitable)
    lȧ·mĕnt'ȧ·b'l for *lăm'ĕn·tȧ·b'l* (lamentable)
    fôr·mĭd'ȧ·b'l for *fôr'mĭ·dȧ·b'l* (formidable)

24. Transposing sounds:
    chĭl'dērn for *chĭl'drĕn*
    hŭn'dērd for *hŭn'drĕd*
    lăr'nĭks for *lăr'ĭnks* (larynx)
    prē·spīr' for *pēr·spīr'* (perspire)
    ĭn'trĕ·gāt for *ĭn'tē·grāt* (integrate)
    plŭ·bĭs'ĭ·tĭ for *pŭb·lĭs'ĭ·tĭ* (publicity)

25. Inserting extra syllables:
    ĕl'ŭm for *ĕlm*
    fĭl'ŭm for *fĭlm*
    ŭm·bēr·rĕl'à for *ŭm·brĕl'à*
    ăth'à·lēt for *ăth'lēt* (athlete)

26. Confusing *i* with *e*:
    mĭn for *mĕn*
    tĭn for *tĕn* (and vice versa)
    sĕns for *sĭns* (since) and vice versa

Tests of Comprehension and Application

IMPROVE YOUR PRONUNCIATION

1 Practice speaking the following words, making especially sure that you are using the correct vowels:

habit	salmon	sew	bird
fable	have	beau	firm
jag	any	rub	term
laden	said	cuff	fern
bracket	meet	rust	stern
valley	reach	does	fir
aging	field	touch	fur
marry	acclimate	double	foe
Mary	handkerchief	cover	girl
safe	dray	other	whirr
tame	say	come	their
rank	obey	love	father
gate	survey	one	rather
waif	veil	flood	laugh
praise	weigh	duel	car
cur	blare	cruel	park
work	snare	jury	army
heard	great	tulip	farm
word	care	due	arch
world	hair	sue	calm
hearse	tear	gruesome	psalm
earth	there	clue	garage
yearn	aeroplane	neutral	hearth
worm	mayor	euphony	beckon
Myrtle	toe	feud	wedge
mad	dough	pert	weigh
plaid	though	irk	steak

gauge	cruise	skid	isle
bare	view	lynch	indict
chary	lieu	nymph	woman
air	beauty	business	women
bear	you	arrive	breeches
heir	mood	defy	English
there	food	England	guild
prayer	soon	pilot	build
father	cool	cry	guillotine
palm	gloom	thine	shoe
hurrah	good	rye	sugar
part	hood	eye	maneuver
heart	foot	toad	daub
aunt	soup	oh	haul
bed	through	yeoman	taunt
head	would	son	vaunt
Derby	route	sun	pause
Windsor	rout	rough	audience
guerilla	do	wood	taught
gorilla	who	full	daughter
blackguard	two	through	naught
accompanist	move	true	awe
guess	blue	sofa	draw
reference	true	soda	gnaw
pleasant	pull	collar	saw
dealt	pulpit	color	sprawl
leisure	fate	draught	ought
saith	fatal	canon	bought
leopard	fail	cannon	fought
jeopardy	play	forbade	ball
many	campaign	amok	call
any	straight	colonel	fall
lenient	they	phlegm	wall
region	reign	sergeant	walk
bury	kneel	lithe	chalk
concede	plead	sign	talk
crew	cease	height	also
pew	brief	night	bald
few	deceit	reply	almost
new	machine	guide	war
brew	intrigue	buy	warden
suit	ravine	aisle	warn
fruit	rib	choir	wharf

dwarf	Chimaera	folk	loud
myth	chamois	yoke	sound
guinea	isthmus	hole	sour
pretty	biscuit	road	plough
like	boatswain	loaf	cow
line	gunwale	soap	brow
iron	Edinburgh	sofa	fowl
time	cough	blow	foul
sign	rough	slow	power
signature	slough	grow	avoid
high	bouquet	bowl	toil
log	ballet	orb	appoint
knock	brusque	pork	noise
boss	cupboard	organ	annoy
bomb	flaccid	park	employ
wasp	lineament	bore	her
watch	liniment	boar	err
squat	mortgage	soar	error
suite	viscount	sore	herd
unique	mischievous	touch	serf
signor	sausage	four	surf
sure	gone	fore	heifer
money	fault	broad	schism
lose	poet	water	yacht
loose	poke	sure	rouge

2 *Homophones.* Words which are pronounced alike although their meanings are different are called homophones. There are a large number of homophones in our language; their meanings are determined only by their context. By failing to make the proper distinction between *w* and *wh* we add unnecessarily to this list of homophones and consequently to the ambiguities of our language. Practice speaking the following pairs of words, making sure that no one could mistake one for the other in your speech:

a whale — wail
b what — watt
c wheel — weal
d where — wear
e when — wen
f whet — wet
g whether — weather
h whey — weigh or way
i which — witch
j whig — wig
k while — wile
l whine — wine
m whinny — Winnie
n whir — were
o whist — wist
p whit — wit

COMPREHENSION AND APPLICATION TESTS

    q   white — wight   t   whop — wop
    r   whither — wither   u   why — y
    s   whoa — woe

3 Practice the following:
    a   He attended divine services regularly.
    b   This is a particular request.
    c   He is universally esteemed.
    d   What a terrible event!
    e   I will support the Constitution of the United States.
    f   He is a formidable adversary.
    g   The men's reputations are ruined.
    h   All things visible and invisible
    i   His countenance fell suddenly.
    j   John and James are friends.
    k   Bound hand and foot
    l   Tufts of grass
    m   We seldom find men who act thus.
    n   Have you found any birds' nests?
    o   The masts of the ships were made of casts of iron.
    p   The world's opinions are errors in mirrors.
    q   He should be drowned in the midst of the depths of the deepest sea.
    r   One should not trust too much to servants.
    s   He devoted his fullest attention to miserable and intolerable pursuits.
    t   He went over the mountain.
    u   Which is the witch?
    v   What awful sounds arise!
    w   The swallows twittered on the eaves.
    x   He begged to be permitted to remain.
    y   They searched the house speedily.
    z   Bursting his bonds, he sprang free.

TEST YOUR PROGRESS

4 Study the action of your lips, tongue, and jaw in a mirror. Lingual and lip laziness spoil our speech.

5 The teacher will dictate a list of polysyllabic words for the stu-

dents to write. Following the dictation, each student will syllabicate and accent the words, using a dictionary when necessary. The papers may then be exchanged and marked in accordance with a correct list put on the board by the teacher.

6   The teacher will write on the board a vowel and a word in which it appears. The students, after consulting their dictionaries for the correct pronunciation of the word, will write as many other words as they can think of containing the same vowel. The papers will then be exchanged and corrected, the teacher serving as arbiter in any differences of opinion which may arise.

7   " How Accurate Is Your Speech? " The passage given below contains fifty words commonly mispronounced. Compute your score by deducting two for each error. The *English Journal* comments as follows:

"It needs to be noted, perhaps, that not all of Mr. Bartlow's words have only a single pronunciation. According to *Webster's New International Dictionary*, *inquiry*, for example, may be accented on either the second or the first syllable. Teachers may well use this list first as a means of teaching students the proper use of the dictionary and something of the philosophy of English usage, then as a pronunciation test. Let them have students test each word in the list by looking it up in Webster and making sure there is not a variant pronunciation. Discuss with them furthermore the process by which the correctness of meaning, spelling, and pronunciation of a word is determined: present to them the procedures outlined in the Introduction to the second edition of *Webster's New International Dictionary*, particularly pp. vii and xii. This method of handling a list like Mr. Bartlow's will make clear to young people the essentially democratic process by which the proper use of a word is determined."

A man's diction, his verbal *address*, whether he is in the midst of alarms in *Moscow*, eating *tamales* in the *San Joaquin*, plucking *acacias* and *gladioli* in *Honolulu* or yucca on the *Mojave*, watching for the ninth wave at *Tintagil*, or wandering at his ease in *Magdalene* close, doing a bit of *research* in the British *Museum*, or pestering the *curator* with endless *inquiries* about the *Elgin* Marbles — whatever his *horizon*, whatever his *vicinage*, his listeners will be *harassed* if he mispronounces his words.

Let his speech be brief and *succinct*. Let him emulate the "*exquisite* veracity of Keats" rather than the *flaccid, deracinated* style of some of our moderns. Whether he be a student in the *Lyceum* or *Bodleian* or a Romeo *ogling* his *Juliet* or *piquant Perdita*, let him beware, for even in *romance* a *plethora* of words brings on *satiety*. Even an *Adonis* may so rouse the *choler* of his hearers that they will be moved to *despicable* and even *homicidal* acts which call for *condign* punishment, or at least a term in *gaol*.

With a little *cerebral* activity on the part of the speaker all such *lamentable* circumstances can be avoided and his *longevity* assured. To *err* may be human, but with an *adult* group inaccuracies in speech are *penalized* as readily as *ribaldry* and *inebriety*. So let him watch his words and seek his *solace* in the *homage* of the *sycophants* who will always grant *precedence* to a man who is *purposive* in speech and whose vocabulary is rich in *resources*.[1]

CHAPTER FIVE *Language and Meaning*

OUR WORD "language" comes from the French *langue*, the equivalent of the Latin *lingua*, which means "tongue." Consequently, the first dictionary definition of the term language is: "Audible, articulate human speech as produced by the action of the tongue and adjacent vocal organs." The second definition is: "The body of words and methods of combining words used and understood by a considerable community, especially when fixed and elaborated by long usage; a tongue, as the Latin language." Using the word in this second sense, there are at a conservative estimate more than one thousand distinct languages in the world. It is interesting to note that, as suggested in the first of the foregoing definitions, "tongue" is frequently used as an equivalent of "language." The dictionary goes on to tell us that language is any means, vocal or other, of expressing

[1] Ned Beatty Bartlow, quoted in *World Study*, copyright, January 1942. Reprinted by permission of the G. & C. Merriam Company. *Word Study* is published periodically, and sent free to all English teachers. You will find a good many interesting bits in it if your teacher will lend it to you.

or communicating feelings or thoughts. Thus language comes to mean a system of conventional signs, visible and audible, used for both communication and thinking.

As in the foregoing paragraph, "language" and "speech" often are used synonymously. However, it would seem that for our purpose certain distinctions should be made between them. Speech is the broader and more inclusive term. Oral language is one of the four elements of speech; the others, as explained in Chapter One, are mental processes, voice, and visible action. In this book we use the term "language" to mean spoken words or written words, although we are only indirectly concerned with the latter. Written language is much younger than spoken language; man spoke for a long, long time before he began to write.

BUILDING A VOCABULARY

The unit of both written and spoken language is the word. Originally "word" meant "name," a fact which suggests that the first words were names of objects and persons. This is certainly true in the language of the child; he begins with nouns and later adds verbs, adjectives, adverbs, pronouns, prepositions, and interjections.

A spoken word, says the dictionary, is "An articulate sound or series of sounds symbolizing or communicating an idea without being divisible into smaller units which can be used independently." Fundamentally, any person's language capacities are limited by the number of words which he understands and can use, either for the purpose of thinking or for that of communicating with others. There are available to each of us something like a quarter of a million perfectly good English words, yet most of us do not have a speaking acquaintance with more than 2 per cent of them. Think of the immense possibilities for improvement in language! Of course we all understand a far larger number of words than we use, but even so, we understand only an extremely small fraction of those which are to be found in the English language, printed and oral, which we encounter every day of our lives.

The way to produce growth in our vocabularies is not to seek out long, difficult, unusual words and attempt to incorporate them into

BUILDING A VOCABULARY

our writing and speaking, but rather to adopt simple, expressive, everyday words which we hear constantly, understand partially, and yet never use in speaking or writing.

With how many of the following words are we sufficiently familiar to use them properly? Let us look up those which we do not habitually use and prepare sentences including them. Then we should read these sentences to the class, inviting discussion of our successes and failures.

1. account
2. acid
3. adjustment
4. agreement
5. amusement
6. angle
7. apparatus
8. approval
9. arch
10. argument
11. attack
12. attraction
13. authority
14. automatic
15. balance
16. base
17. basin
18. behavior
19. belief
20. blade
21. brain
22. brake
23. business
24. canvas
25. cause
26. chemical
27. comfort
28. common
29. comparison
30. condition
31. complex
32. condition
33. connection
34. conscious
35. control
36. credit
37. current
38. decision
39. degree
40. delicate
41. dependent
42. designed
43. detail
44. discovery
45. disgust
46. distribution
47. division
48. education
49. effect
50. elastic
51. electric
52. error
53. event
54. example
55. existence
56. expansion
57. experience
58. expert
59. fact
60. feeble
61. fiction
62. fixed
63. flight
64. force
65. frame
66. frequent
67. future
68. general
69. government
70. group
71. growth
72. harmony
73. healthy
74. history
75. hollow
76. hospital
77. humor
78. ill
79. impulse
80. industry
81. instrument
82. insurance
83. interest
84. invention
85. jewel
86. journey
87. judge
88. knowledge
89. language
90. law
91. learning
92. leather
93. level
94. liquid
95. machine
96. manager
97. mass
98. material
99. matériel

100. medical
101. mind
102. month
103. motion
104. mountain
105. music
106. name
107. narrow
108. nation
109. natural
110. nerve
111. news
112. noise
113. normal
114. number
115. observation
116. operation
117. opinion
118. opposite
119. ornament
120. pain
121. parallel
122. parcel
123. payment
124. person
125. physical
126. plane
127. plant
128. poison
129. polish
130. political
131. porter
132. position
133. power
134. prison
135. process
136. profit
137. property
138. public
139. punishment
140. quality
141. quaint
142. range
143. rate
144. reaction
145. reason
146. receipt
147. regret
148. regular
149. religion
150. representative
151. responsible
152. reward
153. rhythm
154. scale
155. science
156. secret
157. selection
158. sigh
159. slope
160. society
161. stage
162. structure
163. substance
164. suggestion
165. surprise
166. tax
167. tendency
168. theory
169. transport
170. unit
171. value
172. verse
173. violent
174. wound

Note that it is not the number of these words we seem to understand vaguely that matters. It is the number we can use discriminatingly, some of them in five or six different ways, that really counts.

The words above are taken from the vocabulary of what is known as Basic English. We are not necessarily endorsing this particular scheme for simplifying language; we are rather trying to draw attention to simple and useful words a good many of which seem to be wholly absent from the vocabularies of many high-school students. If each of us can get ten or fifteen significant additions to his vocabulary out of the list, we will have profited greatly. The theory of those who have developed Basic English is that if we really can get to know its 850 words thoroughly, we will have made a good beginning in language. For example, it isn't enough to know that the meaning of the first word on the list, " account," is a reckoning, a computation, a calculation, or an enumeration. We should observe that the word also means: (1) a written or printed record of money transactions; (2) a balanced statement of receipts and expenditures or of assets and liabilities; (3) a series of items occurring under a heading in a business ledger; (4) a final balance in a business ledger; (5) a collection of items to be balanced; (6) a statement of one's conduct in money affairs; (7) a discharge of responsibilities; (8) a reckoning of charged purchases and credits; (9) the business involved in a reckoning of purchases and credits; (10) advantage or profit; (11) a statement of reasons, causes, grounds, etc.; (12) a statement of facts or occurrences; (13) an estimation, evaluation, or judgment; (14) worth or value; (15) money on deposit in a bank; (16) and perhaps an unlimited number of combinations of the foregoing! All this for the noun "account." There is a comparable list of meanings of "account" when used as a verb. This kind of an exhaustive listing of meanings will develop ease and efficiency in the use of many meanings for each word and should be of immense value in increasing the number of ideas we have and our skill in manipulating them.

METHODS OF DEFINING WORDS

The great American philosopher and psychologist William James tells an amusing story about an experience he once had in a summer camp. When he went out fishing one morning, a general spirit of friendliness prevailed among his companions at the camp, but when he came back in the evening, he found them divided into two hostile groups and scarcely willing to speak civilly with each other. He found that all the trouble had been occasioned by one of the campers asking another the old riddle of the hunter and the squirrel. It goes as follows: A hunter sees a squirrel which takes refuge on the trunk of a tree. Desiring to get a shot at the animal, the hunter completes a circle about the tree, the squirrel staying on the opposite side of the tree throughout his maneuver. The question which had upset everybody was simply this: When the hunter has "gone around" the tree, has he also "gone around" the squirrel? Some said "Yes," others said "No," and the row was on! The two factions agreed that Professor James should arbitrate the issue.

What do you suppose he did? Well, he proceeded just as any common-sense person should proceed in such a situation. He asked, " What do you mean by ' around '? " One faction said that " around " meant " to be on every side of " while the other group insisted that the term should be interpreted more liberally, meaning " to complete a circle about." Of course William James at once pointed out the obvious fact that so long as the two groups could not agree as to the meaning of the term " around," they could not well give the same answer to the question as to whether or not the hunter had gone around the squirrel. It was impossible to settle the controversy by the simple expedient of looking in the dictionary, for both definitions of " around " appear there.

The upshot of the whole controversy was that the disputants were forced to agree that they were dealing with a problem in definition, that there was equal justification for the positions which the two contending groups had taken, and that there was no sense in getting excited about the argument until the terms were defined. How often we get into just such a predicament! We disagree with someone and do not stop to realize that we are both using words without agreeing upon their meanings. The whole trouble lies in the vagueness of words rather than in fundamental differences of opinion. Nevertheless, it is a matter of very great importance that we should learn how to define terms. By doing so, we may well avoid hours of wrangling which terminate in such a remark as " Oh, is that what you mean? If I had understood that at the beginning, I shouldn't have objected at all. Now, when I use that word, I mean . . ."

One writer on meaning suggests that there are " twenty-five definition routes." [1] While it may not be expedient here to go into the subject elaborately, we can suggest several fundamental ways of defining our words.

At the start, we should note that " to define " is " to fix limits or boundaries." When we fix boundaries, we have to decide what is to be included and what is to be excluded; we have to be clear, and precise in details. One good rule to remember is that in defining a word (or a phrase) we should begin by indicating the general class or division into which it falls. Then we should show how it differs

[1] H. R. Walpole, *Semantics*, pp. 125-35.

from all other members of that class. For example, a " castanet " is properly defined as an instrument (class to which it belongs) consisting of two small concave spoon-shaped shells of ivory or hardwood, fastened to the thumb and beaten together with the middle finger in accompaniment to dances and music (the points of distinction between this instrument and all other instruments).

This is the procedure which the dictionary usually follows in defining words. However, we may go at defining words or phrases in various other ways which, although generally not so effective, nevertheless may shed light on essential meanings. Let us now proceed to consider some of these other " routes " to definition.

Example or illustration. We may define " castanets " by exhibiting a pair of them and saying, " These are castanets." We may define " mammal " by saying, " Human beings, dogs, horses, rabbits, monkeys, and whales are mammals."

Diagrams or pictures. Next to showing the object itself for which the word stands, the best method of definition may be to draw a diagram or a picture of it. We may make a line drawing or a sketch of a building and then point to it saying: " This is what the word ' house ' means."

Synonyms. We may define a word by saying that it has somewhat the same meaning that some other word has. Thus we define " conduct " by saying that it means " deportment," " behavior," or " demeanor." (It should be noted, however, that no two words ever have identical meanings.)

Antonyms. We may define a word by saying that its meaning is the opposite of the meaning of some other word. We say that " somber " means the opposite of " bright," or that " wickedness " means the opposite of " goodness."

Comparison and contrast. We may define a word by showing that its meaning is like that of some other word and yet different. For example, we may define " bat " by saying that it means an animal which is like a mouse in size and general appearance, but that a bat's forelimbs have been modified so as to form wings. Thus a bat is a flying mouse. (Note the German word *fledermaus*.)

Description or explanation. We may define a word by drawing verbal diagrams or pictures of it. We say that the object for which the word stands is of such and such color, size, shape, and weight. We say that it originated at a certain place and time, that it may be used for this or that purpose, and so forth. Using this method, we define a " song sparrow " as a bird about six inches in length, brownish above and white below, with brownish streaks on the breast forming a blotch in the center, and noted for its melodious and cheery singing.

The reactions of human beings. Finally, we may define a word by stating some of the characteristic human reactions to that for which it stands. Thus we may define " calamity " by saying that it means any event or happening which causes human suffering.

Etymology. Before we can understand this method of definition, we may find it necessary to define " etymology "! It means the origin or derivation of a word, the primitive form (or root) upon which it is based, the earlier form in a parent language. We learn the meaning of a word by tracing its ancestry and discovering its original meaning in Latin or French or Anglo-Saxon. To use our first illustration, we derive " castanet " by showing that it is from the Latin *castanea* meaning " chestnut." It is thought that the original castanets may have been the dried halves of a chestnut. At any rate, castanets resemble the halves of a chestnut. The dictionary employs all these methods of definition, usually in combinations. Actually, in discussing the various techniques of definition we have been defining " definition "!

We end as we began by observing that any discipline which helps us to be more accurate and careful in our use of language will improve our thinking and our communication with others.

MEANINGS AND CONTEXT

T. S. Eliot, a contemporary poet, says:
" Words strain,
Crack and sometimes break, under the burden,
Decay with imprecision, will not stay in place,
Will not stay still." [1]

[1] " *Burnt Norton,*" *Collected Poems* of T. S. Eliot, Harcourt, Brace and Company.

We have considered the great variety of meanings which any one word has, and now we find ourselves face to face with the question: How can we employ words so that they will mean just what we want them to and not something else? If one word has twelve well-established meanings, how in the world can we be sure that we are going to stir up in the mind of the person to whom we speak the meaning we intend? The plain answer, of course, is that we never can be absolutely sure. However, by taking certain precautions, we can greatly reduce the ever present possibilities of misunderstanding.

The first fact we should observe is that we always and of necessity interpret words in their settings, or contexts. By context we do not mean merely the words which precede and follow in the sentence, although they are of very great importance always in determining the intended meaning of words or phrases. In the term "context" we must include not only the verbal context of a word but also such contexts as: the occasion on which we are speaking, the experiences which the two parties who are communicating have had (those which have occurred most recently are often most important), the attitudes which we have been expressing just preceding the use of the word, the attitude in which the word is heard, and so on. All these types of context are determiners of word meanings. Even when they are taken into account as completely as possible we may still give and get the wrong meanings. This is why one writer on meaning remarked, "When two people converse, misunderstanding is the rule; understanding is a happy accident." While admittedly this may be an exaggerated statement, we do well to bear in mind the almost infinite possibilities of transmitting unintended and wrong meanings. If in speaking to others we think that the context is not sufficient to guarantee their choosing the correct meanings of the words we use, we will do well to pause and explain the sense in which we are using our words rather than to run the risk of misunderstanding.

One additional warning may be sounded here. When we are quoting what someone else has said, we should be exceedingly careful not to separate a quoted statement from its verbal context. It may be desirable to furnish not only the verbal but the nonverbal context also by telling on what occasion and in what circumstances the statement was made. Some of us remember the situation in which Hamlet gives his famous advice to the players. We know that he had a special interest in using his play for the purpose of proving that the king was guilty of murder. The select audience was to be made up of the king, the queen, and the ladies and gentlemen of the court. Now, to take Hamlet's words out of this situational context and use them as an expression of Shakespeare's views on dramatic production may be extremely misleading. Yet it is frequently done. Perhaps Hamlet would have said something quite different to his actors if they had been putting on their performance for a different type of audience, for instance one made up of the servants in Elsinore castle.

KINDS OF MEANING

Meaning is of two general kinds: (1) denotative, intellectual, or extensional, and (2) connotative, emotional, or intensional. For purposes of our discussion we shall use the terms "denotative" and "connotative." Denotative meaning is characteristic of the language of science. It is accurate dictionary meaning. Connotative meaning is characteristic of the language of art. It is meaning based intimately on the experiences of individuals. The secretary in writing the minutes of a meeting should use denotative language exclusively. The poet uses connotative language primarily.

The denotative meaning of a word is its objective significance. It is more or less the same for everyone. The connotative meaning is its subjective, or implied, significance. It is different for everyone. Every word is capable of carrying both types of meaning, and almost always does so. At times it is difficult to decide which type is predominant. However, in most instances the distinction between primarily denotative and primarily connotative meaning is clear enough. Take the following passage:

"The new tabular heading standard is an accurate measure of work done, infinitely more accurate than the old fifty-five-minutes-per-thousand-handset-ems standard. The new standard is computed from the time per pickup of quad, scabbards, spaces, and type, plus time for other operations such as cutting and inserting downrules, justifying 6-point type line in the stick." Though you may not understand this printer's jargon, such meanings as it has for you are clearly denotative. There isn't anything emotional about these sentences as they appear in print. Their reference is almost exclusively to the objective world, and not to anybody's feelings or emotions.

Now consider the following:

"The second way to divert a part of consumer income before it is spent is for the government to borrow it. If voluntary loans are not sufficient — evidently they are not — compulsory loans can be obtained through pay-roll deductions at the source, a check on consumer buying which does its work surely and promptly."

While the connotative meanings of this passage are a bit stronger than all those in the preceding one, still the meaning is dominantly denotative.

But what a contrast there is between both of the foregoing passages and Tennyson's lines:

CROSSING THE BAR

Sunset and evening star,
   And one clear call for me!
And may there be no moaning of the bar,
   When I put out to sea,

But such a tide as moving seems asleep,
   Too full for sound and foam,
When that which drew from out the boundless deep
   Turns again home.

Twilight and evening bell,
   And after that the dark!
And may there be no sadness of farewell,
   When I embark;

For tho' from out our bourne of Time and Place
   The flood may bear me far,
I hope to see my Pilot face to face
   When I have crost the bar.

There is scarcely a denotative meaning in a carload of such composition, but how rich it is in connotative, emotional, intensional meanings!

We must be sure that we are using language denotatively when we want to emphasize objective realities, and that we are using it connotatively when we desire to stress how we feel. We can save ourselves an immense amount of confusion if we learn to recognize each of these two types of meaning and not to confuse them either in our own speaking and writing or in the speaking and writing of others. When we say, " Our troops have retreated according to plan," and the enemy announces, " American troops have been driven back," we should understand that the difference is fundamentally not in the denotative significance of the language but in the connotative significance, born of the prejudices and the emotions of the two reporters. We need to be skillful in the use of both types of meaning in order to accomplish maximum results in influencing others, and to render ourselves reasonably secure against being unduly victimized by the techniques of " persuaders " who seek to control us.

ORAL AND WRITTEN STYLES HAVE CHARACTERISTICS IN COMMON

" Now we are engaged in a great civil war, testing whether that nation, or any nation so conceived and so dedicated, can long endure. We are met on a great battlefield of that war. We have come to dedicate a portion of that field as a final resting place for those who here gave their lives that that nation might live. It is altogether fitting and proper that we should do this."

What is there about the language in that paragraph that makes it great? The words are not new and unusual. It is not necessary for us

A BOY AND HIS DOG. *This picture furnishes a vivid demonstration of the connotative meaning of the word " dog." The outline drawings on the opposite page convey the idea " dog "; they represent no particular dog. The dog pictured here means something very different from just any dog; this is a very special dog. The meaning of " dog " for this boy is rich in happy connotations which have become a part of the concept.* (H. Armstrong Roberts)

to go to the dictionary for the meaning or the pronunciation of a single one. Yet with those words and sentences Abraham Lincoln brought about a close human relationship between himself and his audience, and many critics from that day to this have pointed to the Gettysburg Address as an example of the greatest style in the American language.

When Mary Ellen Chase, one of America's leading novelists, published *Mary Peters*, she made the following paragraph from Dostoevski's *The Brothers Karamazov* the preface to the novel:

"You must know that there is nothing higher and stronger and more wholesome and good for life than some good memory, especially a memory of childhood. People talk to you a great deal about your education, but some good, sacred memory, preserved from childhood, is perhaps the best education. If a man carries many such memories with him into life, he is safe to the end of his days, and if one has only one good memory in one's heart, even that may sometime be the means of saving us."

Why did Mary Ellen Chase, with her great background of literature, choose that particular paragraph as a foreword to her book? Here again the words are not unusual or difficult. They are familiar and simple. Yet the paragraph is worth reading and rereading; it is as appropriate for high-school students as for adults.

The quotation from Lincoln is part of a speech, intended for listeners. The quotation from Dostoevski is part of a novel, intended for readers. Yet both excerpts have common characteristics fundamental to all great style. We have considered these elements of style in our classes in English. We shall continue to consider them through high school, and after high school. What are these qualities of language which we must use both in writing and speaking if we would stir up in listeners or readers the exact ideas which we wish them to have?

In each of the two descriptions which follow, the author wanted someone else to see the man he had in mind. Charles Reynolds Brown said in a speech:

"Of Lincoln's personal appearance it might have been said as it was said of the promised Messiah: 'There is no form nor comeliness in him that we should desire him.'

"The characteristic gravity of Lincoln's face and the sadness which sat upon him almost overpoweringly during his years in the White House, how it reminds us incessantly of the One who was called 'A Man of Sorrows and acquainted with grief.'"[1]

Count Leo Tolstoy wrote in a novel:

"Pierre was clumsy, stout and uncommonly tall, with huge red hands; he did not, as they say, know how to come into a drawing room and still less how to get out of one, that is, how to say something particularly agreeable on going away. Moreover, he was dreamy. He stood up, and picking up a three-cornered hat with the plume of a general on it instead of his own, he kept hold of it, pulling the feathers till the general asked him to restore it. But all his dreaminess and his inability to enter a drawing room or talk properly in it were atoned for by his expression of good nature, simplicity and modesty."[2]

Why is it that some writers and speakers succeed so well in stirring up just the ideas and feelings they want to stir up in the minds of those whom they address? Why do their words bring to listeners and readers such detailed, vivid, and far-reaching memories of past experiences?

First, successful authors have had vivid experiences about which to write or speak. Second, they recognize their own experiences as similar to the experiences of those with whom they wish to communicate. Third, they have felt their experiences deeply; they are sensitive to fine details and subtle meanings. Fourth, they are able to select words and arrange those words to express ideas or emotions precisely.

Great style grows out of vital experiences. We are all familiar with stories about Lincoln during the Civil War. We know how he hated to call men into the army, away from their homes and families. We know his appreciation of their suffering and sacrifice. We know his high purpose in that conflict and his determination to save the Union.

During the years of trial and imprisonment and the other tragic events of his life, Dostoevski must have felt a steadying security in

[1] *Lincoln, The Greatest Man of the Nineteenth Century*, The Macmillan Company, New York, 1922, p. 75.
[2] *War and Peace*, translated from the Russian by Constance Garnett, Modern Library, New York, p. 17. Reprinted by permission.

memories of his childhood, and because many of his later life experiences were extremely bitter, doubtless these early recollections were markedly important. It is interesting to read biographies of famous authors and to note that frequently their success was delayed because at first they tried to describe people or localities with which they were unfamiliar. Individuals brought up in cities attempted to write about farms; men who had never seen war service spoke for soldiers in army camps; women who had lived in luxury talked about the improvement of the slums; and small-town citizens laid the scenes of their stories in large cities. But what they wrote was not convincing until they turned to their own experiences as source material.

It was as if girls in high school were to talk about how it feels to play on the football team; freshman students to describe the feelings and emotions of teachers; teachers to write of the life of lawyers; or fruit growers to discuss the plans of shipbuilders. Each writer or speaker out of his element is unsuccessful. Let us think over our own lives. What do we know better than other people? If we succeed in using language effectively, it will be to portray the things we know best.

Great style is universal. When Abraham Lincoln chose to talk to the audience at Gettysburg about war, sacrifice, ideals, and freedom, he knew that those things were important to all men everywhere. Dostoevski knew the universality of joy in early memories. He knew that millions before him and millions yet to come would feel satisfaction in recalling what had happened in childhood. To describe Lincoln by comparing him to Christ makes use of experiences common to all inhabitants of Christian countries. Tolstoy's Pierre, clumsy, ill at ease, absent-minded, but good-natured, simple, and modest, appeals to all persons who understand human nature and are moved by sincerity and honesty. These authors had deep vivid experiences. Their listeners or readers have had similar experiences. Therefore, re-creation and real appreciation take place.

Many times we talk to our friends in or out of high school and discover that the things they want very much are exactly the things we want; their sense of humiliation over poor clothes is exactly like ours; their love of family, and their feelings of inadequacy, are just the same as ours. In short, they desire the same things, they appreciate the same things, they fear the same things. If we describe our own deeper experiences exactly, we will be able to communicate our ideas and emotions to others.

Great style grows out of sensitiveness. If a writer or a speaker is not sensitive to the subtle details which make up his experiences, he cannot communicate exact ideas or emotions to others. Lincoln suffered sympathetically with those who sacrificed during the Civil War; if we look at his pictures, we are shocked to see how rapidly he aged. If we read biographies of Tolstoy and Dostoevski, we find records of great joy and deep suffering because of exceptional sensitiveness. Students from the Divinity School at Yale know that Charles Reynolds Brown was never calloused to the life of people about him. We can communicate precisely only those experiences which we live deeply and remember vividly.

Great style is precise. Arthur J. Balfour once said: " Most speakers are content if they find the right word. Mr. Asquith invariably uses what you feel to be the inevitable word." It is the " inevitable word " that brings into the mind of the reader or the listener the whole train of images and memories which give him the real meanings. When we examine the compositions of the authors quoted in this chapter, we feel that the words express the ideas so precisely that they seem to us the very ones we ourselves would have used. We see that to change a word or the place of a word might change the meaning the author intended to convey; the language is exactly right just as it is.

It is clear that if we are to find the inevitable word, the word that expresses the meaning better than any other word, we must have an extensive vocabulary. Great writers and speakers have such vocabularies, and they are continually on the alert to enlarge them. High-school students should likewise try to acquire vocabularies which will be adequate in all situations.

GOOD ORAL STYLE DIFFERS FROM GOOD WRITTEN STYLE

The point of the foregoing discussion is that in many important elements the fundamentals of style for writing are the same as those for speaking. However, there are some important differences between oral language and written language; great rhetoricians have been telling us so for centuries.

Aristotle says: " It should be observed that each kind of rhetoric has its own appropriate style. The style of written prose is not that of spoken oratory."[1] Buffon, the famous French rhetorician, remarks, " Those who write as they speak, though they may speak excellently, write badly." Macaulay says, " Nobody can think it strange that a great writer should fail as a speaker." Clayton Hamilton, in the preface to his *Conversations on Contemporary Drama* writes:

" For twenty years I had practiced the two professions of lecturing and writing; but in all that time, I had never written a single paragraph that I intended to speak, nor dictated a single paragraph that I intended to print. I explained that writing was one thing and talking was another, that the technical processes of the two professions were entirely distinct, that my best writing would be unspeakable and my best talking would be unreadable." [2]

Edward Bok in his autobiography tells us that when he had interviewed Mark Twain he sent the manuscript to Mr. Clemens asking for his approval. It was returned with the following interesting letter:

My dear Mr. Bok:

No, no — it is like most interviews, pure twaddle, and valueless.

For several quite plain and simple reasons, an " interview " must, as a rule, be an absurdity. And chiefly for this reason: it is an attempt to use a boat on land, or a wagon on water, to speak figuratively. Spoken speech is one thing, written speech is quite another. The moment " talk " is put into print you recognize that it is not what it was when you heard it; you perceive that an immense something has disappeared from it. That is its soul. You have nothing but a dead carcass left on your hands. Color, play of feature, the varying modulations of the voice, the laugh, the smile, the informing inflections,

[1] Aristotle, *Rhetoric*, translated by W. Rhys Roberts, Book III, p. 1413 f.
[2] The Macmillan Company, New York, 1924, p. ix. Reprinted by permission.

everything that gave that body warmth, grace, friendliness, and charm, and commended it to your affection, or at least to your tolerance, is gone, and nothing is left, but a pallid, stiff, and repulsive cadaver.

Such is "talk" almost invariably, as you see it lying in state in an "interview." The interviewer seldom tries to tell one *how* a thing was said; he merely puts in the naked remark, and stops there. When one writes for print, his methods are very different. He follows forms which have but little resemblance to conversation, but they make the reader understand what the writer is trying to convey. And when the writer is making a story, and finds it necessary to report some of the talk of his characters, observe how cautiously and anxiously he goes at that risky and difficult thing:

"If he had dared to say that thing in my presence," said Alfred, taking a mock heroic attitude, and casting an arch glance upon the company, "blood would have flowed."

"If he had dared to say that thing in my presence," said the paltry blusterer, with valor on his tongue and pallor on his lips, "blood would have flowed."

So painfully aware is the novelist that naked talk in print conveys no meaning, that he loads, and often overloads, almost every utterance of his characters with explanations and interpretations. It is a loud confession that print is a poor vehicle for "talk," it is a recognition that uninterpreted talk in print would result in confusion to the reader, not instruction.

Now, in your interview you have certainly been most accurate, you have set down the sentences I uttered as I said them. But you have not a word of explanation; what my manner was at several points is not indicated. Therefore, no reader can possibly know where I was in earnest and where I was joking; or whether I was joking altogether or in earnest altogether. Such a report of a conversation has no value. It can convey many meanings to the reader, but never the right one. To add interpretations which would convey the right meaning is a something which would require — what? An art so high and fine and difficult that no possessor of it would ever be allowed to waste it on interviews.

No; spare the reader and spare me; leave the whole interview out; it is rubbish. I wouldn't talk in my sleep if I couldn't talk better than that.

If you wish to print anything print this letter; it may have some value, for it may explain to a reader here and there why it is that in interviews as a rule men seem to talk like anybody but themselves.

Sincerely yours,
Mark Twain [1]

SOURCES OF DIFFERENCES BETWEEN SPOKEN AND WRITTEN LANGUAGE

If we have observed and studied carefully, we doubtless will agree with the authorities that differences between oral and written language do exist. Further to verify this point of view, we should continue to observe conversation and public address, and compare them

with literature, textbooks, and the themes which our English teachers mark "Excellent." The important point to notice is that speaking and writing may be very different and yet each may be proper and satisfactory, in its own place. Before considering the differences, let us ask and answer the question: Whence do they spring?

[1] From *Mark Twain's Letters*, Harper & Bros., New York. Reprinted by permission.

There seem to be six sources, reasons, or causes for actual differences in words and sentences between oral and written language.

The speaker's audience is specific. Generally speeches are prepared for specific audiences; the speaker is informed in advance as to whom he will address. On the other hand, the writer frequently has no such knowledge; he must aim his language at " whom it may concern." The writer's article, essay, or story may be read by a girl on a Wyoming mountain ranch or by a broker in a New York skyscraper — or by both. Some written compositions may have specific " audiences." This is true of personal letters and of articles addressed to special groups. In such writing there certainly will be fewer of the distinguishing characteristics of written language. We tend to write as we speak whenever we are writing to someone or to some group in particular.

The speaker sees the effects of words. The speaker (except the radio speaker) can watch those to whom he speaks. He can see when they agree with him and when they disagree; when they understand and when they are confused. In short, he can observe, in large measure, what the immediate responses to his language are. The writer has nothing but his foresight and general good sense to tell him how his words will affect the reader. This distinction is an important source of differences in language.

Need for instant intelligibility. The reader can go back and reread, the listener must get the meaning at once. The writer knows that the reader can go at his own pace in getting the meaning. The speaker knows that the listener must get the meaning from the language as it is spoken. Unless the listener can do this easily, he usually does not do it at all.

Danger from distractions. Most reading is done in comparative quiet and seclusion. On the other hand, listening usually occurs under conditions far less favorable for getting meanings from language, at least for concentrating on the job. This is especially true in public speeches, where audiences are distracted by sounds, moving people, strange faces. When a reader has been distracted, he can go back and regain his bearings, rereading if necessary. The listener has no such opportunity; when his attention has wandered, the language sounds of the speaker have passed forever beyond his reach, unless he is in a position to ask the speaker to repeat them.

Voice and action affect language. Voice and visible action are mighty helpers in stirring up meanings. Written language must stand or fall alone. People who listen to spoken language usually get important messages from the speaker's posture, movement, gesture, rate of utterance, tone, inflection, and emphasis. The reader has none of these to help him in getting the meanings from language; he has only the poor substitutes of punctuation and other printing devices.

Written language is seen, spoken language is heard. The reader gets his meanings through his eyes. The listener gets his meanings through his ears. Written words and sentences are light-waves. Spoken words and sentences are sound-waves. Written language is made with the arm and hand muscles or with a printing press. Spoken language is made with the vocal apparatus.

DIFFERENCES BETWEEN SPOKEN AND WRITTEN LANGUAGE

Having seen why spoken language and written language may be expected to differ, let us now consider eleven principal differences between the words and sentences of oral language and the words and sentences of written language.

Oral language is adapted to a particular audience. In the first place, a speech needs to be more carefully adapted to an audience than does a written article. The speaker must take into consideration the habits and feelings of a particular listener or group of listeners and refer to them in what he says. A speaker can talk effectively only in terms of the experiences of his audiences, in words which they know, in images with which they are familiar. Therefore he should consider the age, background, training, education, and prejudices of his listeners. In addressing a group of third-graders, he must use language very different from that which he would use in talking to members of a woman's club. Careful adaptation to an audience is the first distinguishing characteristic of oral style.

Oral language is adapted to a particular occasion. In order to be effective, a speech must fit a specific occasion. This may not be possible in a written article, which may be read at any time, but a speech should be prepared for one special occasion and made to serve that occasion. It is easy to see that a speech which is appropriate for Me-

AMERICA HONORS LAFAYETTE. *Impressive ceremonies held before the Houses of Congress in joint session on the centennial of Lafayette's death, May 20, 1934. The President is delivering the memorial address. Note extreme formality of audience, place, and occasion. (Keystone View)*

morial Day may not be appropriate for Christmas; one adapted to a commencement would not make a good funeral eulogy! Speeches should clearly reflect the nature of the occasion.

Oral language is adapted to a particular speaker. The speaker must make the language of his speech fit himself and his own delivery. Says W. B. Cairns: " The more perfectly the two harmonize, the more effective is the impression conveyed. Few orators, even among the greatest, could exchange orations and achieve satisfactory results." An audience wishes to feel that it is fitting for us, and for us alone, to say exactly what we are saying, and that there is a consistency between our personality and our language.

Oral language uses simple words and sentences. Clear, simple sentences are an advantage in spoken language. Listeners find it very difficult to understand involved sentences. The speaker should not try to surprise his hearers with strange words, unfamiliar comparisons, and complicated sentences. For reasons we have already discussed, spoken language must always have that quality called "instant intelligibility." It must be so simple and straightforward that the hearer will find it easy to grasp the meaning immediately. The speaker uses short words and simple sentence structure, for only language which the listener can understand instantaneously can be maximally effective in speech.

Oral language uses greater variety in sentence length. The good speaker generally uses shorter sentences than does the good writer; he also uses fairly long sentences; but, long or short, they are always clear in construction and phraseology. At first thought this may seem like a contradiction, but careful consideration will make clear that in writing, sentences do not vary so much in length as they do in speaking. Just as the speaker uses variety in voice, subject matter, and action, he uses variety in sentence length. We must therefore make some of our sentences short and some long and scatter those of average length among them if we are to use good oral language.

Oral language uses many imperative, interrogative, and exclamatory sentences. The successful speaker asks questions (and answers them), exclaims, and commands his audience to do whatever it is he wants them to.

Oral language is direct. The effective speaker is usually more direct than the effective writer. Directness is that quality which makes each person in the audience feel that the words are spoken straight to him. Our public-speaking style should be the style of our best conversation. Therefore we should make ample use of the pronouns which are so prominent in conversation: *I, me, my, mine, myself; we, our, us, ourselves; you, your, yourself,* and *yourselves*. We should aim to use these pronouns, especially those of the first person singular and plural and of the second person plural, as frequently as we do in animated conversation. The writer who has no definite audience in his mind is necessarily somewhat impersonal. The speaker should be personal. He should be engaged in a spirited conversation, even though only one participant is using language and voice. The attentive audience will be reacting significantly.

Oral language abounds in repetition. The speaker should repeat more than does the writer. We have said that it is impossible for the

MARK ANTONY AT CAESAR'S FUNERAL. "*But here's a parchment with the seal of Caesar; I found it in his closet; 'tis his will: Let but the commons hear this testament — which, pardon me, I do not mean to read —.*" Shakespeare puts into Antony's mouth one of the greatest public speeches of all time. Any student will be repaid for a careful study of its techniques of persuasion. (Culver)

hearer to review spoken discourse; therefore the orator must use enough repetition to be sure that the listeners grasp the meaning as he goes along. Repetition to an extent which might be condemned in writing should be encouraged in speaking. We should try to repeat the ideas in our speech in the same words, in slightly different words, in examples and comparisons, and in stories. We may employ reasoning first and then illustration, now general and now particular examples. The expression of a thought on the printed page may require forty words and on the platform one hundred. If we are skillful, we will not annoy our audience by too much repetition, but we will employ enough of it to make our points clearly understood.

Oral language is markedly euphonious. Spoken language is made up of sound-waves, and it is very important that they stir up only the right meanings. Any word the sound of which draws attention to itself should be avoided. In discussing this point Professor Shurter writes:

" A sentence which cannot easily be pronounced is an inharmonious sentence and should either be thrown out or recast, for men are influenced not only by what is reasonable but also by what is agreeable. The way a sentence sounds depends both upon the choice and arrangement of words. Whatever words are difficult to pronounce are also unpleasant to hear, as *soothedst, inextricableness, incogitation, lowlily, arbitrarily, incalculable, meteorological,* and in general those having either a repetition of syllables of similar sounds or a long succession of unaccented syllables. As to arrangement, words euphonious by themselves may displease the ear on account of their proximity to other words containing similar sounds as *his history, I can candidly say, I confess with humility my inability to decide, how it was was not explained.* Again, while a certain alliteration and rhythm is allowed, any suggestion of rhyme should be avoided as, *then Robert E. Lee began to make history,* avoid any appearance of incoherence, *the sailors mutinied and set him afloat in an open boat.*" [1]

Why are certain words and combinations of words to be avoided in spoken language? Is it merely because in some instances they are unpleasant to hear? Yes, quite so; but the more serious trouble is that they

---

[1] E. D. Shurter, *The Rhetoric of Oratory*, pp. 148-49. The Macmillan Company, New York. Reprinted by permission.

call attention to themselves and away from the meaning. They simply do not work as symbols. Some of them may not detract much from the meaning of written language; but they are all unfit for use in spoken language, where the question always is: How will those to whom the words are spoken react to the sounds they hear?

Oral language is more individualistic. Successful speakers are greater individualists than are successful writers. Careful examination of the works of writers and speakers shows that a good speaker is less like another good speaker than a good writer is like another good writer. This means that if we wish to produce excellent oral language, we must make it reveal us as individuals and make it sound unlike that of anyone else in the world. We must study ourselves to find out how our language can be made to reflect our personalities in our private and public speech.

Oral language is interesting. The problem of securing and holding attention is usually more acute for the speaker than for the writer. The former cannot afford to have any lapses whatever in the attention of his listeners. We have seen that the hearer's attention to language must be much more constant than the reader's. Of course, both written language and spoken language always should be as interesting as possible, but generally a high degree of sustained interestingness is more necessary in speaking than in writing. The successful speaker is concrete. He makes use of variety and suspense. He knows that when attention has been lost, spoken language is so much empty sound.

SUMMARY

Good written style is not good oral style, in spite of the fact that there are certain common fundamental characteristics. Good language for writing is usually poor language for speaking, because the situations to be served are so markedly different. These differences in situations give rise to the rules and suggestions for developing good oral style described on pages 141-146. Together with adequate control of visible bodily action and voice, the ability to select and arrange words for speaking brings us a step nearer to effective communication, which is the contribution of speech to the self-realization for which we are striving.

Tests of Comprehension and Application

MEANING

1   Take your favorite short lyric poem and write out the meaning of it in your own words, eliminating as far as possible all connotative meaning, retaining only the denotative meanings.

2   Make a written analysis of a newspaper editorial, classifying its different meanings as denotative and connotative.

3   Make a strong statement involving both denotative and connotative meanings. Restate the denotative meanings, changing the connotations as completely as possible.

4   An arctic explorer was recently being entertained at dinner. His hostess inquired, " What did you eat up there in the frozen North? " " Why," he replied, " mostly dead fish." " Dead fish," said the hostess. " That must have been dreadful! " " Oh, I don't know," he replied. " How do *you* eat fish? " Explain what makes this funny (if you think it is funny). Somehow it has something to do with the connotation of the term " dead fish," hasn't it?

5   The two columns [1] below show how connotative meanings may be modified while denotative meanings remain much the same:

" Finest quality filet mignon | First-class piece of dead cow
Cubs trounce Giants, 5–3 | Score: Cubs, 5, Giants, 3.
McCormick Bill steam-rollered through Senate. | Senate passes McCormick Bill over strong opposition.
Japanese divisions advance five miles. | Japs stopped cold after five-mile advance.
French armies in rapid retreat. | The retirement of the French forces to previously prepared positions in the rear was accomplished briskly and efficiently.
The governor appeared to be gravely concerned and said that a statement would be issued in a few days after careful examination of the facts. | The governor was on the spot."

[1] S. I. Hayakawa, *Language in Action*, Harcourt, Brace and Company, New York, 1941, p. 71. Reprinted by permission.

"The story is told that during the Boer War, the Boers were described in the British press as 'sneaking and skulking behind rocks and bushes.' The British forces, when they finally learned from the Boers how to employ tactics suitable to veldt warfare, were described as 'cleverly taking advantage of cover.'" [1]

Can you find or construct similar parallel statements?

6 Bring to class a newspaper editorial on some controversial matter. Pick out some ten words which seem to you to show how important an agreement upon definitions is. How can you arrive at it?

7 Give a little talk on the way in which some interesting words have developed their present meanings. Your English teacher may be willing to help you in working out this project.

8 Study the meanings of words as they are used in a motion picture or a stage play. Explain how the actor makes sure that you will get the intended meanings, and not others.

9 Choose some interesting words, a list of say ten or a dozen, ask three or four different persons what each of the words means to him or her, record their answers, and report to the class on what you have learned.

10 What is meant by a "loaded" word? Such words abound in political campaigns. Tell the class about some you have recently read or heard used. How does the propagandist use "loaded" words? Illustrate.

CHARACTERISTICS COMMON TO ORAL AND WRITTEN STYLE

11 (The following is an excerpt from a speech delivered by a high-school girl. Her classmates gave her a superior grade. Judging from the excerpt, do you think they were justified?)

We sit in eleven-o'clock study hall and think of all the luscious food that we would like to have for dinner: pork chops stuffed with savory dressing, a mound of mashed potatoes covered with thick mushroom gravy, a heap of fresh green peas with streams of yellow butter, fresh-fruit salad mixed with whipped cream and marshmallows, and hot pecan caramel rolls. For dessert we imagine plum pud-

---

[1] S. I. Hayakawa, *Language in Action*, Harcourt, Brace and Company, New York, 1941, p. 71. Reprinted by permission.

ding hidden under a layer of hard sauce or perhaps butterscotch pie or ice cream smothered in hot fudge an inch thick, decked with pecans. Suddenly our thoughts are interrupted by the bell, and we tramp home to a well-balanced, vitamin-true menu of liver, creamed carrots or spinach, raw-vegetable salad, and half a grapefruit for dessert.

12   History records for us the names of many writers and speakers who not only communicated successfully with the people of their own time but who, for thousands of years, have continued to be understood and appreciated. The following excerpt from Euripides is an example. Using the criteria for great style, show why this literature has lived.

>   Poor little child!
> Thy curls, these little flowers innocent
> That were thy mother's garden, where she laid
> Her kisses . . .
> And dear proud lips, so full of hope
> And closed forever! What false words ye said
> At daybreak, when he crept into my bed,
> Called me kind names, and promised: " Grandmother,
> When thou art dead, I will cut close my hair.
> And lead out all the captains to ride by
> Thy tomb." Why didst thou cheat me so? 'Tis I,
> Old, homeless, childless, that for thee must shed
> Cold tears, so young, so miserably dead.[1]

13   (Here is a speech delivered more than two thousand years ago by Demosthenes. Are you able to understand it? Name a speech by an American that expresses similar ideas.)

What Greek, what barbarian does not know that the Thebans would have been glad and thankful to let Athens take anything that she liked, besides keeping what she had got, if she would only have done what she was told, and allowed some other power to lead Greece? Such a bargain, however, was for the Athenians of those days neither conditional nor congenial nor supportable. In the whole course of her annals, no one could ever persuade Athens to side with

---

[1] Euripides, *Trojan Women*, translated by Gilbert Murray, Oxford University Press, New York, 1912, pp. 68–69. Reprinted by permission.

dishonest strength, to accept a secure slavery, or to desist, at any moment in her career, from doing battle and braving danger for pre-eminence, for honor, and for renown.

You, Athenians, find these principles so worthy of veneration, so accordant with your own character, that you praise none of your ancestors so highly as those who put them into action. You are right. The Athenians of those days were not in search of an orator or a general who should help them to an agreeable servitude. No. They would not hear of life itself if they were not to live free. Each one of them held that he had been born the son not only of his father and his mother, but of his country also. And wherein is the difference? It is here. He that recognizes no debt of piety save to his parents awaits his death in the course of destiny and of nature. But he that deems himself the son of his country also will be ready to die sooner than see her enslaved. In his estimate those insults, those dishonors which must be suffered in his city when she has lost her freedom will be accounted more terrible than death.[1]

14 (Does the following description recall experiences for you? Does it recall experiences for other members of your class? Are your experiences exactly like those of your classmates? If not, what are the elements that they have in common? What characteristics essential to good style do you find in the quotation?)

Interspersed with the pies of the early season (which we had in plenty) was a strawberry shortcake. Now, strawberry shortcake, as my mother made it, was no mean matter of one small, rangy biscuit split apart and sparingly smeared with a little strawberry juice.

My mother made strawberry shortcake in a small dripping pan and of a very rich biscuit dough. When this was baked to flaky perfection it was turned onto a platter and split in two. The top half was laid aside and the bottom part lavishly spread with butter. Over this the berries (already crushed in a blue and white porcelain bowl) were thickly poured. Then the top half was laid over this (still piping hot), fulsomely buttered, while the remainder of the berries completely canopied the whole. The juice ran off and made a crimson

[1] Demosthenes, "On the Crown," *The Attic Orators, from Antiphon to Isaeos*, ed. by R. C. Jebb, 2 vols., The Macmillan Company, London, 1876, Vol. II, pp. 412–13.

COMPREHENSION AND APPLICATION TESTS

lake on which the shortcake rested. A pitcher of cream stood by, an accompaniment for those who wanted it.

When we had shortcake we had but little else, nor needed more. Here was a dish complete in itself, perfect in quality, adequate in quantity, and presenting a feast sufficient for gods or epicurean men.[1]

15 Make a list of fifty interesting experiences that you have had. Draw a red line through those which you believe your classmates have not experienced in whole or in part. Now draw a blue line through those familiar to your high-school friends but foreign to persons outside of your high school. How many do you have left?

16 Out of the remaining experiences on your list made for project 15 select those in which you were so sensitive and felt so deeply that you still recall them in every detail.

17 By the careful use of language communicate the experiences in exercise 16 to readers or listeners.

VOCABULARY

18 Test your vocabulary by describing precisely ten of the following. If you do them well, you will recall similar experiences for others.

   a Your feeling when you are waiting for your report card
   b Your feeling when you are waiting to receive an award in assembly
   c Your reaction to a beautiful sunset
   d Your first ride on horseback
   e Your first experience on roller skates
   f The taste of some unpleasant food
   g The smell of your home in pickling time
   h Your feeling when the telephone rings and you are hoping for a particular call
   i The sensation when you walk in the mud with bare feet
   j Your feeling when saved from drowning
   k A house on fire
   l The taste of some favorite food
   m Your feeling when you are in a very high place

[1] Della T. Lutes, "The Simple Epicure," *The Atlantic Monthly*, March 1935. Reprinted by permission.

n Your feeling when you are on a train and going around a curve and see the engine of the train on which you are riding
o Your feeling when seasick
p Your feeling when you forget your part in a play, or forget a memorized reading or oration
q Your reaction to a certain teacher for whom you do poor work
r Your desire to " make " the football team
s Your bed when you are very tired
t The state between sleeping and waking

19 Let each student bring a picture or an object to school. Display them in your classroom and have each student write an exact description of one. Place the articles out of sight. Are the word pictures vivid enough to recall the articles precisely?

20 Keep a vocabulary notebook. Add one word every day. This need not be a word you have never heard before, but one you have not used regularly. Make an opportunity to use each word on your list either in speaking or in writing every day. Notice how these words help you to express exact meanings.

21 Play charades in which you act out unfamiliar words.

22 Read literature that you cannot understand without the use of the dictionary. Read until you have looked up ten words and selected meanings appropriate to the context.

23 Find an example of literature intended to be read silently that you consider great style.

24 Find an example of a speech that you consider great style.

25 From the following select one to read and discuss before the class.[1]

a Your Order, Please

Henry James, the great American novelist, never could rest with the phrases that came to his tongue. He simply couldn't leave the English language alone; he would extract a word from his verbal storehouse, drop it, substitute another, then a third, and so on until he had constructed a veritable pyramid of synonyms. This terrible word malady broke out once at a restaurant as he gave the waiter his order.

[1] The six following selections are reprinted from *World Study*, copyright, 1942, G. & C. Merriam Company.

Bring me — fetch me — carry me — supply me — in other words (I hope you are following me) serve me — when it is cooked — scorched — grilled — browned — I should say — a large — considerable — meaty (as opposed to fatty) — chop. (From *The Christian Science Monitor* of August 13, 1941)

b   SYMBOLS — WORDS

O the sudden leaping out of a word!
The hot word torn odorous from the very thing,
Like bark swished from the tree, or the rasp of the receding wave.
O the appropriate image,
Mirrors star-fastened upon the skies, flashing back the earth —
"The morn in russet mantle clad."
O the pretty hedgerow words, blossoming, thrush-noisy —
Tune, purling, murmurous, cymbals, festoon.
O the heavy somber words, like the muffled thunder of horses' feet, as freed, they stampede the pasture —
Doom, moan, dolorous, swamp, dusk, munch.
O the brave sentinel words, scornful, retaliating —
Bludgeoning, courage, canyon, savage.
O the droll words, comically ordered, whimsical —
Pull, pumpkin, egg, pickle.
O the beautiful words, hallowing, chiming —
Chimney, cinder, swallow, abbey, wallflower, building.
O the poignant words, like stars on the vellum ceiling of the palace of Night —
Pang, psalm, melancholy, foam, wan.
O the musical words that must be sung, that jingle like the bells on young horses' necks —
Scintillate, panorama, sickle, flotilla.

— E. E. Johnson (Suggested by Professor Sharon Brown of Brown University)

c   ICONOCLAST

I am an infinitive splitter;
I split to the left and the right.
I'm iconoclastic;

My views quite elastic
When infinitives heave into sight.

I am an infinitive splitter;
I split as my conscience dictates.
   It may be informal;
   I find it quite normal;
I loathe the poor purists' debates.

I am an infinitive splitter;
I split in accord with my whim.
   I break the mad rule
   Taught by tyrant at school,
My nose thumbed benignly at him.

I am an infinitive splitter;
I split, sir, whenever I please,
   Because I defend, sir,
   The right and the end, sir
To constantly *be* at my ease.

To happily *split* an infinitive,
To joyously *write* in that vein,
   To blessedly *split* it,
   To freely *admit* it,
Is *to* proudly *find* freedom again.
      — Ilo Orleans

d   STRONG VERBS

Oh, what a blamed uncertain thing
   This pesky weather is!
It blew and snew and then it thew,
   And now, by jing, it's friz!
— Philander C. Johnson (Quoted in *The Chicago Sun*)

e   A WORD

What is a word?
A word is a pulley
To raise up a city in the wilderness

Or to lift a new star into its place
Or to lift the soul of a man.
A word is a wedge
To separate two friends forever
Or to split a stumbling block.
A word is a lever
To wrench and dislocate
Or to pry open.
These are simple machines.
But a word is also a dynamo, thrusting its subtle power through the hidden filaments of the words;
Or it is a cyclotron, hammering its inquiry at the gates of the ultimate atom;
Or it is an acorn or a time bomb, biding in the soft earth its time to create or destroy;
Or it is sweet peace.
Now, as in the beginning,
Give me for greatest power
In smallest compass,
Not radium,
But a word!

— James Wood

f The following poem won first place in the Walter E. Bryson contest held at Texas Christian University.

I LIKE WORDS

I like words —
Silvery words that tinkle
Across the page like delicate wind chimes;
Like the full-throated shouting of strong men;
Solemn words that bring a catch to my throat
Like kneeling before an altar.
I like pompous, frock-coated words
That puff out their waistcoats like fat politicians
Strutting importantly across the page;
Eager, impetuous words that come racing and tumbling over each other

To reach the end of the sentence;
Comfortable words that purr contently
Like a cat upon the hearth.
I like crisp, scintillant words
Like the flashing cut of a knife;
Artless, carefree words that sing like happy children;
Friendly, folksy words still with the look of homespun on them;
Words that can make a living, breathing thing
Out of a scrap of rag and pulp,
That can make an impassioned oration out of empty air.
I like words. The empty white of paper
Catches at my pen in an insistent plea to be peopled.
I like words.

— Margaret Caskey

SOURCES OF DIFFERENCES BETWEEN ORAL AND WRITTEN LANGUAGE

26 Attend church and observe the clergyman for occasions when he changes his language because of some particular audience reaction as he speaks.

27 For two days keep a record of times when you have gone back to reread material from textbooks because you did not understand it at the first reading.

28 Make a list of speeches you have heard in which you have failed to understand because you could not go back.

29 What distractions do you have that keep you from understanding all of every assembly program?

30 Do you have distractions that keep you from understanding all that is said in class? Does the teacher try to counteract them? Is he successful? Give reasons for your answer.

31 List as many incidents as you can when speakers have used bodily action to help listeners to get the exact meaning intended.

32 Which is easier to understand, what is seen or what is heard? Prepare a speech giving your answer.

33 Make a notebook with explanations and illustrations showing why it is reasonable that language for speaking should be different from language for writing.

ACTUAL DIFFERENCES IN WORDS AND SENTENCES BETWEEN ORAL AND WRITTEN STYLE

34 A high-school English student was asked to read his theme before the class.

"That is unsatisfactory," said the teacher. "You have not made the meaning clear."

"But I did not prepare it to read aloud," objected the student, "it is *written* material intended to be read silently."

"That makes no difference," said the teacher, and she called on the next student to recite.

What is your reaction to this teacher's point of view? Do you get a fair grade when a paper prepared for silent reading is judged by the way it sounds when you read it orally? Explain your answer.

35 Prepare a speech, entitled "Good Oral Language," to be delivered before a group of English teachers, using good oral language to explain why it is not fair to judge written English themes by the way they sound when read aloud before the class.

36 Criticize the following paragraphs with reference to their fitness for speaking aloud.

a Your pedestrian is always cheerful, alert, refreshed, with his heart in his hands and his hand free to all. He looks down upon nobody; he is on the common level. His pores are all open, his circulation is active, his digestion good. His heart is not cold, nor are his faculties asleep. He is the only real traveler; he alone tastes the gay, fresh sentiment of the road.

— John Burroughs

b It is strange that with all the succession of interesting novel experiences I had in Norway, there is none which stands out so clearly in my memory, after an interval of seven years, as a chance meeting with a Norwegian peasant one late afternoon as I pursued my way from Vossevangen to Eide. To give the setting I must begin at the beginning.

— W. L. Richardson

c Why I was christened Thomas Henry I do not know; but it is a curious chance that my parents should have fixed for my usual

denomination upon the name of that particular apostle with whom I have always felt most sympathy. Physically and mentally I am the son of my mother so completely — even down to the movements of my hands, which made their appearance in me as I reached the age she had when I noticed them — that I can hardly find any trace of my father in myself, except an inborn faculty for drawing, which unfortunately, in my case, has never been cultivated, a hot temper, and that amount of tenacity of purpose which unfriendly observers sometimes call obstinacy.
— Thomas Henry Huxley

d Dear Madam:

I have been shown in the files of the War Department a statement of the Adjutant General of Massachusetts that you are the mother of five sons who have died gloriously on the field of battle. I feel how weak and fruitless must be any words of mine which should attempt to beguile you from the grief of a loss so overwhelming. But I cannot refrain from tendering to you the consolation which may be found in the thanks of the Republic they died to save. I pray that our heavenly Father may assuage the anguish of your bereavement, and leave you only the cherished memory of the loved and lost, and the solemn pride that must be yours to have laid so costly a sacrifice on the altar of freedom.

Yours very sincerely and respectfully,
Abraham Lincoln

e Fellow citizens, we cannot escape history. We of this Congress and this administration will be remembered in spite of ourselves. No personal significance or insignificance can spare one or another of us. The fiery trial through which we pass will light us down, in honor or dishonor, to the latest generation. We say that we are for the Union. The world will not forget that we say this. We know how to save the Union. The world knows we do know how to save it.

We, even we here, hold the power and bear the responsibility. In giving freedom to the slave, we assure freedom to the free — honorable alike in what we give and what we preserve. We shall nobly save or meanly lose the last, best hope of earth. Other means may succeed; this could not fail. The way is plain, peaceful, generous, just — a way which if followed the world will forever applaud, and God must forever bless.

— Abraham Lincoln

f If it be affirmed that rhyme and metrical arrangement of themselves constitute a distinction which overturns what has just been said on the strict affinity of metrical language with that of prose, and paves the way for other artificial distinctions which the mind voluntarily admits, I answer that the language of such poetry as is here recommended is, as far as is possible, a selection of the language really spoken by men; that this selection, wherever it is made with true taste and feeling, will of itself form a distinction far greater than would at first be imagined, and will entirely separate the composition from the vulgarity and meanness of ordinary life; and, if meter be superadded thereto, I believe that a dissimilitude will be produced altogether sufficient for the gratification of a rational mind.

— William Wordsworth

g Shakespeare was an intellectual ocean, whose waves touched all the shores of thought; within which were all the tides of destiny and will; over which swept all the storms of fate, ambition, and revenge; upon which fell the gloom and darkness of despair and death, and all the sunlight of content and love, and within which was the inverted sky, lit with the eternal stars — an intellectual ocean toward which all rivers ran, and from which now the isles and continents of thought receive their dew and rain.

— Robert G. Ingersoll

h I would as soon think of bounding a sovereign state on the north by a dandelion, on the east by a blue jay, on the south by a hive of bees in swarming time, and on the west by three hundred foxes with firebrands tied to their tails, as of relying upon the loose and indefinite bounds of commissioners of a century ago.

— Rufus Choate

37 Is the following good style? Is it oral or written? Give reasons for your answers.

He wished he had a dog like Grandma Hutto's. It was white and curly-haired and did tricks. When Grandma Hutto laughed and shook and could not stop, the dog jumped into her lap and licked her face, wagging its plumed tail as though it laughed with her.[1]

38 Bring to class a speech which exemplifies good oral language. Choose one paragraph to read before the class. How do the particular words and sentences used help to make this selection effective when read aloud?

39 Select from a magazine or a book an article of about three hundred words clearly intended to be read silently. Work this over into a speech form, using all of the suggestions given in the text for appropriate oral language. Notice how you will shorten and change the sentences; how you will repeat in a variety of ways; how you will include more of the pronouns of the first and second persons; how you will make the speech fit the audience, the occasion, and the speaker; and how you will choose words which express the thought more clearly because of their appropriate sounds.

40 Attend a church service or a public lecture. List the rules for good oral language which were observed or violated by the speaker.

41 It has been said that newspaper editorials are often prepared in oral rather than in written style. What is your opinion? Give examples.

42 Listen to radio speeches. Do the speakers use effective language? Do they ever seem to violate the rules you have learned? Show how some of the speakers you have heard have exemplified the principles of effective speech.

43 Do radio announcers make use of good oral language? Does your favorite announcer differ on this point from one you dislike?

44 What rules for good oral language can you derive from the following speech?

FIGHTING FOR THE SAME CAUSE

WE MUST ACT TO IMPLEMENT OUR IDEALS

by Madame Chiang Kai-shek [2]

Mr. President, members of the Senate of the United States, ladies and gentlemen: I am overwhelmed by the warmth and spontaneity of the welcome of the American people, of whom you are the repre-

---

[1] Marjorie Kinnan Rawlings, *The Yearling*, Scribner's Sons, New York, 1938, p. 2.

[2] Delivered before the United States Senate, February 18, 1943.

sentatives. I did not know that I was to speak to you today at the Senate except to say "How do you do? I am so very glad to see you," and to bring the greetings of my people to the people of America. However, just before coming here, the Vice-President told me that he would like to have me say a few words to you.

I am not a very good extemporaneous speaker; in fact, I am no speaker at all. But I am not so very much discouraged, because a few days ago I was at Hyde Park and went to the President's library. Something I saw there encouraged me and made me feel that perhaps you will not expect overmuch of me in speaking to you extemporaneously.

What do you think I saw there? I saw many things, but the one thing which interested me most of all was that in a glass case there was the first draft of one of the President's speeches, a second draft, and on and on up to the sixth draft. Yesterday I happened to mention this fact to the President, and told him that I was extremely glad that he had to write so many drafts when he is such a well-known and acknowledgedly fine speaker. His reply to me was that sometimes he writes twelve drafts of a speech. So my remarks here today being extemporaneous, I am sure you will make allowances for me.

The traditional friendship between your country and mine has a history of one hundred and sixty years. I feel, and I believe that I am not the only one who feels this way, that there are a great many similarities between your people and mine, and that these similarities are the basis of our friendship.

I should like to tell you a little story which will illustrate this belief. When General Doolittle and his men went to bomb Tokyo, on their return some of your boys had to bail out in the interior of China. One of them later told me that he had to bail out of his ship, and that when he landed on Chinese soil and saw the populace running toward him, he just waved his arm and shouted the only Chinese word he knew, " Mei-kuo, mei-kuo," which means " America." Literally translated from the Chinese, it means " beautiful country." This boy said that our people laughed and almost hugged him, and greeted him like a long-lost brother. He further told me that he thought that he had come home when he saw our people; and that was the first time he had ever been to China.

I came to your country as a little girl. I know your people. I have lived with them. I spent the formative years of my life among your people. I speak your language, not only the language of your hearts, but also your tongue. So coming here today I feel that I am also coming home.

I believe, however, that it is not only I who am coming home; I feel that if the Chinese people could speak to you in your own tongue, or if you could understand our tongue, they would tell you that basically and fundamentally we are fighting for the same cause, that we have identity of ideals, that the Four Freedoms which your President proclaimed to the world resound throughout our vast land as the gong of freedom, the gong of freedom of the United Nations, and the death knell of the aggressors.

I assure you that our people are willing and eager to co-operate with you in the realization of these ideals, because we want to see to it that they do not echo as empty phrases but become realities for ourselves, for our children, for our children's children, and for all mankind.

How are we going to realize these ideals? I think I shall tell you a little story which just came to my mind. You know China is a very old nation. We have a history of five thousand years. When we were obliged to evacuate Hankow and go into the hinterland to carry on and continue our resistance against aggression, the Generalissimo and I passed one of our fronts, the Changsha front. One day we went into the Heng-Yang Mountains, where there are traces of a famous pavilion called "Rub-the-Mirror" pavilion, which was built over two thousand years ago. It will perhaps interest you to hear the story of that pavilion.

Two thousand years ago near that spot was an old Buddhist temple. One of the young monks went there, and all day long he sat cross-legged with his hands clasped before him in an attitude of prayer, and murmured "Amita-Buddha! Amita-Buddha! Amita-Buddha!" He murmured and chanted day after day, because he hoped that he would acquire grace. The Father Prior of that temple took a piece of brick and rubbed it against a stone hour after hour, day after day, and week after week. The little acolyte, being very young, sometimes cast his eyes around to see what the old Father

Prior was doing. The old Father Prior just kept on his work of rubbing the brick against the stone. So one day the young acolyte said to him: "Father Prior, what are you doing day after day, rubbing this brick on the stone?" The Father Prior replied, "I am trying to make a mirror out of this brick." The young acolyte said, "But it is impossible to make a mirror out of a brick, Father Prior." "Yes," said the Father Prior, "it is just as impossible for you to acquire grace by doing nothing except 'Amita-Buddha' all day long, day in and day out."

So, my friends, I feel that it is necessary for us not only to have ideals and to proclaim that we have them, it is necessary that we act to implement them. And so to you, gentlemen of the Senate, and to you ladies and gentlemen in the galleries, I say that without the active help of all of us our leaders cannot implement these ideals. It is up to you and to me to take to heart the lesson of "Rub-the-Mirror" pavilion.

I thank you.

CHAPTER SIX *Creative Listening*

ALL THROUGH our lives, in school and out, we learn by listening. With the arrival of radio, efficient listening has become even more important. A considerable share of our success in business or professional life, and a very large part of our education after we leave school, will depend on our ability to listen attentively, to analyze accurately, and to discuss intelligently what we have heard. Therefore it is important for us to understand the listening process and to become skillful, creative listeners.

Not a day passes without numerous worth-while opportunities for the practice of right listening habits. At breakfast we listen to radio news. When we arrive at school, we begin a day of adventures in listening. We listen to our teachers and to our classmates. Perhaps at the assembly hour we listen to an entertaining or informative talk by some member of the faculty, by a visiting lecturer, or by a

A LISTLESS LISTENER. *The boy directly in front of the teacher is giving an excellent demonstration of how not to listen. Instead of maintaining an alert attitude he is all set for day-dreaming or " doodling " rather than for creative listening. He probably would be voted by the other members of the class the one least likely to succeed!* (*Lilly Joss from Black Star*)

student. In the evening we hear our favorite radio programs. In short, there is scarcely a waking hour in which we are not expected to listen to something that is important to us. " Well," someone says, " I know all that, and I have no difficulty in listening. I've learned that through long experience." But are we sure that our listening really is reasonably efficient? If it is, we are unusually fortunate; for just as most of us see only a fraction of what is before our eyes, we actually hear only a few of the sound-waves which move our eardrums. Having eyes, we see not, and having ears, we hear not.

CREATIVE LISTENING IS ACTIVE LISTENING

As we have just suggested, the difficulty with most of us is not that we have defective eyes and ears, but that we do not use them efficiently. Seeing and hearing are really mental processes; we see and hear with our minds rather than with our eyes and ears. When two people walk down the street together, we cannot tell by testing their eyesight which one of them will see more than the other. Similarly, when two students sit in a classroom, we cannot tell by testing their ears which one will hear more than the other. Both may have normal hearing and yet in all of the essential situations of life one may hear ten times more than the other does.

Not only is it true that different people in the same situation make very different uses of their hearing apparatus; but, as our own experience has taught us, the same person's hearing of what goes on about him changes greatly from time to time and from situation to situation. We may say, "There's nothing so strange about that." However, it may be well to get some fundamental facts about hearing straightened out before we go further.

Creative listening means more — much more — than just being exposed to sounds; it is a thoroughly active process in which we are stimulated by the sounds into some sort of responses. We are really doing something when we listen, not having something done to us. Ordinarily, by watching a person we can tell whether or not he is really listening. One bad habit into which students get themselves is looking as if they were listening when in reality their minds are elsewhere. They fix their gaze on the teacher intently and then let their thoughts go woolgathering. They think about almost anything but the words that are falling upon their ears. They are just going through the outward forms of listening; real listening is not taking place at all. They may think that they are playing a trick on the teacher, but it frequently happens that the joke is on them!

Real creative listening is active listening. It is a sort of conversation in which we consider what a speaker is saying, think what we might say in reply, and even frame sentences and, in the pauses, speak them to ourselves silently. When we are behaving in this fashion, what we hear is likely to have real meaning for us.

Our capacity for hearing what is said to us depends upon our past experiences and the uses we are able to make of them. Creative listening is a process of fitting what we hear into what we ourselves have felt, believed, and thought. In the final analysis we have nothing to listen with but our experiences, and unless we employ them effectively our hearing will be superficial and shallow.

In creative listening it is a great help to be able to take the proper sort of notes. When we are clumsy in notetaking, we find it impossible to follow a speaker's line of thought, and to get the information he is trying to give us. Moreover, efficient notetaking requires enough physical activity to keep us mentally alert and to guarantee a proper focusing of our attention on what is being said.

CREATIVE LISTENING IS SELECTIVE LISTENING

What we have just said about effective notetaking has a broad application to the whole problem of listening. We cannot hope to remember every detail of any speech; indeed not everything that any speaker says is worth remembering. This being true, it is necessary that we learn to distinguish the more important from the less important matters; for unless we do, we may carefully gather the chaff and lose the wheat. One of the most common faults in notetaking is the attempt to take down everything we hear. We must learn to recognize the main points — the high spots — in a speech or a lecture, and record just enough of what is said to enable us to recall all of it clearly when we go back over our written notes.

Creative listening is selective listening, and selective listening requires: (1) that we learn to recognize the main points or divisions of the speech, and the subheadings which are used to prove or support them; and (2) that we learn to pass critical judgment on the truth or the value of what the speaker is saying as he says it. This evaluating phase of the twofold process involves the critical use of our past experiences. How often we have listened attentively, as we thought, to a lecture, only to find at its conclusion that we were unable to explain the speaker's point of view and to remember what he had said!

A very great help in understanding and evaluating what we hear is the practice of discussing it with someone else immediately after we have heard it. This procedure makes it possible for us to supplement what we ourselves have learned by what others have learned, and it will protect us against misunderstandings and inaccurate judgments.

One great value in the study of speech is that it makes us less susceptible to infection by misinformation, false statements, and propaganda of all sorts. Having learned to listen selectively and critically, we shall not accept so readily unsupported rumors and malicious misrepresentations. We should note that in general we believe everything which we hear unless we have established protective habits of critical appraisal. Belief is a passive process; doubt is active. A democracy needs intelligent believers and doubters; every one of us owes it to himself to be extremely careful as to what ideas he takes into his mind and makes at home there.

If in listening to speakers we have become accustomed to daydreaming and inattentiveness, now is the time to "snap out of it" and establish habits of active and selective listening. We may be amazed to find how much that is really worth while has been getting past us because of our inactive and uncritical listening. When we adopt a dynamic type of listening, we will find ourselves going out mentally to assimilate the thrilling and interesting materials about which we are told. No one ever really develops his full capacities for imaginative and constructive living until he has adopted a positive attitude of mind.

All that we have been saying about listening to lectures and other speeches can of course be applied also to hearing poetry and music. One reason many persons get so little out of listening to good music is that they have never had any training in creating music, and consequently they find it difficult to be active listeners. If we have been trained to play a musical instrument, we are much better prepared for listening creatively to an orchestra concert than we are if we have not been so trained. If we can sing reasonably well, we have the materials out of which we can build an appreciation of an opera broadcast. On the other hand, if we do not have the training to respond to the sounds we hear, our capacity for appreciation must necessarily be extremely limited. Of course, there is always the possibility of talking to ourselves and with others about the music to which we have just listened, and that is certainly far better than wholly passive listening.

There is no substitute for the actual reading of poetry aloud as a preparation for enjoyment when we hear other people read it. We never can acquire full and rich appreciation of poetic forms merely by hearing our teachers or others read poetry. A still better preparation for getting the most out of hearing poetry read aloud is the actual writing of poetry. When we have found out how meaning and music get tied up together in a poem of our own, we are much more able to listen appreciatively to the reading of poetry.

To enjoy music and poetry as adults, we should begin as children to develop simple rhythmic responses, the interpretation of music through general bodily action. Then, so far as we are capable, we should learn to sing and to play musical instruments. Folk dances, choral singing, participation in other musical activities — all of these quicken imagination, deepen emotional responses, and develop powers of discrimination which later may enable us to enter into real appreciation of these art forms through creative, active, and selective listening.

It is amazing what a reputation for ability as a conversationalist can be built on an intelligent use of listening. If we go over in our minds our list of close friends, those with whom we like most to converse, we may well find that many of them talk less than we do. They please us by listening sympathetically to what we say. A drama critic once remarked that in order to have great plays we must have great audiences. It is equally true that to have supremely fine conversation we must have skilled and effective listeners. Without James Boswell, we could not possibly have had Dr. Johnson's remarkable wisdom. What Boswell did was to provide Johnson with a good listener — as well as a recorder.

But we do not want too many one-sided conversations such as those of Boswell and Johnson. The best conversations, the most satisfying in which to participate, are those in which each party to the enterprise has his fair share of both leading and following, talking and listening. We shall have more to say about this matter in the chapter on "Conversation." All that we need to note here is that it will pay us well to learn how to be good listeners in conversations.

TWO KINDS OF SPEECHES

Some speeches are primarily factual and some are primarily emotional. Factual speeches are designed to give information or instruction. Emotional speeches are designed to arouse and modify our feelings.

Factual speeches. When our teachers lecture to us, they usually are making factual speeches. Their purpose is to tell us something we do not already know, to furnish us with facts, figures, and explanations. They are trying to give us an understanding of the subjects they are presenting. Their primary concern is to increase our stock of information and knowledge. When a speaker treats his material in a calm, unemotional manner, when he seems to be motivated mainly by a desire to give us ideas, data, and other information, we usually will be justified in assuming that we are listening to a factual speech.

Emotional speeches. Emotional speeches may be subdivided into: (1) those which aim to arouse our feelings; (2) those which aim to modify our attitudes or to win our acceptance of a proposition; and (3) those which aim to move us into some definite line of action. When we sense the fact that the speaker's personal feelings are playing a large part in what he is saying, when we observe that his concern is not so much that we should see clearly as that we should feel deeply, believe sincerely, or act in some specific way, then we may decide that we are listening to an emotional speech. The sermons to which we give ear on Sunday, the campaign speeches which come to us over the radio, and all the appeals for aid of one kind and another, usually are emotional speeches.

When we are sure that we are listening to a factual speech, the problem of evaluating what is being said is immensely simplified. On the other hand, when we are listening to an emotional speech, we will need to keep all of our critical faculties alert and apply a different scale of values to the speaker's words.

RAYMOND GRAM SWING AT THE MICROPHONE. *A characteristic pose of an eminently successful radio commentator. Such programs as that presented by Mr. Swing furnish opportunities for the practice of the techniques of creative listening discussed in this chapter. (Keystone View)*

HOW TO TAKE NOTES

All through high school and college the ability to take notes effectively is a tremendous asset. The problems involved in taking notes on a lecture or an address are somewhat different from those involved in outlining chapters of a textbook or in taking notes on assigned readings. When we are studying a book, we are free to pause whenever we want to; and when we have difficulty in mastering the sense of a paragraph, we can reread it a second or even a third time. Usually it is not possible for us to stop a speaker and ask him to repeat what he has said. To be sure, in certain circumstances we may feel free to stop our teacher in the midst of a lecture, or we may have an opportunity at the end of the class hour to request a clarification of what we have not understood. But in most public speeches all that we do not get as the speaker goes along is lost.

It is of great importance to know just what and how much of the speaker's material we should try to write down as we listen. Perhaps the most common fault is to be so busy trying to take down complete statements that we have no time to listen carefully to what the speaker is saying. Unless we write shorthand speedily, we cannot expect to take down everything the speaker says — even if we should be so ill-advised as to want to!

Rules for Taking Running Notes

1. Have pencil or pen and notebook ready when the speaker begins.

2. Do not try to make a full word-by-word record of any considerable part of the speech. Listen and note words, phrases, and figures which will help in recalling the most important statements.

3. Be especially on the alert for points which the speaker himself emphasizes in his presentation. If he is a good speaker, he will indicate the relative importance of the various parts of his speech by the way in which he delivers them.

4. When the speaker has finished the discussion of one point, watch carefully for what he says concerning his next point; often he will state this in a topic sentence.

5. It is usually more helpful to put down a striking phrase than it is to write out a complete sentence.

Running notes. The following notes were taken by a college student while listening to a radio address. After some practice any of us ought to be able to do as well, or even better.

Speaker, General John J. Pershing. Place, Washington, D.C. Subject, Red Cross Aid for Sufferers from Drought. Vital to everyone. All Americans morally obligated to help. American Red Cross always faithful. Can be trusted anywhere at all times.

1. Speaker's knowledge A.R.C. goes back to Spanish-American War. Brief history of R.C. — Clara Barton, Cuba, R.C. in World War. Meets emergencies of all types. R.C., U.S. official agency, President of U.S. president of R.C. 10 million dollars needed now.

2. Proportions of drought. Involves 650 counties, 17,000,000 people. Widespread disaster. Food producers hungry! Creeks and wells dry. Thousands starving. Schools closed. Children lack food and clothing. Children worst sufferers. Hundreds of thousands of Americans in misery.

3. R.C. means us. Belongs to all of us. Voluntary. We are fortunate. Democratic ideals at stake. Every dollar goes to needy.

Running notes such as the foregoing are merely intended to furnish clues which enable the listener to recall what the speaker has said. We are now to convert these preliminary notes into a permanent outline of the speech, which should represent the best attempt that we can make to record what the speaker actually said and what our reactions were. The permanent outline for factual speeches is somewhat more flexible than that for emotional speeches. When organizing permanent notes on an emotional speech we will need to bear in mind particularly the logical connections and the structure of the speaker's material.

Rules for Preparing Permanent Notes

1. Be sure to state in one concise sentence the speaker's purpose.
2. Underline in the preliminary notes those words and phrases which seem to mark the main ideas in the speech.
3. Phrase each of these main ideas as effectively as possible in a complete sentence.
4. Under each main idea, place the supporting material — illustrations, examples, reasons, facts, and quotations from authority.
5. Write a paragraph which combines what you already knew with what the speaker has told you. Remember that creative listen-

ing is a co-operative venture to which you must contribute something. Let this paragraph cover your ideas, information, thoughts, and feelings, and the effects of the speech on them.

6. Ask yourself the following question: Was I interested in, indifferent to, or bored by the speech? In a sentence or two explain as nearly as you can the reasons for your answer. In arriving at these reasons we may well consider the following questions:

    a. Was I prejudiced for or against the speaker or his subject?
    b. Did the speaker talk over my head?
    c. During the speech, was I alert and ready to do my part?
    d. Did the speaker seem enthusiastic, well informed, and anxious to influence me?
    e. Did the speaker have any peculiarities or mannerisms which distracted or annoyed me? If so, what?

Permanent notes. The following will furnish an example of permanent notes on the Pershing speech:

Date, 3/24/31. Speaker: General John J. Pershing, General in U.S. Army (retired). Place: Washington, D.C. Served in Spanish-American War, in the Philippines, in the Mexican Campaign of 1916, and as Commander of the American Expeditionary Force in World War I. Interested in the work of the Red Cross for many years. Subject of speech: " The Drought and the Red Cross."

Speaker's purpose: to obtain contributions for the Red Cross Drought Relief Fund. Outline of speech:

1. History of the Red Cross
    a. Clara Barton
    b. The Red Cross in Cuba
    c. The Red Cross in the World War
    d. The Red Cross in the Mississippi Flood Relief
2. Proportions of the present drought disaster
    a. More than 650 counties, with a population of 17,000,000 involved
    b. Much greater than Mississippi flood disaster
    c. Extent of suffering revealed by survey of Dr. D. E. Kleine
3. Why we should support the Red Cross
    a. It is our own agency.

    b. It is voluntary.
    c. It is official.

    I knew very little about the drought situation, and was glad to learn the facts from such a reliable source. I knew that the Red Cross always has been our official relief agency, but I did not know many of the interesting facts about its history. General Pershing showed me how great the need was in the drought area. I felt that the Red Cross was completely justified in asking us for 10 million dollars.

    As I listened to the speech I was distinctly interested because the descriptions of actual conditions were very vivid. I liked the way General Pershing asked for the money. His key sentence, "No one who can afford to give can afford not to give," held a great deal of meaning for me.

    If I want to know more about the Red Cross and this particular relief project I can find material about it in current newspapers and magazines. Further than this, I can talk to one of the Red Cross workers in my community.

Tests of Comprehension and Application

MASTER THE FACTS

1 Pick out what you consider a really good factual speech which takes about ten minutes to read. Prepare it carefully for oral presentation to the class. Let each member of the class take running notes as you read the speech aloud. Then, without any discussion, let each recast his preliminary notes into permanent form. Collect the permanent notes. Study them carefully, and give a little talk to the class on what you have learned from the experiment. Perhaps it will be a good idea to let the class examine the best and the poorest set of permanent notes which have been turned in.

2 How do you account for the fact that different persons listening to the same speech attentively and carefully get widely different meanings from it? Are there greater differences in the meanings of emotional speeches than there are in the meanings of factual speeches? Explain your answer. How much agreement is there among different listeners as to the purpose of speeches? Is this one of the points on which there are great differences? Explain.

COMPREHENSION AND APPLICATION TESTS

3 Listen to a factual speech on some subject concerning which you are rather well informed. Then listen to a factual speech on some subject about which you know very little. What differences in the two experiences seem to you most important?

4 What principles discussed in this chapter seem to you especially helpful in listening to classroom lectures?

PRACTICE TO IMPROVE

5 Take notes on a radio speech of the emotional type. Rework the notes into permanent form and from them attempt to reproduce for the class the speaker's message.

6 Select an editorial from a daily newspaper and try to phrase its purpose in one concise sentence.

TEST YOUR PROGRESS

7 Your teacher will read to you one factual and one emotional speech on some topic of current interest. You will be expected to take notes and to organize the notes into permanent form. These will then be turned in to the teacher, who will put some of them on the blackboard and criticize them for the benefit of the class.

8 Listen to a sermon and make a detailed report on your listening experience. Show clearly how you have applied the principles of this chapter.

Part Two

SPEECH IN HUMAN RELATIONSHIP

"NO MAN *liveth unto himself.*" *After the individual has done all he can to develop his highest possibilities, he must learn to live with others co-operatively and harmoniously. Speech is the cement of the social fabric; without it, society could not exist.*

7   Keys to the Mind

8   Conversation

9   Classroom Speaking

10   Storytelling

11   Interpretative Reading

12   Dramatics

13   Public Speaking

CHAPTER SEVEN *Keys to the Mind*

THERE ARE three fundamental factors in every speech situation; the speaker, the subject matter, and the one who is looking and listening. Put these three together and you have all the essential elements of a typical speech occasion; one person is trying to influence another person (or other persons) with reference to a particular subject. The relations of the speaker to that about which he talks, and to the persons whom he addresses, determine his success or lack of success.

Now of course there is a great deal of informal talking which has little purpose beyond giving us a comfortable sense of companionship and fellowship. In such circumstances we are not talking about any one thing in particular, and we may jump from one topic to another with amazing rapidity and without stopping to say anything really worth while about any of them. We all have noticed a flock of birds sitting on a telephone wire chattering, or several chickens in a coop clucking away as they search for and eat their food. No one would seriously suppose that the birds are engaged in a deep discussion of anything; they are simply " talking " to each other for exactly the same reason that moves human beings to engage in a good deal of their social conversation. This sort of speech is all well enough in its place, but it is not the sort of purposeful, serious activity with which most of this book — this chapter in particular — is concerned. Here we are discussing the problems of planting ideas in other people's minds, and thereby modifying their behavior; of getting other people to do what we want them to do by talking with them. In this enterprise everything which the speaker does must be tested and weighed by its effect on the minds of the persons to be influenced. A speaker can make no more serious mistake than to be egocentric, absorbed with his own concerns and interests to the exclusion of those which are uppermost in the minds of the persons whose actions he is trying to direct and control.

In any normal speech situation there always are at least two "speakers." We often overlook that important fact when we are speaking to others who are not uttering language in reply. No speaker can hope to accomplish much until he understands that those who seem to be playing the passive role of listeners still have opportunity through their actions and physical attitudes to say something to the speaker. A yawn here, a slight raising of the eyebrows there, or an uneasy shifting about on the part of the listener may say something very useful to the speaker if he observes closely and adapts what he is doing to what his hearers are telling him.

PATRICK HENRY'S "CALL TO ARMS." "*Gentlemen may cry 'Peace! Peace!' — but there is no peace.*" This speech in the Virginia Provincial Convention lighted the fires of the American Revolution and furnished it with one of its great slogans, "*Give me liberty — or give me death!*" (*Keystone View*)

When we get up before the class to talk about some interesting experience we have had, to explain some process, or to try to convince our classmates of the truth of some proposition, we should realize that we are face to face with a great variety of mental activities which are not going to stop simply because we have begun to talk. We must do something positive, definite, and effective to get the minds of our audience off what they have been thinking about and onto what we want them to think about. For example, we are going to entertain them (we hope!) by telling them about a motor trip through Glacier Park. As we begin, Tom is thinking of the geometry assignment he has failed to prepare; Susan is worrying about what she is going to wear to the dance tonight; William is formulating the excuse he is going to give for yesterday's absence; Jane is bothered by the thought that somehow she has to tell her father about the crumpled automobile fender which resulted from an unskillful bit of parking as she arrived at school a few minutes before; and so on throughout the entire group. If we cannot manage in some way to get all of these minds off their own problems and onto what we are saying, we cannot hope to succeed in what we are undertaking. As a matter of fact, we cannot even begin our talk until we can win entrance into the minds of at least a considerable number of those whom we are attempting to interest in our story. Our first key to the mind is getting and holding attention.

GETTING AND HOLDING ATTENTION

If we can master some simple principles of focusing the attention of our hearers upon what we are saying, there are practically no limits to what we may be able to accomplish. Everybody readily understands the truth of this statement, but alas! only a few seem to do their speaking in accordance with it.

Too often the speaker knows that in order to make his speaking effective he must be interesting, but he doesn't know how to go on from there and really *be* interesting. The greatest speaker in ancient Greece was Demosthenes. At one time, the story goes, he was addressing the citizens of Athens about the dangers of a threatened invasion by their great enemies, the Macedonians. The day was hot, and the audience was uncomfortable and inattentive. Right in the middle of the speech Demosthenes abruptly stopped his argument and said:

" Once there were two travelers who were on their way down to the harbor to board a ship for a journey to Africa. One of them had a great deal of baggage and had rented a donkey to transport it for him. At the hottest hour of the day the two travelers stopped for rest and refreshment. The one who had the donkey lay down in the shade which it provided. The other suggested that he would like to share the shade. The first man said that the shade belonged to him. They began to argue about this and a quarrel ensued."

Right at this crucial moment Demosthenes stopped and walked off the platform. The audience with one voice demanded that he come back and tell them the rest of the story. Finally, he returned to the rostrum and began: " O men of Athens, when I talk to you about the safety of our country you won't listen, but when I tell you the silly story of two men and a donkey your ears are as long as the beast's." If Demosthenes knew so well how to catch the attention of the people with the story of a donkey, we wonder why he did not use his ability to interest them in the threat to their safety.

Anecdotes and stories. Some of the most successful public speeches which ever have been made have been little more than collections of anecdotes and stories. If we would see how people can be kept alert and continuously interested by an unbroken series of narrative episodes, we should read the most popular lecture ever given in America, Russell Conwell's " Acres of Diamonds." As we listen to radio talks, lectures in our classrooms, political addresses, and conversations, we will find this technique used over and over again. Jesus, the greatest of all speakers, presented his message to his audiences in parables; " and without a parable spake he not unto them." One of Lincoln's biographers in describing the courtroom speeches of the Great Emancipator remarks, " He got more arguments out of stories than he did out of lawbooks." And with most jurors, there is no question, apt stories are more effective than abstract discussions of legal precedents and principles.

How often we find our attention wandering as we listen to a speaker; and then, as he introduces an illustrative incident, we prick up our ears and begin again to pay attention! The old formula " Once upon a time " is the greatest attention-getting device ever discovered. A good story has in it not only all the elements which catch and hold attention, but it may be used to drive home a point more effectively than can any other device. If we think over some of the sermons and addresses we have heard, we probably will agree that the most interesting parts were presented in narrative form.

Perhaps one caution is needed here. We should not tell a story merely to get attention. Sometimes the stories which speakers relate, while highly entertaining and interesting, have nothing whatever to do with their subject or purpose. When this is true, the stories might better be left out. The all-important consideration is to find a story which illustrates the point we want to make. Elbert Hubbard's *Message to Garcia* was not told merely for the purpose of relating how President McKinley's message reached Garcia; it was told to illustrate how important were the characteristics of Major Rowan which enabled him to deliver the message.

Personal interests. Anything which concerns us personally in any vital way has attention value for us. Our own safety and our own health and happiness usually are more interesting to us than anything else in the world. Each one of us can verify this observation by examining his own feelings objectively and fairly. Are we more interested in seeing a newspaper story about ourselves than we are in seeing one about somebody else? If our names are on the honor roll at the end of the term, does not the list interest us more than it would otherwise? One writer on persuasion has made a great point about people's interests in their own names. He says that no syllables in the world are so sweet to us as those which make up our names.

Moreover, we have a way of projecting ourselves into organizations of which we are a part: our own school, our own city, our own state, and our own nation. These are part of us, even as we are parts of them. When a speaker comes from another community and spends his time telling us about his friends, his organizations, and his interests, he does not get our attention nearly so well as he would if he talked to us about our own community or our organizations. If his purpose is to give us information about what is going on elsewhere, he must somehow contrive to do it by making interesting comparisons with what is going on where we are. The elder Senator La Follette made his discussions of railroad freight rates very interesting to his audiences by talking about each audience's own freight rates. Dr. Russell Conwell made it a practice to learn the names of the principal businessmen in every town where he was to lecture and then used these names in his illustrations and stories. Much laughter is always called forth in the theater by simple references to the town in which we live or to one which is smaller than ours but near enough to be a part of our community. This is the principle of personal interests at work in attention-getting.

Novelty and interest. We cannot understand and appreciate anything which is absolutely and completely new. Therefore anything entirely different from what we have known fails to interest us. What

we like most is a skillful combination of novelty and familiarity. A good rule is to deal with old ideas, old sentiments, and old truths, giving them fresh contexts and unusual phrasings. Unless we are able to make comparisons between the novel ideas and the experiences we ourselves have had, we just are not interested.

Contests and struggles. An oft-repeated observation is that a poor dog fight can take the attention off the best speaker. There is excitement in combat. We want to know how the struggle is coming out. Think of the size of the radio audiences which listen to the broadcasts of prize fights, football games, baseball games, and other sporting events, to say nothing of the millions of dollars which people pay annually to witness such contests. Certainly no one needs to emphasize this point with young people of high-school age. We are all tremendously interested in games of various kinds. We can make use of this fact in our speaking. The novelist and the playwright know all about this technique. Even the writers of comic strips and movie scenarios use it constantly. Some of us doubtless follow the exploits of Superman. With others no day is complete without seeing Little Orphan Annie, Red Ryder, or Dick Bradford. Sometimes we can achieve interestingness by presenting what we have to say in terms of competing arguments. Good debates are at their best in the rebuttals, when there is a vigorous and clear-cut clash of contentions. Often we can present our material in the form of a debate, and thus challenge attention.

Manner of speaking. Thus far we have been considering the use of materials in getting and holding attention. Now for a moment we turn to the ways in which we may gain attention to our ideas by the use of voice and visible action.

First of all, we must see to it that we are sufficiently vital and vigorous in voice and action. We pay attention to sounds and actions which demand that we do so. If we are facing a row of lights, we can't keep our eyes off the brightest ones. If we are hearing a barrage of sounds, we inevitably focus on those which are loudest. If we have a panorama of color spread before us, the "loudest" colors are sure to catch our attention. We must remember that everyone to whom we speak is being bombarded by sounds, sights and feelings, both from within their own bodies and from the outside objects within view and hearing. As speakers, we are giving them sounds and sights which have to compete with all these others. We must make it our business to see that our voices and actions compete successfully, or we shall lose the attention of the audience.

The surest way in which to kill attention is by monotony. La Motte-Fouqué, a very wise Frenchman, once said that ennui (that tired feeling) was the natural offspring of monotony. Everybody craves some change in the routines of life; it is meeting the same old thing day after day that bores us. Similarly, if we use an unending succession of similar spoken sounds — if we raise our voices just about the same way along toward the middle of each sentence and drop them again at the end, if we talk at a uniform rate with a tramp, tramp, tramp tempo — we can expect listeners to fall asleep. If audiences when looking at us see nothing but small movements of our jaws and lips, we can't expect them to keep their vision centered upon us. The boughs of a tree swaying in the wind outdoors may be more interesting than a speaker who stands inert and motionless. Nobody ever has to learn to pay attention to loud sounds and moving objects; we do that instinctively. At least, if we do not, we are likely to find ourselves in difficulty very promptly. All of us are descendants of people who did pay attention to these signs of the forces which had to be taken into account in living. This doesn't mean that as speakers we should always shout, and gesticulate wildly. Indeed, if we do that all the time, we will cease to command attention. But we must use sufficient strength of voice and vigor of visible action to remain objects of interest.

It should be added that abrupt and marked changes in vocal patterns and actions are effective also in commanding attention. When we are driving our car and the motor is purring along smoothly we pay no attention to it. Suddenly a strange and different note comes from under the hood. If we are at all mechanically minded, or if we value our car, we will certainly begin to pay attention right away. Similarly, when we are speaking, a lowering of the pitch, a slowing-down of the rate, or a drop in intensity may be quite as effective in getting attention as their opposites. In short, if we want our speaking to attract interest, it must be varied.

Irrelevant attention. It should be noted that it is not difficult to get attention if we do not care how we do it. If one of us were to come before an audience, draw an automatic pistol, and point it toward them, he doubtless would have complete attention instantly! If a public speaker is willing to stand on his head, turn handsprings, or use similar sensational devices, he may get attention. However, the difficulty is that this kind of attention will not be directed toward what the speaker is trying to accomplish. Such attention is irrelevant, and actually damaging to the speaker's cause; it really provides more competition for the speaker's ideas when he doubtless has quite enough competition already. There is a great difference between relevant and irrelevant attention; in many ways they are comparable

A COLLEGE LECTURE AUDIENCE. *Would an observer be justified in drawing any conclusions from the appearance of this audience as to the speaking of the lecturer? What percentage of the class seem awake, alert, and interested? What inferences may be drawn from a detailed study of the various postures of the students? (Library of Congress)*

to fame and notoriety. It is a good deal easier to become notorious than it is to become famous. Just so, it often is a good deal easier to catch the wrong kind of attention than it is to win the proper kind.

ATTENTION AND PERCEPTION

We have just been saying that attention-getting is the key which opens the door into the vestibule of the mind. It furnishes the speaker with the means of stepping into the front hall — but it does not take him on into the locked living room. He must also have the key which will give him access to the inner chambers of the mind. Perception is the key that fits the next lock.

By perception in speech we mean that process by which the voice, the visible action, and the language become meaningful to other people. The problem with which we are now to deal is that of building up in the minds of others the combinations of ideas and feelings

FOOTBALL FANS. *Study the faces of these spectators at a high-school football game. Some excellent illustrations of empathy may be seen. Observe that some of these boys and girls are participating in the action on the field more fully than are others. Does the amount of participation indicate the amount of meaning which is being derived from the situation?* (Library of Congress)

that will guarantee their understanding and appreciation of what we are trying to tell them. We hear a sound, but we cannot identify it; it has captured our attention, but it has no meaning. We continue to pay attention, and eventually we recognize the sound. We know whence it comes, what is producing it, and what it means. We bring our experiences to bear upon what comes to us through our senses.

Needless to say, perception and attention are very closely connected. Neither of them will do us any good without the other. The point is that while we are holding attention, we must find ways of getting those to whom we are speaking to use their memories of what they have seen, heard, touched, and felt in the past to interpret what they are now hearing and seeing.

The very word " attention " suggests tension. And there is at least some degree of tension in the attitude we assume when we are paying attention; we are straining toward something. We may do this either consciously or unconsciously, but do it we must and do it we will under the guidance of an expert speaker if we are to develop the meanings which he wants us to have. We now ask what sounds and sights are likely to be most meaningful. What signs can we present to the eyes and the ears of others which will most speedily and effectively stir up within them the reactions which we want them to get? Through attention we capture the eyes and the ears. Through perception we come into possession of the mind itself. If the explanation of these matters seems complicated, we will do well to remember that the process of influencing the human mind is also rather complicated. No simple explanation can be made which will be at all adequate to our perception of what we are writing about.

Habit in perception. Our habits of thinking have a great deal to do with the meaning we get out of any situation. This fact may be illustrated by the story of the champion chess player who once stood in one of the great art galleries of Europe before a famous painting called " Checkmate." The artist had depicted Satan playing a game of chess with a man. The arrangement of the pieces on the board was intended to represent a hopeless position so far as the man was concerned; one more move and he would have lost the game. The chess player stood in silence for some moments and then an expression of relief came over his features as he turned away, snapped his fingers, and said to himself, " I've got it! " He had figured out a way by which the man could get the better of his adversary. His habits of chess playing made it impossible for him to see what the artist had intended; namely, a human being about to lose his soul to Satan. What he saw was a chess problem. Thus does habit account for the meanings we develop in response to the things which act upon us.

Most of the people standing before the painting probably understood the allegorical meanings which the artist had sought to convey.

Two people are walking in the forest. One of them is a representative of a paper-manufacturing concern which uses pulpwood in its mills. The other is an ornithologist. For the first man the meaning of the forest lies pretty largely in the estimates he is making of the timber available for use in the manufacture of paper. For the other, the essential meaning consists in the bird life that is present in this particular timberland.

Habit controls the meanings we develop. The lesson for us as speakers is that we should know, so far as we can learn them, the habits of those to whom we are going to present our material, so that we may make it as meaningful as possible to them. As Smith and Guthrie say: " Due to the dependence of perception on habit the same combination of stimuli will be perceived differently by two persons. The teataster's perception of tea, the florist's perception of roses, the fancier's perception of dogs, and the entomologist's perception of bugs differ from the corresponding perceptions of untrained persons. Each of us has his private equipment of habit and perceives any situation accordingly." [1]

Attitude in perception. In the quotation just above, we have been told that the meanings which any two people get out of the same situation are likely to be quite different. It is equally important to note that the meanings which the same person may derive from the same situation on two different occasions also may be very different. In other words, our attitude at the moment has a great deal to do with the meanings we develop. Suppose it is 11:45 A.M. and breakfast time seems a long way behind us. We are getting hungry. A tantalizing aroma drifts up from the cafeteria downstairs. " Roast beef," we say to ourselves, and our mouth waters at the thought. But suppose that after eating a hearty lunch we are again back in the classroom. The same odor comes to our nostrils, but how different its meaning now! The change is due to our change in attitude toward food. When we are hungry, we have one attitude. When we have just dined, we have a very different attitude. What in the first instance has meant to us

[1] Stevenson Smith and Edwin Ray Guthrie, *General Psychology*, D. Appleton Company, p. 167.

something very desirable and tempting now means something to which we are neutral or indifferent. So it is with all perception. There are times when we respond vigorously and favorably, and there are times when we respond weakly or unfavorably.

A classic experiment in psychology is to set the attitudes of each of two groups, then put them into the same situation and record their reactions. One group is asked to think of *buildings* while the other is asked to think of *animals*. Letters are then flashed briefly onto the screen before both groups. The letters are H O N S E. Members of the first group report that the word was " house." Those in the second group say that it was " horse."

It is a commonplace that we see what we expect to see. We get into trouble because " we are looking for trouble." We take offense at an innocent remark because we have an attitude of hostility toward the one who makes it. If we can prepare properly the attitudes of those whom we are trying to influence, we will make it a lot easier for them to get the right meanings. Often by controlling attitudes we can greatly reduce the amount of work we have to perform in stirring up meanings. When attitudes are sufficiently favorable, just a partial suggestion may be quite as effective as a long and powerful argument would be in the face of a less favorable attitude.

Personality and perception. One of the best ways for a speaker to get results is to build up a favorable attitude toward himself personally. How easy it is for us to do what we are asked to do by someone whom we like very much! And how difficult it is to comply with requests made by someone whom we dislike! This principle applies to a development of meanings just as it does to any other form of reaction. We stubbornly refuse to see the point when we do not want to see the point. We see it readily enough when we do want to see it. Our wanting to see it — or not wanting to see it — may simply be the result of liking — or not liking — to oblige the speaker. Scientific studies have shown that we consider those whom we admire personally superior in speaking ability to those whom we do not admire. In this book we have said again and again that nothing can be more important in speech than the character and quality of the personal relationship between the speaker and his audience.

Empathy. " Empathy " is perhaps an unfamiliar word. It sug-

HELPING HIM OVER. *As the pole vaulter tries for a record, the two young men on the ground feel the pull of empathy in their muscles. The man to the left seems completely absorbed in the action which he is watching; his position is almost a replica of the pole vaulter's. Which spectator is getting the most vivid meanings out of the athlete's performance? Why? (Press Association)*

gests sympathy, but its meaning is somewhat different. Getting meaning is a very active process; we cannot just sit passively and have someone unload meanings into our minds. We are stimulated by the speaker, we do certain things in response to this stimulation, and what we do furnishes the basis of the meaning we get. If we see a moving object and study it intently, we tend to mimic it. That is, we make muscle movements after the same general patterns as those present in the movement we are observing. As we watch a speaker, we unconsciously and involuntarily take on his muscular activity. This is empathy; doing what we see being done. Empathy is basic in the getting of meaning.

When a speaker stands in an awkward posture; makes abrupt, jerky, and angular gestures and movements; breathes rapidly and shallowly; and shifts about uneasily and aimlessly — then he will stir up in us some very unpleasant feelings. We are doing in a less obvious way what we see him doing, and we do not enjoy it. Therefore we may find ourselves disliking him, although we may not know why. But once we begin to feel that way, our attitude has become extremely unfavorable to the speaker's purposes and meanings. We are likely to say that we did not get his meaning, or that we do not intend to do what he has asked us to do. If someone wants to know why, we may have no better reason than " just because."

While we are on this subject of empathy, we probably should note that indirectly we may imitate (silently) the voices of speakers also. Listening to a pleasant voice may produce within us the kind of muscle activity in our throats which is responsible for that kind of a voice. Hearing a raucous, hoarse, strained voice, we may have unpleasant muscular tensions in our throats which will cause us to react unfavorably to the speaker and his purpose.

To summarize, we may say that if we want to make our way into the minds of other people through speech, we will have to use three keys: (1) attention-getting, (2) attitude-building, and (3) empathy. If we lack any one of the three, we shall find the way barred to the kind of complete sympathy and understanding which is the ultimate goal of all speaking.

Tests of Comprehension and Application

MASTER THE FACTS

1 From your daily experiences give three examples, which you think may be interesting to the class, of the process by which meanings have been enriched and expanded in some subject which you have studied. For example, what did the word "biology" mean to you after you had had a course in it compared with what it meant before you had had such a course?

2 Analyze your personal reactions to someone whom you know rather well and dislike. It may be of great advantage to you to be able to explain your personal reactions to others.

3 Study the behavior of some motion-picture actor who in your judgment is very competent and skillful in stirring up meanings within you. How does he do it?

4 Study some platform speaker whom you have opportunity to hear on more than one occasion, reporting on the way in which he seems to take into account or ignore your habits and attitudes. How could he influence you more effectively by playing up to your habits and attitudes? Be as specific as you can.

5 Analyze the speaking of someone who seems to you especially effective in conversation. Can you become aware of specific and definite tendencies on your own part to imitate his action and his voice as you listen to him and watch him?

6 Analyze for the class a speech you have heard recently which held your attention especially well. How was it done?

7 What news commentator do you hear most frequently on the air? Has his manner of speaking anything to do with the fact that you listen to him more than to others? If so, how would you describe his vocalization?

8 Study every public speaker whom you have opportunity to hear in an effort to understand the ways in which he employs voice and visible action to focus attention on what he is saying. Describe a good speaker and a poor one you have heard, for the purpose of bringing out the essential contrasts in manner.

9 What advertising devices have you seen recently which illustrate

the principles of getting attention through loud sounds, variations in sound patterns, moving objects? Can you apply these in your own speaking?

10 See if you can find a speech or an editorial which is especially effective in its use of struggle and conflict as attention values. Where does the writer or speaker succeed best, where does he fail, and why?

PRACTICE TO IMPROVE

11 Give an example of how a change in attitude has changed the meaning of some situation for you.

12 State a point or a principle and then make it vivid by telling a story which illustrates it.

13 Pick out the most interesting article you can find in a newspaper or magazine, bring it to class, explain why you have chosen it, and read the portions of it which you consider most interesting. Do the members of the class agree with your analysis and evaluation? If not, why not?

14 Find a story you think would be useful in a speech designed to secure funds for the Red Cross. Tell it to the class as effectively as you can and use it purposively.

15 Read the following bit of facetious " advice " to the class as effectively as you can and then comment seriously on the points which it is intended to make:

When you tell a joke, stop occasionally to remark, " This'll slay you," or some other appropriate witticism. When you have finished with your joke, be the first to laugh, and try to laugh louder than anyone else present. Then start immediately on another joke or anecdote before anyone else gets a chance. If anyone else present does try to get a word in, cut him out, glower at him a split second, then go ahead with your talk. Ignore any others who try to edge a word in.

Don't laugh at other people's jokes, no matter how humorous they may be. This conveys to them the thought that you occupy the higher strata. To laugh at their jokes or to register amusement would allow them to think you may be in their class and would somewhat lower your dignity in their sight, and hamper your efforts.

Carrying this thought through is sure to impress and influence your acquaintances.[1]

16 Select what you consider a particularly good example of magazine advertising which secures attention by appealing to personal interests. Be sure your advertisement is large enough to be seen easily by all members of the class. Place it before them, and analyze its effectiveness as an attention-getter. Could you use the same appeal in a speech?

17 Pick an item from the society page of your daily paper which interests you. Present it to the class and explain why. Can you make it interesting to the class as well as to yourself? How?

18 Listen to a good news commentator on the radio and analyze his methods in getting and holding your attention. Report to the class on your experience.

19 Write a speech of your own trying to make use of stories, personal interests, and struggle in keeping attention focused on the points you want to make.

CHAPTER EIGHT *Conversation*

A HIGH-SCHOOL sophomore wrote the following description of a good conversationalist. Let us examine it. What that she has omitted should be included in her description? Should anything be left out?

THE IDEAL CONVERSATIONALIST

In my opinion the ideal conversationalist is one who is able to talk about a great variety of subjects and to make his conversation interesting. He should know what topics will interest his listeners and have the ability to discuss them fluently. He should be able to talk to any class or type of people and adapt his conversation to their interests and manners.

[1] E. A. Rogers, "How to Influence People," *Gags*, September 1942. Reprinted by permission.

He should be able to listen as well as to talk, for it is human nature to enjoy talking more than listening. One who does not monopolize the conversation is more popular than one who does.

A good conversationalist should study his voice and manner so as to hold attention and convey the impression he wishes to convey.

In his conversation he should be tactful and be sure that what he says or the way he says it does not embarrass anyone. A good conversationalist is courteous at all times.

How do we measure up to the ideal conversationalist? Are we skilled in the sort of speech we use more often than any other kind? Conversation is a way of living with others; it lies at the heart of those satisfactory human relationships which we are considering in this part of our text. Conversation is a form of mental and spiritual fellowship, and should conform to the same standards as those which apply to other forms of human association.

It is easier to recognize a good conversationalist than to be one. Most of us have a fairly clear picture of what makes successful conversation, but how many of us have given conscious attention to acquiring the qualities we look for in others? Generally, ability in conversation is an accident rather than an achievement. But whatever our skills may be, they can be improved by giving them our conscious attention. The purpose of this chapter is to lay out a plan which will accomplish just that.

THE GENERAL TEST OF GOOD CONVERSATION

If we were asked to state in one short sentence a general test that we could use to judge the quality of each conversation in which we participate, what would it be? It would not be glibness and fluency, for they do not ensure success in the fine art of conversation. It would not be the quantity of talk, for it is quite as possible to fail in conversation because one talks too much as because one talks too little. Is not the most important general test that of mutual advantage and satisfaction? The only desirable kind of fellowship is that which makes those who participate in it better and happier than they would be without it.

It is well to avoid the type of talk described by the New York State Department of Education: "The ordinary conversation begins and ends with safe, shallow, profitless inanities, nothing given, nothing received." Some people feel that this sort of speech is essential if one is to be polite. They know that such artificiality and superficiality keep the speaker out of trouble; if he never commits himself to any definite stand or policy, it will not be necessary for him to defend his principles or his attitudes. We should not forget that if one is giving nothing to his associates, he may be on the way to losing them. Intelligent people are not willing to waste much time in bandying empty phrases back and forth. To make conversing with people interesting and worth while, we must interchange information and points of view. To say that we should seek substantial values in communication with others does not mean that we should not be considerate of the feelings of our associates and continue the customary pleasantries which relieve the daily grind. However, it does suggest that insincere, meaningless phrases cannot be substituted successfully for sincere worth-while conversation. Shakespeare refers to "companions that do converse and waste the time together." Most of us do not need any help in wasting time. Conversation should offer a way of conserving and improving time and of making those who converse more comfortable and happier in their relations with each other.

TEN CONSIDERATIONS IN IMPROVING CONVERSATION

Careful, continual, and conscientious practice will improve any person's conversational skill. Let us lay out a systematic program which will bring us nearer to perfection. Such a plan will include ten points, each important, and all interrelated:

1. Be sincere.
2. Know human nature.
3. Be courteous.
4. Consider the interests of others.
5. Be a good listener.
6. Improve action.
7. Improve voice.
8. Improve language.
9. Find interesting things to say.
10. Adapt conversation to the occasion.

Be sincere. Just as sincerity is fundamental to all happy and successful living, so is it essential in conversation. Honesty of mind and honesty of intention can be recognized by those with whom we associate, and they always count in our favor. We all know that there is little chance of having a pleasant conversation with a person who is affected and artificial. Unless conversation brings us into contact with real personalities, we do not obtain much satisfaction from it. No one cares to have fellowship with a person who is insincere. To pretend to be different from what we really are is a futile struggle, because what we are always shows through what we pretend to be. The deep tragedy of insincerity lies in the fact that if our associates once discover dishonesty in us, they are likely to expect more of it whether it is there or not. Because they dislike insincerity so much, they avoid us and do not give us a chance to show that we have mended our ways. We must be honest, frank, friendly, and sincere if we want others to enjoy conversing with us.

Know human nature. We have said that conversation is one way of getting on with other people, and a very important way too. We are but calling attention to the obvious when we say that a sympathetic understanding of the people about us is of the greatest help in adjusting ourselves to them. Generally, those who know what others are thinking and feeling succeed best in conversation. They also know what other people have thought and felt, how they have acted in the past and why; in short, they understand human nature. Without this understanding, no one can expect any considerable success in conversation. Therefore to improve in conversation, become a student of human nature.

Be courteous. If we are courteous, we are as considerate of the other person's feelings and comforts as we are of our own. Anyone can be courteous if he understands human nature and remembers to be kind. In fact, all of the rules of social form in the etiquette books were developed in just that way. Most of them are so reasonable that we would follow them even if we had not read them in a book.

Let us examine a few sections of a book on social form just to illustrate how unnecessary some of the rules are for a thinking boy or girl. First take the matter of introductions. We are told that we usually: (1) present men to women, (2) younger people to older people, (3) the individual we know better to the individual we know not so well, and (4) less famous persons to more famous persons. Let us take the most commonly used form of making an introduction: " One, may I present Two? " We will put in place of One: (1) women, (2) older persons, (3) the person we do not know so well; and (4) the more famous. It is absurd to reverse the procedure. Imagine that our grandmother is visiting in our home. One of our classmates walks home from school with us and we introduce him to our grandmother. Since our grandmother is our house guest and much older than our friend, would we be likely to say, " John, may I present my grandmother? " Let us take a more extreme example. The President of the United States has talked in our town. We have been introduced to him. Our mother is standing near and we would like to introduce her. Would it be reasonable for us to say, " Mother, may I present the President? "

It is not necessary to memorize any exact phraseology for making introductions. The purpose is to bring two persons together. How can that be done best? We may merely give the names, or we may say, " Mr. Blank, I am eager to have you meet Mr. Doe." Anything is appropriate which will please the persons being introduced, especially the one whom we most wish to honor. It is courteous to make some comment, to show why we think the two persons will enjoy meeting, and to speak a few words to start the conversation.

In the same way, we must figure out a response when we have been introduced. It is courteous to show our pleasure at the meeting and to do our part to get a conversation under way. If we have originality, we will be able to meet the situation with something better than a trite phrase discovered in some book or a quotation from some other person. Furthermore, if we are considerate of the feelings of the person to whom we have been introduced, we will take pains to get his name as it is given to us, and to fix it in our minds by speaking it several times during the conversation. Then we will know him the next time we meet him.

In any etiquette book we will find long lists of suggestions for the conversation of the host or hostess, for conversation at meals, at the theater, and in hotels and restaurants. If we read them carefully, we see that they all aim at the same thing — courtesy and consideration.

If we always put the other person's pleasure ahead of our own, we will avoid being the chronic conversational bore whose chief characteristic is his egotism. The bore may be fluent enough, but he is forever talking about himself and his own affairs. Out of his egotism grow the other faults of a bore: his inability to leave out of the conversation the irrelevant, inconsequential details of his own concerns; his desire to drag in everything even remotely connected with whatever interests him; and, worst of all, his complete lack of courtesy, a characteristic which always spells disaster in conversation.

Consider the interests of others. With whom do we most like to converse? Is it not invariably someone who is able and willing to discuss matters which interest us? If so, we should be thoughtful of others, find out what they are interested in, and talk intelligently and sympathetically about those matters. Then people will rate us as pleasant conversationalists. While this point might very reasonably have been included under the discussion of courtesy, it is so important that it is well to emphasize it by considering it separately. If we happen to be in conversation with a boy whose hobby is boatbuilding while ours is photography, we should lead the talk around to boatbuilding. He in turn, if he is considering our interests, will give us a chance to talk on photography. The result will be a well-balanced conversation satisfactory to both of us.

Be a good listener. Many a man has earned a reputation as a master of the art of conversation simply by being a good listener. We must not regard conversations as "talkfests" in which we are the star performers. A conversation is a joint or group undertaking, in which each party should show himself willing to do his part both as speaker and as listener. The surest way to spoil a conversation is to monopolize it, refusing to let anyone else get in a word edgewise. We cannot be "at bat" all the time. Unless we give the other fellow his innings and listen to him as we want him to listen to us when our turn comes, we shall fail in conversation. Above all, we must not seem impatient for our next chance to talk. Writing in the *New Republic* recently, Bruce Bliven made this comment: "The world of conversationalists, in my experience, is divided into two classes: those who listen to what the other person has to say, and those who use the interval to plan their next remark."

Charles Lamb tells an interesting story about the poet Coleridge, who was always a great talker and occasionally a rare conversationalist. When he met an acquaintance on the street, he had the habit of seizing a button of the friend's coat and then closing his eyes and beginning to talk. While his eyes were closed, he would pour out a torrent of words concerning subjects which interested him very much, whether or not they interested the one to whom he was talking; and being unable to see the distress signals of the other man, he charged straight ahead. One day Coleridge met and literally " buttonholed " a friend who, waiting until the poet had got well under way with his talk, took out his knife, carefully cut the button off his coat and left Coleridge standing, with his eyes closed, " conversing with " the button. After some time, having gone about his errands, he came back and found Coleridge still talking to the button! Coleridge was not really conversing with his friend; he was talking for his own pleasure regardless of his victim's feelings. The button served his purpose just as well as, or better than, the person, so long as the poet did not know that the person had gone.

In learning to be good conversationalists we must practice being good listeners; we must be careful how much of the time we use and how much we allow for others.

Improve action. Almost everything that can be said on the subject of speech in general applies to conversation. Conversation is usually the least formal kind of speaking; yet it too has its conventions and proprieties, which may not be lightly disregarded. In trying to improve ourselves in the art of conversation, we should strive for competence in the management of our bodies (See Chapter Two). The way we stand, walk, and sit; our facial expressions; the movements of our arms and hands — these are all a part of the communicative process in conversation. As in all other speech activities, the most appropriate bodily action is that which helps to stir up the right ideas in the minds of the listeners, but does not call attention to the action as such.

Improve voice. We have all entertained guests who talked louder than others at the party. Whether they were near us or far from us, they used the same shouting, raucous voices. On the other hand, we have all had guests who spoke so softly that we could not hear what they said. They mumbled away, in dull, monotonous, expressionless voices seemingly talking for their own amusement rather than for communication. If we have any of these faults, we should attempt to get rid of them, and the suggestions in Chapter Three will help us to do it. Let us each find the particular sections that apply to us, and improve our voices.

Improve language. Most of what we have learned about improving language for speech in general (see Chapter Five) can be applied to language for conversation. Drill on the pronunciation and the meaning of new words, practice in selecting appropriate words, and reading precisely phrased literature will all help us to improve our language for conversation.

Find interesting things to say. Professor Howes says: " The development of a fund of interesting things to say cannot be made an object of a course in conversation, for conversation has no definite subject matter. Any subject within the range of human knowledge or speculation may under given circumstances become a topic of conversation. Preparation for general conversation includes the whole range of the individual's experience; his reading, thinking, travel, contact with interesting persons, with the theater, with business, with politics — in short with all phases of life. The best one can do, therefore, is to keep informed on subjects about which his circle of friends have shown particular interest." [1]

Other things being equal, the best conversationalist is the man with the largest fund of interesting experiences. Careful observation, coupled with the habit of putting into words what one has observed, forms an indispensable background for success in conversation. Many people fail in the fine art of conversation because they have not taken the pains to form contacts with those things which are of particular interest to their associates. We are living in a day of specialization, and one of the consequences of specialization is that each of us is less and less able to talk about anything except his specialty. The

---

[1] Raymond F. Howes, "Training in Conversation," *Quarterly Journal of Speech,* Vol. XIV, No. 2, p. 256. Reprinted by permission.

demand of the present is that every man should come as near as possible to knowing everything about something. To be a good conversationalist he must also know at least something about everything. If one is to be able to play both the active and the passive rôles in conversation, he must have both a thorough understanding of some subjects and a general knowledge of many others.

This combination of wide knowledge and intensive specialization suggests that, on certain occasions, anyone may be asked for his opinion on a subject about which he is more or less of an authority. At such times he will probably do most of the talking, his associates being content to listen and to make an occasional contribution or to ask intelligent questions. The "parties of the second part" will be receiving more information than they are giving; their eager queries and comments will serve as a means of tapping the fund of information possessed by the specialist and thus may help to mold their hazy ideas into definite and well-grounded opinions.

Adapt conversation to the occasion. Just as certain types of behavior, clothes, and food are appropriate on some occasions and not on others, so certain types of speech fit better into some situations than into others. When we were preparing for our first formal parties, perhaps our mother advised us about our manners; she tried to show us that our behavior should not seem out of place in a beautifully decorated room and among carefully dressed guests. If we conducted ourselves successfully, then from the time we arrived until we said good-by our manners were formal. We did not lounge against the furniture. We did not play rough jokes on our friends. We did not run and slide across the dance floor. Everything about our conduct was in keeping with our attire, with which we had taken pains in every detail. We hoped most sincerely that we looked our very best, and we endeavored to act in such a way as to create a favorable impression.

Now let us recall an informal social situation; for example, a meeting of our class at a street corner when we were going picnicking. We felt that we were well dressed at the formal party, but we did not appear in the same gown or suit on this very different type of occasion. For the picnic we probably wore an outfit that did not hamper us in hiking, in running, in building fires, and in playing

A SIDEWALK CONVERSATION. *Two farmers are talking with a popcorn man. Does the merchant seem interested in what the farmer is telling him? What is the role of the second farmer in the conversation? Does the setting have any effect on what the participants are saying and how they are saying it? (Library of Congress)*

games. To behave with extreme formality at a picnic is just as much out of place as to behave with informality at the junior prom; wieners which are consumed with enthusiasm at the former would be considered " impossible " at the latter.

Everyone recognizes the need for adapting behavior, food, and clothing to the nature of the social occasion; very reasonable, we all say. But fewer people appreciate the same important point in matters of speech. To illustrate: We make a general rule to the effect that it is rude to say, " If you don't want to get hurt, get out of my way! " As a matter of fact, that statement may well be less rude on the football field than to say, " I beg your pardon, may I pass? " When a boy comes to football practice in the spirit of the latter remark, his comrades usually feel a powerful urge to " take it out of him." Speech, like manners, food, and clothing, should fit the occasion. When we are with our school friends, talking or playing games, our language may be more effective if we speak with less obvious precision and care. But when we are with adults or at a formal party, appreciation and respect are revealed by carefully chosen words, a well-modulated voice, and more delicate and subtle bodily action.

Practice intelligently. The suggestions laid out for us in this chapter will, if followed, improve our conversation, and in improving our conversation will improve our human relationships. We should try to learn something about the process every time we converse. We should study others in conversations. We should be honest with ourselves in estimating our ability to establish and keep up mental commerce with others. We should decide to be better tomorrow than we are today. We should try to improve. The only weakness that can make our situation hopeless is a foolish spirit of self-satisfaction.

Tests of Comprehension and Application

MASTER THE FACTS

1 Would a conversation be mutually advantageous and satisfactory if all participants had the characteristics of the individual described in " The Ideal Conversationalist," pages 196–197? Give reasons for your answer.
2 Describe a conversation from which you derived great pleasure. Did other participants enjoy the occasion too? Give reasons for your answer.
3 Recall a conversation from which you learned a great deal but which you considered unsuccessful. Justify your answer.
4 Recall a conversation from which you learned nothing new but which you still consider a successful conversation. Give reasons for your answer.
5 In your reading, find two examples of insincere persons who were ineffective conversationalists.
6 Observe other students in high school. See how skillful you are in picking out those who are honest and sincere.
7 Watch the reactions of teachers and of other students to members of your classes. Are they able to recognize insincerity? Do they prefer the trustworthy person? How do you know?

8 Pick out five famous historical characters who were much beloved largely because they were believed to be sincere.
9 Pick out two well-known persons who lost popularity when their insincerity was discovered.
10 List all the ways in which you can discover insincerity.
11 Write a paper explaining what you mean by " intellectual honesty."
12 Attend a tea and pick out four sincere and four insincere persons.
13 Attend a legitimate play or a movie and notice how actors suggest sincerity and insincerity.
14 Study the members of your own family. Do you know why they react as they do? Are you always able to converse with them successfully? Remember, in conversation you cannot excuse yourself by saying the fault lies with the other person! *You* must make the conversation a success.
15 Find examples in literature where conversations were unsuccessful because participants did not understand human nature.
16 When is it more courteous to eat, and when is it more courteous to wait, if a guest is late for a meal? Explain your answer.
17 What will you do if one of your guests insists on telling long uninteresting stories?
18 What will you do if one of your guests does not talk at all?
19 Advise a person on how to accept a compliment.
20 Advise a person on how to apologize.
21 Name four famous persons you would like to meet. Decide on a topic of conversation that you could discuss with each.
22 Discuss all of the ways you can think of which will help you to discover when a topic being discussed in a conversation is boring to the participants.
23 Name ten topics which vary so greatly that familiarity with each will assure you of an appeal to any person's particular interests.
24 Find a literary selection containing a conversation in which each participant does his share of listening.
25 From the following list select those which will usually help conversation and those which will hinder it.

    a Standing in a slouchy position when all others are standing straight and poised
    b Listening with your mouth open
    c Showing facial changes appropriate to the ideas of the speaker
    d Continually moistening the lips
    e Picking at fingernails
    f Using the hands to clarify an explanation
    g Showing interest and enthusiasm over the topic of conversation
    h Slouching down in a chair when everyone else is sitting more formally
    i Sitting very straight when most participants are relaxed and at ease
    j Holding a cup of tea while speaking so that no one notices how it is being held
    k Sitting down when all others are standing
    l Waiting until all older persons are seated before sitting
    m If you are a boy, rising when the girl you are with rises
    n Rising when an older person enters the room
    o If you are a boy, entering a room ahead of the girl you are escorting
    p Pulling at your dress or tie
    q Letting your whole body help to express your ideas
    r Giggling continually when others do not know what is funny

26 Collect pictures of people engaged in conversation. Classify them according to desirable and undesirable uses of bodily action.

27 From your reading of literary material, select descriptions of the use of good and poor bodily action in conversation.

28 Listen to the voice of each member of your family when engaged in conversation. Write a paper describing their voices.

29 How would each of the ten characteristics of good conversation differ in a call after a death in a home and a call on a return from a vacation?

30 Show how your conduct would differ when you are attending a party given in your honor from when you are a guest at a party given in someone else's honor.

COMPREHENSION AND APPLICATION TESTS

31 How does streetcar conversation differ from theater conversation? How from drawing-room conversation?

32 Attend a school party. Watch the persons who appear most at ease. Write a paper describing the way they act.

PRACTICE TO IMPROVE

33 Practice adjusting yourself to people with a great deal of formal education and to those with very little formal education. Make every effort to have both groups feel satisfaction.

34 Talk to high-school students who have lived in very large cities, small cities, villages, or on farms. Try not to bore any of them.

35 Observe people as you walk on the street, ride in busses, shop in stores, or sit in study hall. Try to discover how they differ. Think of ways in which you can adapt your speech and behavior to stir up favorable reactions from each person.

36 Attend a school dance, tea, or dinner. Write a description of each person with whom you converse. In each case consider: which individuals were formal and which were informal; which wanted you to talk a great deal and which wanted you to listen most of the time; which wanted you to be very precise in your diction and very careful about grammatical errors or words hurriedly spoken; which wanted you to speak in a very quiet voice and which in a voice with more volume; which wanted you to talk about general world problems and which preferred to have you discuss intimate personal matters.

37 When attending some social function, see if you are able to hold a mutually satisfactory conversation with someone who seemed bored before you came. Account for your success.

38 Select some student in high school who seldom talks to other students. Without his knowledge, study methods of interesting him in communicating with others. Try out your plans and see how they work.

39 If you can secure a copy of the February 1927 *St. Nicholas Magazine* or *Challenge to Explore* by Luella B. Cook, Walter Loban, George V. Norvell, and William A. McCall (p. 155), read the story of "The Lame Duck" by Thomas A. Curry. Analyze the story carefully and decide whether you think Paul Miller was sincere and

whether he really understood human nature. Make your decision without reading the suggestions at the end of the story.

40 From the people who converse with you, select five who understand you very well and five who understand you very poorly. Explain why you have selected these particular persons.

41 How would you deal with each of the following if you were a host or hostess to one of your school clubs?

  a Someone spills a cup of chocolate and makes long and repeated apologies.
  b Someone misunderstands and comes without an invitation.
  c Someone starts to eat before all are served.
  d One person is very quiet and does not mingle with the rest.
  e In playing games the party gets rough and you are afraid furnishings may be marred or broken.
  f Two persons become angry over a difference of opinion on some civic problem.
  g Someone asks a very personal question about your father's income.
  h Someone asks one of your guests about his father and you know his father and mother have separated and he is sensitive about it.

42 Write a paper on "Handling the Silver at a Dinner Party." Explain how the topic is related to speech.

43 For the girls: Make a booklet called "Social Life for Girls at —— High School." Give detailed helps on how to behave, dress, and conduct yourself for all of the social events of the school. Illustrations will make the discussion clear and interesting.

44 For the boys: Make a booklet called "Social Life for Boys at —— High School." Do for boys what exercise 43 suggests for girls.

45 Phrase ten questions each of which could be used to discover the interests of the persons with whom you are conversing.

46 In conversation at home, practice turning the attention away from a topic you enjoy to one some other member of the family enjoys.

47 Watch yourself at the dinner table tonight. Do you take more than your share of the conversation? Are you more considerate in the living room after dinner than you were during dinner?

COMPREHENSION AND APPLICATION TESTS

48 At some dinner at home when the family is alone, try monopolizing the conversation. Later, get the reaction of your family to what you have done.
49 Study the bodily action of the most interesting conversationalist you know. Prepare a talk on the subject, pointing out how appropriate action is an asset.
50 Engage in conversations in the corridors at school. Observe effective and ineffective use of the body.
pronunciation is in conversation.
51 Review Chapters Four and Five. Notice how important correct
52 Use new words in your conversations.
53 Work out a list of ten interesting ways to acknowledge an introduction.
54 Find substitutes for such overworked words as:

grand	marvelous	funny	thrilling
swell	super	you know	dumb
wonderful	mad	awful	gorgeous

55 Find examples of the effective use of words in the literature you are asked to read.
56 Listen to a good conversationalist and note his use of words.
57 By lists, illustrated booklets, stories, or any method you choose, show all the ways you can think of in which individuals should change methods of conversations to make them fit all situations.
58 Make a reading list for the year. Include some material about which you are at present uninformed.
59 Remembering the old saying that it is not so much what you say as the way you say it that offends people, select a student with whom you disagree about certain important matters. See if you can make an occasion for talking about those controversial issues. Try to do this in such a way that he gets your point of view and you his, and that both of you enjoy the meeting.
60 Attend a tea or a dinner and leave one group and join another without changing the trend of conversation in either group and without calling attention to yourself.
61 Study ten students in your class. Decide on a topic of conversation which would be of special interest to each.

62 Divide the class into groups of five or six students. Let each student take a turn passing from one group to another, and pick out those persons who do too much talking and those who do too much listening. Compare notes later in a class discussion.

63 In what instance in exercise 62 was your listening most creative? Write a short paper on creative listening in conversation.

64 Choose a partner in your speech class. Ask him to help you to correct unfortunate mannerisms in the use of visible action. In return, help him to correct those which he has that are unpleasant.

65 Divide the class into groups of four or five. Dramatize good and poor use of the body for conversation. Let the class decide which is good and which is poor.

66 Have moving pictures taken at a social gathering. Analyze your bodily action and set out to correct your weaknesses.

67 Two conversations follow. Divide the class into groups and dramatize them. When your group is performing, let the rest of the class listen and criticize you. Help the other groups yourself in the same way when they are performing.

a   Travel in Central and South America

CONVERSERS

Dorothy Turner   *Anne Pulling*

(Dorothy Turner *and* Anne Pulling, *two teachers in Puerto Rico, are taking a Christmas cruise. As this conversation occurs, they are standing at the boat rail waiting for the health officers to finish their inspection and to permit them to go ashore.*)

Dorothy. So this is Fort-de-France! I had no idea Martinique would be so hot. Puerto Rico is going to seem like Alaska when we get back. Just think how many bits of the Old World we have seen in replica — St. Thomas with its picturesque harbor came first; then what was next?

Anne. Oh, you could not forget Saint-Martin last Sunday. When I think of Saint-Martin, I shall remember that old Negress standing on the pier all decked out in her Sunday best.

Dorothy. Wasn't it queer how she had her skirt draped?

Anne. But you know why, don't you?

Dorothy. I hadn't thought about it. Probably she wished to show her gorgeous underskirt; with all that handwork it was surely worthy of being displayed. It really was a crime to cover it at all. And did you notice how accurately she balanced that huge tray of cakes and bread on her head?

Anne. Yes, I noticed that point particularly, for I have tried that stunt in Puerto Rico, with rather disastrous results.

Dorothy. And I also; I truly believe Americans are a bit envious of the Latin poise. It really was a pity to cover that gay kerchief on her head by a tray of cakes.

Anne. Yes, wasn't it? One place I shall not forget is Philippsburg.

Dorothy. But why? I found nothing there but the huge salt piles ready for export; they looked like huge snowbanks of the Far North.

Anne. Maybe you didn't find anything striking, but I suffered that most embarrassing moment. Several of us reached the church just as the bell rang. It was a queer-looking church which made us all anxious to enter. Just as it happened, I was the only one wearing a sleeveless dress.

Dorothy. Just what difference did that make?

Anne. Difference! Why, the priest marched down the aisle in person to tell me to go out and dress myself. He said, " It is disgraceful to enter the house of God in such clothes."

Dorothy. What did you do?

Anne. There are times when one has an advantage in a foreign country. First he spoke to me in Dutch, which I did not understand; next he spoke to me in English, which I pretended not to understand. Since those two seemed to be the extent of his languages, he turned in disgust, but much muttering was heard as he returned to the altar. That was one time I had no need for artificial coloring.

Dorothy. Basse-Terre in Guadeloupe was wild with local color, wasn't it? What are those women doing?

Anne. I wonder why the black gowns. There must be more mourning here than in Puerto Rico. Just watch the swing of that walk.

Dorothy. Those feet surely never felt the controlling power of leather. Why, do you see what they are doing? Those huge baskets they are carrying on their heads are filled with coal.

Anne. Right you are. Then wait — why, Dorothy, they are carrying coal into the hold of our ship! They must be the coal heavers I heard two men talking about last night. What powerful bodies they have! It looks as if this is the country where the women do the work.

Dorothy. Do you notice the rhythmic swing of their bodies? Kipling should be here to write a poem on " Feet, Feet, Feet." I am beginning to understand just what his soldiers were feeling. Come, let's get away from this eternal beat of feet climbing up the gangway. At last the bars are down!

Anne. I feel as if I had an excellent picture of Martinique, but I presume we must see the usual landmarks as checked in the guidebook; the market, Josephine's statue, and so on through the day.

Dorothy. Yes, it would be a pity to let the rest of the cruisers have more to tell this evening than we do. I have a feeling this is going to be a very enriching addition to our knowledge of the West Indies.

b   THE RADIO BOYS TRAILING A VOICE [1]

CONVERSERS

| Mr. Preston, principal of the high school | Herb
Joe
Bob
Jimmy } high-school students |

Mr. Preston. How are you, boys? You seem to be having a good time.

Herb. Jimmy is. . . . We're making the most of the snow and ice while it lasts.

Mr. Preston. Well, I don't think it will last much longer. As a matter of fact, winter is " lingering in the lap of spring " a good deal longer than usual this year.

Joe. I suppose you had a pleasant time in Washington?

Mr. Preston. I did indeed. To my mind it's the most interesting city in the country. I've been there a number of times, and yet I always leave there with regret. There's the Capitol, the noblest

[1] Allan Chapman, *The Radio Boys Trailing a Voice*, Stratemeyer Syndicate, East Orange, New Jersey, pp. 11-15. Reprinted by permission.

building on this continent and to my mind the finest in the world. Then there's the Congressional Library, only second to it in beauty, and the Washington Monument soaring into the air to a height of five hundred and fifty-five feet, and the superb Lincoln Memorial, and a host of other things scarcely less wonderful. But the pleasantest recollection I have of the trip was the speech I heard the President make just before I came away. It was simply magnificent.

Bob. It sure was. Every word of it was worth remembering. He certainly knows how to put things.

Mr. Preston. I suppose you read it in the newspaper the next day.

Bob. Better than that. We all heard it over the radio while he was making it.

Mr. Preston. Indeed! Then you boys heard it even before I did.

Joe. What do you mean? I understood that you were in the crowd that listened to him.

Mr. Preston. So I was. I sat right before him while he was speaking, not more than a hundred feet away, saw the motions of his lips as the words fell from them and noted the changing expressions of his features. And yet I say again that you boys heard him before I did.

Herb. I don't quite see. You were only a hundred feet away and we were hundreds of miles away.

Mr. Preston. And if you had been thousands of miles away, what I said would still be true. No doubt there were farmers out on the Western plains who heard him before I did. You see, it's like this. Sound travels through the air to a distance of a little over a hundred feet in the tenth part of a second. But in that same tenth of a second that it took the President's voice to reach me in the open air, radio could have carried it eighteen thousand six hundred miles.

Jimmy. Whew! Eighteen thousand six hundred miles! Not feet, fellows, but miles!

Bob. That's right, though I never thought of it in just that way before. But it's a fact that radio travels at the rate of one hundred and eighty-six thousand miles per second.

Mr. Preston. Equal to about seven and a half times around the earth. In other words, the people who were sitting in the presence of the President were the very last to hear what he said. Put it in still another way. Suppose the President were speaking through a megaphone in addition to the radio and by the use of the megaphone the voice carried to people in the audience a third of a mile away. By the time those persons heard it, the man in the moon could have heard it too — that is, supposing there really were a man in the moon and that he had a radio receiving set.

Joe. It surely sounds like fairyland.

Mr. Preston. Radio is the fairyland of science in the sense that it is full of wonder and romance. But there the similarity ceases. Fairyland is a creation of the fancy or the imagination. Radio is based upon the rock of scientific truth. Its principles are as sound as those of mathematics. Its problems can be demonstrated as exactly as two and two make four. But it's full of what seem to be miracles until they are shown to be facts. But there's scarcely a day that passes without a new one of these miracles coming to light.

Joe. He is a thirty-third-degree radio fan.

Bob. Just as most bright men are becoming. The time is coming when a man who doesn't know about radio or isn't interested in it will be looked on as a man without intelligence.

68 Put on a program of talks on voice in the speech class. Assign one speaker to each of the following topics. Hold a general discussion after the program:

  a The voice in conversation at the theater
  b The voice in conversation at the restaurant
  c The voice in conversation on a streetcar
  d The voice in conversation at a dinner table
  e The voice in conversation at a football game

69 List grammatical errors that you make habitually. Ask members of your family and members of your class to help you to correct them.

70 Work out a list of ten different expressions to use when entering a group of conversationalists, and ten different expressions to use when leaving a group of conversationalists. Arrange to try them out in your class.

71 Survey the class and find each person's particular interest. Ask each to give a five-minute talk before the class on the fundamentals of that topic. Talks on music, art, sports, sewing, cooking, travel, sci-

COMPREHENSION AND APPLICATION TESTS

ence, homemaking, agriculture, and government will help each listener to talk intelligently on these topics in some future conversation.

72   Attend a picnic and notice the conversation. Write a careful report of the speech and behavior of individuals who seemed to be making a favorable impression. Notice particularly members of your speech class.

73   Attend a formal dance and notice the conversation. Write a careful report of the speech and behavior of individuals who seem to be making a favorable impression. Compare this report with the one you made in exercise 72.

74   Select some topic about which you have so little information that you could not even ask an intelligent question if it happened to come up in conversation. Read enough about it to give a three-minute talk before the class.

75   Take part in several conversations, and as you listen contribute brief remarks (questions or comments) that will make what the speakers are saying more effective. Later, think back over the conversations and decide when you got most from the conversation. Find out whether or not there was a relationship between what you brought to each conversation and what you took away.

76   Attend four lectures for the purpose of getting information to use in conversation.

77   Use the information from other classes in conversation.

78   Are you able to join a group of little children without spoiling their game? Remember, the most cultured person is one who can adapt himself to the conversations of old and young, rich and poor, well educated and illiterate. He does not try to change each group, he makes everyone more comfortable and happy because he has come. The children in the next conversation are playing at being grown up. Try to remember how you felt when you did that and act out the entire story, assigning parts of various characters to members of your class.

"Daisy's Ball"[1]

CONVERSERS

Tommy Daisy
Demi Nan
Nat

(" Mrs. Shakespeare Smith would like to have Mr. John Brooks, Thomas Bangs, and Mr. Nathaniel Blake come to her ball today.

" P.S. — Nat must bring his fiddle so we can dance, and all the boys must be good, or they cannot have any of the nice things we have cooked."

This elegant invitation would, I fear, have been declined but for the hint given in the last line of the postscript.)

Tommy. They have been cooking lots of goodies, I smelt 'em. Let's go.

Demi. We needn't stay after the feast, you know.

Nat. I never went to a ball. What do you have to do?

Tommy. Oh, we just play be men, and sit round stiff and stupid like grown-up folks, and dance to please the girls. Then we eat up everything, and come away as soon as we can.

Nat. I think I could do that.

Demi. I'll write and say we'll come. (*Writes:* We will all come. Please have lots to eat. — J. B. Esquire)

[*Great was the anxiety of the ladies about their first ball, because if everything went well they intended to give a dinner party to the chosen few.*]

Daisy (*as she sets the table and surveys the store of refreshments with a rather maternal air*). Aunt Jo likes to have the boys play with us, if they are not rough; so we must make them like our balls, then they will do them good.

Nan (*shaking her head over the cake basket she is arranging*). Demi and Nat will be good, but Tommy will do something bad, I know he will.

Daisy (*with decision*). Then I shall send him right home. People don't do so at parties; it isn't proper. I shall never ask him any more.

---

[1] Adapted from: Louisa M. Alcott, *Little Men*, Chap. IX.

Nan. That would do. He'd be sorry not to come to the dinner ball, wouldn't he?

Daisy. I guess he would. We'll have the splendidest things, won't we? Real soup with a terreem (*She means "tureen."*) and a little bird for turkey, and gravy and all kinds of nice vegytubbles.

Nan (*having arranged a fine costume for the occasion, and anxious to wear it*). It is 'most three, and we ought to dress.

Daisy (*putting on a nightcap ornamented with a red bow, one of her aunt's long skirts, a shawl, and a large pocket handkerchief*). I am the mother, so I shan't dress up much.

Nan (*with a wreath of artificial flowers, a pair of old pink slippers, a yellow scarf, a green muslin skirt, and a fan made of feathers from the duster; also, as a last touch of elegance, a smelling bottle without any smell in it*). I am the daughter, so I rig up a good deal, and I must sing and dance, and talk more than you do. The mothers only get the tea and be proper, you know.

[*A sudden knock causes* MISS SMITH *to fly into a chair, and fan herself violently, while her mamma sits bolt upright on the sofa, and tries to look quite calm and proper.* LITTLE BESS, *who is on a visit, acts the part of maid and opens the door, saying with a smile*]

Little Bess. Wart in, Gemplemum, it's all weady.

[*Boys wear high paper collars, tall black hats, and gloves of every color and material, not one boy with a perfect pair.*]

Demi (*in a deep voice*). Good day, mum.

[*Everyone shakes hands and then sits down, looking so funny and yet so sober that the gentlemen forget their manners and roll in their chairs with laughter.*]

Mrs. Smith (*much distressed*). Oh, don't!

Miss Smith (*rapping* MR. BANGS *with her bottle because he laughs so hard*). You can't ever come again if you act so.

Bangs (*gasping with most uncourteous candor*). I can't help it, you look so like fury.

Miss Smith. So do you, but I shouldn't be so rude as to say so. He shan't come to the dinner ball, shall he, Daisy?

Mrs. Smith. I think we had better dance now. (*Trying to preserve her polite composure*) Did you bring your fiddle, sir?

Nat. It is outside the door.

Tommy (*winking at* DEMI). Better have tea first.

Mrs. Smith (*sternly*). No. We never have supper first; and if you don't dance well, you won't get any supper at all, *not one bit, sir. I* will take Mr. Bangs and teach him the polka; for he does not know it fit to be seen. (*This sobers* TOMMY *at once.*)

[NAT *strikes up, and the ball opens with two couples, who go conscientiously through a somewhat varied dance. The ladies do well because they like it, but the gentlemen exert themselves from a more selfish motive, for each feels that he must earn his supper and each labors toward that end. When everyone is out of breath, they are allowed to rest; the little maid passes around molasses and water in such small cups that one guest empties nine.*]

Daisy (*to her brother*). You must ask Nan to play and sing now. (*Her brother sits looking very much like an owl.*)

Brother. Give us a song, mum.

Miss Smith (*sailing up to an old secretary which stands in the room, and accompanying herself with a vigor that makes the old desk rattle, she sings*):

> Gaily the troubadour
> Touched his guitar
> As he was hastening
> Home from the war.

[*The gentlemen applaud so enthusiastically that she gives them " Bounding Billows " and " Little Bo Peep," and other gems of song, until they are obliged to hint that they have had enough. Grateful for the praises bestowed upon her daughter,* MRS. SMITH *graciously makes an announcement.*]

Mrs. Smith. Now we will have tea. Sit down carefully, and don't grab.

[*It is beautiful to see the good lady do the honors of her table, and the calmness with which she bears the little mishaps that occur. The best pie flies wildly onto the floor when she tries to cut it with a dull knife; the bread and butter vanish with rapidity calculated to dismay a housekeeper's soul; and worst of all, the custards are so soft that they have to be drunk up instead of being eaten elegantly with the new tin spoons.* MISS SMITH *squabbles with the maid for the best jumble, which causes* BESS *to throw the whole dish into* the air, and burst out crying in a rain of cakes. She is comforted by a seat at the table and the sugar bowl to empty; but during this flurry, a whole plate of patties is mysteriously lost and cannot be found.]

Mrs. Smith (*threatening her suspected guest with a milk pot*). You hid them, Tommy, I know you did.

Tommy. I didn't!

Mrs. Smith. You did!

Nan. It isn't proper to contradict. (*Hastily taking advantage of the fray to eat up the jelly*)

Tommy. Give them back, Demi.

Demi (*roused by the false accusation*). That's a fib. You've got them in your own coat pocket.

Nat (*finding his first ball to be more exciting than he had expected*). Let's take 'em away from him. It's too bad to make Daisy cry.

[DAISY *is already weeping, and* BESS, *like a devoted servant, mingles her tears with those of her mistress;* NAN *denounces the entire race of boys as "plaguey things." Meanwhile the battle rages, for, when the two defenders of innocence fall upon the foe, that hardened youth entrenches himself behind the table and pelts them with the stolen tarts, which are very effective missiles, being nearly as hard as bullets. While his ammunition holds out, the besieged prospers, but the moment the last patty flies over the parapet, he is dragged howling from the room and cast upon the hall floor in an ignominious heap. The conquerors return, flushed with victory, and while* DEMI *consoles poor* MRS. SMITH, NAT *and* NAN *collect the scattered tarts. But their glory has departed, for the sugar is gone and no one cares to eat them after the insult offered to them.*]

Demi (*suddenly*). I guess we had better go.

Nat (*dropping a stray jumble he has picked up*). P'raps we had.

[*But* MRS. JO *is among them before the retreat is accomplished, and into her sympathetic ear the young ladies pour the story of their woes.*]

TEST YOUR PROGRESS

79 Test yourself on the following list. Could you contribute to, or ask intelligent questions about, the following topics?

a	Greek music	o	Indian mounds
b	Supreme Court	p	Coin collecting
c	Landscape painters	q	Mohammedanism
d	Soybeans	r	Valley Forge
e	Raphael	s	Seismometer
f	Plato	t	Wool production
g	Photography	u	Australia
h	New Orleans	v	Tariff
i	Archaeology	w	Wild flowers
j	Silversmiths	x	Hunting
k	Dress designing	y	Modern drama
l	Folk dancing	z	Architecture
m	Fingerpainting	aa	Radar
n	Taj Mahal		

80 Make records of the conversation at some party without letting your friends know the machine is working. Study the records. Are the speaking and the listening evenly balanced for all? Play the record in class and hold a discussion on " give and take " in the conversation.

81 With two other persons, make a record of an original conversation. Listen for voice qualities. How does your own voice compare with the others in quality, force, time, pitch, and pronunciation?

82 Rate yourself on voice. Place a check at that point on each of the scales below which best represents your voice. Rate some member of your class in the same way.

Quality very inexpressive	Quality fairly expressive	Quality very expressive
Not loud enough	Right volume for occasion	Too loud
Pitch noticeably low	Pitch not noticeable	Pitch noticeably high
Pronunciation slovenly	Pronunciation easily understood	Pronunciation too precise

83 Take moving pictures of the class in conversation. Show the pictures and follow with a discussion of the good and weak points.
84 Apply the general test to a conversation which took place while you were walking to school with a friend or an acquaintance.
85 Apply the general test to a conversation in the corridor at school.
86 Apply the general test to the conversation when someone accepted your invitation to a movie.
87 Apply the general test to the conversation at the next dance you attend.
88 *Test yourself.* Do you say things that are not exactly true in order to make a more favorable impression? Is your behavior ever intended to give a false impression because you believe that the true one will not be favorable? What have the reactions of others been when you have been insincere? Make this study of yourself for your own enlightenment. Do not tell anyone about it. If you have discovered some insincerity and artificiality in your behavior and talk, try conversing without it.
89 Prepare a class report on a talk with some person you have seen for the first time. Give an honest account of your success or failure in the meeting. Show how you can do better next time.
90 Using mutual advantage and satisfaction as your criteria, write an evaluation of a conversation in which you have participated.
91 Apply the general test to the conversation at your dinner table. Did every member of your family enjoy himself during the entire meal? What did you do to make the conversation successful or unsuccessful?
92 Make a list of topics to which you could make a contribution in conversation. Test the members of the class on your list.
93 Get one of the popular question-and-answer books. Divide the class into small groups and test one another on the questions in the books.
94 Listen for the sound of your own voice in your next conversation. Is it expressive? If not, why not?

CHAPTER NINE *Classroom Speaking*

IN PART THREE of this book we will study some of the principles and techniques of discussion in a democracy. There we shall be concerned with the uses to which discussion may be put in the solving of social and political problems. In this chapter we are to examine more especially the effects of classroom speaking upon those who participate in it. While it is true that in the classroom we may practice the types of discussion presented in the later chapter, here we are dealing with other more restricted and limited uses of the discussion method. Self-improvement and satisfactory human relationships are the real goals of most discussion which goes on in classroom groups. This kind of discussion proceeds under special conditions.

Normally the chairman of a classroom discussion is the teacher; he directs the talk into profitable channels, makes available his superior information and knowledge, corrects errors, and does his best to provide each member of the group with an opportunity to make a maximum contribution. In the nature of things, no other member of the classroom group is so able as he is to make helpful, constructive criticisms and comments. Obviously, on most subjects no other equally authoritative leader is present in the classroom. But there are occasions when a student will know more about a certain subject than does the teacher. At such times the teacher will resign his leadership to the student. Even then the teacher, as the wisest and most experienced person on the scene, will guide and supervise the entire procedure.

Another way in which discussion in the classroom differs from other forms of discussion is that it proceeds with a background of common information and purpose not usually present in other situations. For example, when a speaker in a discussion group outside the classroom undertakes to explain a principle or a process, he generally does so with the genuine purpose of giving information to others. In the classroom, however, much of the speaking is done not primarily

A TEACHER DEMONSTRATES. *A geometry teacher explains a geometrical figure to her class. Note that the paper models in her hands are so placed that she can easily divide her visual attention between them and her audience. It seems clear that she is commanding the complete interest of the members of the class. (Library of Congress)*

for the purpose of enlightening others, but to perfect the speaker's understanding of the subject which he is discussing, or merely to demonstrate his understanding to his teacher and his classmates. Unquestionably, it is always desirable for a classroom speaker to add what he can to the knowledge of his classmates. Nevertheless, his chief concern frequently will be to strengthen his own mastery of his material.

Suppose that our history class is discussing the causes of the Civil War. The purpose of the whole discussion is to clarify and analyze the conflict of forces and opinions which culminated in the struggle. If one of the members of the group has only partially grasped the causes underlying the war, he may carry the discussion as far as he can, to show what he has learned, and to demonstrate what he has

AN EXPOSITORY SPEECH. *A college freshman discusses the skeleton of a pig before his class in anatomy. Note that the eyes of the speaker are where they belong — right on the class. There is always a strong temptation for the speaker who is presenting an oral exposition to keep his eyes on the exhibit and neglect his contact with his audience. This speaker is using his hands to direct attention to the skeleton and his eyes to facilitate his communication. (Library of Congress)*

failed to understand. With this background, he can be led to a fuller appreciation of the topic. Of course, if a student already understands the whole situation exceptionally well, he becomes a teacher as he participates in the discussion.

Finally, let us note that the objective of the typical classroom discussion is to foster understanding rather than to incite action. Group discussions outside the classroom usually aim at the formulation of available courses of action. In the classroom this is less frequently true. This difference manifests itself in the predominance of expository over convincing and persuasive speaking in classroom discussions; clarity, not group action, is usually the end sought.

With these considerations in mind, we should plan our speaking to fit the classroom situations of which we are a part. If our social-science teacher asks us to explain the method by which a bill is enacted into a law in the Congress of the United States, we must know whether we are expected: (1) merely to demonstrate that we understand the procedure, or (2) to enlighten our classmates who may not understand it. Most of the speaking we will do in our various classrooms will be primarily for one of these two purposes. To aim at one when the other is expected is to get off on the wrong foot.

PRACTICE GOOD SPEECH IN ALL CLASSES

There is an old story of a boy who insisted on using the ungrammatical form " have went." His teacher kept him after school one day and assigned to him the task of writing " I have gone " five hundred times. When he had finished, not seeing the teacher anywhere about, he laid his paper on the teacher's desk with an appended note which read, " Seeing that you had went out, I have went home." The point of this little story is that a correct form is worth knowing only when we use it habitually in the real business of living. One of the most unfortunate features of speech training is that we are likely to make the mistake of thinking that good speech is something to be used exclusively in the speech classroom or on " dress-up " occasions. All too seldom does it appear in our communication with others on the playground and in our mathematics, history, and English classrooms. Just as some students write correct English sentences and pay careful attention to spelling in the English classroom, and then become extremely careless when they write papers for the science teacher, some of us use correct speech in the speech classroom and forget all about it in biology and chemistry recitations. If our newly improved speech habits are going to flourish and take deep root in our lives, they must be cultivated and made the objects of constant attention and use. Only in this way can they become second

SPEECH IN A MATHEMATICS CLASS. *A member of a high-school class in geometry gives a demonstration. He is looking at the geometrical figure on the board rather than at the audience. Perhaps he just happened to be doing this as the picture was taken. It is all right to make sure that the pointer is rightly placed in such a demonstration but the speaker should not neglect his audience entirely; he should look at them as much as he can and still be accurate in the handling of his pointer. (Library of Congress)*

nature to us. Every classroom experience furnishes excellent opportunities for the practice of better speech.

On the playground we sometimes feel self-conscious and artificial about being careful and exact in our speech. But in the schoolroom the teacher and all our fellow students are more than ready to coöperate with us in the development of efficient speech habits. All that we need to do is to resolve that every time we speak we will use the best speech of which we are capable. If we will stick to this resolution for a few weeks, we shall find our grades in all our school subjects rising. We should remember that teachers, just like other people whom we meet, consciously or unconsciously form their most fundamental and lasting impressions of our ability from the speaking which we do in their presence.

COMMON WEAKNESSES IN CLASSROOM SPEAKING

As a basis for the preparation of this chapter hundreds of teachers all over the United States were asked to send in lists of the defects in speaking which in their judgment most seriously interfere with the effectiveness of classroom discussion. Let us take up some of the faults named most frequently in these reports.

Poor material. The first essential of good speaking is to have something worth saying. This means a careful preparation of the subject matter with which the discussion is to deal. It is true that individuals have been known to cover up lack of information on a subject by good bodily action, expressive voices, and fine attitudes. But content is an indispensable element of every type of speaking. In our high-school classes more than in most speech situations we are likely to be criticized harshly for deficiencies in subject matter. In mathematics, history, English, languages, science, art, physical training, agriculture, home economics, and music we are seldom the only ones who have studied a given topic. Usually the other students are prepared to participate in the discussion, and the teacher, an expert in the subject, also contributes. Under these conditions, mistakes are quickly discovered, and bluffing is resented. The high-school boy or girl who is recognized as a bluff by classmates and the teacher often earns that reputation by repeatedly forgetting that the best speech is impossible without sound ideas and knowledge.

Indirectness or uncommunicativeness. Very frequently the most damaging fault of the classroom speaker is a seeming inability or unwillingness to get into real communication with the group. When he is asked to make his contribution to the discussion, he looks at nobody in particular and gives the impression of meditating out loud rather than of talking with those about him. Frequently he looks at the ceiling, at the floor, or out the window. When he behaves in this fashion, he cannot possibly make a good impression, either on the teacher or on his classmates. All that we have learned about being straightforward, direct, and communicative in speech should stand us in good stead in remedying this defect.

Lack of physical co-ordination. How rare it is to have a classroom speaker stand up and recite as if he meant business! By assuming an easy, graceful posture, a speaker adds all of his resources of visible action to those of voice, language, and thought. It is distressingly common to see the student slouched over his desk and going through a lot of meaningless and wholly irrelevant visible action while he is attempting to communicate with his fellows. He plays with a piece of chalk, twiddles a pencil in his fingers, thrusts his hands into his pockets and pulls them out again, leans against the wall in such a way as to suggest that if the wall were to disappear suddenly he would fall down; in short, he demonstrates a complete lack of being able to pull himself together and use his visible action in a coordinated and unified way. How can anything other than a bad impression result from such habits?

Weak voice. How many of us have tried to tune in a very distant radio station when the signal was just too weak to be heard clearly even though we strained our ears as much as possible? Was not that an unpleasant experience? Yet we often seem to forget the desirability of being heard easily when we speak in the classroom. We pay little attention to the comfort of others when we speak with a weak voice. As a matter of fact, our classmates will not exert themselves very long to try to hear what we are saying. They will quit listening and pay attention to something else that is going on around them. It is hard to overestimate the value of a voice sufficiently strong to be heard without difficulty in all parts of the classroom. And there is absolutely no excuse for failing to develop such a voice.

Vocal monotony. Almost as bad as a weak voice is a monotonous and uninteresting voice. Everything we have studied in Chapter Three should be of assistance to us in getting rid of vocal monotony. Most of this difficulty results from emotional indifference to, and lack of enthusiasm for, what we are saying. We usually have appropriate vocal variety when we are saying things in which we really are interested. The answer, then, is to get interested in what we are going to talk about in the classroom. There isn't any adequate substitute for genuine interest in our material.

We may remember the story of the minister who was preaching in a singsong voice and found that one of the members of his congregation had fallen asleep. He stopped and requested one of the ushers to wake the man up. The usher replied: "Wake him up yourself. You put him to sleep." If we expect to do well in our school subjects, we must resolve not to make any vocal contribution to the sleepiness of those who listen to us. We must learn to use sufficient vocal variety to keep our classmates alert and wide-awake. If we do not, they will not be much impressed either by us or by what we say.

Mispronunciations. Correct pronunciation is indispensable to all speaking, but particularly so to classroom speaking, where we are supposed to be on our good behavior. How can we expect to create an impression of competence in the eyes of our fellow students, to say nothing of our teachers, if we mispronounce the words we use? In preparing our lessons, one of the first matters to which we should attend is the vocabulary we are going to need in classroom discussions. If we are reading a chapter in American history about the Mexican War, we should look up all the proper names, as well as all the other unfamiliar words we find used in the text, because they serve better to convey essential meanings about the period than will any others. If we are going to discuss a poem or an essay in our English class, we should get ready to do the job with maximum effectiveness by mastering the pronunciation of all of the words we may want to use. We must not be satisfied with a hazy and vague notion as to these pronunciations and then find that we have handicapped ourselves hopelessly for any adequate presentation of the material in class. Above all, when we have looked up the words, we should say them aloud a number of times. Then we should use them in correct context until they fall trippingly from our tongues with such a degree of naturalness that we are not self-conscious about using them.

Lack of fluency. Halting and hesitant speech is almost always ineffective; it suggests uncertainty and confusion of mind. If we want to give an impression of competence and grasp of subject matter, we will have to speak fluently. Of course the best way to develop such fluency is actually to master what we are going to talk about. In part this mastery can be accomplished by talking over, either with someone else or with ourselves, what we are planning to say in various situations which may arise in the classroom.

At some time in our school life we have been members of classes which have made special advance preparation for visits of school administrators, parents, teachers, or other classes. Despite the added strain on everybody, the exercises went off with unusual smoothness and ease. Every class period could be a good deal more like that if students would only get themselves ready beforehand. The trouble is that too frequently we wait to formulate what we want to say until the moment we are called upon. The result is that the speaking is filled with awkward pauses, repetitions, false starts, and clumsy phrasings. When anyone speaks his mind fluently and smoothly, we are likely to say, " Ah, there is someone who really knows his stuff."

Stage fright. How often many of us have come to the end of a class period conscious of the fact that we have made a poor showing simply because we were too nervous to do ourselves justice when we were called on! We have already been given advice as to what to do in alleviating this malady, which afflicts everybody, more or less. About all that we can do here is to focus our attention on the necessity for diligent and thorough preparation of every assignment if we would come into the classroom with a fair chance of escaping the baleful effects of stage fright. We should remember that fear

AN INSTRUCTIONAL SPEECH. *A high-school chemistry student becomes teacher for the time being as he explains and demonstrates an experiment before his class. What may be inferred from the faces of members of the class as to the degree of success with which the speaker is meeting? How are the marked differences in the attitudes of various auditors to be accounted for?* (Library of Congress)

arises primarily from a sense of inadequacy. Even our teachers, who seem so calm and self-possessed, experience stage fright when placed in difficult speech situations. For example, if called upon to discuss some educational theory before an audience of one thousand fellow teachers, they might well have a serious case of " jitters." Obviously, the best way to reduce a feeling of inadequacy is to become less inadequate! The surer our grasp of subject matter, the less cause we have to be fearful that we may fail in telling others about it. We must not be discouraged if after we have done everything we can reasonably be expected to do by way of preparing our assignments, we still find ourselves troubled by some slightly unpleasant feelings of fear when we come to the recitation hour. Every time we make a successful recitation, we are closer to triumph over this bogey which besets us all.

Tests of Comprehension and Application

PRACTICE TO IMPROVE

1 Select a book on the list of required readings in your English class and prepare a ten-minute talk for or against its inclusion in the list.
2 Give a five-minute talk on the preparation you would make if you were to have the opportunity for an interview with some important person in the world of letters.
3 Suppose you were to have a chance to interview one of the following, what questions would you most like to ask, and why? George Washington, Benedict Arnold, Alexander Hamilton, Thomas Jefferson, Daniel Webster, Abraham Lincoln, Dwight L. Moody, William J. Bryan, Calvin Coolidge
4 Tell the class about some contemporary novel you have read. Your object is to get them to read it.
5 Prepare a brief talk for your physics or chemistry class on the lifework of some great figure in modern science.
6 Prepare to furnish your history class with background information they would find helpful in understanding and appreciating the Webster-Hayne debate, or the Lincoln-Douglas debates.
7 Prepare to participate in a physics-class discussion of frequency-modulation broadcasting in America.
8 Discuss the life of John Keats and compare it with that of Henry Wadsworth Longfellow. What similarities and what differences do you find?
9 Compare Lord Tennyson with Robert Browning. Which of the two do you enjoy more, and why?
10 Were the conspirators in Shakespeare's *Julius Caesar* justified in their action?
11 In your judgment, which is the better story, George Eliot's *Silas Marner*, or Dickens's *Oliver Twist*? Why?
12 Which scenes from Shakespeare's *Macbeth* would you most like to see on the stage or in the movies?

COMPREHENSION AND APPLICATION TESTS 235

13 Who said "The gift without the giver is bare"? Is it true? Can you illustrate?

14 What are the comparative effects of peace and war on the production of literature? Give examples.

15 A great mathematician once remarked, "Mathematics is language." In what sense is that true?

16 State three rules of punctuation you consider very important. Can you show what happens when these rules are disregarded?

17 Bring to the class some novel on your English reading list which has no chapter titles, and indicate the titles you would use, and your reasons.

18 Is it true that Shakespeare always strikes the keynote of a play in the first act? Illustrate by reading brief passages. Bring to class a short lyric poem which you like particularly. Read it aloud and comment on it.

19 Which do you think will be more valuable to you in later life, biology or history? Explain.

20 What was happening in America when John Milton was writing *Paradise Lost*?

21 Which American author do you think is most like Thomas Carlyle? Why?

22 Prepare to discuss one of the following as interestingly as you can.

  a Confessions of a bluffer
  b The benefits of laziness
  c Educating my parents
  d Interesting birds I have known
  e The faults of my little brother (or of my little sister)
  f Future possibilities of aviation
  g Figures of speech
  h Color combinations in apparel
  i An interesting profession
  j Duties of citizenship at the present moment
  k Jacques' philosophy
  l The character of Polonius
  m Camouflage in war and in peace
  n Television

23 Prepare to lead a discussion on one of the following topics. Check your selection with your teacher to make sure that it is not being duplicated.

a Soil-erosion problems
b Co-operatives in Scandinavia
c Heredity and environment
d Properties of gases
e Disinfectants and preservatives
f Sedimentation
g Women in politics
h Health problems
i How the stock market works
j Oil products
k Synthetic rubber
l Taxation problems
m Where the styles come from
n Submarine disasters
o How we think
p Statistics
q Written and oral tests
r Bacteria
s Study habits
t Technological unemployment
u Tolerance
v Chromosomes
w Great discoverers
x The meanings of words
y Values and dangers in curiosity
z Laboratories
aa The social life of ants (or bees)
ab Food poisoning
ac Why keep animals in the zoo
ad Tragedies of childhood
ae Values and dangers in ambition
af Raising money for charity
ag Tank farming
ah Relations of government to industry
ai The Babcock test
aj Mendel's law
ak Color blindness
al The dye industry
am Patent medicines
an Musical instruments
ao Heroes of the air
ap The Alaska purchase
aq Forensic contests
ar The F.B.I.
as Francis Parkman
at Guns that weren't loaded
au Quaint customs of other lands
av Learning a foreign language
aw Circumstantial evidence

24 Prepare a program on magazines. Each one in the class should present a magazine, explaining its special features, the public which it reaches, advertising rates, subscription price, and so forth.

25 Read up on some engineering project such as the Grand Coulee Dam, the TVA, the San Francisco bridges, or the Holland Tunnel, assigning some particular phase of the undertaking to each of several

members of the class. Then discuss what you have found out, for the benefit of the other members of the class.

TEST YOUR PROGRESS

26 Evaluate the discussion in one of your classes other than speech. What are its strong points and what are its weaknesses? On the basis of what you have observed, what would you add to the list of weaknesses discussed in this chapter?

27 Check yourself on the list of faults in classroom speaking and estimate your effectiveness. Which are your particular besetting sins? What sort of a remedial program can you work out?

28 Rehearse in the speech class a long report you are to give in some other class. Try to get as much help as you can in improving it.

CHAPTER TEN *Storytelling*

ONE OF THE best ways to retain old, friendly human relationships and to form new ones is through cultivating and practicing storytelling. This is one of the oldest arts in the world, and it is just as popular today as it was a thousand years ago. Everyone likes to hear a good story well told, and can recall occasions when a sale has been made, a difficult problem understood, a quarrel averted, contracts signed, friendships sealed, or dull parties made interesting by the telling of appropriate and worth-while stories. We shall get along with people more successfully if we are good storytellers.

AIMS IN STORYTELLING

If we set out to tell stories, we will have one of six aims in mind. These are: (1) to give pleasure, (2) to give information, (3) to make a point, (4) to develop imagination, (5) to enlarge vocabularies, and (6) to gain social ease. Let us examine each purpose and see how it may contribute to a general program of speech training in the realm of human relationships.

STORY-READING TIME. *The reading seems to be claiming the pleased attention of all the children. The setting is the library of an elementary school. The storybook from which the reading is being given is held open toward the audience so that they may see the pictures. If this procedure is followed, the reader must "read" the story from memory.* (Library of Congress)

Telling stories to give pleasure. The telling of stories does give pleasure to listeners — otherwise, storytelling would have died out long ago — and because it gives pleasure it is safe to assume that human beings will tell stories until the end of time. The public speaker most in demand is the one who uses anecdotes to entertain, to instruct, and to persuade his audience. The traveler who can make his experiences seem vivid and interesting to other people is always asked to relate them. There is no surer way to win the confidence and affection of little children than through judicious use of the opening " Once upon a time."

Telling stories to give information. The second purpose in telling stories is to give instruction. Teachers whose classes we most enjoy illustrate many points with interesting narratives. Frequently we can teach best by telling appropriate stories. The parables of the New Testament illustrate this point. Listening to informative stories is an excellent way to collect worth-while material for conversation.

Telling stories to make a point. Many public speakers have achieved unusual success in changing the beliefs and the actions of their audiences by skillful storytelling. They have learned how to use this old device of illustrating a point or supporting an argument by reducing to story form what they want to demonstrate or prove. Abraham Lincoln was a master at making points clear by the use of stories.

Telling stories to develop imagination. There are few better ways to develop lively imagination than through telling stories. By relating incidents effectively we participate in them, and thus indirectly achieve experiences which may be denied to us in real life. Of all man's mental powers, imagination deserves to rank first. Read what Robert Green Ingersoll has to say of a great storyteller:

" Shakespeare exceeded all the sons of men in the splendor of his imagination. To him the whole world paid tribute, and Nature poured her treasures at his feet. In him all races lived again, and even those to be were pictured in his brain.

" He was a man of imagination — that is to say, of genius — and having seen a leaf and a drop of water, he could construct the forests, the rivers, and the seas. If Shakespeare knew one fact, he knew its kindred and its neighbors. Looking at a coat of mail, he instantly imagined the society, the conditions, that produced it and what it, in turn, produced. He saw the castle, the moat, the drawbridge, the lady in the tower, and the knightly lover spurring across the plain.

" He lived the life of all. He was a citizen of Athens in the days of Pericles. He listened to the eager eloquence of the great orators, and sat upon the cliffs, and with the tragic poet heard ' the multitudinous laughter of the sea.' He saw Socrates thrust the spear of question through the shield and heart of falsehood. He was present when the great man drank hemlock, and met the night of death, tranquil as a star meets morning.

"He walked the ways of mighty Rome and saw great Caesar with his legions in the field. He stood with vast and motley throngs and watched the triumphs given to victorious men, followed by uncrowned kings, the captured hosts, and all the spoils of ruthless war. He heard the shout that shook the Colosseum's roofless walls, when from the reeling gladiator's hand the short sword fell, while from his bosom gushed the stream of wasted life.

"The Imagination had a stage in Shakespeare's brain, whereon were set all scenes that lie between the morn of laughter and the night of tears, and where his players bodied forth the false and true, the joys and griefs, the careless shallows and the tragic deeps, of universal life."

Without imagination there can be no effective storytelling. And without some form of storytelling it is difficult to keep the imagination alert and alive.

Telling stories to enlarge vocabularies. A pleasant way to become familiar with new words is to meet them in the context of an absorbing story. Even listening attentively to stories enlarges our vocabulary. But when we ourselves prepare a story for oral presentation, we have a rare opportunity to use new words for the expression of the exact thought and feeling we wish to convey; and by speaking these words aloud we fix them firmly in our own vocabularies.

Telling stories to gain social ease. Storytelling helps us to feel at ease in social situations. The capable storyteller is always in demand socially. At formal dinners he is popular; in family gatherings he puts himself and others at ease; with little children he is the center of attention; and on the public platform he is listened to with interest. Because people are constantly drawn to him and anxious to hear what he has to say, he loses his feeling of self-consciousness and anxiety and gains confidence and social poise.

THE HISTORY OF STORYTELLING

The history of mankind is preserved in stories. Homer's tales, told over and over throughout many generations before they were ever written down, record the traditions of the people of ancient Greece. Such myths furnish important clues to the spiritual development of the race. In its narratives, the Old Testament embodies the remains of Hebrew-Chaldaic culture; the New Testament presents in its stories the early history and doctrines of Christianity. Aesop's *Fables* tell us much about the most brilliant period of Athenian literature. *Beowulf* gives us a picture of Anglo-Saxon life. The great legends of King Arthur and his knights of the Round Table portray the sturdy national virtues of the medieval Englishman. The *Fables* of La Fontaine suggest a significant era in the national life of France, and *The Song of Hiawatha* epitomizes the romance and the customs of the Indian inhabitants of North America. These and thousands of other thrilling stories and fables have been transmitted to us and kept alive because there always have been storytellers, and listeners to well-told tales.

Medieval minstrels, ballads, and stories. In medieval days, when there were no newspapers, an enthusiastic welcome was accorded everywhere to the minstrel who tramped from village to village, singing stories of current events to the unlettered people of his age. In such circumstances, it is not surprising that audiences became enthusiastic participators in these performances, to the extent of assisting the reciters by changing and adding phrases to the growing tales of truth and fiction which became more and more interesting and romantic as they passed from mouth to ear and from generation to generation.

In England and in neighboring countries no medieval fair or castle festivity was considered complete if it did not boast the presence of these minstrels with their ballads. These singing storytellers were honored and rewarded not only by the common people, but by the nobles and the kings. They were received hospitably, entertained as privileged individuals, and often more amply paid than the clergy. They recited and sang whatever tales seemed to them appropriate for given occasions. They quoted from one another freely, and then improvised new stanzas to fit new audiences. Often these minstrels picked up news in one town and set it to music for the entertainment of the people in the next one. These stories, founded on truth but given increased popular appeal by the embellishments of romance and adventure, did not differ widely from the newspaper articles of today. They were intended to interest all sorts of people, and they succeeded admirably, because when the audience's interest seemed to decline, the minstrel exaggerated his visible bodily action and his vocal inflections until he once more secured the listeners' attention. Much of the storytelling was carried on at table, and it was not unusual to have the whole dinner company join in the songs and stories. This practice encouraged repetition and rhythm, and may account in part for the form of the ballad as it has come down to us.

Folk stories. Every people and every race have their folk stories. Some authorities believe that many of these tales were started by mothers as warnings to their children. For example, when children were very young, their mother told them not to touch fire lest they be burned, and in order to make the point more impressive, she may have added: " Once upon a time a little baby *did* touch the fire, and . . ." Then the mother's imagination built a dramatic story which she and they repeated to other children. We can all remember such stories told to us by our own mothers. Most naturally, these stories often were " set " in the community in which we lived, and their characters were like the people we knew best. In the same way, the warning tales of the French, the German, and the Norwegian mothers were based on the customs and the scenes familiar to the people of their respective localities. So folk stories have been built up by the people in every age and in every community.

Other folk tales have lived because they embodied important human experiences. Fathers passed them on to sons, and leaders to followers. When writing and printing were unknown, there was no way except storytelling to make sure that important events would be remembered and transmitted to future generations.

There is little doubt that the Paul Bunyan tales of northern Wisconsin, Minnesota, and Michigan grew up because in many of the lumber camps there were men of unusual size and strength. There actually may have been one such of giant stature named Paul Bunyan.

who became the hero of the stories the lumberjacks told around the fire after the day's work was done. Characteristically, the storyteller is reluctant to boast too much about his own ability and skill; he feels that the listener is often a bit skeptical. It seems much easier, therefore, to make the audience believe a tall yarn about a fictitious character. So, as these unlettered storytellers made up their exaggerated tales of strength and daring, Paul Bunyan came to be the central figure of many exciting incidents. With each story he grew taller, stronger, and more courageous, until now he towers above buildings and forests, steps from Wisconsin to Maine in a single stride, and with his fall shakes the whole earth!

Myths. The stars in the heavens, the waters of the rivers and the sea, the hills and the mountains, the animal and plant life of the earth, have always been and no doubt always will be in part unexplained mysteries to us. Myths grew out of man's attempt to penetrate such mysteries. For example, he looked at the heavens and saw that the stars were arranged in forms that seemed to him like those of bears and dippers. Then he invented stories about these constellations which have been told and retold ever since.

It is interesting to take a puzzling problem like that of the origin of the world and gather from every age and every people stories intended to explain the beginning of things. The Greeks had several different accounts. So did the Egyptians and the ancient Hebrews. Other peoples before and after them have had their own creation myths. From the legends of the red and the black races of our own country, we can make a most interesting compilation of stories about the origin of the universe.

CHOOSING THE STORY

In choosing a story to tell to an audience, it is well to ask ourselves the questions of the ten following paragraphs. (In formulating these questions, the authors have dealt with the problem of selecting stories from books, magazines, and other printed sources; the queries do not apply to original stories or personal experiences.)

Is the story good literature? In selecting printed material as the basis for storytelling, it is well for us to keep in mind the fact that audiences may be bored by stories that are below standard in literary quality. By this time we know that our classmates have many ways of occupying themselves during the hours of the day, and if we try to tell them stories which are trite and dull, they will soon be using their time to better advantage than in listening to us. What is true of high-school boys and girls is also true of little children and adults. They will not tolerate stories they consider beneath them. When there is such limitless opportunity for selecting fine stories from real literature, it is unfortunate to waste one's talents in telling trashy stuff. The application of this principle does not mean that we should never use story material from nonclassical sources. We do not need to be "high-brow" in order to avoid being "low-brow." Nevertheless, it is always well to ask ourselves: "Does this story which I am to tell possess genuine literary quality? Is the language good enough to affect my own language habits favorably?"

Is the plot plausible? Next we should be sure that the plot of our story is plausible. This rule means that if the storyteller expects the listener to believe that the story actually might have happened, he must confine himself to events that could have happened, and make his characters behave as they would have behaved in similar real-life circumstances. Boys and girls in stories should act as normal boys and girls act, and not like either angels or demons. However, a fairy story, with supernatural characters, will be received with enthusiasm if it is properly presented; that is, if we ask our audience to go with us on a make-believe trip to never-never land. What we object to is being led to suppose that we are on the firm ground of fact and then, unexpectedly, finding that we are hobnobbing with goblins and witches somewhere in the cloudland of phantasy. We all demand consistency in both plot and characters when we read or hear a story.

Does the language of the story express the thought accurately? In a well-told narrative the words say exactly what the teller wants them to say. The characters are described so vividly that they "come alive" as we listen. The descriptions are so accurate that there is no mistaking situations or events. When these qualities are present, we know that we are dealing with real literature.

Is the story worth repeating? Any piece of good literature reveals new and richer meanings at each reading or hearing, while poor material becomes less meaningful when read or heard for the second time. Some of our very best tales have been told over and over for thousands of years and yet they are appreciated as much now as they were at the first telling. If after we read a story a dozen times, we like it better than we did when we read it first, we may be pretty sure that it is worth telling to others.

Is the story of proper length? Many stories are not of the proper length for oral telling. Some are too long and must be abridged if they are to be presented in the available time; some are too short, and several must be combined to make a good program for the scheduled period. In " cutting " or arranging material it is important to keep in mind the characteristics of good stories, in order not to lose the more fundamental values in fitting the material to time limits. Time limits should be scrupulously observed, but we can do this best by finding stories which do not have to be hopelessly mangled in order to keep them within prescribed bounds.

Does the story have a climax? When each scene and each adventure in a story are completely unified in a final and satisfying turn of events, we say that the story has a strong climax. Carolyn Sherwin Bailey cites an example of perfect climax. She says:

" Hans Christian Andersen's inimitable allegory of ' The Ugly Duckling ' owes a measure, at least, of its popularity to its perfect climax. In the beautiful word pictures of the story we follow its hero, The Ugly Duckling, through his series of perilous and sorrowful adventures, sympathizing with but not anticipating the outcome of them. In no single one of the scenes of the story do we have a hint of the glorious ending of the hero's journeying. Finally comes a quick, artistic curtain falling.

" ' Then he flew toward the beautiful swans. As soon as they saw him they rushed to meet him with outstretched wings.

" ' " Kill me! " said The Ugly Duckling: but as he bent his head, what did he see reflected in the water? It was his own image — not a dark, gray bird, ugly to see — but a graceful swan.

" ' Then the great swans swam around him and stroked his neck with their beaks for a welcome. Some little children came into the garden.

"'"See," they cried, clapping their hands. "A new swan has come and he is more beautiful than the others!"'"

"This story's climax is perfect also, because it carries the element of surprise to the story hearers and to the story hero, The Ugly Duckling, as well."[1]

Is something happening all the time in the story? In a good story, something happens all the time. There are no uneventful moments; action is present from start to finish. Long descriptions of scenes, people, attitudes, or feelings cause audiences to lose interest. In the best stories for telling aloud, events rather than descriptions follow one another in rapid succession.

Are the scenes, incidents, and characters distinct? If the scenes and incidents of our stories are confusing, if the characters are not clear-cut and vivid, we should choose another story. Otherwise, our audiences probably will be bored by our efforts. Every scene must stand out distinctly, every incident must have its peculiar place in the plot, and every character must be sharply etched.

Does the telling of the story require changes in bodily action and voice? We should be sure that the story we choose gives us opportunity — nay, compels us — to use changes in bodily action and voice as we tell it. Variety in posture, facial expression, movements of the hands, trunk, and feet, will help us to hold the interest of the audience when other elements fail. Appropriate changes in voice will help our listeners to get the story exactly. The wise storyteller evaluates stories in terms of opportunities for expressional activities, interpretation, and impersonation.

Is the story appropriate to the audience? In selecting stories for children in the primary grades and of preschool age, it is well to remember that jingles, repetition of sounds, and refrains are very interesting to little people. If we have had experience in telling stories to children, we may recall that in the repeated hearings of a tale a child is quick to notice the slightest changes in language. If the chorus or refrain does not remain word for word as it was in former tellings, the child will correct us. He will chant with us the rhythmic bits that he likes. Both adults and high-school students, as well as children,

---

[1] *For the Story Teller*, The Milton Bradley Company, New York, p. 87. Reprinted by permission.

AROUND THE CAMPFIRE. *Storytelling in Texas. A group of ranchers and their friends are gathered around a campfire. For what sort of a story is this setting ideal? What kind of stories could not be told very effectively in such a place and to such a group? Not all the members of the group are looking at the storyteller. How is this fact to be explained, if we assume that he is a successful teller of tales? (Meisel from Monkmeyer)*

are intrigued by repetition and rhythm. Such lines as "the great gray-green, greasy Limpopo River, all set about with fever trees"[1] charm young and old.

For little children, all language must be very clear and simple; remember that we want them to understand every detail of the story. For the small child the ending of a story is extremely important; he insists upon having his story well rounded out. It is typical of the child to want his villains killed and his heroes to live happily ever after. It may well be added that most grownups never get far beyond this stage!

One of the outstanding characteristics of the stories which appeal to high-school students is that they have a forward rather than a backward look. Life is ahead of the high-school boy, and he reads all literature in the light of what he thinks or dreams that he will do when he meets the situations portrayed in the stories. He sees himself as the discoverer of the gold, the hero of the romance, the victor in the battle — all in a roseate future.

The older person adopts a somewhat opposite attitude. He enjoys reminiscence. He pictures himself as one who might have met the story situations as the characters do. He looks back on what might have been. He realizes that much of his life is behind him, and he mildly regrets the fact that he will not now be able to do all the things he once had hoped to do.

PREPARING THE STORY

Knowing that there are the following different types of stories may be helpful in finding the ones we wish to tell. However, this list should not limit our choice. It is our privilege to find our own stories, sometimes best of all in our own experiences.

Ballads	Bible stories	Travel stories	Allegories
Myths	Adventure stories	Anecdotes	Personal
Fables	Romances	Historical	experiences
Fairy stories	Stories of science	narratives	

Read the story carefully and repeatedly. When we have selected our story, the first step in preparing it for telling is to read it aloud

[1] Rudyard Kipling, "The Elephant Child," *Just-so Stories.*

carefully. We must be sure that every part of the meaning is perfectly clear to us before leaving this first step in preparation. If we understand it thoroughly, we will be better able to describe the setting, we will know when the action took place, and we will have the characters clearly in mind and the outstanding incidents in their proper sequence. By reading and rereading aloud to ourselves we will get the "feel" of the material, its mood, and the unity of impression that the author intended.

Plan each scene. When we have gained this preliminary understanding, we should decide whether all or part of the story will serve our purpose more effectively. With this question in mind, we should select the leading incidents that we wish to tell to our audience. It is important here to tie each group of incidents into a subclimax and to see that these subclimaxes culminate in one final main climax. In selecting the incidents and characters we wish to bring into the final telling, it is well to remember that a few scenes and characters are less confusing than are many scenes and characters. It is difficult for the audience to keep in mind a mass of details, and the skillful storyteller knows this. The art of eliminating irrelevant or inconsequential side excursions, once learned, is mightily helpful to the storyteller.

Adapt the language of the story to the audience. Since we have selected a story with careful attention to the quality of its language, we will want to retain many of the words and phrases of the author. Seldom should our story be memorized, but when the author has used a particularly apt phrase, we may rightly desire to pass that on to our listeners. We must try to keep the freedom, the communicativeness, the flexibility, and the conversational directness of extemporaneous speech and at the same time to suggest the author's characteristic style of language.

Make the story interesting throughout. Remember that the first sentence is extremely important; so, too, is the last. We must plan to hold the attention of the audience all the time. We must plan the introductory sentences so carefully that they will not fail to interest the listeners at once and direct their train of thought to the next point in the story. We must not expect to force our listeners to listen; we must strive for their involuntary, almost unconscious, attention. Presumably, we have chosen a plot that has in it the elements of curiosity and suspense. These should be emphasized by changes in voice and action. Suspense is effective in holding the attention of normal human beings of any age.

TELLING THE STORY

When the time for the final performance has come, we must keep the central idea of the story in mind. If we have practiced conscientiously, it will not be necessary for us to worry about our standing posture, our action, our voice, and our language. The time to be concerned about such techniques is in practice. When we stand before the audience, our thoughts should be on what we are telling rather than on how we are telling it.

The expert storyteller has had so much practice that his body and voice respond adequately and correctly without conscious effort. So long as we are more or less inexperienced, it may be necessary for us to check on certain techniques we are using, as our story progresses. We must see to it that our position before the audience is helping us. In some groups, we may be more successful if we sit; in others, an easy standing position will be more effective. Whatever we do, we must make sure that we can see, and be seen by, our audience without uncomfortable strain. The good storyteller is sure that he uses enough volume to be heard easily without attracting attention to his voice.

Always watch the audience. Remember that the success of any story depends on whether or not it is heard and understood. If we see by the expressions of the listeners' faces that they are not following us, we must do something different from what we are doing. We must try to show our hearers that the story is really interesting, letting visible action, voice, and language indicate our own feeling about the various episodes. We can scarcely expect others to react properly unless we do so ourselves.

Tests of Comprehension and Application

MASTER THE FACTS

1 Recall an occasion when someone told a story to give pleasure, but did not accomplish his purpose. Explain what was wrong and how the failure might have been avoided.
2 Give five specific examples of stories told in other classes for the purpose of giving information; for example, as an aid to the understanding of an incident in history, some principle in cooking, a theorem in mathematics, the spelling of a word, or the mastery of a technique in music.
3 Cite three instances in which stories have given you information.
4 From literature, find each of the purposes of storytelling exemplified.
5 Recommend two stories which develop the imagination.
6 Give an example of an occasion when a speaker gained ease and poise through use of a well-told story.
7 Make a scrapbook in which you illustrate the history of storytelling.
8 Find two stories you have never read before, both by authors you have not known. Apply the tests of good literature given in this chapter and evaluate the stories.
9 Select a story that has a climax which makes it appropriate for telling.
10 Select two stories, one of which is dull, and one which is interesting because something is happening all the time.
11 Find a story in which the scenes and the incidents are clear and distinct. Write a report on why you have selected it and how it fulfills this requirement of a good story.
12 Report on an anecdote you have heard told ineffectively. Point out what step or steps in preparation apparently had been neglected.
13 Recall some story that lost the attention of the audience at a particular point. Try to discover how the mistake might have been avoided through better preparation.
14 Make a comprehensive storytelling scrapbook. Write up all the suggestions you have learned about aims in storytelling and the history, selection, preparation, and presentation of stories. Include

your favorite stories. Remember to include material suitable for telling to people of various ages and on different occasions.

15 Find out all you can about the history of storytelling in Greece, Rome, Spain, Germany, France, England, Norway, Sweden, Denmark, or America. One or more class periods may be devoted to stories on the beginnings of storytelling.

16 Add to the information in this chapter on the early history of storytelling. Present your material in a general classroom discussion.

17 Bring in pictures illustrating the history of storytelling. Display them on the bulletin board while working on this project.

18 From your reading bring in the plots of three stories that are not true to life. Explain to the class the reasons for your selection.

19 Bring in two stories, one which illustrates good language and one which illustrates poor language.

PRACTICE TO IMPROVE

20 Bring to class a story that has added at least five new words to your vocabulary. Before the class, pronounce the words correctly, explain the meaning of each, and use each in a sentence.

21 Tell a story which illustrates a truth or a principle. After you have told it, apply it.

22 What story would you say has challenged your imagination more than any other story? In a three-minute talk to the class justify your choice.

23 Give an example of an occasion when a well-told story helped you to gain social ease.

24 Using the suggestions given above, prepare each of the three stories selected in exercise 2.

25 Listen to a story told over the radio and determine whether each of the steps in "Preparing the Story" has been carefully observed. If not, show how the ones omitted weakened the effectiveness of the story.

26 Practice one of your stories before a mirror at home. Criticize your performance honestly.

27 Read supplementary material on how to prepare a story for telling. Report to the class.

28 If possible, get an interview with a good storyteller. Get his

suggestions for effective storytelling. Write them up in organized form for other members of the class.

29 Devote an entire class period to "backgrounds of storytelling." Elect a chairman and have him arrange the program. Include talks on storytelling from the earliest times down to the present. See that all types of stories are discussed. Add new material to that presented in the text. Every student will wish to participate.

30 Bring in folk stories gathered from individuals of various nationalities in your communities. Present them in a class program.

31 Let each student make up an original myth.

32 Make a collection of ballads for storytelling.

33 Listen to at least one story over the radio. In a speech before the class, criticize it from the standpoint of plot and language.

34 Select four stories of varying lengths, one a short anecdote appropriate to tell in a dinner conversation, one appropriate to tell to children from three to six years old, one to illustrate a point in a lecture, and one to tell to your class.

35 Using a story you consider a good one, show how appropriate bodily action and voice can help to make the story clear to the audience.

36 Bring in three stories, each appropriate to tell to a different audience.

37 Choose a novel worth telling. Let each student tell the story of one chapter.

38 Devote all or part of a class period to the telling of stories on the courage of individuals. Do the same with dog stories, mystery stories, and anecdotes.

39 Offer the services of your class to some social-service group. Prepare appropriate stories, and schedule the best ones.

40 Tell the story of some book you have read recently. You will be stopped at the end of seven minutes. Be sure you include the essentials and omit the nonessentials. Try to make all members of the class want to read the book.

41 Tell the story of your ancestry.

42 Tell the story of the smartest animal you have ever known.

43 Tell a "tall" story like those about Paul Bunyan or Baron Munchausen.

44   Devote one class period to six different kinds of stories, each kind presented by a student who has shown special ability in telling it.
45   Tell the story of your most interesting experience.
46   Prepare and tell a Bible story.

TEST YOUR PROGRESS

47   Tell two different kinds of stories, one in class and the other before some other audience. Write a report of your experience before the outside audience. Was it better or worse than your class presentation? Upon what do you base your opinion? Ambitious students may find opportunities to tell from two to four stories before outside audiences.
48   Arrange to tell stories before Sunday-school groups. Practice in class and profit by the criticisms of your friends.
49   Imagine that the members of your class are little children of first- or second-grade age. Prepare a story and tell it to them. Let the best storyteller go to the first and second grades and tell the story.
50   Tell an interesting anecdote in one minute. Which students were successful and which unsuccessful? Why?
51   Practice one of your stories before your mother or a good friend. Ask for frank criticism.
52   Make an occasion for telling a story to a group of small children. When you have finished, write a report showing in detail how your listeners reacted. If they were interested from start to finish, analyze the techniques you used. If they were not interested and did not derive pleasure from your story, try to discover your shortcomings.
53   Get permission to have one member of your class tell a story in assembly. Let all members compete for the honor. Choose the best.
54   Report to the class on a story told in a sermon. What point did it support? Could it have been made more effective? How?

CHAPTER ELEVEN *Interpretative Reading*

HOW MANY times each week do we or members of our families read aloud to others? Thoughtlessly some of us may answer, " Not at all," but let us see if we are accurate. Let us see how well we remember what happened last week. Begin early in the morning on Sunday. Did anyone read aloud from the newspaper? Did anyone else share a part of a book or a magazine article? Was there reading from the Bible at home or in Sunday school? Did we meet for a reading hour in the evening? Let us recall Monday. Let us think over the preparation and presentation of all of our lessons in all subjects at school, family letters, club meetings, tryouts for plays, daily papers, directions for making a dress, cake recipes, government advice on farm projects, advertisements, a new poem, a favorite story or play — did any of us communicate these aloud to our friends, our families, or a public audience? Let us follow through the rest of the week and add the reading for those days to that of Sunday and Monday. After such a survey, few people can report " No reading aloud at all." What we have been doing is interpretative reading; that is, speaking to others what we have found on the printed page.

PURPOSE AND NATURE OF INTERPRETATION

What is the purpose of any interpreter? Suppose that one of us were asked to act as an interpreter for two persons one of whom speaks English only and the other Spanish only. What knowledge or abilities would the interpreter have to possess in order to perform his task satisfactorily? Clearly, he would need to know both languages; he would have to understand the meanings expressed in Spanish and translate them adequately into English, and vice versa. In other words, he would have to be proficient in two different language codes. Just so with the interpretative reader; he must be a master of the two codes, writing and speaking, and be able to make an effective one-way translation — from the written to the spoken symbols.

In most of the reading that we have done we have looked first at the language symbols on the printed page and from them have discovered the facts we are going to report in history, the thoughts and emotions we plan to express in English, the ideas and feelings of the letter writer, the incidents of the daily news, the steps in making a dress or a cake, and the story of the play in which we wish to act. There is no meaning whatever in the printed page except that which, by means of suggestions and guides from the writer, we as readers put into it. We ourselves as readers decide what and how much meaning there is to be. Once having developed these meanings, we are ready to stimulate others through speech until we have stirred up in them the same or similar meanings.

Thus we see that reading prose and poetry aloud to others — interpretative reading — is important in improving human relationships and therefore appropriate to consider while we are concentrating on that aim in education. But why should anyone read to others? Why not let each individual do his own reading? The answer is that an effective interpretative reader can save his hearers an immense amount of labor and bring them much pleasure by substituting the symbols of speech for the symbols of print. The aim of a good interpreter of literature is to cause his hearers to respond as the author would want them to respond to what he has written. Longfellow puts it in a nutshell:

> Then read from the treasured volume
>   The poem of thy choice,
> And lend to the rhyme of the poet
>   The beauty of thy voice.

Do the problems of the interpretative reader differ from those of the speaker? The whole duty of the reader is to determine what meanings the language is intended to convey and then to utter the language with such vocal modulations and visible actions as may be helpful in stirring up the intended meanings. The use of the speech mechanism in reading is not essentially different from its use in speaking.

UNDERSTANDING THE WRITTEN CODE

The first problem in learning to read is understanding the written code. This is not so simple as it at first appears. True, when reading a recipe, excerpts from a letter, or a bit of news from the daily paper, it is seldom necessary to spend much time in analyzing the written code. Usually its meaning is obvious almost at once, and the oral presentation of that meaning can take place immediately. However, it is important to understand the written code completely before any attempt at communication is made. It will be well to review carefully the material on meaning in Chapter Five.

At this point it may be interesting to analyze some short literary selections in order to become familiar with a systematic method of getting meanings from what has been written. Literature created by high-school students has special appeal for high-school students, doubtless because students have certain characteristics in common, and are able to understand the written codes used by each other more easily than the written codes used by older authors.

The following is a poem created by William Sargent, a high-school boy. It is used here as an example to show how to prepare literature for reading aloud. The steps followed with this poem should be applied in getting other selections ready for oral presentation. We must thoroughly understand and appreciate the material before we can expect to make others understand and appreciate it. The analyses given on pages 258–265 will help us to do that.

THE BLACKFEET OF MONTANA

I met the chiefs in the morning (and oh, but I am old!)
Where roaring down the canyon the summer west wind rolled.

I heard them lift the war whoop that quelled the gray wolf's song,
The Blackfeet of Montana — two thousand voices strong!

The cry of warring nations along Montana's plain,
The whoop of scalping squadrons that stripped the bleeding slain,
The chant of frenzied dances that churned the heart to flame —
The Blackfeet of Montana — before the paleface came!

I met the braves in the morning (I'll meet them ne'er again);
They came and went in parties that dotted all the plain.
And as the pioneers came West, their squatter homes to make,
We slew the scattered vanguard, and burned them at the stake!

The plains of old Montana — the badland buttes so tall,
The great-browed, red-eyed bison, the flint-clawed puma's call,
The game trails of our hunting grounds, all shining smooth and worn!
The plains of old Montana — the home where we were born!

The Blackfeet met in the morning, a broken, scattered band,
The white men shoot us down like dogs, to rob us of our land.
They drive us from our homeland, broken and cowed and tame;
But we recall Montana before the paleface came!

Wheel out, wheel out to the eastward; oh, prairie falcon, go!
And tell the Eastern nations the story of our woe;
Ere, empty as the clamshell the river flings ashore,
The plains of old Montana shall know their sons no more.[1]

— William Sargent

Read the selection. The first step in attempting to understand what is on the printed page is to go over it silently from beginning to end. We must watch carefully for parts that are meaningful and for those not absolutely clear to us. We must make notes of words, references, and examples that need further study.

Study the title. If the title of a piece of literature is well chosen, it holds the very essence of the meaning. The name " The Blackfeet

---

[1] Reprinted from Hughes Mearns' *Creative Youth*, with the permission of Hughes Mearns and Doubleday, Doran and Company.

of Montana," if studied carefully, will reveal much more than the careless observer sees at first. Let us think of some of the poems and stories that we have liked best and notice how well chosen the titles are: " The Great Stone Face " by Nathaniel Hawthorne, *The Adventures of Huckleberry Finn* by Mark Twain, " The Code " by Robert Frost, " The Fool's Prayer " by Edward Rowland Sill, " Caliban in the Coal Mines " by Louis Untermeyer, " God's World " by Edna St. Vincent Millay, and *What Men Live By* by Leo Tolstoy. The title often helps a reader to understand the author's meaning.

Use the dictionary. For most of us there are some unfamiliar words in " The Blackfeet of Montana." Some we cannot pronounce and some we do not understand. We must use the dictionary until we can pronounce every word without the slightest hesitation and until we have discovered meanings appropriate to the context of the poem.

Let us recall what we have learned in Chapter Four about the use of the dictionary, and make sure that we have acceptable pronunciations for:

Montana	scalping	vanguard	bison
canyon	squadrons	buttes	puma's
quelled	squatter	browed	falcon

Let us look up in the dictionary the meanings of each of the following words, and make sure we select one appropriate to the context of the poem.

Blackfeet	gray wolf	paleface	stake
Montana	scalping	braves	buttes
chief	squadron	pioneers	bison
canyon	stripped	squatter	puma's
war whoop	frenzied	slew	falcon
quelled	churned	vanguard	clamshell

Use the encyclopedia and other reference books. Many times it will be worth the extra effort required to use an encyclopedia, even though we have secured a brief definition of a word from the dictionary. For "The Blackfeet of Montana" the *Encylopaedia Britannica* gives us detailed and interesting information about Montana, Blackfeet Indians, North American Indians, gray wolves, bisons, badlands, pumas, falcons, and buttes. Since we are looking for a complete understanding of what is found on the printed page, additional details and interesting illustrations found in various source books will help us. Let us go to the high-school library and search for detailed information on the places and things referred to in "The Blackfeet of Montana." We will notice how much more meaningful the poem becomes with added information to help us in building images.

Study the structure and composition. Before we can get meaning from a page efficiently, we must know not only separate words, but also sentence structure and punctuation. The order of words in a sentence and the punctuation marks are signs of meaning sometimes far more important than the words themselves.

The schoolboy who wrote on the board the words "The teacher says the principal is a fool," and then added commas, quotation marks, and capitals resulting in "The teacher," says the principal, "is a fool," changed the meaning of the original sentence drastically. We must understand not only the elementary laws of grammar and punctuation, but also the principles of *unity, coherence,* and *emphasis.* We must know how to analyze paragraph structure, and how to see all the units of composition in their proper interrelations.

In acquiring the mastery of the technique of reading, few exercises can be more profitable than letter writing and theme work. By understanding how meanings are put into written symbols we can learn how to get meanings out of them.

Use geographical knowledge. Even though we know approximately where Montana is and something about it, it will be worth our while to study a map. We should notice the mountain ranges, the plains, and the cities. We should read about the topography, the people, the minerals, the raw materials, the farm products, and the scenery. A rich background of such information will make us see more vividly what the author is trying to describe.

The interpretative reader seldom can give his listeners experiences and pictures that are as vivid as the ones he himself possesses. Thus, if the reader barely understands what he is attempting to interpret, the chances are that the ideas will be even more vague to his listeners. The successful reader gets too much background rather than just enough. He takes great pains to know all of the details. He works until his pictures are vivid and clear-cut. Through travel or reading, the State of Montana should be familiar to him if he plans to read " The Blackfeet of Montana." Such understanding of geography is an aid in getting the meaning of much literature.

Use historical background. In attempting to understand " The Blackfeet of Montana," it will be helpful to study the history of the North American Indians in Montana. We should find out all about the different tribes, how long they held the land, and when and how the white people got it away from them. We must know the names of some of the warriors and leaders; we must visualize the struggles between the pioneers and the Indians if we hope to make our listeners see them. What is true of the value of an understanding of the historical background for the particular poem we are studying is also true of all literature. What American lad could fail to improve his reading of " Sheridan's Ride " by looking up the facts concerning it — the issues involved, and the forces engaged in the battle?

Know the author. We must find out about the author and see the relationship between the incidents of his life and what he has written. William Sargent, who wrote " The Blackfeet of Montana," knew Montana well. He had lived among the Indians there. He understood their problems. Anyone is better prepared to read a poem or a story if he has acquired some kind of acquaintance with the author. Reading then becomes a personal matter, and the meanings come more easily and more richly. One who has been in Cambridge and visited the homes of Lowell and Longfellow, or one who has met John

Masefield or Alfred Noyes, should have improved his ability to read what these poets have written. How much more meaning one gets from a book like Hamlin Garland's *A Son of the Middle Border* after having seen the author and heard him speak of those boyhood experiences which are so delightfully recorded in the book!

Most of us can never meet the great masters of literature in the flesh, but we can all become informed concerning the facts of their lives. It is hard to imagine what the Gettysburg Address would mean separated from a knowledge of who and what Abraham Lincoln was, and of the circumstances under which the speech was delivered. What a man writes is always closely and directly related to what he is. In addition to developing a familiarity with the general facts of an author's life, it is helpful to know the special conditions under which the particular composition was written.

Examples showing relationship of author to poem. Following are some more poems written by high-school students.[1] Accompanying each are biographical notes. This information shows why these boys and girls wrote as they did, and it helps us to understand their poems:

1. ON LEAVING WYOMING
by Ben Newcomer
Cody High School, Cody, Wyoming

("Ben Newcomer is the son of a Wyoming sheep raiser. All his summers previous to his graduation from high school were spent in the mountains and on the range. During his senior year he was planning to go to college in California; and the more he thought of it, the more homesick he became. 'On Leaving Wyoming' was written at that time after some study of free verse in his English class.")

> I shall miss you, Wyoming —
> I shall miss your vistas of sagebrush plains,
> Shimmering in the summer sun.
> I shall miss the red of your early sunrise,
> Sharp-cut against the buttes;
> Your glorious sunsets, pink and gold,

---

[1] These three poems are from *Younger Poets*, ed. by Nellie B. Sergent, D. Appleton and Company, New York. Reprinted by permission.

Bathing the blue mountains —
I shall miss you, Wyoming.

I shall miss the bands of wild horses,
Manes wind-tossed; painted horses,
Loping to water holes to drink
And be away again.
I shall miss the sight of upland pastures
In the summertime;
Green pines against an azure background,
Blue as lapis lazuli —
I shall miss you, Wyoming.

You are a man's country, Wyoming!
Yet you are hard on men;
I have seen you make them and break them, Wyoming.
You are hard, and yet, for one who knows you,
You have a glamour, a primitive appeal,
Drawing men back to you,
Though they half hate you.
I have caught your magic and mystery
And I'll be back to you,
For I'll miss you, Wyoming.

2. DUSK ON THE ROOF
by Mary Ann Barry
Evander Childs High School, New York City

(Mary Ann Barry whose home was in New York City, " explained that she really went up to bring the clothes down from the roof, and her mother thought she was gone an awfully long time! ")

I journeyed to the roof one twilight deep,
To watch the weary world go hustling by;
There, through the noise, a silence seemed to creep,
Its calm and balm gold-threaded with a sigh.

A few faint lights shone dimly through the haze,
I saw the last swift swallow southward fly —

> The trees and houses faded to a maze,
> And trails and veils of smoke rose up the sky.
>
> I stood and gazed until the evening star
> Came stepping timidly into the night,
> And thought I heard its music from afar,
> That sings and rings through firmaments of light.

3. ROYALTY
Margaret Griffith
James A. Garfield High School, Los Angeles, California

(Margaret Griffith " is a great lover of the out-of-doors — the hills, the sea, trees, and everything natural. She also has a great love for all animals, especially dogs and horses. Her pets include a dog, a squirrel, a bird, a goldfish, and a turtle. Her poems were first inspired by the views and surroundings of a tiny mountain cabin purchased by her parents when she was fifteen.")

> Born to the Purple? Not I!
> Born to the blue of the sky,
> To the ancient green of the trees,
> Born to the joy of these —
> Born not to the Purple was I.

Look up literary references. When an author has referred to something written by someone else, it is necessary to understand that reference before attempting to give the idea. There is no such reference in " The Blackfeet of Montana," but frequently in reading it is necessary to look up such literary allusions. In " The Ransom of Red Chief " by O. Henry, with which most of us are familiar, the Biblical reference to the boy David killing the giant Goliath with a sling must be clear for an understanding of the war whoop " such as David might have emitted when he knocked out the Champion Goliath."

Recall the legend of Romulus, the first King of Rome. When a child, he was thrown into the Tiber with his twin brother Remus but was saved and suckled by a wolf. That story clarifies these lines from " Horatius at the Bridge " by Thomas Babington Macaulay.

> Quoth he, " The she-wolf's litter
> Stands savagely at bay."

We should be on the alert for these references. To appreciate them, we need to read the old legends and myths, the Bible stories, and the other masterpieces which have become a part of our literary heritage, allusions which other authors have made a part of what they have written.

Read the entire selection from which the excerpt is taken. Sometimes the material we wish to read is an excerpt from a longer selection. " The Blackfeet of Montana " is a complete selection, but sometimes we may choose to read a chapter or part of a chapter from a book, several stanzas from a long poem, or a few paragraphs from a short story. Then we will profit by knowing the whole selection even though we do not intend to present it all to our audience. Omitted parts may have a bearing on the particular sections to be read aloud, and an understanding of them may determine the interpretation.

Get the central idea. A story, a poem, or a speech always has a main point and a dominant theme which are the essence of its meaning. Until we have grasped this central idea we are not prepared to give the meaning to others. How might we phrase the central idea of " The Blackfeet of Montana "? " The Blackfeet Indians in Montana present a tragic picture today." Or, " The Blackfeet of Montana are a vanishing race with a glorious past." The ability to condense meanings into such statements is a guarantee that the reader has done his preliminary work conscientiously.

GIVING THE MEANING TO OTHERS

Paraphrasing. Only after we ourselves understand, are we ready to help others to understand. We now turn to the process of putting the ideas we have derived from our study of the printed page into an audible and visible code which will stir up those ideas in others. Here paraphrasing may be a useful technique. Putting the meaning of a passage into different language is paraphrasing. Expressing meanings in our own words makes for surer and clearer comprehension. Paraphrasing is essentially a matter of definition by synonyms. It is one of the surest ways to make our voices and actions communicative. Quite often it is difficult to know exactly what inflection to use when giving the words of the author, but when we give his ideas in our own words, we are unconsciously communicative.

Let us tell the story of " The Blackfeet of Montana " in our own words, sentence by sentence. Then let us read the lines of the author. We can notice how much more communicative we are now when we read the lines as Sargent wrote them.

Using voice to bring out meanings. In our daily talk and conversation we have learned to standardize certain tones of voice as signs of certain emotional attitudes. For example, we can detect anger, fear, hatred, or affection in the voice of one whose words we do not understand. The voice tells the story by its tone. By reading over a troublesome passage and arriving at a tentative notion as to what tones would best express the author's meanings, we can communicate meanings more fully.

The language of poetry is addressed to the ear and not to the eye. The meaning of the author comes to the reader most completely when he hears the sounds of the poem. Hiram Corson says in his book *The Voice and Spiritual Education:* " To him [Shakespeare] language was for the ear, not for the eye. The written word was to him what it was to Socrates, ' the mere image or phantom of the living animated word.' " Again: " Reading must supply all the deficiencies of written or printed language. It must give life to the letter. How comparatively little is addressed to the eye in print or manuscript, of what has to be addressed to the ear by a reader! There are no indications of tone, quality of voice, inflection, pitch, time, or any other of the vocal functions demanded for a full intellectual and spiritual interpretation. A poem is not truly a poem until it is voiced by an accomplished reader who has adequately assimilated it — in whom it has, to some extent, been born again, according to his individual spiritual constitution and experiences. The potentialities, so to speak, of the printed poem must be vocally realized. In silent reading, an appreciation of matter and form must be largely due to an imaginative transference to the ear of what is taken in by the eye." [1]

[1] The Macmillan Company, 1896, p. 114.

When a poet writes, he talks to himself. He applies these tests to his work: " What will this sound like to other people? How will they like it? Will it mean to them what it means to me? " And while answering these questions he talks to himself. Often enough he speaks his poem to himself to test it. Lord Tennyson had a fine voice, and whoever came to visit him was fairly sure of hearing him read aloud the latest verses he had written. And it is to be noted that Tennyson's poetry reads very well aloud.

It is in revealing the connotative meanings of literature that reading aloud furnishes the greatest help. While denotative meaning is necessary in what anybody writes, still the great differences between the bad and the good, the good and the better, the better and the best, are in the feelings expressed, the sentiments, and the emotions — in short, in connotative meanings. It is in the comprehension and grasp of the emotional side of literature that reading aloud helps most.

How do we show our emotions in everyday affairs? Is it not by the way our voices sound — by their fullness or thinness, their loudness or softness, their harshness or smoothness? If we are describing something we admire, our voices become smooth and rich and full; if somebody makes us angry, our voices get harsh and rough and strident; if we are embarrassed, our voices become faint and almost whispery, or perhaps shrill and throaty.

What has this association of sound with sense to do with good literature? If an author is honestly and sincerely feeling what he writes and is talking to himself as he writes it, he will imagine himself talking roughly when angry, talking smoothly when full of admiration, and talking gently when expressing kindness. If he actually makes the sounds aloud thus and if he is sincere in what he is doing, his vocal mechanism makes the changes necessary for whatever mood he is in. And — here is the point — he chooses words that have the sounds in them that help him to express the sentiments he is feeling. Then, by using appropriately voiced sounds, we can give those feelings to others.

Let us take a plain case. When Lord Byron wants us to understand that he loves the ocean and that he thinks it is the most tremendous thing in the universe, so great and vast that it leaves him overcome with its awe and majesty, he does not say, " Well, the sea is a great thing, the biggest object on the map; it is so big that we just can't get it." No, what he says is:

> Roll on, thou deep and dark blue Ocean — roll!
> Ten thousand fleets sweep over thee in vain;
> Man marks the earth with ruin — his control
> Stops with the shore — upon the watery plain
> The wrecks are all thy deed, nor doth remain
> A shadow of man's ravage, save his own,
> When, for a moment, like a drop of rain,
> He sinks into thy depths with bubbling groan,
> Without a grave, unknelled, uncoffined, and unknown.

Notice that the sounds we make in reading this poetry aloud are round, full, broad, and deep — sounds easy to hold with a ringing tone. These sounds carry a feeling of awe, of worship, and of reverence. In the absurd sentence suggested just above Byron's words, notice how light and flickering and fluttering the sounds are, and how utterly unsuited to the feeling the ocean inspires.

When Milton wants us to feel the spirit of the dance, he invites us out to play in the following words:

> Haste thee, Nymph, and bring with thee
> Jest and youthful jollity,

> Quips, and cranks, and wanton wiles,
> Nods, and becks, and wreathèd smiles,
> Such as hang on Hebe's cheek,
> And love to live in dimple sleek:
> Sport that wrinkled care derides,
> And Laughter holding both his sides.
> Come, and trip it as you go,
> On the light fantastic toe.

The sounds of this poem, we readily observe, are easy to make quickly and lightly.

In reading aloud "The Blackfeet of Montana" we see the importance of the voice in interpretation. Here, as with the language of Lord Byron and Milton, the words must be intoned by the voice to be understood by listeners. Our voices will help others to hear the west wind roaring down the canyon and the war cry of the Indians, and to see the broken, scattered band of red men.

Using visible action to give meaning. In earlier chapters, we have discussed the importance of visible action in communication. Visible action is also of great assistance in interpretative reading. With our voices we have attempted to interpret the meanings of poetry. Now we will try to enrich those meanings by using visible action as well. In this visible action we supply more of the speech signs which written language lacks. Before we can use our visible action successfully we must have bodies that respond as we wish them to respond. This capacity to respond comes as the result of training and practice in numerous speech situations.

Rhythm versus meter in poetry. An important factor in the reading of poetry, not present in the reading of prose, is an understanding of the difference between rhythm and meter. Meter is a matter of accented and unaccented syllables following each other in certain definite patterns. We can get the rocking-horse, hippety-hop effect of the meter and still not know the sense or be able to convey it to others when we read aloud. Such reading is childish singsong, as typified in Mother Goose:

> Jack and Jill
> Went up the hill

>   To fetch a pail of water.
>   Jack fell down
>   And broke his crown,
>   And Jill came tumbling after.

Or:

>   Hippety-hop
>   To the barber shop
>   To buy a stick of candy.
>   One for you,
>   And one for me,
>   And one for Sister Mandy.

In these verses the rollicking meter gives us our chief delight, and we do not care much whether there is any sense or not.

Rhythm, however, is inseparably linked to sense. Rhythm always subordinates meter to ideas and feelings. Rhythm is thought and feeling made smooth, easy-flowing, and harmonious. Meter is as rigid as marching. Rhythm is as free as the wind in the trees. Take this by Thomas Hood:

>   I remember, I remember
>   The house where I was born,
>   The little window where the sun
>   Came peeping in at morn;
>   He never came a wink too soon
>   Nor brought too long a day;
>   But now, I often wish the night
>   Had borne my breath away.

We can readily see how easy it is to make this into a mere nursery jingle. But to do that is to destroy its meaning.

The following lines of Walt Whitman can also be made a jingle or can become something rich and full of feeling. In reading them we will have to be careful.

>   O Captain! my Captain! our fearful trip is done,
>   The ship has weathered every rack, the prize we sought is won,
>   The port is near, the bells I hear, the people all exulting,
>   While follow eyes the steady keel, the vessel grim and daring;
>   But O heart! heart! heart!

> O the bleeding drops of red,
>> Where on the deck my Captain lies,
>>> Fallen cold and dead.

If we read the foregoing so that it sounds like a man dancing a jig, we will be one of those who declare that there is nothing in it. If we take special pains to break up the jingle, we suddenly discover that it means something very deep and interesting. As we become more and more familiar with poetry we discover that a poet uses a certain rhythm because he can best express his thought, mood, or feeling in it. We should not ignore it, but neither should we emphasize it so much that it overshadows what the author wants expressed. It must be given just enough emphasis to bring out the meaning.

Notice how the rhythm in "The Blackfeet of Montana" helps to communicate the spirit of the poem. Keep that spirit, but see that the most important words are emphasized even if the rhythm is not very metrical.

The suggestions about rhythm also hold for oratorical prose. All eloquence has rhythm, as is shown in these lines from Lincoln's second inaugural:

"With malice toward none; with charity for all; with firmness in the right, as God gives us to see the right, let us strive on to finish the work we are in; to bind up the nation's wounds; to care for him who shall have borne the battle, and for his widow, and his orphan — to do all which may achieve and cherish a just and lasting peace among ourselves, and with all nations."

Phrasing important. One of the worst of the common bad habits which mar much interpretative reading of verse is the tendency to phrase it (to group the words) not according to the meaning, but rather according to its typographical arrangement on the page, making each line a complete unit, terminating in a definite falling inflection and followed by a mechanical pause. Thus we read:

> I *come* from *haunts* of *coot* and *hern*, (*Pause*)
>> I *make* a *sud*den *sal*ly, (*Pause*)
> And *spar*kle *out* a*mong* the *fern*, (*Pause*)
>> To *bick*er *down* the *val*ley.

If these stanzas were written out in prose form, no sensible person would group the words in this way. More than likely we then should phrase them as follows:

I come from haunts of coot and hern, (*Pause*) I make a sudden sally, and sparkle out among the fern (*Pause*) to bicker down the valley.

Perhaps we will prefer other phrasings. Whatever we do, let us try not to let the singsong of the meter run away with the sense. We should not be tricked into pausing simply because we are at the end of a line. We should note that pauses at the ends of phrases usually should be made following a rising or a sustained pitch rather than a falling inflection. We should also note that punctuation is not an infallible guide to correct phrasing.

Associated with, and possibly a part of, this fault of failing to carry phrases past the end of lines is a temptation to overstress the final rhyming words. These end rhymes often do not contain the ideas of major significance; moreover, even without a special effort to give them emphasis, they inevitably derive considerable prominence from the fact that they carry the rhyme scheme. A good way to break up this bad habit of stressing the rhymed words is to write poems out in prose form and practice reading them with emphasis distributed according to meaning, letting verse form be stressed only so far as it helps to make the meaning clear.

Shakespeare's *Midsummer Night's Dream* furnishes a most amusing example of bad phrasing in the reading of verse. We all recall the scene in the Duke's palace when the amateur players are presenting their version of *Pyramus and Thisbe*. The fun begins with the Prologue's speech. He phrases it as follows:

Prologue. If we offend, it is with our goodwill. (*Pause*)
        That you should think, we come not to offend,
But with goodwill. (*Pause*) To show our simple skill,
        That is the true beginning of our end. (*Pause*)
        Consider then, we come but in despite. (*Pause*)
        We do not come as minding to content you,
Our true intent is. (*Pause*) All for your delight,

GIVING THE MEANING TO OTHERS

>We are not here. (*Pause*) That you should here repent you,
>The actors are at hand; (*Pause*) and by their show
>You shall know all that you are like to know.

Lysander. He hath rid his prologue like a rough colt; he knows not the stop. A good moral, my lord: it is not enough to speak, but to speak true.

Hippolyta. Indeed he hath played on his prologue like a child on a recorder; a sound, but not in government.

Theseus. His speech was like a tangled chain; nothing impaired, but all disordered.

Hudson comments: " Had ' this fellow ' stood ' upon points,' his speech would have read nearly as follows:

" If we offend, it is with our goodwill
   That you should think we come not to offend; (*Pause*)
But with goodwill to show our simple skill: (*Pause*)
   That is the true beginning. (*Pause*) Of our end
Consider then: (*Pause*) we come, but in despite
   We do not come: (*Pause*) as minding to content you,
Our true intent is all for your delight. (*Pause*)
   We are not here, that you should here repent you. (*Pause*)
The actors are at hand; (*Pause*) and, by their show,
You shall know all that you are like to know."

Not the ends of lines, not the punctuation marks, but the thought, determines how words should be grouped. True, the punctuation marks often help the reader to get the thought, but to phrase solely according to those marks is often a great hindrance in communicating what the author intended.

In " The Blackfeet of Montana," we notice how the thought of the first line of the first stanza is not completed until the second line is uttered. The same thing is true of the third and fourth lines. In the second stanza, the thought is not completed until all four lines have been read; the first three are a description of the Blackfeet of Montana before the paleface came. This poem illustrates admirably what we have been saying about grouping the words to express the thought the author intended.

Summary of suggestions for getting and giving meaning. If we have followed this chapter carefully, we have found helps for understanding the full meaning of literary material, and suggestions for giving that meaning to others. We have seen the value of studying the title, of getting the meanings and pronunciations of all words, and of making use of reference books for background appreciation. We recognize the importance of understanding punctuation and the structure of sentences. We also know the value of geographical, historical, and literary references. We see the role of the author's experiences in what he writes. Finally, we know that without the central idea clearly phrased in our own minds, we cannot give the thought and feeling of prose or poetry to others. Having a thorough mastery of the full meaning of a selection, we will use effective action and voice to convey that meaning to others.

INTERPRETATION AND IMPERSONATION

A question which often puzzles one who wishes to read aloud is: How much shall I act? Shall I try to use the voices and gestures of the characters, or shall I just be myself? The answer to that question is found in the answer to another question: What is the central idea of the selection to be read? If the author intended to portray characters primarily, we can probably accomplish that purpose best by trying to act and sound like the characters. But if he wanted primarily to present incidents and occurrences, we must be careful not to let characters get in the way.

The point can be made clear by examining some selections from this text. Let us turn to " Georgha da Wash " on page 294 and " A Wee Little Verse " on page 317. In the first selection, it is clear that the author wants to picture a character, an Italian who has not been in America very long. By having the man talk and give his reactions to a familiar American story, Richard Henry Little shows what kind of man the Italian is. If we are reading the poem and wish to show the character to an audience, we want our listeners to forget that we are high-school boys or girls and think of us as an immigrant

RUTH DRAPER. *Study this portrait of a great character actor and compare it with the one on page 277. How are such striking changes brought about?* (Culver Service)

getting used to American ways. If we are trying to be like the immigrant, we will try to act and speak as he would. We will do more than suggest the visible action and the voice of the Italian; we will try to make our action — our walk and gestures — and our voice exactly like his. This method of reading is called impersonation. It should be used only when the speaker in the selection is a distinct and definite character. In impersonation we act a great deal, because the character is more important than the other ideas; we may say that the character *is* the idea.

Who is the speaker in " A Wee Little Verse "? Is it the wee little boy? No, because the speaker quotes the wee little boy, but does not do this until the last verse. Is it an old man, an old woman, a child, a high-school boy or girl, an Italian, or a German? It may be any of these. As a matter of fact it makes no difference who reads it, just so that person does not stand in the way of the central idea of the poem — the knife is useful, but not to convey food to the mouth! In this poem, the important consideration is not the character. In fact, if the reader tries to act like someone other than himself, the chances are that the listeners will remember the character rather than the point of the poem. Therefore in reading " A Wee Little Verse," we will act like ourselves — high-school students, interpreters, storytellers. When we come to the place where we quote the little boy, we may change our voices and actions slightly to make clear that we are quoting him, but we will only *suggest* his voice and his actions. This method of reading to others is called interpretation.

The audience must never be confused about which we are trying to do, to interpret or to impersonate. In dealing with the two poems with which we have illustrated our point, it is clear that one should be impersonated and the other interpreted. But some material may be handled either way; we may interpret or impersonate as we see fit.

Turn to *He Knew Lincoln*, page 307 or to " Jim Bludso," page 296. In each of these there is a definite and distinct speaker, but in each case the speaker is important only because he is the kind of person who can make the story effective. Billy Brown, Lincoln's friend, is definitely the " homespun " type, because Ida Tarbell wanted to show that " Mr. Lincoln was like one of us." We feel that the man telling the story about Jim Bludso has many of the characteristics of the man

"GRANDMOTHER IN COURT." *This is Ruth Draper in one of her inimitable character portrayals. All of the differences between what is to be seen here and what is to be seen in the portrait on page 275 are produced without the aid of make-up and with only an old shawl added to an evening dress. (Culver Service)*

he is describing, and therefore he is an appropriate person to present the description. But in both of these selections, the persons being described — "Mr. Lincoln" and Jim Bludso — are much more important than the speaker, and their characters must overshadow the storyteller's. If when we have finished, the listeners see Billy Brown more clearly than they do Abraham Lincoln, or the storyteller more clearly than they do Jim Bludso, we have not been successful. Our method has been wrong. We must be a Billy Brown who can make Abraham Lincoln important, or a storyteller who can make Jim Bludso seem to be a good man.

We should analyze our own skills and the situations in which we wish to read before we decide whether we will act out a character literally or be ourselves, merely suggesting the character's voice and action. Frequently, a girl is more successful in suggesting a male character (interpretation) when a boy could act it out literally (impersonation). And a boy can suggest a female character which a girl can act out literally. These facts are true because it does not attract the attention of the audience to the performance quite so much when an individual impersonates one of his own sex as when he attempts to impersonate one of the opposite sex.

The point of this discussion is that there is some material which must be impersonated to give the author's essential meaning; some that must be interpreted to give the author's meaning; and some that may be interpreted or impersonated, depending upon the reader's skill, the situation, and the tastes of the audience.

Shall material be memorized or read from the printed page? Another question which confronts the person who wishes to learn how to read aloud effectively is: Shall the material be memorized, or read from the printed page? The answer is: It depends on the material, the reader, the occasion, and the audience.

Impersonative material is usually more effective when memorized. The reason for this is obvious. The Italian in "Georgha da Wash" is telling the story, not reading it from a book; and if we want to be just like the character, we must have the freedom that he would have in that situation. Sometimes, when we are reading with the book in our hands or before us on a stand, our arms and hands are left free for literal gestures, and our bodies for characteristic posture and movements, but usually the characterization is not so realistic as it is when we have no book.

Our greatest concern in this course should be in learning to read well with the page before us, because most reading is done that way. We will read from a book hundreds of times more often than we will recite from memory. If we are inexperienced readers, we may consider this easier because we believe it requires less study. In that we are mistaken; the same thorough analysis of material is required. After careful study, the individual who reads from the page the same material that he might "read" from memory knows the selection so well that it is practically memorized; and the manuscript merely relieves him of the danger of forgetting, a misfortune that often detracts from a memorized performance.

In short, to know our material well is at the very heart of successful reading. When we have memorized a selection, the words must follow one another without a single hesitation in action or utterance. When we read from manuscript, we must be so free that our contacts with the lines are never noticeable to our listeners. This, like all of the steps in learning to interpret effectively, requires practice.

Tests of Comprehension and Application

GETTING THE MEANING

1 Pick out your favorite story, your favorite novel, and your favorite poem. Give a short talk to your class showing why and how the title of each one is significant.

2 Bring in two titles which you consider inappropriate. Explain.

3 Write an original poem, play, or story and select an appropriate title. Show why it is appropriate.

4 Divide the class into groups of five or six. Let each person bring a poem or prose selection of not more than ten lines. Let each listener give the material a title. Select the most appropriate one. Show why it is the best.

5 Make lists of stories, poems, and plays which have especially appropriate titles.

6 Use the encyclopedia and other reference books to help you to a better understanding of a poem or prose selection you have chosen to prepare for reading aloud.

7 Use the dictionary to get the meanings of all words which you do not understand fully in the selection you have chosen for exercise 6.

8 Find some piece of literature that you would like to interpret for others. Read it silently.

9 Turn to the material on pages 282–318. Select one poem and one piece of prose for oral interpretation. Read each silently.

10 Show how a knowledge of sentence structure clarifies meaning in the poem chosen for 9.

11 Report to the class on your experiences in getting meanings in the following:

a   *Hamlet's Advice to the Players*

O! it offends me to the soul to hear a robustious, periwig-pated fellow tear a passion to tatters, to very rags, to split the ears of the groundlings, who for the most part are capable of nothing but inexplicable dumb shows and noise; I would have such a fellow whipped for o'erdoing Termagant; it outherods Herod; pray you, avoid it.

— William Shakespeare

b   *Lord Chatham's Eloquence*

But that which gave most effect to his declamation was the air of sincerity, of vehement feeling, of moral elevation, which belonged to all that he said. His style was not always in the purest taste. Several contemporary judges pronounced it too florid. Walpole, in the midst of the rapturous eulogy which he pronounces on one of Pitt's greatest orations, owns that some of the metaphors were too forced. Some of Pitt's quotations and classical stories were too trite for a clever schoolboy. But these were niceties for which the audience cared little. The enthusiasm of the orator infected all who heard him; his ardor and his noble bearing put fire into the most frigid conceit and gave dignity to the most puerile allusion.

— Thomas Babington Macaulay

12   Bring to class two selections from this book, or from other sources, illustrating how an understanding of geography will help the reader to get the author's intended meaning.

13   Turn to Longfellow's poem *Evangeline*. Look up the geography of Acadia. Notice how much more meaningful the descriptions become.

14   Go to your high-school library and see if you have the volume *Challenge to Grow* by Cook, Loban, Norvell, and McCall. Read the following stories and in class discussion show how an understanding of geography will help in the interpretation of each.

    a   "Dark Flight" by John J. Floherty, p. 488.
    b   "Cher Ami" by Alice Gall and Fleming Crew, p. 523.
    c   "A Tale of Two Lumber Towns" by Joseph Gaer, p. 541.

15   Examine the poems you have selected to read (pages 282–318). Will a knowledge of geography help you to interpret them?

16   Turn to "The Admiral's Ghost" by Alfred Noyes, page 298.

Get the historical background for the poem and notice how it aids you in complete understanding.

17   Read *He Knew Lincoln* by Ida Tarbell, page 307. Prepare a talk on Civil War history that will help the members of your class to understand the selection.

18   Bring to class one literary selection of your choice in which a knowledge of some incident in history is essential to understanding the author's intention.

19   Read Walt Whitman's " O Captain! my Captain! " What historical background is necessary for an understanding of the poem?

20   The title of the following poem contains a reference to Shakespeare's *The Tempest,* in which Caliban is a slave of Prospero, or to Browning's " Caliban upon Setebos," in which Caliban gives his views on deity. Which reference helps more in understanding the real meaning of the poem?

CALIBAN IN THE COAL MINES [1]
by Louis Untermeyer

God, we don't like to complain;
　We know that the mine is no lark.
But — there's the pools from the rain;
　But — there's the cold and the dark.

God, You don't know what it is —
　You, in Your well-lighted sky —
Watching the meteors whizz;
　Warm, with the sun always by.

God, if You had but the moon
　Stuck in Your cap for a lamp,
Even You'd tire of it soon,
　Down in the dark and the damp.

Nothing but blackness above
　And nothing that moves but the cars. . . .
God, if You wish for our love,
　Fling us a handful of stars!

[1] Louis Untermeyer, *Challenge,* Harcourt, Brace and Company. Reprinted by permission.

COMPREHENSION AND APPLICATION TESTS 283

21 Bring in allusions to the Bible from readings assigned in English.
22 Bring to class references to early mythology found in your reading.
23 Bring to class references from Shakespeare's writings which you have read in your work in literature.
24 Read all of Ida Tarbell's *He Knew Lincoln*, and then read the excerpt on page 307. Notice how much richer your understanding is now.
25 Bring in three examples from your literature books in which excerpts are used. Read the entire selections from which the excerpts are taken and report on your improved appreciation of the parts.
26 Bring in two poems from your outside reading. Give the central idea of each in one sentence.
27 Bring in two stories from your outside reading. Give the central idea of each in one sentence.
28 Give the central idea of each of the poems you selected to read in the first step in understanding the written code (page 257).
29 From the following selection, write a paper on Robert G. Ingersoll's attitude toward his brother. After you have finished, secure the facts from a biography of Robert G. Ingersoll. How close were you to the facts?

My Friends: I am going to do that which the dead oft promised he would do for me.

The loved and loving brother, husband, father, friend, died where manhood's morning almost touches noon and while the shadows still were falling toward the west.

He had not passed on life's highway the stone that marks the highest point, but, being weary for a moment, lay down by the wayside, and using his burden for a pillow, fell into that dreamless sleep that kisses down his eyelids still. While yet in love with life and raptured with the world, he passed to silence and pathetic dust.

Yet, after all, it may be best, just in the happiest, sunniest hour of all the voyage, while eager winds are kissing every sail, to dash against the unseen rock, and in an instant hear the billows roar above a sunken ship. For, whether in midsea or 'mong the breakers of the farther shore, a wreck at last must mark the end of each and all. And every life, no matter if its every hour is rich with love and every moment jeweled with a joy, will at its close become a tragedy as sad and deep and dark as can be woven of the warp and woof of mystery and death.

This brave and tender man in every storm of life was oak and rock, but in the sunshine he was vine and flower. He was the friend of all heroic souls. He climbed the heights and left all superstitions far below, while on his forehead fell the golden dawning of the grander day.

He loved the beautiful, and was with color, form, and music touched to tears. He sided with the weak, and with a willing hand gave alms; with loyal heart and with purest hands he faithfully discharged all public trusts.

He was a worshiper of liberty, a friend of the oppressed. A thousand times I have heard him quote these words: "For justice all place a temple, and all seasons summer." He believed that happiness was the only good, reason the only torch, justice the only worship, humanity the only religion, and love the only priest. He added to the sum of human joy; and were everyone to whom he did some loving service to bring a blossom to his grave, he would sleep tonight beneath a wilderness of flowers.

Life is a narrow vale between the cold and barren peaks of two eternities. We strive in vain to look beyond the heights. We cry aloud, and the only answer is the echo of our wailing cry. From the voiceless lips of the unreplying dead there comes no word; but in the night of death hope sees a star, and listening love can hear the rustle of a wing.

He who sleeps here, when dying, mistaking the approach of death for the return of health, whispered with his latest breath, "I am better now." Let us believe, in spite of doubts and dogmas, and tears and fears, that these dear words are true of all the countless dead.

And now to you who have been chosen, from among the many men he loved, to do the last sad office for the dead, we give his sacred dust. Speech cannot contain our love. There was, there is, no greater, stronger, manlier man.

— Robert G. Ingersoll

30 Bring in some original writing you have done in your English class. Tell the class what experiences and events of your life motivated it.
31 Write a poem out of your own experiences.
32 Read "Crossing the Bar" and decide at what time in Tennyson's life it was written. Look up the facts.
33 Paraphrase the poems you have selected to read.
34 Paraphrase some selection from your English class. Notice how the meaning is clarified.
35 Write out prose paraphrases of the following poems.[1]

a
MARSH MORNING

The thuribles of beauty burn
   Along the brook at break of day;
Their incense rises with the wind
   And broods above the seeded hay.

And there between the aster tops,
   With fantasy and beauty frail,
Mocking the worker, lovely hangs
   The spider's pearl-encrusted veil.

So I have faith that when the breath
   Of God lifts all my whirling dreams,
Some eye may mark the woven skein
   Of light beside long-hidden streams.
              — Bennett Weaver

b
THE BRIDGE

Dull thunders troubled the great hills
   And moanings lay upon the land.
Close where the Beaver outward spills
   I saw the cantilever stand.

I saw him take ten thousand tons
   Of charging steel across the flood;

[1] Three poems reprinted from "Sussex Poems" and "Pittsburgh Poems" by permission of the author.

There where the strong Ohio runs
  I saw him make his purpose good.

The poisoned fathoms of the stream
  Licked at the piers and lost their prey;
I saw the lightning gild the stream
  As the great engines fled away.

Beneath a heaven whose crowding power
  Bellowed and struck the thickened earth,
I saw this giant hour by hour
  Doing a mighty thing with mirth.

And then I thought, What power is there
  To take the soul across the flood?
The drifting atoms of despair
  Gathered and sank within my blood.
              — Bennett Weaver

ANODYNE

When beauty lingers at the wrist
  And will not flow into the hand,
Send me a marsh wind blowing
  And a breath from the meadowland.

When vision settles in the eye
  And will not run into the brain,
Send me a storm from the marshes
  And the wild hawks blown again.

When rapture thickens in the blood
  And will not pass into the heart,
Send me a zephyr of clover
  From the flounce of a farmer's cart.

When worship sinks within my breast
  And will not rise into the soul,

> Send me a star from the meadow,
> Two stars to make me whole.
> — Bennett Weaver

36 Show how the rhythms in the following are appropriate to the meanings.
  a "Sweet and Low," Alfred, Lord Tennyson
  b "Boots," Rudyard Kipling
  c "The Highwayman," Alfred Noyes
  d "The Mountain Whippoorwill," Stephen Vincent Benét

  e

>   MARY ANNE'S LUNCHEON [1]
> Here comes Mary Anne
> With a shining clean face.
> She tucks in her bib
> And climbs in her place.
>
> And says quite politely,
> "I'm ready now, cook,"
> And looks at us all
> With a very pleased look.

For we are her luncheon, yum yummy, yum yummy,
And we're all going down to visit her tummy.

The Poached Egg Says:
> I'm a poached egg.
> I sit on my toast
> And wonder which fork stab
> Will tickle the most.

And the Milk Says:
> I am the milk
> In her own little cup
> And soon Mary Anne
> Will drink me all up.

[1] This, the three poems following, and those on pages 294 and 317 are used with the permission of the compiler of the *Linebooks,* from the "Line o' Type or Two" column of the *Chicago Tribune.*

*For we are her luncheon, yum yummy, yum yummy,
And we're all going down to visit her tummy.*

And the Carrots Say:
    We are the carrots.
    We like little girls,
    And when we're inside them
    We grow rows of curls.

And the Custard Says:
    I am the custard
    Who makes a quick trip
    Off the edge of her spoon
    With a slide and a slip.

*Oh, we are her luncheon, yum yummy, yum yummy,
And we're all going down to visit her tummy.*

Then the Egg Speaks Again Very Sadly:
    Oh, what a mean fork!
    Oh, what a thrust!
    My beautiful yellow
    Middle is bust.

And the Milk Says:
    I'm almost all gone
    Down her little red lane —
    In a minute her cup
    Will be empty again.

And the Carrots Speak Cheerfully:
    Just one more bite
    Of us carrots to chew
    And then pretty soon
    Mary Anne will be through.

And the Custard Sounds Surprised:
    It's certainly strange
    The way I disappear;

I was in her saucer
And now I am here.

*For we once were her luncheon, yum yummy, yum yummy,
But now we are all dancing around in her tummy.*

Then good Mary Anne
Gets down from the table
And folds up her bib
As well as she's able.

She walks very straight
So as not to upset;
And she's glad that it isn't
Her suppertime yet.

— Dorothy Aldis

f   THE WANDERER

Dusk on a prairie farm, a thousand miles from the sea,
 The cows are in and the chores are done.
 The stars are coming one by one,
And a prisoned soul is free.
The farmhouse fades like a fairy thing, and a fettered soul goes free.

There's an offshore wind tonight. The tide will turn at ten.
 The scudding moon is cutting its way
 Through billows of cloud. We only stay
For the tide, my merry men.
So man the capstan. Yo, heave ho! Heave ho! my bully men.

We have filled the hold with copra. We have piled the deck with bales
 Of silks from every road that ran
 From Tokio to Ispahan,
From Malabar to Wales,
The riches of the Orient lie beneath our purple sails.

There's ivory and incense. There's indigo and tea.
 There's sandalwood from Mandalay,

    And pearls like eggs from Arabay,
And Persian tapestry,
And we've treasures in the cabin men would give their eyes to see.

Oh, bravely have we voyaged through tempest and typhoon,
    By Polynesian coral isles,
    Through jungle rivers, miles on miles,
Beneath the tropic moon.
We're homeward bound, but we shall make another voyage soon.

g   THE FOOL'S PARADISE

  I know there are onions in heaven,
    For they have a heavenly smell,
  A smell like the smell of a long-lost friend
    Who has good news to tell.

  Roses are lovely and fragrant,
    But who ever tasted them fried?
  And lilies are nice to lay on the breast
    Of one who has lately died.

  But onions — aroma immortal! —
    That smother a steak done well!
  I know there are onions in heaven,
    For they have a heavenly smell!
              — The Phantom Lover

h   HALLOWE'EN

I would not walk alone if I were you
   Tonight when shadows lurk and gaunt black cats
Sail past the moon and eerie night winds slough
   Off dead black branches hung with evil bats.

I would not wander far if I were you
   Tonight when darkness comes, for strange dark hags
Will flavor well and stir their baleful brew
   As weird shapes ride the wind on broomstick nags.

I would not step outside if I were you
   Tonight when unseen fingers tap " tick tack . . . tick tack."
Although it's said a few brave people do
   Sometimes: I've heard, they never do come back.

— Jayhawker

37 Use the dictionary for the correct pronunciation of words in the material which you have selected to read.

38 Attend a public reading and note the contribution that bodily action makes to the meaning.

39 Try different ways of reading the following passages, and notice that as soon as you have found the right way to bring out the author's sense and feeling, and not merely the meter, you begin to like the poems better.

a   Thou, too, sail on, O Ship of State!
    Sail on, O UNION, strong and great!
    Humanity with all its fears,
    With all the hopes of future years,
    Is hanging breathless on thy fate!
    We know what Master laid thy keel,
    What Workman wrought thy ribs of steel,
    Who made each mast, and sail, and rope,
    What anvils rang, what hammers beat,
    In what forge and what a heat
    Were shaped the anchors of thy hope!
    Fear not each sudden sound and shock,
    'Tis of the wave and not the rock:
    'Tis but the flapping of the sail,
    And not a rent made by the gale!
    In spite of rock and tempest's roar,
    In spite of false lights on the shore,
    Sail on, nor fear to breast the sea!
    Our hearts, our hopes, are all with thee,
    Our hearts, our hopes, our prayers, our tears,
    Our faith triumphant o'er our fears,
    Are all with thee — are all with thee!

— Henry Wadsworth Longfellow

b As we cover the graves of the heroic dead with flowers, the past rises before us like a dream. Again we are in the great struggle for national life. We hear the sounds of preparation — the music of boisterous drums — the silver voices of heroic bugles. We hear the appeals of orators; we see the pale cheeks of women, and the flushed faces of men; we see all the dead whose dust we have covered with flowers. We lose sight of them no more. We are with them when they enlist in the great army of freedom. We see them part from those they love. Some are walking for the last time in the quiet woody places with the maidens they adore. We hear the whispers and the sweet vows of eternal love as they lingeringly part forever. Others are bending over cradles kissing babies that are asleep. Some are receiving the blessings of old men. Some are parting from mothers who hold them and press them to their hearts again and again and say nothing. And some are talking with wives and trying with brave words spoken in the old tones to drive from their hearts the awful fear. We see them part. We see the wife standing in the door with the babe in her arms — standing in the sunlight sobbing; at the turn of the road a hand waves — she answers by holding high in her loving arms the child. He is gone and forever.

— Robert G. Ingersoll

40 Bring in ten short excerpts (from one to five sentences). Demonstrate to the class how the use of voice helps listeners to understand them.

41 Read excerpts from the poems you have selected (pages 294–317) to show the importance of voice changes in giving clear meaning.

42 Analyze the selections in this chapter and decide whether you as a reader should impersonate or interpret. Arrange the material in three groups.
   a Those selections which *must* be interpreted.
   b Those selections which *must* be impersonated.
   c Those selections which may be impersonated or interpreted. Which method will you use?

43 Experiment with the memorized and the manuscript methods of delivery. Write a paper on your reactions to each.

44 From your English class and other sources, find material that you will enjoy reading aloud. If possible, find an actual occasion for these readings. Memorize some and give others with the book. Describe the audience reactions.

45 From the following selections choose several to read aloud. Follow the steps in preparation laid out in this chapter.

a   FOOTNOTE TO HISTORY [1]

In September 1777, Patrick Ferguson, commanding officer of His Majesty's Rifle Corps, and the best shot in the British Army, lay concealed with a few of his men on the outskirts of a wood near Brandywine Creek, Pennsylvania.

Suddenly his fingers tightened on his rifle. Only 100 yards away were two mounted enemy officers. The first was dressed in hussar outfit; the other, who rode a large bay horse, wore a dark-blue uniform and a remarkably large cocked hat. Both men were in easy range. Ferguson signaled to his men to fire, then hesitated and recalled the order. He couldn't shoot two defenseless men in the back.

The enemy officers swung around, bringing the big man in the cocked hat even nearer. Ferguson called to him. The rider looked at Ferguson, but calmly proceeded on his way. Again the Englishman's trigger finger tightened, but again he relaxed. He couldn't shoot in cold blood. In a moment the two officers were out of sight.

The next day Ferguson was talking with a group of fellow officers when the army surgeon, who had been attending to wounded enemy prisoners, came by. "We've learned from rebel prisoners that their commanding general was in this vicinity yesterday," he said. "He was accompanied only by a French officer in hussar dress. The general rides a bay horse and wears a large cocked hat."

Ferguson looked up. Realization came quickly. The man whose life he had spared was George Washington.

[1] Adapted from Adam Ferguson's "Biographical Sketch of Lt. Col. Patrick Ferguson," *Reader's Digest*, February 1944. Reprinted by permission.

b
GEORGHA DA WASH [1]

Oh, Georgha da Wash, he gretta da man,
He makka no bluff, playa no granda stan'.
Hees pop geev him ax, say, "Leesten to me,
Go choppa weeth ax all theengs wot you see.
Choppa down theesa house, go choppa da barn,
Choppa down da pee-ann, I no geev a darn.
But Georgha wan theeng, makka prom now to me,
You no choppa down thata neece cherry tree."
Poppa go way an' he come home to sup,
He lookka da tree — eet all choppa up!
And poppa so mad, he no talk — justa hees.
He say, "Cussa dam, wotta Blackhan' do thees?"

Now Georgha da Wash no shedda da tear,
An' say, "Notta know, too bad I no here,
Maybe bird chop eet down, maybe beeg honeybee";
Naw! Georgha da Wash, he jess say, "Eetta me!"

Oh, Georgha da Wash, he fighta da war
An' makka da Breetish to feel gooda sore.
Da Breetish say, "Georgha, you playa da game,
Keepa da rules for da war an' no be ashame.
All summertime fight, een wintertime bes'
Ever'bodie go home an' takka good res'.
Een winter da Hesh you musta no touch.
Now, Georgha, be good, lay offa da Dutch."
But Georgha he wait till da river all froze —
An' thenna he hitta da Dutch on da nose.
Da Breetish get mad an' makka da shout
An' say, "Georgha, who lay all these Hessian boys out?"

Now, Georgha da Wash mighta talk theesaway,
"Mebbe drink mucha whisky an' getta too gay,
An' shoota themselves, you waitta, I see."
Naw! Georgha da Wash he jess say, "Eetta me!"

— Richard Henry Little

[1] From the *Linebooks* (see footnote, page 287).

c   CANOPUS [1]
  When quacks with pills political would dope us,
   When politics absorbs the livelong day,
  I like to think about the star Canopus,
   So far, so far away!

  Greatest of visioned suns, they say who list 'em;
   To weigh it science always must despair,
  Its shell would hold our whole dinged solar system,
   Nor ever know 'twas there.

  When temporary chairmen utter speeches,
   And frenzied henchmen howl their battle hymns,
  My thoughts float out across the cosmic reaches
   To where Canopus swims.

  When men are calling names and making faces,
   And all the world's ajangle and ajar,
  I meditate on interstellar spaces,
   And smoke a mild seegar.

  For after one has had about a week of
   The arguments of friends as well as foes,
  A star that has no parallax to speak of,
   Conduces to repose.
        — Bert Leston Taylor

d   THE DINOSAUR
  Behold the mighty Dinosaur,
  Famous in prehistoric lore,
  Not only for his weight and strength,
  But for his intellectual length.
  You will observe by these remains
  The creature had two sets of brains —
  One in his head (the usual place),

---

[1] This and the next poem are reprinted from *Motley Measures* by permission of and special arrangement with Alfred A. Knopf, Inc., authorized publishers.

The other at his spinal base.
Thus he could reason a priori
As well as a posteriori.
No problem bothered him a bit;
He made both head and tail of it.
So wise he was, so wise and solemn,
Each thought filled just a spinal column.
If one brain found the pressure strong,
It passed a few ideas along;
If something slipt his forward mind,
'Twas rescued by the one behind;
And if in error he was caught,
He had a saving afterthought.
As he thought twice before he spoke,
He had no judgments to revoke;
For he could think without congestion,
Upon both sides of every question.
Oh, gaze upon this model beast,
Defunct ten million years at least!
— Bert Leston Taylor

JIM BLUDSO OF THE PRAIRIE BELLE

Wal, no! I can't tell whar he lives,
  Because he don't live, you see;
Leastways, he's got out of the habit
  Of livin' like you and me.
Whar have you been for the last three year
  That you haven't heard folks tell
How Jimmy Bludso passed in his checks
  The night of the *Prairie Belle?*

He war'nt no saint — them engineers
  Is all pretty much alike —
One wife in Natchez-under-the-Hill
  And another one here, in Pike;
A keerless man in his talk was Jim,
  And an awkward hand in a row,

But he never flunked, and he never lied —
  I reckon he never knowed how.

And this was all the religion he had:
  To treat his engine well;
Never be passed on the river;
  To mind the pilot's bell;
And if ever the *Prairie Belle* took fire,
  A thousand times he swore,
He'd hold her nozzle agin the bank
  Till the last soul got ashore.

All boats has their day on the Mississipp,
  And her day come at last —
The *Movastar* was a better boat,
  But the *Belle* she *wouldn't* be passed.
And so she came tearin' along that night —
  The oldest craft on the line —
With a deck hand squat on her safety valve,
  And her furnace crammed, rosin and pine.

The fire bust out as she clar'd the bar,
  And burnt a hole in the night,
And quick as a flash she turned and made
  For that willer bank on the right.
Thar was runnin' and cussin, but Jim yelled out,
  Over all the infernal roar,
"I'll hold her nozzle agin the bank
  Till the last galoot's ashore."

Through the hot, black breath of the burnin' boat
  Jim Bludso's voice was heard,
And they all had trust in his cussedness,
  And knowed he would keep his word.
And, sure's you're born, they all got off
  Afore the smokestacks fell —
And Bludso's ghost went up alone
  In the smoke of the *Prairie Belle*.

He war'n't no saint — but at jedgement
   I'd run my chance with Jim,
'Longside of some pious gentlemen
   That wouldn't shook hands with him.
He seen his duty, a dead-sure thing —
   And went for it thar and then;
And Christ ain't a-goin' to be too hard
   On a man that died for men.

— John Hay

THE ADMIRAL'S GHOST [1]

f

I tell you a tale tonight
   Which a seaman told to me,
With eyes that gleamed in the lanthorn light
   And a voice as low as the sea.

You could almost hear the stars
   Twinkling up in the sky,
And the old wind woke and moaned in the spars,
   And the same old waves went by,

Singing the same old song
   As ages and ages ago
While he froze my blood in that deep-sea night
   With the things that he seemed to know.

A bare foot pattered on deck;
   Ropes creaked; then — all grew still,
And he pointed his finger straight in my face
   And growled, as a sea dog will.

"Do'ee know who Nelson was?
   That pore little shriveled form
With the patch on his eye and the pinned-up sleeve
   And a soul like a North Sea storm?

[1] Reprinted by permission, from Alfred Noyes, *Collected Poems*, 2 vols., copyright, 1910, J. B. Lippincott Company, Vol. II, pp. 26–29.

"Ask of the Devonshire men!
  They know, and they'll tell you true;
He wasn't the pore little chawed-up chap
  That Hardy thought he knew.

"He wasn't the man you think!
  His patch was a dern disguise!
For he knew that they'd find him out, d'you see,
  If they looked him in both his eyes.

"He was twice as big as he seemed;
  But his clothes were cunningly made.
He'd both of his hairy arms all right!
  The sleeve was a trick of the trade.

"You've heard of sperrits, no doubt;
  Well, there's more in the matter than that!
But he wasn't the patch and he wasn't the sleeve,
  And he wasn't the laced cocked hat.

"*Nelson was just — a Ghost!*
  You may laugh! But the Devonshire men
They knew that he'd come when England called,
  And they know that he'll come again.

"I'll tell you the way it was
  (For none of the landsmen know),
And to tell it you right, you must go a-starn
  Two hundred years or so.

* * * * *

"The waves were lapping and slapping
  The same as they are today;
And Drake lay dying aboard his ship
  In Nombre Dios Bay.

"The scent of the foreign flowers
  Came floating all around;

'But I'd give my soul for the smell o' the pitch,'
  Says he, 'in Plymouth Sound.

"'What shall I do,' he says,
  'When the guns begin to roar,
An' England wants me, and me not there
  To shatter 'er foes once more?'

"(You've heard what he said, maybe,
  But I'll mark you the p'ints again;
For I want you to box your compass right
  And get my story plain.)

"'You must take my drum,' he says,
  'To the old sea wall at home;
And if ever you strike that drum,' he says,
  'Why, strike me blind, I'll come!

"'If England needs me, dead
  Or living, I'll rise that day!
I'll rise from the darkness under the sea
  Ten thousand miles away.'

"That's what he said; and he died;
  An' his pirates, listenin' roun',
With their crimson doublets and jeweled swords
  That flashed as the sun went down,

"They sewed him up in his shroud
  With a round shot top and toe,
To sink him under the salt sharp sea
  Where all good seamen go.

"They lowered him down in the deep,
  And there in the sunset light
They boomed a broadside over his grave,
  As meanin' to say 'Good night.'

"They sailed away in the dark
   To the dear little isle they knew;
And they hung his drum by the old sea wall
   The same as he told them to.

          * * * *

"Two hundred years went by,
   And the guns began to roar,
And England was fighting hard for her life
   As ever she fought of yore.

"'It's only my dead that count,'
   She said, as she says today;
'It isn't the ships and it isn't the guns
   'Ull sweep Trafalgar's Bay.'

"D'you guess who Nelson was?
   You may laugh, but it's true as true!
There was more in that pore little chawed-up chap
   Than ever his best friend knew.

"The foe was creepin' close,
   In the dark, to our white-cliffed isle;
They were ready to leap at England's throat,
   When — O, you may smile, you may smile;

"But — ask of the Devonshire men;
   For they heard in the dead of night
The roll of a drum, and they saw him pass
   On a ship all shining white.

"He stretched out his dead cold face
   And he sailed in the grand old way!
The fishes had taken an eye and his arm,
   But he swept Trafalgar's Bay.

"Nelson — was Francis Drake!
   O, what matters the uniform,

Or the patch on your eye or your pinned-up sleeve,
If your soul's like a North Sea storm? "

— Alfred Noyes

g   THE MOUNTAIN WHIPPOORWILL [1]

Up in the mountains, it's lonesome all the time.
(Sof' win' slewin' thu' the sweet-potato vine.)

Up in the mountains, it's lonesome for a child,
(Whippoorwills a-callin' when the sap runs wild.)

Up in the mountains, mountains in the fog,
Everythin's as lazy as an old houn' dog.

Born in the mountains, never raised a pet,
Don't want nuthin' an' never got it yet.

Born in the mountains, lonesome-born,
Raised runnin' ragged thu' the cockleburrs and corn.

Never knew my pappy, mebbe never should.
Think he was a fiddle made of mountain-laurel wood.

Never had a mammy to teach me pretty-please.
Think she was a whippoorwill, a-skitin' thu' the trees.

Never had a brother ner a whole pair of pants,
But when I start to fiddle, why, yuh got to start to dance!

Listen to my fiddle — Kingdom Come — Kingdom Come!
Hear the frogs a-chunkin' " Jug o' rum, Jug o' rum! "
Hear that mountain whippoorwill be lonesome in the air,
An' I'll tell yuh how I traveled to the Essex County Fair.

Essex County has a mighty pretty fair,
All the smarty fiddlers from the South come there.

[1] *Ballads and Poems: 1915–1930*, copyright, 1931, and reprinted by permission of Farrar and Rinehart, Inc., publishers, pp. 18–23.

Elbows flyin' as they rosin up the bow
For the First Prize Contest in the Georgia Fiddlers' Show.

Old Dan Wheeling with his whiskers in his ears,
Kingpin fiddler for nearly twenty years.

Big Tom Sargent, with his blue wall-eye,
An' little Jimmy Weezer that can make a fiddle cry.

All sittin' roun', spittin' high an' struttin' proud,
(Listen, little whippoorwill, yuh better bug yore eyes!)
Tun-a-tun-a-tunin' while the jedges told the crowd
Them that got the mostest claps'd win the bestest prize.

Everybody waitin' for the first tweedledee,
When in comes a-stumblin' — hillbilly me!

Bowed right pretty to the jedges an' the rest,
Took a silver dollar from a hole inside my vest,

Plunked it on the table an' said, "There's my callin' card!
An' anyone that licks me — well, he's got to fiddle hard!"

Old Dan Wheeling, he was laughin' fit to holler,
Little Jimmy Weezer said, "There's one dead dollar!"

Big Tom Sargent had a yaller-toothy grin,
But I tucked my little whippoorwill spang underneath my chin,
An' petted it an' tuned it till the jedges said, "Begin!"

Big Tom Sargent was the first in line;
He could fiddle all the bugs off a sweet-potato vine.
He could fiddle down a possum from a mile-high tree.
He could fiddle up a whale from the bottom of the sea.

Yuh could hear hands spankin' till they spanked each other raw,
When he finished variations on "Turkey in the Straw."

Little Jimmy Weezer was the next to play;
He could fiddle all night, he could fiddle all day.

He could fiddle chills, he could fiddle fever,
He could make a fiddle rustle like a lowland river.

He could make a fiddle croon like a lovin' woman.
An' they clapped like thunder when he'd finished strummin'.

Then came the ruck of the bobtailed fiddlers,
The let's-go-easies, the fair-to-middlers.

They got their claps an' they lost their bicker,
An' settled back for some more corn licker.

An' the crowd was tired of their no-count squealing,
When out in the center steps Old Dan Wheeling.

He fiddled high and he fiddled low,
(Listen, little whippoorwill, yuh got to spread yore wings!)
He fiddled with a cherrywood bow.
(Old Dan Wheeling's got bee honey in his strings.)

He fiddled the wind by the lonesome moon,
He fiddled a most almighty tune.

He started fiddling like a ghost,
He ended fiddling like a host.

He fiddled north an' he fiddled south,
He fiddled the heart right out of yore mouth.

He fiddled here an' he fiddled there.
He fiddled salvation everywhere.

When he was finished, the crowd cut loose.
(Whippoorwill, they's rain on yore breast.)

An' I sat there wonderin', " What's the use? "
(Whippoorwill, fly home to your nest.)

But I stood up pert an' I took my bow,
An' my fiddle went to my shoulder, so.

An' — they wasn't no crowd to get me fazed —
But I was alone where I was raised.

Up in the mountains, so still it makes yuh skeered,
Where God lies sleepin' in his big white beard.

An' I heard the sound of the squirrel in the pine,
An' I heard the earth a-breathin' thu' the long night-time.

They've fiddled the rose, an' they've fiddled the thorn,
But they haven't fiddled the mountain corn.

They've fiddled sinful an' fiddled moral,
But they haven't fiddled the breshwood laurel.

They've fiddled loud, and they've fiddled still,
But they haven't fiddled the whippoorwill.

I started off with *dump-diddle-dump.*
(*Oh, hell's broke loose in Georgia!*)
Skunk cabbage growin' by the bee-gum stump,
(*Whippoorwill, yo're singin' now!*)

Oh, Georgia booze is mighty fine booze,
The best yuh ever poured yuh,
But it eats the soles right offen yore shoes,
For hell's broke loose in Georgia.

My mother was a whippoorwill pert,
My father, he was lazy,

But I'm hell broke loose in a new store shirt
To fiddle all Georgia crazy.

Swing yore partners — up an' down the middle!
Sashay now — oh, listen to that fiddle!
Flapjacks flippin' on a red-hot griddle,
An' hell's broke loose,
Hell broke loose,
Fire on the mountains — snakes in the grass.
Satan's here a-bilin' — oh, Lordy, let him pass!
Go down Moses, set my people free,
Pop goes the weasel thu' the old Red Sea!
Jonah sittin' on a hickory bough,
Up jumps a whale — an' where's yore prophet now?
Rabbit in the pea patch, possum in the pot,
Try an' stop my fiddle, now my fiddle's gettin' hot!
Whippoorwill, singin' thu' the mountain hush,
Whippoorwill, shoutin' from the burnin' bush,
Whippoorwill, cryin' in the stable door,
Sing tonight as yuh never sang before!
Hell's broke loose like a stompin' mountain shoat,
Sing till yuh bust the gold in yore throat!
Hell's broke loose for forty miles aroun'
Bound to stop yore music if yuh don't sing it down.
Sing on the mountains, little whippoorwill,
Sing to the valleys, an' slap 'em with a hill,
For I'm struttin' high as an eagle's quill,
An' hell's broke loose,
Hell's broke loose,
Hell's broke loose in Georgia!

They wasn't a sound when I stopped bowin',
(*Whippoorwill, yuh can sing no more.*)
But, somewhere or other, the dawn was growin'.
(*Oh, mountain whippoorwill!*)

An' I thought, "I've fiddled all night an' lost.
Yo're a good hillbilly, but yuh've been bossed."

So I went to congratulate old man Dan,
— But he put his fiddle into my han' —
An' then the noise of the crowd began.
— Stephen Vincent Benét

h   HE KNEW LINCOLN [1]

"Did I know Lincoln? Well, I should say. See that chair there? Take it, set down. That's right. Comfortable, ain't it? Well, sir, Abraham Lincoln has set in that chair hours, him and Little Doug, and Logan and Judge Davis, all of 'em, all the big men in this state, set in that chair. See them marks? Whittlin'. Judge Logan did it, all-firedest man to whittle. Always cuttin' away at something. I just got that chair new, paid six dollars for it, and I be blamed if I didn't come in this store and find him slashin' right into that arm. I picked up a stick and said: 'Here, Judge, s'posin' you cut this.' He just looked at me and flounced out, mad as a wet hen. Mr. Lincoln was here, and you ought to heard him teehee. He was always here. Come and set by the stove by the hour and tell stories and talk and argue. There wan't never no United States Senate that could beat just what I've heard right here in this room with Lincoln settin' in that very chair where you are this minute.

"Tell stories? Nobody ever could beat him at that, and how he'd enjoy 'em, just slap his hands on his knees and jump up and turn around and then set down, laughin' to kill. Greatest man to git new yarns that ever lived, always askin', 'Heard any new stories, Billy?' And if I had I'd trot 'em out, and how he'd laugh. Often and often when I've told him something new and he'd kin' a forgit how it went, he'd come in an' say, 'Billy, how was that story you'se tellin' me?' and then I'd tell it all over.

"You know I felt kind of sorry for Lincoln when they began to talk about him for President. It seemed almost as if somebody was makin' fun of him. He didn't look like a President. I never had seen one, but we had pictures of 'em, all of 'em from George Washington down, and they looked somehow as if they were different kind of timber from us. I couldn't imagine George Washington

[1] Reprinted, by permission of the publishers, from *He Knew Lincoln* by Ida M. Tarbell. Copyright by The Macmillan Company. Arranged by Gertrude E. Johnson.

or Thomas Jefferson settin' here in that chair you're in teeheein' over some blamed yarn of mine. None of us around town took much stock in his bein' elected at first — that is, none of the men, the women was different. They always believed in him, and used to say, ' You mark my word, Mr. Lincoln will be President. He's just made for it, he's good, he's the best man ever lived and he ought to be President.' I didn't see no logic in that, then, but I dunno but there was some after all.

" ' Was there much talk about his bein' killed? ' Well, there's an awful lot of fools in this world and when they don't git what they want they're always for killin' somebody. Mr. Lincoln never let on, but I reckon his mail was pretty lively readin' sometimes.

" Of course he seemed pretty cheerful always. He wan't no man to show out all he felt. Lots of them little stuck-up chaps that came out here to talk to him said, solemn as owls, ' He don't realize the gravity of the situation.' Think of that, Mr. Lincoln not realizing. They ought to heard him talk to us the night he went away. I'll never fergit that speech — nor any man who heard it. I can see him now just how he looked, standin' there on the end of his car. He'd been shakin' hands with the crowd in the depot, laughin' and talking, just like himself, but when he got onto that car he seemed suddint to be all changed. You never seen a face so sad in all the world. I tell you he had woe in his heart that minute, woe. He knew he was leavin' us for good, nuthin' else could explain the way he looked and what he said. He knew he never was comin' back to us alive.

" ' Ever see him again? ' Yes, once down in Washington, summer of '64. Things was lookin' purty blue that summer. Didn't seem to be anybody who thought he'd git re-elected. I kept hearin' about the trouble he was havin' with everybody, and I just made up my mind I'd go down and see him and swap yarns and tell him how we was all countin' on his gettin' home. So I jest picked up and went right off.

" ' Well, I footed it up to the Soldiers' Home where Mr. Lincoln was livin' then right among the sick soldiers in their tents. There was lots of people settin' around in a little room, waitin' fer him, but there wan't anybody there I knowed, and I was feelin' a little funny when a door popped open and out came Mr. Lincoln. He saw me first thing, and his face lit up, and he laid holt of me and jest shook my hands fit to kill. 'Billy,' he says, ' now I am glad to see you. Come right in. You're going to stay to supper with Mary and me.'

" Didn't I know it? Think bein' President would change him — not a mite. Well, he had a right smart lot of people to see, but soon as he was through we went out on the back stoop and set down and talked and talked. He asked me about pretty nigh everybody in Springfield. I just let loose and told him about the weddin's and births and the funerals and the buildin', and I guess there wan't a yarn I'd heard in the last three years and a half he'd been away that I didn't spin for him. Laugh — you ought to a heard him laugh — just did my heart good, for I could see what they'd been doin' to him. Always was a thin man, but, Lordy, he was thinner'n ever now, and his face was kind a drawn and gray — enough to make you cry.

" Well, we had supper and then talked some more, and about ten o'clock I started downtown. Wanted me to stay all night, but I says to myself, 'Billy, don't you overdo it. You've cheered him up, and you better light out and let him remember it when he's tired.' So I said, ' Nope, Mr. Lincoln, can't, goin' back to Springfield tomorrow.'

" Well, sir, I never was so astonished in my life. Mr. Lincoln just grabbed my hand and shook it nearly off, and the tears just poured down his face, and he says, ' Billy, you never'll know what good you've done me. I'm homesick, Billy, just plumb homesick, and it seems as if this war never would be over. Many a night I can see the boys a-dyin' on the fields and can hear their mothers cryin' for 'em at home, and I can't help 'em, Billy. I have to send them down there. We've got to save the Union, Billy, we've got to.'

"' Course we have, Mr. Lincoln,' I says, cheerful as I could, ' course we have. Don't you worry. It's most over. You're going to be re-elected, and you and old Grant's goin' to finish the war mighty quick then. Just keep a stiff upper lip, Mr. Lincoln, and don't forget them yarns I told you.' And I started out. But seems as if he couldn't let me go. 'Wait a minute, Billy,' he says, 'till I get my hat and I'll walk a piece with you.' It was one of them still sweet-smellin' summer nights with no end of stars and you ain't no idee how pretty 'twas walkin' down the road. There was white tents showin' through the trees and every little way a tall soldier standin' stock-still, a gun at his side. Made me feel mighty curious and solemn. By-and-by we come out of the trees to a sightly place where you could look all over Washington — see the Potomac and clean into Virginia. There was a bench there and we set down and after a while Mr. Lincoln he begun to talk. Well, sir, you or nobody ever heard anything like it. Tell you what he said? Nope, I can't. Can't talk about it somehow. He just opened up his heart if I do say it. Seemed as if he'd come to a p'int where he must let out. I dunno how long we set there — must have been nigh morning, fer the stars begun to go out before we got up to go. 'Good-by, Billy,' he says. 'You're the first person I ever unloaded onto, and I hope you won't think I'm a baby,' and then we shook hands again, and I walked down to town and next day I come home.

"Yes, that's the last time I seen him — last time alive.

"Wan't long after that things began to look better. War began to move right smart, and, soon as it did, there wan't no use talkin' about anybody else for President. I see that plain enough, and just as I told him, he was re-elected, and him and Grant finished up the war in a hurry. I tell you it was a great day out here when we heard Lee had surrendered. Somehow the only thing I could think of was how glad Mr. Lincoln would be.

"We began right off to make plans about the reception we'd give him — brass band — parade — speeches — fireworks — everything. Seems as if I couldn't think about anything else. I was comin' down to open the store one mornin' thinkin' how I'd decorate the windows and how I'd tie a flag on that old chair, when I see Hiram Jones comin' toward me. He looked so old and all bent over. I didn't know what had happened. 'Hiram,' I says, 'what's the matter? Be you sick?'

"'Billy,' he says, and he couldn't hardly say it, 'Billy, they've killed Mr. Lincoln.'

"Well, I just turned cold all over, and then I flared up. 'Hiram

Jones,' I says, ' you're lyin', you're crazy. How dare you tell me that? It ain't so.'

"'Don't, Billy,' he says, 'don't go on so. I ain't lyin'. It's so. He'll never come back, Billy. He's dead!' And he fell to sobbin' out loud right there in the street, and somehow I knew it was true.

"For days and days 'twas awful here. Waitin' and waitin'. Seemed as if that funeral never would end. I couldn't bear to think of him bein' dragged around the country and havin' all that fuss made over him. He always hated fussin' so. Still, I s'pose I'd been mad if they hadn't done it.

"Of course they got here at last, and I must say it was pretty grand. All sorts of big bugs, Senators and Congressmen, and officers in grand uniforms and music and flags and crape. They certainly didn't spare no pains givin' him a funeral. Only we didn't want 'em. We wanted to bury him ourselves, but they wouldn't let us.

"Ma and me didn't go to the cemetery with 'em. I couldn't stan' it. Didn't seem right to have sich goin's on here at home where he belonged for a man like him. But we go up often now, Ma and me does, and talk about him.

"Yes, I knowed Abraham Lincoln; knowed him well; and I tell you there wan't never a better man made. Leastwise, I don't want to know a better one. He just suited *me* — Abraham Lincoln did."

— Ida M. Tarbell

i THE PLAINT OF THE CAMEL [1]
Canary birds feed on sugar and seed,
  Parrots have crackers to crunch;
And as for the poodles, they tell me the noodles
  Have chicken and cream for their lunch.
    But there's never a question
    About *my* digestion —
Anything does for me!

Cats, you're aware, can repose in a chair,
  Chickens can roost upon rails;

[1] Reprinted by permission of, and arrangement with, Houghton Mifflin Company.

Puppies are able to sleep in a stable,
　　And oysters can slumber in pails.
　　　　But no one supposes
　　　　A poor Camel dozes —
Any place does for me!

Lambs are enclosed where it's never exposed,
　　Coops are constructed for hens;
Kittens are treated to houses well heated,
　　And pigs are protected by pens.
　　　　But a Camel comes handy
　　　　Wherever it's sandy —
Anywhere does for me!

People would laugh if you rode a giraffe,
　　Or mounted the back of an ox;
It's nobody's habit to ride on a rabbit,
　　Or try to bestraddle a fox.
　　　　But as for a Camel, he's
　　　　Ridden by families —
Any load does for me!

A snake is as round as a hole in the ground;
　　Weasels are wavy and sleek;
And no alligator could ever be straighter
　　Than lizards that live in a creek.
　　　　But a Camel's all lumpy
　　　　And bumpy and humpy —
Any shape does for me!
　　　　　　— Charles Edward Carryl

j　　　　　　JODY AND FLAG [1]

　Jody wandered west with Flag beside him. He carried Penny's [2] shotgun over his shoulder. His heart beat and stopped and beat again.
　He said under his breath, "I'll not do it. I'll jest not."

[1] From Marjorie Kinnan Rawlings, *The Yearling*, Chas. Scribner's Sons, New York. Reprinted by permission.
[2] Penny was Jody's father.

He stopped in the road.

He said out loud, "They cain't make me do it."

Flag looked at him with big eyes, then bent his head to a wisp of grass by the roadside. Jody walked on again slowly.

"I'll not. I'll not. I'll jest not. They kin beat me. They kin kill me. I'll not."

He threw himself in the grass under an old chinaberry tree and sobbed until he could sob no more. Flag nuzzled him and he clutched him. He lay panting.

He said, "I'll not. I'll jest not."

He was dizzy when he stood up. He leaned against the rough trunk of the chinaberry. It was in bloom. He was ashamed of himself for having taken time to cry. It was no time to cry. He would have to think. He would build a pen for Flag. A pen ten feet tall. He would gather acorns and grass and berries and feed him there. But it would take all his time to gather feed for a penned animal. Penny was on his back in the bed. . . . The crops would have to be worked. . . . There was no one but himself to do it.

He was flooded with excitement. He turned from the clearing up the road to the Forresters', trotting. His throat was dry and his eyes were swollen and smarting. His hope refreshed him and in a little while, when he swung up the Forresters' trail under the live oaks, he felt all right again. He ran to the house and up the steps. He rapped at the open door and stepped inside. There was no one in the room but Pa and Ma Forrester. They sat immobile in their chairs.

He said breathlessly, "Howdy. Where's Buck?"

Pa Forrester turned his head slowly on his withered neck, like a turtle.

"Been a long time since you was here," he said.

"Where's Buck, please, sir?"

"Buck? Why, Buck and the hull passel of 'em has rode off to Kentucky, hoss tradin'."

"In plantin' time?"

"Plantin' time be tradin' time. They'd ruther trade than plow. They figgered they'd make enough, tradin', to buy our rations." The old man spat. "And likely, they will."

"They're all gone?"

"Ever' one of 'em. Pack and Gabby'll be back in April."

Ma Forrester said: "Heap o' good it do a woman to birth a mess o' young uns and raise 'em and then have 'em all go off to oncet. I will say, they left rations and stacked wood. We won't need nothin' 'til some of 'em's back in April."

"April . . ."

He turned dully from the door.

"Come set with us, boy. I'd be proud to cook dinner for you. Raisin' puddin', eh? You and Fodder-wing allus loved my raisin' puddin'."

"I got to go," he said. "I thank you."

He turned back.

He burst out desperately, "What would you do, did you have a yearlin' et up the corn and you couldn't keep it out noway and your Pa told you to go shoot it?"

They blinked at him. Ma Forrester cackled.

Pa Forrester said, "Why, I'd go shoot it."

He realized that he had not made the matter clear.

He said, "Supposin' it was a yearlin' you loved?"

Pa Forrester said: "Why, love's got nothin' to do with corn. You cain't have a thing eatin' the crops. Lessen you got boys like mine, has got other ways o' makin' a livin'."

Ma Forrester asked, "Hit that fawn you carried here last summer?"

"That's him. Flag," he said. "Cain't you-all take him?"

"Why, we got no better way'n you o' keepin' him. He'd not stay here, nohow. What's four mile to a yearlin' deer?"

They too were a stone wall.

He said, "Well, good-by," and went away.

He was glad to get away again. Jody found himself tired with a fatigue born of hunger. He fell asleep. When he awakened, Flag had gone. He followed his tracks. They led in and out of the scrub, then turned back to the road and continued evenly toward home. There was nothing to do but follow. He reached Baxter's Island after dark. A candle burned in the kitchen. Supper was over. His mother sat in the candlelight, sewing her endless patchwork pieces.

He was trying to make up his mind whether to go in or not when Flag galloped across the yard. He saw his mother lift her head and listen.

He slipped hurriedly beyond the smokehouse and called Flag in a low voice. The yearling came to him. He crouched at the corner. His mother came to the kitchen door and threw it open. A bar of light lay across the sand. The door closed. He waited a long time until the light went out in the kitchen. He allowed time for her to go to bed and to sleep. He made a bed in a stall at the lot with an armful of the scant remaining marsh-grass hay. He slept there with Flag beside him, not quite warm enough through the chill March night.

He awakened after sunrise, stiff and miserable. Flag was gone. He went reluctantly but compelled to the house. At the gate he heard his mother's voice raised in a storm of anger. She had discovered the shotgun where he had leaned it against the smokehouse wall. She had discovered Flag. She had discovered, too, that the yearling had made the most of the early hours and had fed, not only across the sprouting corn, but across a wide section of the cowpeas. He went helplessly to her to meet her wrath. He stood with his head down while she flailed him with her tongue.

She said finally: " Git to your Pa. For oncet, he's with me."

He went into the bedroom. His father's face was drawn. Penny said gently, " How come you not to do what I told you? "

" Pa, I jest couldn't. I cain't do it."

" Come here clost to me, boy. Jody, you know I've done all I could to keep your leetle deer for you."

" Yes, sir."

" You know we depend on our crops to live."

" Yes, sir."

" You know they ain't a way in the world to keep that wild yearlin' from destroyin' 'em."

" Yes, sir."

" Then why don't you do what's got to be done? "

" I cain't."

Penny lay silent.

"Tell your Ma to come here. Go to your room and shut the door."

"Yes, sir."

There was a relief in following simple orders.

"Pa says to go to him."

He went to his room and closed the door. He sat on the side of the bed, twisting his hands. He heard low voices. He heard steps. He heard a shot. He ran from the room to the open kitchen door. His mother stood on the stoop with the shotgun smoking in her hands. Flag lay floundering beside the fence.

She said: "I didn't want to hurt the creetur. I cain't shoot straight. You know I cain't."

Jody ran to Flag. The yearling heaved to his three good legs and stumbled away, as though the boy himself were his enemy. He was bleeding from a torn left forequarter. Penny dragged himself from his bed. He sank on one knee in the doorway, clutching it for support.

He called: "I'd do it if I could. I jest cain't stand up. . . . Go finish him, Jody. You got to put him outen his torment."

Jody ran back and snatched the gun from his mother.

He screamed: "You done it o' purpose. You allus hated him."

He turned on his father.

"You went back on me. You told her to do it."

He screeched so that his throat felt torn.

"I hate you. I hope you die. I hope I never see you again."

He ran after Flag, whimpering as he ran.

Penny called: "He'p me, Ory. I cain't git up . . ."

Flag ran on three legs in pain and terror. Twice he fell and Jody caught up to him.

He shrieked: "Hit's me! Hit's me! Flag!"

Flag thrashed to his feet and was off again. Blood flowed in a steady stream. The yearling made the edge of the sinkhole. He wavered an instant and toppled. He rolled down the side. Jody ran after him. Flag lay beside the pool. He opened great liquid eyes and turned them on the boy with a glazed look of wonder. Jody pressed the muzzle of the gun barrel at the back of the smooth neck and pulled the trigger. Flag quivered a moment and then lay still.

Jody threw the gun aside and dropped flat on his stomach. He retched and vomited and retched again. He clawed into the earth with his fingernails. He beat it with his fists. The sinkhole rocked around him. A far roaring became a thin humming. He sank into blackness as into a dark pool.

TEST YOUR PROGRESS

46 Divide your class into pairs. Work with a partner who will tell you how successful you are in expressing meanings through visible action.

47 Have moving pictures taken as you read a selection. What is your own reaction to your use of your body in interpretation?

48 Observe other members of the class as they read. Work out a rating sheet recording the strong and weak points of each reader.

49 Notice the bodily action of members of your family as they read aloud at home.

50 State the central ideas in each of five selections in this chapter. Compare your statements with those of other members of the class.

51 Listen to someone read the following and criticize his use of voice. Did he make his ideas clear by the skillful use of voice?

a   A WEE LITTLE VERSE [1]
A wee little knife, and a fork and a spoon
   Set out for adventure one day;
And the fork and the spoon to the wee little mouth
   Of a wee little boy found their way.

The wee little knife, left alone by the plate,
   Just felt that he'd wasted his life;
For somebody's mother had firmly announced
   That a boy mustn't eat with his knife!

"But never you mind," said the wee little boy,
   "I'll use you to butter my bread;

[1] From the *Linebooks* (see footnote, page 287).

318 INTERPRETATIVE READING

    And I can't do that with a fork or a spoon."
  "God bless you!" the little knife said.
          Marjorie F. W.

b   It is an ancient Mariner,
    And he stoppeth one of three.
  "By thy long gray beard and glittering eye,
   Now wherefore stopp'st thou me?"
      — Samuel Taylor Coleridge

c   I wind about, and in and out,
    With here a blossom sailing,
   And here and there a lusty trout,
   And here and there a grayling.
     — Alfred, Lord Tennyson

52 Bring to class a selection that can be meaningless if the meter is too strongly accented, but in the effective reading of which the rhythm helps to convey the meaning. Ask the class to evaluate your ability to present it effectively.

CHAPTER TWELVE *Dramatics*

"ALL THE WORLD'S a stage, And all the men and women merely players," wrote Shakespeare long ago. This analogy between the theater and life has a special meaning for us as we take up our study of dramatics. Dramatic activities at their best always have in them many of the high values of social living. We include this chapter in the part of the book which has to do primarily with the development of satisfactory human relationships because it deals with the most completely socialized of all speech forms. When people get together to put on a play, their behavior reflects the characteristics of all social structure and organization. First of all, the drama group, like all other organized groups, has a common objective — the goal of the drama group is the presentation of the play as a finished product. Second, the objective is reached when every member of the group contributes his own part to the common enterprise. Each person must carry out his part, big or little, to the best of his ability if the objective is to be realized. Finally, harmonious coöperation is the indispensable key to success in play production, as it is in all other human relationships. So far as the professional theater is concerned, Hamlet's observation " The play's the thing " may be

correct. But, from our viewpoint in this chapter, it is more important to assume that the playing is the thing. We are seeking primarily the social values of working with our fellow human beings in a common enterprise. Acting and play production furnish us with interesting adventures in social living.

Since we were old enough to walk and talk we have liked to play that we were someone other than ourselves. As children we dressed like grownups; we mimicked our mothers and fathers and their friends. When we had grown old enough to listen to stories, we imagined that we were the different characters in them and, with other children in our neighborhood, we acted them out.

Now that we are in high school, we do not wish to drop makebelieve as a pleasant and effective method of enjoying literature and of grasping the subject matter of other courses. We shall find that we understand *Silas Marner* better when we put ourselves into the characters of Dunstan Cass, Mrs. Winthrop, and the others in the story. So too, when our social-studies class organizes itself into a "state legislature" to dramatize the processes of making laws, we appreciate more fully the workings of our government. We may learn more of a foreign language by acting in a play than by spending the same amount of time in drill on vocabulary, sentence structure, and idiom. Participation in dramatics gives us the opportunity to learn by doing. In dramatics, we *use* language instead of merely studying *how* to use it. We actually *conduct* a council meeting instead of just finding out *how* to conduct one.

It is the most normal thing in the world to work with enthusiasm on dramatic production. It is great fun — fun for the actors and fun for the audience. One of our strongest desires is to do something that will make us the center of favorable attention. We all crave audiences. Dramatic activity provides a proper and satisfactory way of getting audiences.

If we feel uncomfortably bound by the rules of home, school, and society in general, dramatization gives us a chance for freedom. Here, without risk of unfortunate consequences, we may experience many things we have dreamed of. We may return from the well of death with Richard Halliburton, fly over the South Pole with Byrd, call the Senate to order, become a member of the royal family of England, sing in the courtyard with a minstrel of the Middle Ages, or live the life of an ancient princess of Egypt. Stories we have read come to life as we dramatize them and live among their characters. Through the medium of dramatics, we may dwell in every age, in every stratum of society, and in every country of the world, which our study and imagination can construct for us.

Dramatization is almost certain to improve our speech. It is hardly necessary to explain how dramatics may contribute to our fund of worth-while things to say. No normal person can take part in interesting dramatic situations without having more to talk about than has the individual without such experiences. By dramatizing fine literature and using some of the author's best phrases we receive drill in speaking precise and vivid language. Dramatization also gives us valuable voice training. We have to become skillful users of voice if we are to make characters seem true and interesting. Finally, dramatization makes us more effective in expressing our ideas through visible action. To play the Hunchback of Notre Dame one day and Godfrey Cass or Shylock the next requires proficiency in the use of every part of the body from the face to the tips of the fingers and the toes. With an improved understanding of diverse personalities, with enhanced language ability, with a more adaptable voice and a better-controlled body, we shall discover that we have gained much in general speech competence. We shall be more at ease when invited out for dinner; we shall have more courage in asking our employer for an increase in salary; and we shall dare to express our opinions on political and social issues.

There are two kinds of dramatic production — informal and formal. In formal presentations, we give the audience a play, word for word as the author has written it. In informal dramatic production we do not necessarily use the exact words of the author. We keep the story clearly in mind; we decide what scenes we wish to play; we catch the flavor of the language, but we make up most of the actual dialogue. Although the final performance of an informal dramatic production does not achieve the finish of a formal presentation, nevertheless it does give us greater opportunity for originality.

INFORMAL PLAY PRODUCTION

Study the backgrounds of the story. To say that we must *know* the story if we are to dramatize it effectively means that we must study it more thoroughly than many of us at first may be inclined to think. To begin with, it is necessary to understand background materials. We may start by studying the properties and costumes of the period in which the story is set. Some books have illustrations that are very enlightening. Each new bit of information about the life of the period may enrich the story for us as we play it. Where is the scene laid? What can we find out about the country where the story takes place? We should look up words that are unfamiliar to us, especially those containing historical, Biblical, or other literary allusions. In short, we should do everything we can to prepare ourselves for getting and giving the full meaning of the story.

Plan the scenes. If we have chosen a long story or a novel, it will probably not be possible to produce it all. We must decide what scenes taken together will make a unified story. For example, one high-school freshman chose *The Prince and the Pauper* by Mark Twain. Obviously he could not present every scene of the story. But he did select scenes which led to a climax and carried the main plot. He dramatized the story in the following scenes: I. Tom Canty's Lodging; II. The King's Palace; III. Westminster Abbey.

It is easy to understand that when parts of a story are omitted, it may be necessary to reorganize the remaining parts so that everything vital to the plot can be retained. This point may be illustrated with O. Henry's short story, "The Ransom of Red Chief." Those who have not read it have a pleasant half-hour in store for them. It is about a boy who was kidnapped by "Two Desperate Men," and held for a $2500 ransom. The boy made the kidnappers so miserable that they were glad to get rid of him, and they finally paid his parents $250 to take him off their hands! This play might open with the men taking the boy from a street in the small village of Summit, where he lived. The second scene might be in the cave where they tried to conceal him. And the third might be at the boy's home when he is returned by the kidnappers and forced to remain with his father. Since more than half of the action of this narrative takes place in the cave, we also could easily arrange to dramatize the whole story in one act. By means of a dialogue between the two men as they sit before the cave, the audience could be told how the kidnappers caught the boy. By having the father come to the hiding place for the money and his son, the return could be made clear to the audience at the end of the play. Such changes do not injure the essentials of the plot; they make the dramatization more interesting, and they stimulate originality.

Impersonate the characters. We should begin by asking ourselves: How does each of the characters look? How does he walk? How does his voice sound? What are his characteristic mannerisms? How can we bring these characters to life for those who look and listen as we present our play? Since voice plays such an important part in the success of any type of dramatic production, each actor should assure himself that he is able to make his vocal sounds express joy, fear, anger, and other emotions. If we are to portray different characters, we must cultivate the ability to sound like different characters. Some preliminary concentration on voice as such will greatly strengthen the final performance.

Prepare the dialogue. While we should preserve freedom in the use of language, yet we should make it our concern to reproduce the essential flavor of the author's expressions. For example, the dialogue between Tom Canty and the Prince, or that between "Red Chief" and his kidnappers, should not be fixed and memorized as it is in print, but the audience should always hear language characteristic of the story as it was written. We should retain certain phrases verbatim because they express the thought or the feeling so aptly. In the Coronation scene from *The Prince and the Pauper*, we should keep the dialogue very close to Mark Twain's wording. The contrast between the King and Tom will be more effectively revealed by the King's own words, "How used you the Great Seal of England?" and Tom's blunt and confused answer, "To crack nuts with," than by any improvised lines we could invent.

When most of the dialogue is original, there is some danger that it may not be interesting; plays may drag, and what should be witty, clever repartee may become slow, boring talk which fails to hold the attention of the audience. The best way to learn how to invent good dialogue is to read authors who have done it exceptionally well and to examine the actual conversation heard in similar situations.

Devise movement and grouping. All stage action should be so placed as to call attention to important incidents and to lead up to the climax of the story. The way we stand and move about on the stage should help to make our dramatizations effective. Remember that we are playing for an audience; therefore it will be necessary to stage the action where it can be easily seen by that audience. Try to make and keep the stage picture effective at all times. Avoid crowding on the stage. Keep in mind the relative importance of the characters, and place them so as to keep a balance of interest between the two sides of the stage. The hero or the heroine alone on one side of the stage may balance a number of relatively unimportant characters on the other. The center opening at the back furnishes the most effective

"THE DEVIL AND DANIEL WEBSTER." *Daniel Webster (Edward Arnold)* and "*Old Scratch*" (*Walter Huston*) in "*All That Money Can Buy*," the movie version of Stephen Vincent Benét's story. What seems to be the relationship between the two characters and how do they seem to feel toward each other? (*Culver Service*)

entrance, and the doors at the side nearest the audience the least effective.

Present the dramatization. It is fun to put on a final performance, but it is impossible to make the event as significant as it should be without the full co-operation of every person in the group. First, there are the actors, who have been cast in the several roles because, in the opinion of the group, they can play them best. The actors should not treat their responsibilities lightly. Second, the stage crew has been selected to set the stage and to provide the necessary properties. The average classroom provides the largely make-believe set and imaginary properties. The emphasis should be on the play and the playing, not on the set and the properties. The stage crew should see to it that the stage is ready for the actors at all times. When a chair is necessary, it must be in place, and when the stage is supposed to be vacant of furniture, the actors should not be expected to push the furniture out of their way. Third, those not chosen as actors or as members of the stage crew may serve as critics. The success of future productions depends largely upon the tact and skill of the critics in analyzing performances and suggesting improvements. Constructive criticism is indispensable in learning to do anything well.

FORMAL PLAY PRODUCTION

We are now to consider the acting and staging of a ready-made play, one in which the scenes have been worked out and the dialogue prepared for us. It is our prime object in producing such a play to make it come alive for the audience so that it will be for them not a story in a book, but a counterpart of life itself. In Hamlet's words, we are " to hold, as 'twere, the mirror up to nature."

Choosing the play. Choosing the play is our first task. There are plays and plays, but there are always only a few that will suit a particular purpose. Obviously, the more we know about the general field of drama, the more wisely we can choose a play which suits our purpose.

It pays to put on a good play. It is a mistake to assume that any sort of play will do. The better the play, the greater are the chances for a good production. As amateur play-producers it is good for us to try to do a better play than we think we can do. We may be surprised to find how well we can do it. The very saddest spectacle in all the world of dramatics is to see a cheap, badly written play produced poorly. For high-school groups in particular, we can be sure that Shakespeare and Sheridan and Goldsmith are good. *The Rivals*, *She Stoops to Conquer*, and *A School for Scandal* have been given successfully thousands of times. The Shakespearean plays that audiences like best when they are given by high-school students are: *The Merchant of Venice*, *Julius Caesar*, *As You Like It*, *Twelfth-Night*, *A Midsummer-Night's Dream*, *Much Ado about Nothing*, *The Merry Wives of Windsor*, *The Winter's Tale*, *The Tempest*, *The Comedy of Errors*, and *The Taming of the Shrew*. Of modern drama there is a plentiful supply. Plays by Barrie, Shaw, Wilde, Pinero, Henry Arthur Jones, Clyde Fitch, Augustus Thomas, George

"ELIZABETH THE QUEEN." *Fontanne and Lunt in a costume play with elaborate make-up. It is difficult to believe that these are really the same actors shown in the picture on page 445. Compare with the two pictures of Ruth Draper on pages 275 and 277. (Culver Service)*

Kelly, Maxwell Anderson, and other contemporary playwrights are of good caliber and very actable.

Casting the play. In casting the play, height must be kept in mind. For example, suppose a boy and a girl are to play opposite each other in " straight " parts, a " juvenile lead " and an " ingénue." The boy should be taller than the girl, and both should be of average stature, or only slightly above average. It is better for the actor of a heroic part to be an inch or two taller than the other characters. In extreme comedy parts, the characters should be extremely tall or short, or extremely fat or thin. On the stage a son is supposed to be slightly taller than his father, a daughter slightly taller than her mother. When a father is very much shorter than his son, a mother very much shorter than her daughter, or a husband shorter than his wife, the situation is inevitably understood by the audience as meant for comedy. If we have a husband taller than the wife by a wide margin, again comedy is suggested. Characters that are set off against each other on the stage should not be very different in size except when we seek comic or tragic effects.

Father   Son   Daughter Mother   Husband Wife   Hero Heroine

Understudies. When casting a play, we should provide a sufficient number of understudies. There is a fine moral effect in this; being chosen for a part frequently seems to work like strong wine — it goes to the head! It helps to have a substitute ready to step into the role of an actor who gets the idea that he is indispensable and so becomes unteachable.

Reading the play. After the play has been chosen and the cast is selected, the next step is for the director to read the play aloud to the cast. Let the actors assemble and sit around the director while he reads the play to them, putting into it as much interpretation and characterization as possible. During this reading the various potential actors may discover suggestions for success in acting their roles.

Memorizing cues and lines. There are at least three stages in learning a role in a play. First, the actor should memorize the lines so that he can speak them at home by himself. This of course is a helpful beginning, but it will not get the actor through a rehearsal. The second stage in the learning has been reached when the actor can go into rehearsal, pick up his cues, and get through his speeches. Yet this degree of memorization will not permit much real acting. The third and final stage is to have the lines and the cues *wholly committed to memory.* Then the actor can go ahead confidently, with vigor and abandon, and *play* the part. Until he has perfected his learning of lines to this last stage, he is not ready to give a performance. Many an otherwise good production has been ruined by actors who have not gone further than the first or second stage of committing their parts to memory.

Scheduling rehearsals. The scheduling of rehearsals needs careful attention. The director should post a definite announcement of meetings, so that every member of the cast and production staff will know when and where he is expected to be on hand. Rehearsals should begin promptly, proceed without waste of time, and close on the minute. Participants in a play must not come straggling in late, or leave before a rehearsal is over. If they are not ready at the proper moment, let their understudies have their chance. It will not take many such substitutions to bring about a perfect record of attendance.

Conducting rehearsals. Everyone not on the stage must be quiet during rehearsal; any person familiar with producing plays knows that the general excitement of the occasion is likely to set everybody talking. Such disturbances "offstage" may seriously injure the whole rehearsal. At the final or dress rehearsal it is well: (1) that the whole play should be run straight through; (2) that it go on without any interference from the director, proceeding with the help of stage manager, property man, electrician, and prompter; (3) that as far as possible the players should maintain the tempo of the play; and (4) that the rehearsal should be completed in the *same length of time* that the actual performance will require.

Organizing production personnel. The following outline of the organization and distribution of duties may prove helpful to those who wish to present plays with a minimum of confusion and waste effort.

The director must be supreme. Directing a play effectively does not permit of divided authority. The director must be master. He makes out a promptbook showing all the movements of the actors, their groupings, the location of the furniture, the changes in lighting, the off-stage effects, the use of music, and everything else necessary to the production. The director must have helpers. The most important of these are:

1. The stage manager, who is responsible to the director for scenery, off-stage effects, the operation of doors, windows, lights, and so on. He must have the stage ready for the actors.

2. The property man, who furnishes the movable things needed on the stage: furniture, lamps, telephones, dishes, books, and the rest. *It is the duty of the property man to return properties after the play is over!*

3. The stage carpenter, who prepares whatever is to be constructed with hammer, saw, and nails.

4. The electrician, who attends to the lighting.

5. The prompter, who holds the book during rehearsals and on the night of the play, thus freeing the director's hands and eyes.

6. The chief musician, who gets the music ready and fits it into the director's general scheme.

7. The advertising manager, who interests the public in the play and stimulates them to buy tickets.

8. The box-office man, who has the tickets in orderly array so that he can lay his hands on just the tickets he wants at any moment.

9. The ticket takers and the ushers, who are on hand promptly the night of the performance and who keep things moving smoothly and expeditiously.

10. The back-stage organization, which provides one job for every person and one person for every job. The stage manager is head of the back-stage organization. Working under him are: stage crew, electrical staff, property staff, wardrobe mistress, curtain man, doorman. Note especially that no functions overlap and that all workers

are individually and collectively responsible to one head — the stage manager. The stage manager in turn is responsible to the director. The actors are subject to the stage manager's call. On a well-organized stage, during both rehearsals and performance the actor remains in his or her dressing room until called by the stage manager.

The stage manager must make certain that the stage is set ready for the first curtain. He should see to it that scenery, properties, and off-stage effects are in their places. He must make sure that the changes of scenery and costume have been rehearsed carefully. It is his responsibility to make sure that each stagehand knows his job. *He can leave nothing to chance, for if anything goes wrong, the stage manager must bear the responsibility.*

Some Important Back-Stage Rules

1. Attend to your own business.
2. Stage crew: Don't bother actors.
3. Actors: Keep clear of stage when scene shifts are taking place.
4. Don't talk off stage.
5. Have a fire extinguisher on hand.

THE PRINCIPLES OF ACTING

Many people think of acting as merely speaking the lines the author of the play has written. Acting is very much more than just uttering sentences. Then too, we often hear people say that they have enjoyed this or that dramatic production because it was so true to life, because it was so " natural." As a consequence many people are confirmed in the conviction that the best way to act on the stage is to do as one would do in everyday life, that the actor's supreme duty is to " be natural." If there is one thing that acting is above everything else in the world, it is make-believe. By our very use of the terms " theatrical " and " stagy," we indicate our appreciation of the fact that what happens on the stage should be different from what it would be in real life. Good acting should not *be* natural; it should *seem to be natural,* which is a very different matter!

The actor's voice. First of all, the actor's speech must be distinct. In most rooms where plays are produced, distinctness is much more

THE PRINCIPLES OF ACTING

"JIM DANDY." *An unusual stage setting for Saroyan's strange play. This production, directed by Alan Schneider, was given at Catholic University, Washington, D. C. The scene designer has caught the spirit of the dramatist. Compare this scenery with the conventional type and discuss the relative merits of the two styles. When should each be used? (Jordan Studio)*

than a matter of enunciating words clearly and pronouncing them correctly; it is also a matter of what is known as projecting the voice. When acting, we must remember that we are talking to many people. Those in the back of the room have just as much interest in getting what we say as have those in the front row. We must *project* our voices so that they will carry to the persons in the last row. Stage speech is always exaggerated; it cannot be exactly like parlor chat or office gossip. It is well for beginners to practice overdoing rather than underdoing distinctness and projection. Let them put it down as a safe rule to overdo until the director or some competent critic tells them their voices are too strong or their articulation too painstaking and exact. Note what was said of "stage diction" on page 102.

A specific piece of advice to follow in improving the projecting of the voice is to make sure to " talk front " as much as possible. Talking front means facing toward the audience. This rule applies especially to acting in rooms where it is not easy to hear and where the person in the last row is far from the stage. In smaller, more intimate places there may be more opportunity for talking to one side or to the rear.

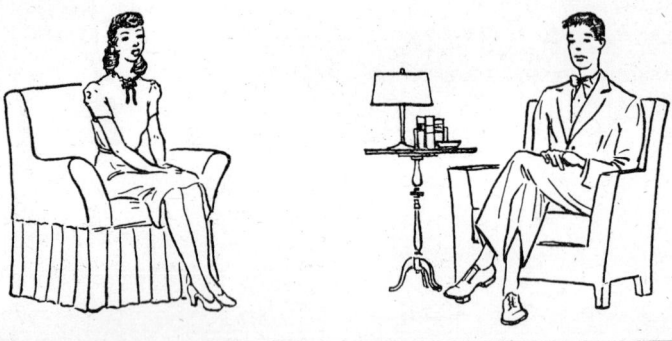

The actor's visible code. The hands of the actor can accomplish wonders in the presentation of feelings and ideas. The ordinary man in everyday life is awkward with his hands. If he should go onto the stage and use them in precisely the same way that he does around the house or at his place of business, he would look odd.

The actor's walk on the stage tells the audience a great deal as to what sort of person he is representing. Every time an actor comes onto the stage he ought to suggest what sort of person he is supposed to be by the way he carries himself. His walk ought to be a revelation of the inner nature of the character he is playing.

We have all seen amateur actors. What is it that makes us call some of them " amateurish "? We have seen some of our own friends do so well that we have considered them as good as professionals and we have said of them, " Well, do you know, I just couldn't believe that was John (or Mary); he just made me think that I was looking at that character in the play." This is the standard for the actor to aim at: to make his audience forget who he is, and to think only of the character he portrays. This result can be achieved only when an actor " acts all in one piece " — when he plays his part *all over.*

If we are to be a "no-count" character, we must have the right jerk of the shoulder, the proper projection of the chin, the appropriate flapping of the hands, the characteristic wriggle of the body, the natural shuffling of the feet, and all the other specific elements of visible and audible behavior which the audience will recognize as belonging to that sort of an individual. If one is to be a dashing young hero, one must walk and move with the precision of a person of distinction.

Beware of just "walking on." Be sure that the audience always will be studying the actor to pass judgment on what they think he is, or ought to be. Now if he merely "walks on" and behaves the way he does in real life, there is every chance in the world that he will be only ridiculous.

Seem to ignore the audience. When it is evident that the actor sees the audience, illusion is dispelled. However, turn often toward the audience during conversation, especially when some important word or phrase is to be uttered.

Observe proper tempo. Good actors speak their lines with wide variety in rate; pauses are brief and pauses are long; some characters are speedy and others are slow; certain parts of a scene are hurried up and others are slowed down. This change of pace has a great deal to do with the kind of impression the acting makes on the audience.

Study action values. A fundamental of acting is "business" — intelligent and meaningful actions with hands and feet, shoulders and hips, head, face and eyes. A sure mark of crudeness is for an actor to stand inert, merely spouting memorized lines. Those in the audience often learn more through their eyes than through their ears. So study lines to discover how many intelligent actions they suggest — walking, turning, changing position, using hands, head, and the whole body. Furniture on the stage is there for a purpose. It is not there, as one might expect from watching most amateurs, to be dodged. If you want to create the impression of naturalness, use the furniture. There are scores of things that an ingenious actor can do with the furniture and thus help to send his meaning across the footlights.

Gesture with the "upstage" hand. Rarely should an actor gesture with the hand nearer the footlights. This is a simple principle, and when once understood and practiced, it overcomes many of the awkward movements noticeable in amateur acting.

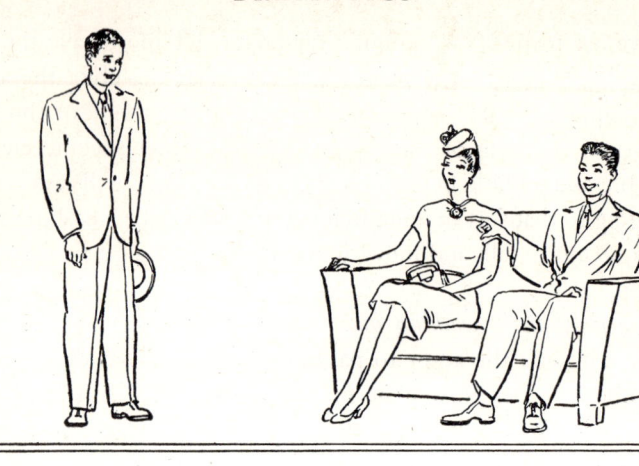

Similarly, in kneeling drop down on the knee nearer the audience, the "downstage" knee. This rule applies whether one is going to remain on one knee or to kneel on both knees. The same principle suggests that the shorter of two persons should be nearer the front. This must be taken with limitations, but it is a valuable general rule.

Permit only one event at a time. The basic rule for bringing out dramatic values is to allow only one major event on stage at a time. Attention needs to be focused; otherwise the audience is distracted and does not know to which of the simultaneous happenings to attend. This does not mean that only one person at a time should move, or that only one person at a time should talk; it means that the audience should get a unified impression.

In general, no actor should walk while another actor is speaking; to do so is likely to give the audience two centers of attention. We will get more value out of the lines and the action if most of the walking is done between speeches. When we move about, we should do it in such a way that the audience can see us "thinking" our way around.

Pick up cues quickly. The most approved way of speaking lines is almost to interrupt the preceding speech. As soon as the last word of a cue is heard, the next speech should begin — except when a pause is needed for dramatic effect. The mastery of this dramatic technique takes practice. It has much to do with getting the right tempo into the play.

Know how to " cross." The manner of passing another person on the stage is important; it is called crossing. There is a definite technique of crossing, which should be followed:

1. The person initiating the cross passes nearer the audience than does the person whom he crosses.

2. The person crossed must make some kind of movement by way of recognizing that he has been crossed. He commonly does this by moving in the opposite direction. It is possible, however, that he may be in such a position as to find such a movement awkward. He can then register his recognition of a cross by a turn of his body or a shift of his weight or by some other movement of his hands or head. This rule applies in moving forward and backward as well as in moving sidewise.

3. Generally, cross in front of the furniture.

Face the right way. When does an actor face toward other characters on the stage and when does he turn his back on them? This is an important question, for the audience reads meanings from the relative positions of the characters. If we dislike a person, but are not definitely fighting or opposing him, we register this attitude best by turning away from him; likewise if he embarrasses us, we turn our face away, even though he may be talking to us. If we like him, and trust him, and are eager to hear what he says, we face toward him when he speaks. Many subtle meanings and intentions can be conveyed by this device of facing the right way.

Work out effective groupings. The way characters cluster together, or stand apart, suggests subtle meanings to the audience. People who dislike each other or are fighting should not be in the same stage group unless they are almost ready to come to blows. When a character enters the room and it is intended that the audience shall understand that he is strange to the group, he should be set apart. A sinner or an outcast should be put by himself. Many effects can be worked out by means of grouping.

Do not speak lines during laughter or applause. About the surest mark of the amateur is to go right on talking when those in the audience are doing their best to enjoy the laugh that has been so carefully prepared for them. It is a wise procedure in the final rehearsals to have stationed in the house spectators who have been coached to break into laughter at points where laughter may be anticipated, and at any other points where the actors should be on guard. Then let the actors wait until the laughter dies down. Nothing is more exasperating to an audience than to have to stop laughing in order to hear the next line of an over-eager actor. The skillful actor will not only wait, but during the laughter will employ business to redouble the laughter and to keep it going. It is only the amateur who becomes embarrassed and charges ahead when the audience wants to laugh.

This same rule applies to sadness, terror, and suspense. Once we have established atmosphere, we should hold it; let the audience freeze, or jell, or tremble before we go on. That is what they came for; let us give them their money's worth. It is the true artistic way.

Study entrances and exits. Entrances and exits are always important. They must not appear to be accidental. Actors should not just drift on or wander off. When they enter, they should be in character. They should tell the audience by their walk and actions why they have come in and what mood they are in. They should know just what impression ought to be made at each entrance and exit. They should get near the exit before speaking the last line. They should prolong a walk before the exit only when the object is to draw unusual attention to the departure; that is, when the departure is especially important to the action. They should turn before going out, to say the last line toward the audience or the others on the stage — except in indicating extreme excitement, when they may face in any direction appropriate to the expression of the emotion. Definite meaning and character should be indicated by actions which reveal feelings.

Let action precede voice. As in all other forms of speech, it is a rule that gesture, movement, and facial expression should tell the audience what we are about to say and precisely how we feel. For example: Someone has just said to us, " That's not so "; our back has been toward the speaker, and his remark angers us. Will we say " Sir! " and then turn on him? Not if we are good actors; we will turn first, and then say " Sir! " People see more quickly than they hear; so to keep their interest at a maximum, we must engage their eyes first and then their ears.

Use dramatic preparation. Remember the principle that the audience usually must be prepared in advance for what is going to take place; they must anticipate what is going to happen. True, there must be some element of suspense in the denouement, but most matters of detail must be forecast by " dramatic preparation." Seldom should stage characters have secrets from the audience. It is all very proper for them to have secrets from each other, as the story so often demands; but usually they should let the audience make as many correct guesses as possible as to what is going to happen next. This is a principle not readily understood by amateurs. But to give an audience the greatest degree of satisfaction, we must not keep them too much in the dark; we must have them just on the point of knowing completely what is going to happen next. Suppose a certain letter is to be found on a table at a critical moment; in general, let the audience be aware that a letter is on the table. If a pistol is to be drawn at a given juncture, it is well to let the audience know that it is in the drawer or in the actor's pocket. If a wall safe is behind a picture, some means must be devised of letting the audience know it is there: a furtive peek behind the picture by one of the actors when no one else — on the stage — sees it, a reference to it during conversation, a significant glance, or an inspection of it to see that it is all right. An audience completely baffled is an audience that is very unhappy, but an audience that has secrets which the stage characters do not share enjoys its superior knowledge.

The true character of each stage personage should be suggested to the audience at his first appearance. One of the most uncomfortable things than can be done to an audience is to compel them to revise their first impression of a character.

Trust memory. The best advice that can be given for making sure to remember lines is to trust memory, and the best way to increase confidence in memory is to keep the body free. The actor who gets stiff and tense all over his body is the one most likely to miss his cues and forget his lines. If we make sure to keep our bodies doing what they ought to do to represent the characters we are portraying, there is every likelihood that our lips and tongues will pronounce the words that go with the actions.

STAGING A PLAY

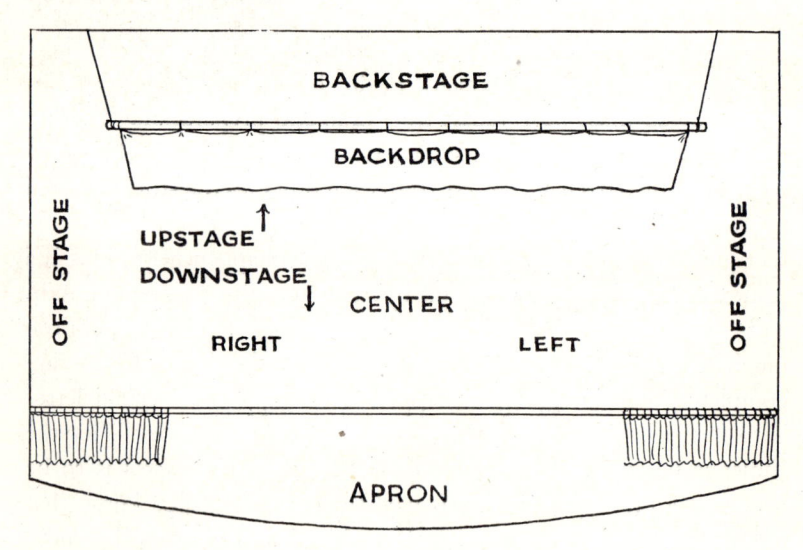

```
                    BACKSTAGE
                    BACKDROP
   OFF    UPSTAGE ↑              OFF
   STAGE  DOWNSTAGE ↓  CENTER    STAGE
          RIGHT          LEFT
                     APRON
```

Second only to the acting in dramatic production is the disposal of characters on the stage and the handling of the nonhuman factors — the curtain, the furniture, all the " properties."

Very important to the enjoyment of the audience is the way the stage is balanced. Balance is usually not symmetry. A stage is symmetrical when there are two pieces of furniture on one side and two pieces just like them on the other side, similarly placed; or a man and woman on one side and a man and woman on the other, in like positions. One of the surest marks of amateur play-producing is the symmetrical placing of characters to look like a church choir or a male quartet. Most of the time balance is a matter of getting more people on one side of the stage than on the other, or more people forward than back, or more back than forward, because balance is a matter of weight of interest. A character who holds interest strongly can be alone at one side of the stage and yet balance five people on the other side. Furniture helps out in balance. If the table holds objects of interest, two people seated near it at the left of the stage can balance four people in the open at the right. One side of the stage can even be almost empty and yet balance a group of people and furniture on the other if the interest of the audience is sharply directed to something on the vacant side; for example, a hidden necklace, a wall safe, or a concealed revolver. The person of the greatest psychological importance for the moment should have the center, and the others should be grouped to balance on either side of him according to their relative importance. The actor who can keep his head thoroughly can " trim " the stage; if he finds the balance has been lost, he will take a position to restore it.

In a good dramatic performance it is necessary to have a few " big scenes." These are moments in the play when excitement reaches a high pitch. Big scenes are almost always achieved by a rapid tempo joined with loud talking, or by a slow tempo linked with talk that is unusually quiet, tense, and subdued. Every successful play should have one point of highest interest, its climax — usually at the close of the next to the last act. This should be extra-fast, or extra-loud, or extra-subdued, or extra-deliberate — something different from what has been going on in other portions of the play.

An important factor in avoiding the amateurish touch is that of holding the tableaux. When the action has moved up to a climax, then almost always the players and the director have a chance to get the very best effect of all — a tableau. This means that when they have achieved this high point of interest, they can give their audience a maximum of enjoyment by holding the effect. Often a striking stage picture, with perfect balance, coming at the moment of highest excitement gives the audience its finest enjoyment of the evening.

The curtain plays a very important part in rounding out a scene. A well-planned scene usually ends with a good deal of emotion and tension; and the way the curtain is handled has a great deal to do with bringing this tension to just the right point. On a scene portraying the death of a character, the curtain is usually very slow; on a scene that has been fast and snappy, the curtain should be quick. There are many degrees of speed with which the curtain can be lowered, and all of them are needed for various kinds of scenes. With good effect, on the proper occasions, the curtain can start down slowly and end speedily, or start speedily and end slowly. Great care should be taken that the curtain begins to fall at just the right instant and that it reaches the floor at just as precise an instant.

A simple principle, but one worth noting, is that lights which are a part of the stage setting should be so placed that they are not between the audience and the actors, getting in the eyes of the spectators. This rule applies mostly to candles on tables and desks and to electric bulbs on the walls. Akin to it is the rule: When placing a mirror on the stage, try to set it on a side wall rather than the back, so that it does not throw a reflection of the footlights or any other light into the eyes of the audience. It may be well to " fix " the mirror by soaping or waxing its surface so that it will not reflect light.

Many kinds of projects can be devised by the use of scenes from classic drama, and by the use of one-set plays; that is, plays that need only one stage set for all the action.

The objective in formal dramatics is to bring out " dramatic values " by extracting from the printed play all the possibilities for entertainment, profit, and charm. Among the values that can be achieved in class are:

1. *Interpretation of lines:* bringing out the full value of the spoken part of the acting

2. *Impersonation:* characterization — catching the spirit of the personage to be represented; using the whole body to good effect; responding all in one piece

3. *Business:* using hands, clothing, furniture, other properties, to serve the situations and the action

4. *Crossing:* moving the actors about the stage successfully
5. *Balancing the stage:* devising effective stage pictures; changing effectively from one picture to the next
6. *Setting and scenery:* preparing the stage for the play
7. *Tempo:* securing the best rate and change of pace
8. *Tableaux, climaxes, curtain:* all done with the best of stage technique
9. Drilling a staff of workers for play production

Tests of Comprehension and Application

INFORMAL DRAMATICS

1 After each student has told the class about his favorite selection from literature and his plan for producing it, select by vote the material best suited for informal dramatization.
2 Impersonate the characters of the stories you have selected. See how quickly and completely you can change from one to another in characteristic voice, action, and language.
3 Walk across the stage as each of the following characters:

Autolycus, from *The Winter's Tale*
Silas Marner, from *Silas Marner*
Shylock, from *The Merchant of Venice*
Long John, from *Treasure Island*
David Balfour, from *Kidnapped*
Sydney Carton, from *A Tale of Two Cities*
Scrooge, from *A Christmas Carol*
Roderick, from *The Lady of the Lake*
Elaine, from *Idylls of the King*
Father Felician, from *Evangeline*
Ichabod Crane, from *The Sketch-Book*
Rebecca, from *Ivanhoe*
Red Queen from *Alice's Adventures in Wonderland*
Huck Finn, from *The Adventures of Huckleberry Finn*
Nokomis, from *The Song of Hiawatha*
Bottom, from *A Midsummer-Night's Dream*
Joan of Arc, from *Saint Joan*
Mrs. Wiggs, from *Mrs. Wiggs of the Cabbage Patch*

4 Speak in the characteristic voices of each of the characters in **3**.
5 Give informal dramatizations of some of the following:
Pyramus and Thisbe, from *A Midsummer-Night's Dream*

The courtroom scene, from *The Merchant of Venice*
Huck Finn and the Duke on the raft, from *Huckleberry Finn*
Christian and Hopeful in the dungeon, from *The Pilgrim's Progress*
The rescue of the sheep, from *Lorna Doone*
The finding of Friday, from *Robinson Crusoe*
"The Death of the Hired Man," Robert Frost
"Michael," William Wordsworth
Scenes from *Evangeline*, Henry Wadsworth Longfellow
Scenes from *The Princess*, Alfred, Lord Tennyson
"The Vision of Sir Launfal," James Russell Lowell
"The Dauber," John Masefield
"The Eve of St. Agnes," John Keats
"Tam O'Shanter," Robert Burns

6 Prepare a critic's score card to help you in criticizing informal dramatic productions.

7 Prepare a notebook on famous characters from literature. Use your originality in making the people live for the reader.

8 Impersonate characters from plays and have your classmates identify the characters.

9 Collect interesting, character-revealing dialogue from literature.

10 Collect accurate descriptions of scenes and characters from literature.

11 Dramatize a story from the Bible. The following suggestions may be helpful:

    The story of Moses   The story of Haman
    The story of Esther   The story of Naboth's vineyard
    The Christmas story   The story of Gehazi

12 Make a dramatization of one of the following:
Pride and Prejudice, Jane Austen
Kenilworth, Sir Walter Scott
Henry Esmond, William Makepeace Thackeray
Les Misérables, Victor Hugo
The House of Seven Gables, Nathaniel Hawthorne
The Pilgrim's Progress, John Bunyan
A Christmas Carol, Charles Dickens
The Moonstone, Wilkie Collins

A Man for the Ages, Irving Bacheller
The Adventures of Tom Sawyer, Mark Twain
The Three Musketeers, Alexander Dumas
Jane Eyre, Charlotte Brontë
Don Quixote, Miguel de Cervantes
Alice's Adventures in Wonderland, Lewis Carroll
Vanity Fair, William Makepeace Thackeray
" The Ransom of Red Chief," O. Henry
" Little Brother," Madeleine Z. Doty
" Wee Willie Winkie," Rudyard Kipling
" How Mr. Rabbit Was Too Sharp for Mr. Fox," Joel Chandler Harris
" Little Kaintuck," Margaret P. Montague
" A Parable for Fathers," Julia F. Wood
" A Bird out of the Snare," Dorothy Canfield
" The Devil and Tom Walker," Washington Irving

FORMAL DRAMATICS

13   Present a comedy scene from Shakespeare. Have all the actors assume the limit of awkward attitudes and postures, outlandish costumes, eccentric voices — squeaky, rough, guttural, and shrill. Let each participant devise a walk and manner of general carriage that suit his particular character.

14   Have each member of the class present some odd character. Let the exercise be particularly focused on the idea of acting all in one piece; plunge in fearlessly.

15   Invent characters and make up conversation to fit the following:
 a A high, shrill voice, and grasping hands
 b A Southern drawl, and very lazy motions
 c A tired, weak voice, lame joints, and sore feet
 d A musiclike lilt of voice, dancing, eager feet, and quick, restless hands
 e A rough growl, hardened muscles, and a slovenly gait
 f The firm, clear tone of perfect health, abounding spirits, and a well-poised body
 g The honeyed tones of insincere politeness and a manner that suggests an attempt to be overnice and too ingratiating

  h A bawling shout, a swagger, and an air of boastfulness
  i A hushed tone and an air of fear and awe

16 Invent dialogues between any two of the characters suggested in the preceding exercise. Many surprising and interesting results can be achieved.

17 Make up dialogues to fit the following characters and situations; act them out fully.

  a An agent is trying to sell a patent wall blackboard to a mother whose two children are looking on eagerly.
  b A foreman is " firing " a mill hand who has been caught stealing.
  c A local politician is trying to win the vote of a man who frankly says he doesn't believe in the politician's ability.
  d An Italian and a Negro are digging a ditch and discussing a proposed cut in wages.
  e A " society lady " is complaining to a ribbon clerk that he does not show her enough courtesy.

18 Following is a list of scenes from classic drama which furnish almost endless opportunity for training in the arts of dramatic presentation. The comments suggest the dramatic values for which each scene is serviceable as classwork.

The Merchant of Venice, Shakespeare
 Act I, sc. II: interpretation and impersonation
 Act I, sc. III: interpretation and impersonation
 Act II, sc. II: especially good for characterization
 Act III, sc. I: quick change of mood and feeling in impersonation
 Act III, sc. II: setting stage, balance, interaction of characters, interpretation — all stage values, in fact
 Act IV, sc. I: court scene; excellent for all dramatic values
 Act V, sc. I: setting, atmosphere, dialogue in the finest strain of " high " comedy

Julius Caesar, Shakespeare
 Act I, sc. II: balancing numerous characters, handling of full stage, superior interpretation and characterization
 Act II, sc. I: characterization, balancing a full stage
 Act III, sc. I: elaborate problem in balancing stage and shifting the stage picture

COMPREHENSION AND APPLICATION TESTS 345

Act III, sc. II: mob scene, Antony's speech; study of stage interaction and balance

Act IV, sc. III: the famous quarrel scene between Brutus and Cassius; also the appearance of Caesar's ghost. Excellent for many values

Macbeth, Shakespeare

Act I, sc. III: the witches' caldron; characterization, atmosphere, excellent chance for careful interpretation

Act I, sc. V: interpretation of Lady Macbeth's thoughts

Act I, sc. VII: interpretation

Act II, sc. I–II: murder scene; very difficult, but the height of great drama

Act III, sc. IV: banquet scene; excellent problem in setting, interaction of characters, crossings, balance

Act V, sc. I: sleepwalking scene; interpretation and setting, stirring action

A Midsummer-Night's Dream, Shakespeare

Act I, sc. I: dialogue, stage balance

Act I, sc. II: excellent study of clowning; impersonation

Act II, sc. I: impersonation of fairies, interpretative value in superior poetry; delicacy in interpretation and acting

Act III, sc. I: mingling of clowns and fairies, excellent study in contrasts

Act III, sc. II: elaborate, difficult, but worth trying

Act V, sc. I: mingling of high and low comedy; needs good acting

The Rivals, Sheridan

Act I, sc. II: excellent character delineation; interpretation

Act III, sc. I: excellent dialogue

Act III, sc. III: characterization, action

Act IV, sc. I: intricate; many stage values

Act V, sc. III: the famous duel scene, offering all dramatic values

She Stoops to Conquer, Goldsmith

Act I, sc. II: character study

Act II, sc. II: character study; excellent comedy of interpretation

Act III, sc. I: complicated action; excellent characterization

Act IV, sc. I: all dramatic values

CHAPTER THIRTEEN *Public Speaking*

WE HAVE BEEN preparing and practicing speech in human relationships in and out of high school. We have learned how to get and hold the attention of others in conversation, classroom speaking, storytelling, reading, and drama. Now we are approaching a new speech activity, public speaking. Most of us have already made a good many public speeches. All of us have made some, and as time goes on the number we will be called upon to make will increase.

Almost every day in our classes, teachers and students make expository speeches — speeches which give information. We make campaign speeches during an election campaign. We deliver speeches to get contributions, or to make sales. Commemorative speeches such as eulogies, inaugurals, and those at dedications and anniversaries are common in connection with school organizations. Speeches of introduction, welcome, farewell, presentation, acceptance, and response are delivered at special school assemblies. After-dinner speeches are the main feature of school banquets. In some respects the most challenging speech of all is the contest oration prepared by students who have a special interest in public speaking and messages of importance to give to the public. Every public speech, no matter what its type, should be presented for a definite purpose on a specific occasion. Therefore both purpose and occasion must be considered in deciding what we are going to say and how we are going to say it.

STEPS IN PREPARING A SPEECH

Consider the occasion. Suppose we have been asked to make a public speech, that no subject has been assigned, and that we are ready to begin our preparation. What shall we do first? Would it not be sensible to start by asking and answering some of the following questions?

What is the reason for the meeting?
Who are to be in the audience?

Are there other speakers on the program?
How much time has been assigned to me?

Determine the purpose. On the basis of our answers to such self-questioning, we should find ourselves in a position to choose a subject and to make a one-sentence statement of our purpose or objective; that is, to determine just what response we expect from our audience as a result of what we say.

Do we desire to entertain our audience?
Do we wish to impress them?
Do we hope to explain something so that they may understand it clearly?
Is our intention to make them believe something?
Do we hope to persuade them to act in some specific way?

True, we may seek any combination of these five kinds of responses; but in every speech we should have one dominant purpose to which the others will be subordinate and contributory. The purposes of all speeches can be classified under one of five aims: entertainment, impressiveness, instruction, belief, and action.

Phrase the topic sentence. After deciding on the general aim, the next step is to decide what particular subject or phase of the subject we shall discuss. We can do this most effectively by phrasing a good topic sentence.

Such a topic sentence:
1. Is declarative in form.
2. Commits us to a definite stand.
3. Is unmistakable in aim and direction.
4. Shows us how to subdivide the subject.
5. Keeps us from scattering our fire.
6. Is the very essence of keen and accurate thinking.

To illustrate, let us take a subject and a general purpose and arrange a number of topics derived from it:

General purpose: to inform
   Subject: Dolls

Now we proceed to construct possible topic sentences.
   "Following these directions we can make paper dolls."
                              or
   "Following these directions we can collect foreign dolls."

or

"Following these directions we can make acting dolls."

or

"Following these directions we can rejuvenate worn-out dolls." Many other variations are possible, all of them clear, direct, and specific. With the topic sentence formulated, we are in a position to begin our speech.

It is important to note the difference between a subject and a topic sentence. A subject may be compared to a broad area in which we are looking for a certain house, field, or building; the topic sentence indicates clearly just what we are seeking. The topic sentence commits us to a definite attitude on our subject. Before we begin to prepare our speech, we must make sure that we have not merely a subject, but also a topic sentence — one limited enough so that our speech will be directed to a definite end. The person who is preparing a speech cannot be sure where he is going unless he can put his purpose into a definite declarative topic sentence, with a subject, a predicate, and whatever modifiers are needed. If we are not ready to do this, our thinking is hazy. We never shoot ducks by banging away at the whole flock or the wide sky. We pull the trigger when the bird is in line with the gun sights. In terms of preparing to make a speech, this means: Use a topic sentence to get your sights on the target and reserve your fire until you are prepared to make a bull's-eye.

Get worth-while subject matter. After we have phrased our topic sentence, we must assemble some worth-while subject matter. Whatever material we gather will fall into one of two classes: facts or opinions. If we are using facts and opinions to accomplish our purpose, we will have to make sure that our listeners will accept as authoritative the sources from which we quote, and that they will consider our arguments valid.

There are four methods of getting worth-while material for a speech: thinking, observing, questioning, and reading. The resourceful speaker uses all of them, to avoid audience comments like "Old stuff," "I knew all that," "Not one new idea."

First let us take time to recall everything that we know about the subject we plan to discuss. We may begin by organizing that material as well as we can. We want to be sure that it is crystal-clear to us.

When we really remember what we know, we are often surprised at how well informed we are. This procedure will also help us to discover on what phases of the topic we need more information.

Let us look around. It is not necessary to get from others what we can observe for ourselves.

In questioning, letters and interviews are two good ways of getting information from authorities. Here we can make use of what we have learned about letter writing, and then turn ahead to Chapter Twenty for additional useful information.

Reading is the final method of getting worth-while material for speeches. We should all become familiar with our school library, and find out how to get what we want from magazines and books. Skill in the use of the card catalogue is important. Encyclopedias and dictionaries are invaluable as sources of information. Daily papers should not be neglected. Almost all the information that we fail to get through thinking, observing, and questioning we can get through wise reading.

Record what has been found. A good method for making a permanent record of the material we gather is to write it on 4" by 6" cards. Cards are superior to notebooks because they can be sorted and re-sorted to suit the particular needs of the user. The following is a sample:

Subject	Writer	Where found
Television	John T. Williams Television Dept. National Broadcasting Company	Quarterly Journal of Speech, Vol. XXX, No. 2, p. 136

Television as a public service in the United States became a fact on April 30, 1939, when Television Station WNBT, New York, owned and operated by the National Broadcasting Company, Inc., carried as its first program President Franklin D. Roosevelt's address opening the New York World's Fair.

Develop the topic sentence. There are many ways in which topic sentences may be amplified, supported, and developed. The following examples will illustrate seven methods: narration, description, illustration, argument, statistics, authority, and personal experience.[1]

Narration: Amid the bleak foothills of Scotland before a corps of soldiers stands a group of condemned Christians. They are ruthlessly led to the funeral pyre — the torch is applied. But as their blazing bodies are silhouetted against the crimson sky a song is heard above the crackle of the flames. It is the battle hymn of a coming republic. As the "blood of the martyrs has ever been the seed of the Church," so forth from the Old World come the survivors of this oppressed people to found a new home and a free nation on American soil.

In that very century in the Royal Gardens at Fontainebleau we find Louis XIV, his soul fear-stricken because of the havoc he has wrought and the blood with which his hands are stained. He sees now the handwriting on the wall and, in the shadow, the white specter of waiting death. A priest whispers in his ear that there is yet a way to win eternal salvation. Louis feverishly clutches at escape and with trembling hands revokes the Edict of Nantes. France is then plunged into such a carnage of blood as the world has seldom known. Men are crucified until there cannot be found wood enough for crosses. As a result of this cowardly persecution 200,000 of the noblest sons of France push off from the shores of their beloved motherland to seek the land of liberty — America. — *Frank S. Hodge,* "Is America Safe?"

Description: Look at the Pacific Ocean as pictured by a writer in a recent issue of the *Survey*. It has become a mere pond, dividing two different cultures and races. On one side are nations with teeming populations; on the other, vast areas of relatively vacant territory. One rim shelters the oldest and the most stable of living civilizations; the other the most recent and the most progressive. On one side lives a race which feels itself superior and destined to lead and dominate the world; on the other lives another race which is smarting under a sense of wrong and injustice, and is becoming more determined not to accept the brand of inferiority without a decisive demonstration.

[1] From Winston H. Ashley, ed., *Fifty Orations That Have Won Prizes,* Noble and Noble, New York. Reprinted by permission.

The shadow of misunderstanding darkens both shores, and the dreaded race conflict seems to threaten. — *Glenn Ginn*, " The Yellow Peril "

Illustration: Ladies and gentlemen: A few years ago a newspaper account of crime was unusual — a phenomenon to pique one's curiosity. But times have changed. Every front page emphasizes the fact. *Night before last* four-inch headlines proclaimed the daring robbery of a Portland church. *Last night* the *Capital Journal* was aflame with the gruesome massacre of a whole family. *Tonight* it is bandits bombing an armored car. And even as I speak to you, criminals throughout this country are furnishing new sensations for *tomorrow's* headlines. These newspaper accounts are indicative of a general situation which exists throughout our society.

These youthful lawbreakers, like all criminals, are most common in the larger cities. They are not isolated unfortunates, as one might expect; but as a rule are deliberately organized gangs. Four such gangs engaged in systematic robbery were apprehended by the police of Portland in a single night! And only last night just such a gang plundered the gymnasium here at Willamette University! A few weeks ago in Chicago nine such boys ranging from fourteen to nineteen years of age were found guilty of deliberate robbery and murder. When the prosecution demanded the death penalty, the youthful defendants snickered in derision! These boy criminals increase steadily in number. During the year ending June 1926, there were in New York eleven thousand of them committed to the county and city courts alone! A nine-year-old automobile thief expressed his defiance of law — " I ain't afraid of no cops! I ain't afraid of nuthin'! " — *R. S. Griffin*, " The Strange Drama "

Argument: We accept Mr. Tillman's assertion that the Negro is not the equal of the white. It is not remarkable that the white race, with centuries of development in an environment of freedom, has risen superior to a race whose only inheritance is ignorance and oppression. But is the Negro capable of acquiring a culture equal to that of the white? Remember, yesterday the Negro was a chattel in the market, beaten by lashes and bound by chains, the child of hopeless, unrewarded toil. In him ambition was an evil, education a crime; every faculty of his mind and soul was rigidly suppressed. Today the world is moved by the pathos of Dunbar; it thrills with the powerful fiction of Chesnutt and Dumas; it listens, entranced, to the rhythmic cadences of Coleridge Taylor; it praises the superior generalship of Toussaint L'Ouverture; it applauds the forceful energy and sterling character of Bowen, Vernon, Gaines, Du Bois, and it thunders with enthusiasm before the inspiring eloquence of Bruce, Douglas, Mason, and Booker Washington. The genius of these individuals is the gift of God to black men — men whose stupendous labors have been performed with hands marked by manacles and scarred by chains. We point to their achievements as indications of the cultural possibilities of the race. — *Henry F. Coleman,* " The Philosophy of the Race Problem "

Statistics: The new constitution provided that all land in Mexico belonged inherently to the people and that all subsoil rights belonged to the sovereign state of Mexico. Under this constitution, the petroleum law was passed in 1925, which declared that the owners of petroleum properties should apply for fifty-year exploitation leases. Now at the time when the property was being taken away from the villagers and sold into the large estates, the "Belshazzars" of the American oil companies were busy at the feast. Of the 824 large estates which were created, 127 were owned by American petroleum companies. When the new petroleum law was passed, 126 American companies immediately conformed with it and transferred their titles for fifty-year exploitation leases. But 21 companies chose to defy the laws of Mexico and even the sovereignty of Mexico itself. The leaders among the rebel companies were those of Harry F. Sinclair and Edward L. Doheny, both notorious names to the American public. If we resent Sinclair and Doheny in the Teapot Dome affair, imagine what must be the sentiment of Mexico — for hers seems not to be a teapot but a modern percolator. Why do these men refuse to exchange their titles for exploitation leases? During the creation of the large estates, most of the Doheny and Sinclair properties were acquired in escrow, pending confirmation of the title, which has never taken place. Like the Teapot episode, the pivot of the whole difficulty is dubious Doheny and Sinclair titles. They fear that the Mexican Government would refuse to recognize their dubious titles if they applied for leases. Rather than run this risk, they chose to defy the petroleum laws of Mexico. — *Alfred A. Klitz*, " America Goes Abroad "

Authority: Is it not high time that we rid ourselves of this moth-eaten legal apparel, which has proved itself to be such a failure? A comparison of our crime records with those of England points to a decided superiority in English criminal jurisprudence. Should we not therefore accept a system which has proved to be so successful? The answer comes to us from the pen of William Burdick, professor of law at the University of Kansas; from Roscoe Pound, dean of the Harvard Law School; from Elihu Root and Chief Justice Taft; and finally from the American Bar Association. We must bring our criminal court procedure up to date; we must take from the English system, or any other system, anything which will aid us and fit our needs. — *Lyman S. Judson*, " Crime and the Criminal Court "

Personal experience: This is a homecoming. It hardly seems an occasion for a lengthy political speech — rather it is an opportunity to recall old associations and renew old friendships.

I am glad, a son of Iowa, to come back to the place where I was born. Here I spent the first ten years of my boyhood. Here my parents and my grandparents toiled, worshiped God, did their part in building this community, and now lie in the cemetery over the hill.

During forty-four years I have returned from time to time that I might pay respect to their memory, that I might express my appreciation of those kindly and sympathetic folk who, taking a boy to their hearts, wiped away the one grief of childhood. One of my vivid recollections was my earnest interest in the debate between neighbors and relatives when they were discussing not who was to assume me as a burden, but who was to take the boy as member of their own flock. That is the spirit of the people of Iowa. It is the spirit of the thousands of villages and towns in all this wide land.

And I have no apology for even a more personal note. There is present here today a lady who took part in that debate and who was for years my teacher in our public school. She embodies the spirit of that vast body of women who not only teach and inspire our children but watch over their widest destinies. You have come to do me courtesy as a son of Iowa. I take this occasion to acknowledge my debt to that lady — Mrs. Curran.

There is no imprint upon our minds so deep as those of early boyhood. Mine are the joys of Iowa — the glories of snowy winter, the wonder at the growing crops, the joining of the neighbors to harvest, the gathering of apples, the pilgrimage to the river woods for the annual fuel and nuts, the going to school, the interludes from work, in the swimming hole, fishing in creeks, the hunting for prairie chickens and rabbits in the hedges and woods. It is the entry to life which I could wish for every American boy and girl.

Again, today, I have had refreshment of spirit in return to these scenes. The swimming hole still is in use. It has the same mudbank. It still is impossible to dress without carrying mud home in one's inner garments. As an engineer I could devise improvements for that swimming hole. But I doubt if the decrease in Mother's grief at the homecoming of muddy boys would compensate the inherent joys of getting muddy.

I have been to see the old Quaker meetinghouse. It has been moved across the street and replaced by a more modern structure. The old building appears at some time to have been turned into a moving-picture house, which reminds me of the time I heard Aunt Hannah, moved in meeting, bitterly denounce the rise of modern ways and prophesy that if they were persisted in, that edifice dedicated to God would some day be transformed into a place of abomination. I do not place the movies in that class, but knowing Aunt Hannah's views on any form of human recreation, even to the Godlessness of sliding downhill, I suspect that if she knew of this she would get great satisfaction at the consummation of her warnings.

This always was a Republican village. It was here that I received my first touch of national life. I well recollect the hoisting of the flag at half-mast over my father's blacksmith shop on the assassination of President Garfield. I also recollect well the torchlight procession in the Garfield election. I was not high enough to be permitted the conduct of a torch, but I participated by walking alongside for miles. At that time there were two or three Democrats in the town. I do not know today whether what seemed to me an enormous torchlight parade was instituted for their conversion or not, but I believe it was hopeless, because one of my boyhood friends and opponents in battle, who I expect is in this audience today, is a descendant of one of those Democrats and has been regenerated only in the last month.

I am proud to have been born in Iowa. I have ofttimes said that the good Lord made it the richest stretch of agricultural land that ever blessed any one sovereign government. It was settled by the adventurous, the courageous, who fought their way across the ever extending frontier. They have builded here in so short a period as seventy-five years a state with the least poverty, the highest average intelligence, the most generous education, which ever blessed a single commonwealth. —*Herbert Hoover*, speaking at his birthplace, West Branch, Iowa, August 22, 1928

Adapt material to audience attitudes. In deciding upon devices and means for the development of topic sentences or propositions, it is of prime importance to know what attitude our audience will probably take toward our ideas and purposes. There are three typical attitudes: (1) friendly or favorable, (2) hesitant, doubtful, neutral, or indifferent, and (3) antagonistic or hostile. The rule is: Study the audience and decide whether they believe as we do, are in doubt, or are against us. Once we have reached a decision on this point, we may discover things to do, and other things not to do.

When the attitude of the audience is favorable, it is wise to stress ideas the audience likes to hear, especially old beliefs, familiar pictures, and well-beloved quotations. When the attitude of the audience is doubtful, we should rely more heavily on logic and authority. When the attitude is antagonistic, we can usually get the support of the audience by proceeding tactfully from the known to the unknown and from the accepted to the unaccepted.

Examples of topic sentences of the kind audiences already accept or are willing to accept without argument are:

Old friends are best.
Man is the highest of animals.
Lincoln is the ideal American.
" Peace hath her victories no less renowned than war."

It is not useless to talk about a point just because the audience already believe it. If we listen to sermons, " pep " talks, political speeches, trade and business talks, we notice that a good half or more

SPEAKER WITH MICROPHONE. *This lady is addressing an audience which is shown in the picture on the opposite page. The microphone is not connected with a radio station but merely with a loudspeaker system in the auditorium. What changes in platform speaking have arisen from the introduction of public-address mechanisms? (Library of Congress)*

of their content is material which everybody already knows but still delights to hear spoken out in meeting. We all are like that, every one of us. We get a real "kick" out of hearing someone else utter ideas we have long accepted. Most of us would not find it hard to listen to someone telling us that we are wonderful fellows, that we live in a beautiful city, or that we attend a fine school. It is pleasant to hear all over again about the championship game our team won or about how we put a big deal across. It is just this sort of talk that makes up half of the conversation and the public speeches the world opens its ears to daily. And everybody succumbs to it, everybody!

THE AUDIENCE. *These people are listening to the speaker shown on the preceding page. With very few exceptions the members of this audience give evidence of creative listening to what the speaker is saying. Which members of the group are distracted by the photographer and are watching him instead of the speaker?* (Library of Congress)

To gain the interest of people when they already accept the topic sentence:

1. Illustrate with a suitable story.
2. Draw word pictures of nature and life: the out-of-doors, birds, animals, wind, trees, flowers.
3. Employ pictures and narratives of familiar scenes: home life, friendship, love, family affection, loyalty, success, victorious struggle.
4. Quote revered and accepted leaders, heroes, and books.

Here are examples of topic sentences that probably will need explanation and support before audiences will accept them:

Our minister should seek a new charge.
Taxes are going down next year.
The press is becoming too powerful.

ANOTHER AUDIENCE. *In what significant ways does this audience differ from that pictured on page 357? Is there any evidence of inattention here? Is the subject humorous or serious? Does the woman second from the left in the second row seem to be in agreement with what is being said? How about the woman directly behind her? Are there any expressions which might worry the speaker?* (James H. Stone)

    This school is ably managed (or badly managed).
    History books should be frank and unexpurgated.
    The price of corn is less than (or more than) it ought to be.
    The "movies" do more good than harm (or more harm than good).
    Armaments will lead to war.
    When the listeners want more facts before they can agree wholeheartedly with the speaker, it is necessary to be especially logical and coherent. For this type of situation:

1. Define terms accurately.
2. Classify ideas in orderly fashion.
3. Support generalizations with specific instances.

4. Argue from effect to cause; explain present situations by what has happened heretofore.

5. Quote good authorities and sound experts.

Examples of topic sentences that are likely to be opposed (always depending on the audience) by those named in parenthesis are:

Children should be allowed to do as they please. (By parents)

The loafer is the ideal citizen. (By industrious people)

Reading is a waste of time. (By teachers or citizens generally)

Saving money does little good. (By a serious-minded group)

You farmers are getting high enough prices. (By a grange or farm bureau)

Your wages are too high. (By workingmen)

Vacations need not be so long as they now are. (By a school assembly)

The present administration is a success (or failure). (By those at a political rally)

When the audience disapproves of our stand and is set to reject it, we will make little progress by painting word pictures or telling its members how wonderful they are; we do not gain by arguing against fixed opinions and feelings. Rather we should avoid direct collision by somehow disarming our opponents. The best way to do this is to make the audience like us personally. Get the listeners to do this and then if we are reasonable and honest, they will be more likely to believe what we say. After we have gained the confidence of the audience we can safely argue a little. Through argument, through narrative and descriptive excursions, and reliving old experiences, we may win the audience over to our point of view.

The following methods of developing points are helpful in dealing with audiences hostile to our topic sentence:

1. Go carefully from the known to the unknown.

2. Show learning, wit, keenness of observation in selecting and presenting facts.

3. Support the topic by quoting widely accepted authorities and experts; writers, poets, scholars, Presidents, Senators, church dignitaries.

4. Use statistics, government reports, textbooks.

5. Make good use of the occasion on which the speech takes place:

talk about the place, the audience, local happenings, other speakers, the presiding officer. Use compliments tactfully and honestly.

6. Indulge in witty deprecating remarks about yourself, your troubles, your embarrassments. Do it modestly, and with a sense of humor.

7. Use the art of storytelling to " break the ice " and to melt opposition.

Outlining. In preparing a speech, it is always expedient to make an outline. The speaker may or may not use this outline while he is delivering the speech, but it will aid him greatly to organize his material. It will help him to concentrate on the main point and it should prevent scattered thinking.

In using letters and numbers to designate headings, subheadings, and sub-subheadings, the rule is: Let the symbols consistently represent logical relations and values. Use the same kind of letters and numbers, capitals, and small letters, Roman and Arabic numerals, for ideas of the same relative importance in the outline. The following is the commonly accepted scheme; with main items closer to the margin than subitems:

  I. (Major item)
    A. (Subhead under I)
      1. (Subhead under A)
        a. (Subhead under 1)
        b. (Subhead under 1)
          (1) (Subhead under b)
            (a) (Subhead under (1))
            (b) (Subhead under (1))
          (2) (Subhead under b)
      2. (Subhead under A)
    B. (Subhead under I)
  II. (Major item)

Words, phrases, or sentences may be used as headings in outlining. Assume that we have the topic sentence " Americans believe strongly in education." This phrasing obviously is better than merely " Education " or " American education," which are not sentences. The complete sentence is more concrete and specific. With the general direction of our speech indicated, it is safe to fill out the outline in detail with words and phrases, provided our talk is to be short. For example: Americans believe strongly in education.

I. The common schools
    A. Number
    B. Cost
    C. Efficiency

II. The high schools
    A. Increase in number
    B. Equipment
    C. Social significance
    D. " The poor man's college "

III. Colleges and universities
    A. " Main Street has gone to college."
    B. Endowments
    C. State support
    D. Effects on the populace

Another example: Assume that we have the broad subject of American politics and have focused on this topic sentence, " The type of politician has changed in America." It may be safe to proceed then with these one-word markers and guides:

I. Webster   III. Cleveland   V. F. D. Roosevelt
II. Lincoln   IV. Wilson

Here the mere arrangement of names in the order desired helps make our thinking orderly and provides guides for developing the speech.

The sentence outline is the most effective aid to accurate thinking, because a sentence points in one direction, whereas a phrase permits us to wander off in any one of several directions. If we take the sentence " Improvements in our town are badly needed," we will be far more certain to follow a direct line of thought than if we speak on " Improvements in Our Town," " Local Improvements," or just " Improvements."

For a two-minute speech on local improvements we need the full declarative sentence to start with: " Many improvements are needed in our community." We will do well to subdivide this into two or more topic sentences, such as:

I. We need better paving.
   II. We need more adequate school buildings.
For a longer speech we may need ten or a dozen such sentences:
   I. Local improvements are always needed.
      A. At present more than the usual number of enterprises seem necessary.
         1. Certain dirt streets need to be paved.
         2. Considerable old paving needs repair.
         3. Two school buildings are unsafe and crowded.
         4. A third school should be supplanted entirely.
   II. The objections to this program should not be regarded too seriously.
      A. While it is natural, of course, to object to any plan which will raise the taxes, the rewards to the community will repay the expense.
      B. This program will place us on an equality with other near-by communities.

The introduction and the conclusion. A speech usually is made up of an introduction, a body, and a conclusion. Because what is said first and what is said last are more likely to be remembered than what is in the middle of a speech, let us turn our attention to the opening and close of a speech.

What is the purpose of the introduction?

1. It should make the audience favorably disposed toward the speaker.

2. It should direct the attention and understanding of the audience to the subject.

These purposes may be accomplished in a number of different ways. We may be able to achieve them with a clever story; an apt illustration from life or literature; a startling fact; a reference to the place, the audience, the speaker; or by bodily action, gesture, and facial expression. Whatever method or combination of methods we use, we must make our listeners eager to hear us on the particular subject we have chosen to discuss.

In a speech delivered at the Green Pastures Rally, Charlotte, North Carolina, September 10, 1936, just after a thunderstorm had subsided and a rainbow had appeared in the sky, Franklin Delano Roosevelt combined a startling fact; references to place, audience, speaker; and an apt illustration from literature in the following introduction. The general topic sentence is: " Your life and mine, though we work in the mill, the office, or the store, can still be a life in green pastures and beside still waters."

" I notice that the rainbow shines in the sky; and it is a fitting climax to two of the most delightful days I have ever spent in my life.

" I am grateful, Governor Ehringhaus, for your hospitality; and may I, through you, thank the people of the Old North State for the welcome that they have given me?

" I am told that this is a Green Pastures meeting. And the showers that we have passed through today prove that the pastures of North Carolina are green.

" Green pastures! What a memory those words call forth! In all our schooling, in every part of the land, no matter to what church we happen to belong, the old Twenty-third Psalm is in all probability better known to men, women, and children than any other poem in the English language.

" And in this great lyric, what do we best remember? Two lines:

> ' He maketh me to lie down in green pastures;
> He leadeth me beside the still waters.'

" It does not greatly matter whether that symbol of an ideal of human physical and spiritual happiness was written in its original three thousand or five thousand or ten thousand years ago. It might have been written as well in the twentieth century of the Christian era.

" Have you ever stopped to think that happiness is most often described in terms of the simple ways of nature rather than in the complex ways of man's fabrications? Perhaps it is because peace is necessary to ultimate happiness. Perhaps therefore, when we seek a symbol of happiness, we do not go to the rush of crowded city streets or to the hum of machinery to find the simile."

The conclusion to a speech is important because it plays a large part in determining whether the listeners will remember what the speaker wants them to remember. In a good conclusion the central idea of the speech is left vividly with the audience. The method may be a summary, a comparison, or an apt quotation. The conclusion is successful if after the speaker has finished the members of the audience are thinking of the heart of the speaker's message.

President Roosevelt closed his address at the Green Pastures Rally with the following paragraph:

"I speak to you today as common-sense American men and women. You will agree that from the material aspect, based on the sound concept of restoring purchasing power and prosperity to the great mass of our citizens, this nation's consuming power has been and is being rapidly restored. I trust, therefore, that you will likewise agree that better conditions on the farms, better conditions in the factories, better conditions in the homes of America, are leading us to that beautiful spiritual figure of the old psalmist — green pastures and still waters."

TYPES OF SPEECHES

In learning how to organize materials for public speaking, it may be helpful to classify speeches according to the specific kinds of occasions they are designed to serve.

Speeches of courtesy. Speeches of introduction, presentation, welcome, farewell, and response are almost invariably made before audiences distinctly friendly to the speaker and ready to agree with his topic sentence. The more closely a speech of courtesy is connected with the occasion out of which it grows, the better it is. Such speeches should embody the following types of material:

1. Narratives
2. Descriptions
3. Personal recollections
4. Personal feelings and attitudes
5. Discussion of mutual interests and relations
6. Quotations from literature
7. Accepted beliefs and convictions: religious, patriotic, civil, moral

If we select from these judiciously, we probably will not bore our audiences. If we arrange our ideas well and speak them skillfully, we should make a successful speech.

Mark Twain once said that the purpose of a *speech of introduction* is to give the speaker "a good unbiased start before an audience."

Speeches of introduction are best when they bring the person introduced to his feet feeling comfortable and glad to be present, and when they stimulate the interest and friendliness of the audience. The besetting temptation in introducing a speaker is to say too much; the occasion belongs to the main speaker, not to the introducer. Introductions should never so overstate the virtues or abilities of the speaker as to embarrass him. While it is permissible and proper to say that the speaker's subject is one which he has special qualifications for discussing, in no circumstances should the introducer himself enter into the subject at length.

The purpose of a *speech of presentation* is to bestow some token upon an individual or organization gracefully and graciously. The speaker should beware of attempting to steal the occasion for himself. Good taste should restrain him from overdoing his praise of the person or group to whom he is presenting the gift. Such a speech may contain:

1. A statement of the reasons for the presentation
2. Some description of the gift and the reasons for selecting it
3. A well-phrased tribute to the recipient of the gift

In speeches of presentation the main points to be made and amplified are already known and approved by the audience. They are expressed in topic sentences like these:

This gift represents our loyalty, affection, faith. (Describe.)

With this award goes a responsibility; we know you will carry it successfully. (Explain.)

The history and origin of this gift is a stimulating story. (Recite it.)

There are vital principles suggested by this object. (Specify them.)

When I look at this I am reminded of (narratives, personages, events, ideas, and ideals). (Recite names, picture, explain.)

This is an unworthy token of our true esteem. (Show how great the esteem is and why.)

May this serve to strengthen the bond between you and us. (Picture what this bond is and means.)

Let me tell you where this came from. (Tell.)

You have done well, and richly deserve all we can give you. (Show what the good deeds were and what we can give.)

We delight to offer this recognition of your services. (Picture the services.)

The *speech of welcome* should do for the public guest precisely what a cordial and genuine informal greeting does for the private guest. It should be manufactured out of such materials as the following:

1. A well-constructed but moderate tribute to the person or persons being welcomed.
2. References to the significance of the occasion.
3. An explanation of the nature and purposes of the organization in whose behalf the welcome is being extended.

Suppose that at the commencement exercises the principal gives a talk about the graduating class, its members, and their record of service to the school. It then devolves upon some representative of the class to deliver *the valedictory (farewell) address*. Or, it may be that the minister of the church has accepted a call elsewhere and, at a congregational meeting, makes a farewell speech. Usually, brevity is the distinguishing mark of excellence on such occasions, although extraordinary conditions may sometimes justify more extended remarks. The all-important consideration is that what is said and the manner of its saying should be appropriate to the special occasion. In a farewell speech we may:

1. Say all the complimentary things that can be said with honesty and sincerity about those who are leaving (or who are remaining behind).
2. Be a bit sentimental about the occasion and its significance.
3. Take a hopeful look into the future and predict a happy reunion.

Speeches of response usually serve either: (1) to acknowledge a greeting such as may have been expressed in a speech of welcome or (2) to accept some gift or token which may have been the subject of a speech of presentation. The keynote of a response should be appreciation. Speeches of response resemble speeches of presentation and welcome, and are to be developed in the same mood. Such topic sentences as these are helpful:

I accept this gift (award) with a feeling of responsibility. (Describe the feeling.)

This occasion awakens in me many memories. (Tell of them.)

The honor this carries brings a determination to live up to it. (What I will do.)

Others deserve this honor with me. (Tell about the others.)

Speeches on special occasions. The *eulogy* is a speech of personal tribute usually in praise of someone no longer living. Eulogies are of two general types: (1) the biographical, or chronological, in which the events of the subject's life are arranged in time sequence, and (2) the topical, in which the major aspects of the subject's career are stressed in a logical rather than in a time order. Usually the second type is superior to the first.

In eulogies, the chief necessity is to say things people like to hear. Accordingly there should be little arguing or going against the current of opinion. Such topics as these are the right kind to use:

Many incidents in his life show his character. (Recite them.)

Here we have an example for others to follow. (Explain; tell who may follow.)

This life was spent in heroic days. (Narrate it.)

Such a life teaches many lessons. (Indicate and picture them.)

One incident shows his whole character. (Recite it and tell why.)

He was a devoted friend. (Illustrate.)

Having known such a man we can do our work better. (Tell why.)

The *nominating speech* is closely related to the eulogy; the main difference is that it is likely to contain a good deal of controversial material, which the eulogy carefully avoids. Some nomination speeches are made where there is no opposition. In such situations, we should select and express the pleasant points which make our candidate look good to the voters. But where there is a struggle among candidates, it may be necessary to plan a speech which is:

1. Very strict as to facts
2. Diplomatic, tactful, and courteous
3. Graceful and kindly
4. Orderly and sensible
5. Careful of language
6. Not too heavy or solemn

Speeches of inauguration are best when they subordinate the speaker and his office to the society he represents, its needs, its policies, and its principles. An inauguration gives a newly appointed leader a chance to review the activities of the society, to outline the program of duties and projects, or to present and develop some principles or policies. The materials are usually:

1. Outlines of policies and plans
2. Definitions of what the society stands for
3. Predictions of various happenings or conditions
4. Explanations of past events and situations

After-dinner speeches. The best type of after-dinner speaking is the treatment of a sensible idea in a vein just as light as our wit can manage. We should be as funny as we can, but have a worth-while idea; we let the fun carry the idea. One of the best after-dinner speakers in the United States, when asked for the formula of his never-failing success, gave it as " a narrative, a bit of verse, a sentiment." What he meant was that he had a good story or two, some poetry to support his point, and a serious idea behind it all.

Contest orations. Writing a speech for a contest calls for a special procedure. The speech is to be written out ahead of time, constructed and worded with great care, and then committed to memory.

Here are some suggestions that apply to the writing of contest speeches:

1. Choose a timely subject.
2. Select a subject which offers a chance for an appeal to emotions.
3. Take the constructive rather than the destructive side.
4. Give a good analysis of the origin of the problem and its present status.
5. Present your solution as persuasively as possible.

METHODS OF DELIVERING SPEECHES

What are the possible ways of presenting a speech effectively? There are five common methods:

1. Impromptu
2. Extempore
3. Memoriter (reading from memory)
4. Reading from manuscript
5. A composite method

Impromptu delivery. Most speaking — daily conversation, and a great deal of classroom discussion — is necessarily impromptu. Impromptu speaking is the kind that is given no special preparation; the speaker talks offhand as well as he can. In a way it is the most dangerous kind of speaking; it looks so easy and yet can be done well by so few. In a real sense, the impromptu method is not a method at all; it is simply the only way out when a speaker has no opportunity to choose another method.

The impromptu "method" is to be used only when we know thoroughly what we are going to talk about. If we have just come in from a football game, we probably can give an interesting account on the spur of the moment, for we are full of the subject. We may ramble and backtrack and sidestep and fumble and get out of bounds; yet we can tell what has happened. Or perhaps our teacher chances to know that we are putting an old Ford together and asks us to talk about it. Again we "know our stuff," and therefore are ready to discuss the subject intelligently. In other words, impromptu speaking can be successful when it presents the ideas of a person who is an expert on the subject he is talking about. For example, an expert at assembling an old Ford, an expert at making fried cakes, or an expert at directing motor traffic knows his specialty well enough to speak about it without formal preparation.

Extempore delivery. "Extempore" comes from Latin words meaning "from the time," "on the spur of the moment." Some people use "extempore" synonymously with "impromptu," but modern practice makes a very definite distinction between the two. "Impromptu" means "without preparation." "Extempore" implies that we have made careful, definite, and special preparation for this particular speech. We have read carefully, studied sensibly, and organized our material skillfully before we stand up to speak. We have known for some time what we were going to talk about and have done what we can to be ready. We have not prepared our speech word for word, but we know what we are going to say — how we are going to start, how we intend to continue, and how we expect to close. Everything is ready but the wording, and we provide that as we go along. In a way this is the hardest kind of speaking, but it is usually the most effective. Lively people can often choose words more appropriately and speak better sentences when they stand face to face with an audience than when they are at their desks. A facile speaker is one who gets his brightest inspirations right in the process of speaking. The extempore method gives us a chance to react to what we see while studying our audience. When we are looking at our audience and observing their moods, we are in a much better position to get into close communication with them.

Memorized delivery. The speech which is committed to memory is fairly common, but the method should be used with caution. In the first place, it is not really a speech; it is a reading from memory. The memorized speech is likely to be dull, stiff, or high-flown. As with other reading, before it can be delivered effectively it must be thoroughly understood and felt. Yet many who deliver memorized speeches merely pronounce the words without realizing and feeling what they say.

On formal occasions, the memorized speech may be useful. If the speaker can keep the thought and the language vital and communicative, then speaking from memory is all right. In fact, it has this advantage, that we can be sure of just what we say. It is most valuable when the speaker finds it necessary to be extremely accurate in his facts and language; when he cannot afford to take the chances involved in the impromptu or the extempore method.

Probably the commonest use of the memoriter method for high-school students is in the oratorical contest. This type of speech teaches boys and girls to be careful of language, to build up ideas skillfully and effectively, and to make the written page sound sensible and alive. The same general purposes may be served by declaiming speeches of Webster, Lincoln, or Bryan. The advantage of the oratorical contest over the declamation contest is that we write the orations ourselves.

Reading from manuscript. This is both the easiest and the hardest manner of presenting a speech. It is the easiest because all we have to do is to read the words without any effort at finding them except with our eyes, the hardest because most readers are tempted to do nothing more than find the words with their eyes and say them with their mouths. But audiences cannot be interested this way; they have to feel that the speaker is alive, awake, and caring about what he says. Probably more dull speeches are made by reading from manuscript than by the other three methods combined. Even men who are lively enough as impromptu or extempore speakers slump down into grade-school habits of reading when they try to read a report, a poem, or a written speech. But there are occasions when reading from manuscript is the best method. If we decide to read from manuscript, we must take special pains to see that our mind is centering actively on the meaning, and that voice and action are as lively as they would be in conversation. We must not forget to look at the audience often.

A composite method of delivery. No one of these methods is ideal for all occasions. In choosing which one we are to use, much depends on the particular conditions under which we are to speak. Sometimes we will be called suddenly to our feet and asked to express our opinions on a matter which has not been uppermost in our minds, and our speech will have to be impromptu. If it is a matter that we have thought over rather carefully, it will be, in part, extempore. Again, in preparing definitely for extempore delivery, we may find it advisable to prepare carefully beforehand some of our sentences word for word just the way we want to give them. Accordingly we will either memorize these sentences or else write them out to be read from the page. This is a very common practice in debating. Good debaters prepare their points, know what they are going to say, and have some of the language in mind ahead of time. They have to deal with many ideas that they must express exactly: quotations, figures, and, most important of all, the repetition of what their opponents have said. Therefore they find it advisable to read certain statements from cards. Even skilled impromptu speakers, when suddenly called to their feet, are likely to break forth into memorized quotations or to fish something from their pockets and read it.

It is obvious that the ideal method is to employ whichever of these techniques best suits the special occasion. It is well to confine our impromptu remarks to matters in which we are expert. When we propose to speak extempore, let us be sure that we have had adequate preparation. When we recite from memory, let us be sure that we give a good interpretation. When we read from manuscript, let us be as wide-awake and lively as we are when speaking impromptu or extempore.

Tests of Comprehension and Application

1   Test your ability to recognize speaking purposes and state topic sentences.
    a   Which one of the five general purposes of speeches seems most appropriate for each of the following topic sentences?
        1. The Pilgrims were a brave courageous people.
        2. You should vote for John Smith for senior president.
        3. Superintendent Rowe has made a great contribution to the schools of Valley City.
        4. These adventures are unusual and interesting.
        5. Every student should attend the all-school play.
        6. These suggestions will show you how to build a boat.
        7. I will give an accurate description of Niagara Falls.
        8. The colonists suffered in Jamestown in 1607.
        9. You can help to prevent forest fires.
    b   In which sentences under a do you think the general ends or purposes were not clear? Show why you selected the one you did.
    c   Phrase a topic sentence for each of the following:

COMPREHENSION AND APPLICATION TESTS

1. When the general purpose is to entertain and the general subject is "High-School Juniors."
2. When the general purpose is to persuade and the general subject is "High-School Publications."
3. When the general purpose is to convince and the general subject is "Presidents of the United States."
4. When the general purpose is to impress and the general subject is "Parents."
5. When the general purpose is to instruct and the general subject is "History."

   d Bring in a speech exemplifying each of the five general ends or purposes in public speaking.

   e Bring in one speech which accomplishes all of the five purposes, with one purpose predominating over the other four.

2 Test your ability to select worth-while material.

   a In the following, check those facts or opinions which you probably would accept in support of a topic sentence and those which you might refuse to accept.

1. Statistics from the *Encyclopaedia Britannica*.
2. Opinion of a faculty member who is opposed to reorganizing the curriculum, and who will lose his job if it is reorganized.
3. Opinion of a faculty member who is in favor of reorganizing the curriculum, in spite of the fact that he may lose his job if it is reorganized.
4. Opinion of a famous mathematics instructor on facts in mathematics.
5. Opinion of a famous mathematics instructor on facts in history.
6. Figures from the *World Almanac*.
7. The opinion of a student who has failed an examination in history, and contends that there was something wrong with the teaching methods.
8. The fact that every student failed the examination in history.
9. The opinion of the President of the United States on coffee recipes.
10. Dates from *Webster's New International Dictionary*, 2d ed.

b Bring to class three opinions that you would accept in support of a proposition and three that you would not accept.

c Select a good speech and evaluate the facts and opinions used to support the topic sentences.

d Name ten sources from which you would accept opinions as authoritative.

e In a five-minute speech discuss: acceptable sources, valid arguments, and well-informed authorities.

3 Test your ability to gather and record material.

a Using some phase of one of the following general subjects that is of interest to you, gather and record material by thinking, observing, questioning, and reading.

1. Gold
2. Clocks
3. Football
4. Drama
5. Russia
6. American cities
7. Cooking
8. Architecture
9. Forms of government
10. Ancient Greece
11. Physical education
12. Farming
13. Science
14. Home decorations
15. Oriental rugs
16. Painting
17. Music
18. Metals
19. Organized labor
20. Honor systems

b Select some topic for investigation and gather material by using each of the following:

1. Dictionary
2. Encyclopedia
3. *Reader's Guide*
4. *Poole's Index*
5. *Congressional Record*
6. Newspaper

c Discover topics on which other members of the class have information. Divide into pairs and hold interviews to get and give desired material.

d Have class reports on "How Scholars Gather and Record Facts."

e If you like to use some means other than cards to record material, prepare a short talk in which you demonstrate your method and show why it is preferable.

4 Test your ability in outlining.

a Make sentence outlines to fit the following:

1. Reciprocal trade agreements will benefit the world.
2. World federation is the best means of preserving peace.
3. Educational opportunities should be restricted.

4. All high-school students should choose their vocations before graduation.

b Try the following:

Part I. This is to test your ability to make a good logical outline. Several topics are listed together in each group. You are to arrange them in logical order.

First pick out the topics which are most important. Place the numbers of these topics in the space beside the Roman numerals, I, II, etc. Then pick out the topics which should be included under each main heading and place their numbers under each main heading. When you do this, you may find that you have made some mistake in the order of the main topics. You should then correct the order so that the topics will fit into the outline.

Example:

Abraham Lincoln
1. Lincoln as President of the United States
2. The early life of Lincoln
3. Lincoln's parents and home
4. His education

I.___2___
A.___3___
B._____
II.___1___

The Digestive and Circulatory Systems
1. The organs of the digestive system
2. The circulatory system
3. The digestive system
4. The organs of the circulatory system
5. How blood circulates through the body

I._____
A._____
II._____
A._____
B._____

Wisconsin High School
1. The interior of the building
2. The work of the school
3. The school building
4. "Reading, writing, and arithmetic"
5. The teachers
6. The materials used in the building
7. The subjects studied

I._____
A._____
B._____
II._____
A._____
1._____
B._____

The Oil Industry
1. Preparing crude oil for use
2. How the Indians secured oil from streams

I._____
A._____

3. Preparation of lubricating oils   B.____
4. How men learned to pump oil from wells   II____
5. Distilling gasoline: the first product   A.____
6. Historical development of the oil industry   B.____
7. Other products from crude oil   C.____

The Leather Industry
1. Tanning the hides   I____
2. For what is leather used?   A.____
3. Recent improvements in the tanning process   B.____
4. How is leather made?   C.____
5. Shoes and gloves   II____
6. Other uses for leather   A.____
7. Cleaning the hides   B.____

Building a Home
1. Selection of a suitable location   I____
2. The roof   II____
3. The advantages in planning of employing an architect   A.____
4. Making the plans for the house   III____
5. Construction of the house   A.____
6. The foundation   B.____
7. The walls   C.____
8. Finishing the interior of the house   D.____

Organization of the State Government
1. The governor   I____
2. The executive department   A.____
3. Other state courts   B.____
4. The lower house   C.____
5. The judiciary   II____
6. How laws are made   A.____
7. The supreme court   III____
8. The senate — the upper house   A.____
9. The lower house   B.____

Some Facts about Furs
1. Furs, expensive and inexpensive   I____
2. Seal   A.____

3. How furs are prepared for the market   B._____
   4. Cutting furs for garments   C._____
   5. Rabbit   II._____
   6. Cleaning the animal furs   A._____
   7. The skunk   B._____
   8. Stretching and dyeing the skin   C._____
   9. Raccoon   D._____

The Development of Civilization
   1. The Greeks   I._____
   2. The importance of the Christian Church   A._____
   3. Modern civilization   B._____
   4. The Romans   C._____
   5. Characteristics of modern civilization   II._____
   6. The civilization of the Middle Ages   A._____
   7. The earliest civilizations: the Near East   III._____
   8. Ancient civilizations   A._____
   9. Have we progressed?   B._____

Early History of Our Country
   1. The period of discovery   I._____
   2. Virginia — the first colony   A._____
   3. Taxation and other difficulties   B._____
   4. The revolt from England   II._____
   5. Columbus' voyage   A._____
   6. The period of colonization   B._____
   7. Spain's search for gold   III._____
   8. The Declaration of Independence   A._____
   9. The New England colonies   B._____
  10. The Revolutionary War   C._____

The Second World War
   1. Events of the war   I._____
   2. The causes of the war   A._____
   3. The Nazi policy of expansion   B._____
   4. Japan seizes the Philippines.   II._____
   5. Germany marches into France.   A._____
   6. Germany attacks Russia.   B._____
   7. Japan wishes an Eastern Empire.   C._____

8. The effect of the war in America   III_____
9. The shortage of rubber tires   A._____
10. Sugar rationing   B._____

Part II. This is a test of your ability to form a logical outline, and to exclude from that outline all materials which do not aid in developing the main points. The main points in the following topics are indicated as I, II, and III. Go through the topics and check with ( ) the points which do not apply to the main points. Then letter the other topics in the order in which they should appear. The letters for the subtopics should be preceded by the Roman numeral of the main topic to which they belong, as I A, II A, etc.

Maintaining a Democratic Government
 ___I___ The characteristics of the kind of government we wish to maintain
 ___II___ Difficulties in maintaining democracy
 ___III___ Ways to maintain democracy
 _____ In a democracy people vote for their representatives.
 _____ Democracy can be maintained by educating children.
 _____ Democracy is a form of government.
 _____ We do not always get the best men as representatives.
 _____ Children should be taught self-control from the cradle up.
 _____ In a democracy people have freedom of action within the law.
 _____ Democracy can be maintained by keeping people informed.
 _____ Democracy is a way of living.
 _____ We must elect our representatives more intelligently.
 _____ Some people do not live democratically.
 _____ The newspapers should give all the facts to the people.
 _____ The schools should give students an opportunity to live democratically.
 _____ Wars threaten the independence of democratic peoples.
 _____ We must abolish the ideas that people in high places can violate principles of democracy.
 _____ Some people vote at every election.

COMPREHENSION AND APPLICATION TESTS

Aviation in the Second World War
- __I__ The importance of airplanes in this war
- __II__ Some new types of airplanes
- __III__ Armaments carried by modern airplanes
- __IV__ The future of aviation
- _____ Airplanes will be used to carry heavy freight.
- _____ The Germans announced a new dive bomber.
- _____ The Mustang pursuit plane is not produced in America.
- _____ Blockbusters, or two-ton bombs
- _____ The Mosquito boat endangers shipping.
- _____ Submarines are a menace in this war.
- _____ The 50-caliber machine gun is a deadly weapon.
- _____ The British Lancaster bomber
- _____ The Spitfire, a modern fighting plane
- _____ The Wright brothers invented the airplane.
- _____ Airplanes have become the best weapon of the navy.
- _____ Airplanes are used for spotting gunfire.
- _____ Airplanes will be used to tow freight trains of gliders.

Free Speech
- __I__ Freedom of speech is needed in a democracy.
- __II__ Free speech should be maintained during wartime.
- __III__ Free speech does not mean the right to say anything.
- _____ Free speech does not give one the right to falsify about other people.
- _____ Free speech was not practiced by the ancient Greeks.
- _____ Democracy rests on the right of the people to say what they think about problems of government.
- _____ If the people fight the war, they should be permitted to express opinions about it.
- _____ Free speech helps to eliminate injustice from government.
- _____ Free speech will make for more efficient production of war goods.
- _____ Free speech does not give you the right to incite people into destroying property.
- _____ Not all people should have the right of free speech.

Race Equality
    __I__ All races have made great contributions to civilization.
    __II__ America is made up of many different races.
    __III__ Equality of all races is a principle of democracy.
    _____ The Negroes have had many great musicians and scientists.
    _____ German scientists have added much to human knowledge.
    _____ Ten per cent of the population of the United States is Negro.
    _____ The Constitution guarantees equality to all persons regardless of race, color, or creed.
    _____ Japan attacked the United States at Pearl Harbor.
    _____ One of the world's greatest composers is a Russian.
    _____ Democracy believes that all persons have equal rights.
    _____ Language differences make it hard to communicate with persons of other races.
    _____ Many Chinese and Japanese people are citizens of the United States.

5 Test your ability in each of the following. Note how helpful each device is in preparing speeches discussed in this chapter.
   a Use appropriate narrative
     1. Honesty pays.
     2. You can be your own worst enemy.
     3. To be a farmer you have to have good sense.
     4. This town is a pretty good place to live in.
     5. The team is putting up a hard fight.
   b Draw word pictures in support of these topic sentences; use imagination.
     1. The view quite took our breath away.
     2. Behind the fence lay an old-fashioned garden.
     3. The family used to get together every evening around the fireplace.
     4. The view from there was magnificent.
     5. A Roman triumph was a wonderful spectacle.
     6. The moon was beautiful on the river last night.

COMPREHENSION AND APPLICATION TESTS

c Support these topics with statements made by men who are well honored or beloved or known to be experts:
1. The Federal income tax has become a great success.
2. This school ranks high in various ways.
3. There is great need of efficient doctors in the country districts.
4. Hope springs eternal in the human breast.
5. Peace is a possible ideal.

d Define accurately the following terms, each in a good-sized paragraph; that is, a two-minute talk.

1. Anthropology
2. The grandeur that was Greece
3. The survival of the fittest
4. Rotogravure
5. Good form in golf
6. The newspaper deadline
7. Preventive medicine
8. Pari-mutuel betting
9. Drumfire
10. A 4–11 alarm
11. Needlepoint
12. A soufflé
13. A double steal
14. Echelon formation
15. Cutting a stencil
16. Purling

e Classify ideas and things in orderly fashion. Name, describe, and explain the different types that come under each of these headings. Then make short speeches of from two to five minutes.

1. Cats
2. Quitters
3. Modernistic ideas
4. Grinds
5. Antiques
6. Feature stories
7. Postures
8. Pests
9. Stop signals

f Support the following generalizations with specific instances; each one should make a talk of from three to five minutes. This is the commonest form of argumentative speaking.
1. Central America is unstable politically.
2. Our school plays are improving.
3. New styles in dwelling-house architecture are interesting.
4. High schools should watch the eligibility of their athletes.
5. Stunt airplane flights are unwise.
6. The new styles are delightful (or trying, or comfortable, etc.).
7. Many of our graduates have made good.

g Argue from the known facts to what you think is going to happen. Argument "from cause to effect," or predicting consequences, is a very common way of arguing. Gather facts on the following or similar subjects and then state them clearly; predict what the facts point to.
1. Present happenings and tendencies in high-school life
2. Abuses in athletics
3. Recent advances in airplane navigation
4. The condition of the farmer and the price of his products
5. The great decrease in the number of millionaires in America

h Give your idea of the causes of known conditions: a common type of argument, known sometimes as "effect to cause," or explaining causes. From the following known facts or accepted convictions find and argue the causes:
1. Present conditions in China
2. Why our football team is not winning games
3. The trouble with the Democratic party (or the Republican, or any other)
4. The lack of school spirit
5. Why the law isn't enforced in our town
6. What's wrong with the Christian Church
7. The reasons why Americans are losing interest in voting
8. The growth of the moving-picture industry

i Use authority, quotations, and testimony of experts. Get statements from books, articles, reports, quoting persons considered as experts.
1. America leads in radio.
2. The public library is not used as much as it should be.
3. Tobacco injures the heart.
4. A scarcity of print paper is not far distant.
5. The Solid South is growing less solid.

j Tell a story that fits in well with the audience, the subject, the occasion, and yourself as a speaker. Practice this art; it is very valuable and very much used by skillful speakers. Many try it and fall flat. Such failure merely argues that when poorly done a story is pretty painful. But when it is well done, it "goes over big." Cultivate the art of good storytelling, and you can get a favorable

COMPREHENSION AND APPLICATION TESTS 383

hearing where others are ignored or defied (see Chapter Ten).
6 Test your ability to prepare good introductions and conclusions.
  a Turn your attention to introductions.
    1. Write introductions for two speeches.
    2. Find introductions in which listeners were motivated to hear the speaker and his speech by:
      a. A story
      b. A startling fact
      c. A reference to the audience
      d. A reference to a previous speaker
      e. A remark shocking to the audience
    3. Bring in the best introduction that you can find. In a short report, show why you consider it good.
    4. Listen to the introductions of radio speakers. Rate each one according to its success in accomplishing the two purposes of an introduction.
    5. Attend a public speech. Make a report on the relation of the introduction to the speech.
    6. Criticize the introduction of a sermon.
  b Turn your attention to conclusions.
    1. Write conclusions for the two speeches from earlier exercises for which you wrote introductions.
    2. Find examples of conclusions in which the speaker:
      a. Gave a summary of the main parts of the speech.
      b. Left his final message in the minds of the audience with a story.
      c. Concluded with a quotation.
    3. Bring to class an example of an excellent conclusion.
    4. Listen to the conclusions of radio speeches. Give your estimates of three.
    5. Attend a public speech and make a report on the relation of the conclusion to the entire speech.
    6. Criticize the conclusion to a sermon.
7 Test your ability to prepare and deliver speeches of courtesy.
  a Make a short speech introducing one of the following:
    1. The first president of a school club formed some years ago
    2. A former principal of the school

3. A member of the state legislature
4. The county superintendent of schools
5. The president of the local Chamber of Commerce
6. A member of Congress asked to preside over a debate
7. The captain of the football team
8. An orator after he has won a contest for the school
9. A missionary just returned from China
10. A former minister visiting his old congregation
11. The newly elected president of any organization
12. The speaker of the day at a service club
13. A visitor from a foreign country
14. An assembly speaker

b Make a presentation speech for one of the following situations. Do not be long-winded. Be in the picture, but not too close to the camera. Use your imagination and your wit.

1. The president of a social service club is presented with a special button in honor of his labors.
2. A sales manager has won a prize in his district.
3. A beauty queen gets a trip to Hollywood.
4. A member of a class in literature receives a book for excellence in the year's work.
5. The assembly recognizes the fairness of its chairman during the convention.
6. Winning athletes are given their medals.
7. A hero medal is pinned on a boy (or girl) at a meeting of the local City Council or Chamber of Commerce.
8. A church presents a resolution of thanks to a prosecuting attorney for enforcing the law.
9. The cast of a play presents the director with a watch.
10. The blue ribbon is awarded at a showing of paintings.
11. Gold footballs (or baseballs or basketballs) are awarded to members of the championship team.
12. Diplomas are given at commencement.
13. Sweaters are given to a courageous, but not always winning, team.

c Make a one- or two-minute speech of welcome on one of these occasions:

1. A graduate of your school who has won collegiate athletic renown returns to address your assembly.
2. A distinguished educator comes to your class.
3. A new principal takes charge of your high school.
4. The newly elected mayor of the city speaks at your school.
5. The chief of police comes to discuss problems of law enforcement before your church group.

d Prepare a speech of farewell for the following occasions:
1. The senior class graduates from your high school.
2. The junior-high students pass into senior high.
3. You are leaving one high school for another.
4. A popular teacher leaves your school.
5. You leave a club of which you have been a member all through high school.

e Select appropriate situations in the exercises under **b, c,** and **d** above, and give the responses suitable for the various occasions there suggested.

8 Test your ability to prepare and deliver speeches for special occasions.

a Eulogy
1. Study the following. It is a beautiful tribute to a great scientist and teacher. Read it aloud to get the swing and the feel of it. Memorize and deliver it, or at least parts of it.

A LAUGHING SAINT OF SCIENCE [1]
Stephen Moulton Babcock
1843–1931
by Glenn Frank

Expressing the mood of myriads of men and women throughout the world who have known the boon of his spirit or the beneficence of his science, the University of Wisconsin today bares its head and bows its heart before the memory of Stephen Moulton Babcock.

Inventor of a device and a formula that emancipated the dairy farmer from the injustice of the rule of thumb that long prevailed in the market place!

Trail blazer in the crucially important field of vitamin research!

[1] Reprinted by permission of Mrs. Glenn Frank.

Symbol of the best that the pursuit of science generates in the scholar and gives to the state!

Joyous comrade!

A friend beloved beyond measure!

Inspirer incomparable of the vast army of young scholars serving as acolytes at the altar of science!

Like the great seminal minds of the Renaissance, this grand old doctor of science was himself greater than anything he did, and thus, in death, he gives to us, the legatees of his spirit, a goal toward which to point the education and the science of our time.

This merry man of many years was made of the stuff that gives mankind its saints and its martyrs. But he was a saint without seriousness, and he could have gone to martyrdom without a murmur of self-pity, as part of the day's work.

For his was a casual greatness!

He pursued the most painstaking research as if he were playing a game. He brought to his tasks that gaiety of spirit which authentic greatness can afford. His spirit never surrendered that incorrigible playfulness which so often marks men of power. He brought laughter into the laboratory, for there was about him that deceptively careless air which creative spirits have as they go about their business.

But there was toughness to the fiber of his mind!

He was a teacher who scorned the tyranny of the textbooks, and he did not think it impertinent to doubt the authorities. Each morning he met the universe with a question. His was the creative heresy of an insatiable curiosity. The cleansing winds of the critical spirit swept freely and forever through his mind.

He belongs to the apostolic succession of the great pioneers of research — Pythagoras, Aristotle, Archimedes, Copernicus, Galileo, Harvey, Newton, Lavoisier, Dalton, Faraday, Helmholtz, Darwin, Pasteur, Gregor Mendel, and Einstein — for, like them, he was an adventurer into the unknown to whom research was an intellectual passion rather than an institutional ritual, to whom creative thinking was more important than elaborate equipment, and for whom there was no barricaded frontier between pure and applied science.

In an age when scholars all too often hasten to publish even before they prove their findings, he was content to let his greatest work speak for itself, for perhaps the most illuminating fact of his career is that he never published so much as a word about his part in the discovery, definition, and defeat of that "hidden hunger" from which man and beast might die while eating their fill.

In an age smitten with the passion for publicity, he forgot himself into immortality!

And in the midst of the sickness of an acquisitive society, his spirit remained unsullied even by legitimate personal considerations!

> Scholar of a great university!
> Servant of a great state!
> Shy benefactor of mankind everywhere!
> Laughing saint of science!
>
> Being dead he yet speaks!

    2. Prepare a eulogy five minutes in length on some person of your own choosing.
    3. Bring to class a eulogy written by someone else that exemplifies the principles laid down for a good eulogy.

b Nomination
    1. Select a candidate for some office and make a suitable nominating speech.
    2. Nominate some boy or girl for president of a debating or dramatic club.
    3. Prepare and deliver a speech nominating a class president.
    4. Study your local community and prepare a speech of nomination for someone you would like to have elected to office.
    5. Prepare a speech of nomination for your preferred candidate for President of the United States.

c Inaugural
    1. If any member of your class is elected to office, help him to prepare an inaugural address.
    2. Assume that you have been elected to some position of leadership, and deliver a brief inaugural address.
    3. Prepare an inaugural address for a class president.
    4. Prepare an inaugural address for the president of a debating or dramatic club.

5. Prepare an inaugural address for the president of a sorority or a fraternity.
9. Test your ability to prepare and deliver after-dinner speeches.
   a Hold a class banquet. Use your knowledge of parliamentary law in appointing committees and speakers. Use what you have learned about interviews to arrange for the dinner. Use your training to help you prepare after-dinner speeches. Make it a real occasion.
   b. Bring to class one example of a good after-dinner speech.
10. Test your ability to prepare and deliver an oration.
   a Examine contest orations written by high-school students. Evaluate them, using the criteria presented in this chapter.
   b Listen to a high-school or college oratorical contest. Judge the speakers. Compare your ratings with those of an expert judge.
   c Write an oration in which you present in your best manner some idea very important to you.
11. Test your ability to deliver all types of speeches.
   a Practice each of the five ways for delivering speeches discussed on pages 368–372.
   b Try to find occasions outside of class for delivering speeches.
   c Select and use the type of delivery most appropriate for each speech prepared for this chapter.
   d What suggestion for improvement can you get from the following quotation?

> By hearing him often I came to distinguish easily between sermons newly composed and those which he had often preached in the course of his travels. His delivery of the latter was so improved by frequent repetitions that every accent, every emphasis, every modulation of voice was so perfectly well turned and well placed that without being interested in the subject one could not help being pleased with the discourse, a pleasure of much the same kind with that received from an excellent piece of music. This is an advantage itinerant preachers have over those who are stationary, as the latter cannot well improve their delivery of a sermon by so many rehearsals.
> — Benjamin Franklin

Part Three

SPEECH IN CIVIC LIVING

THE INDIVIDUAL *is not only an integral part of the body social; he is indispensable also to the body politic. How shall governments derive their just powers from the consent of the governed if the people are inarticulate? Free speech furnishes the only climate in which democracy can flourish, and speech is really free only in proportion to the degree of its own excellence. Free speech is a personal achievement, not a power bestowed by the Constitution.*

14 Discussion

15 Debating

16 Parliamentary Procedure

17 Radio Speaking

CHAPTER FOURTEEN *Discussion*

OF WHAT do we think when we hear the word " parliament "? Do we see the venerable Gothic towers of the Houses of Parliament in London? Or do we hear in our imagination the deep-throated tones of Big Ben as they come to us with the words " This is London "? Let us stop and think a moment about the word " parliament." It comes from the French word *parler*, meaning " to speak." Parliament is not a building; it is the governing body of a free people, operating through free speech. It is well said that democracy is government by discussion, and it is with this essential technique of self-government that we are to deal in this chapter. Anything which interferes with the speech of a free people threatens their institutions.

Now of course a great deal of the talk in which the citizens of a democracy engage has little or nothing to do directly with the processes of government. Yet in critical matters of great consequence there is little or no hope of arriving at right decisions in a democracy unless every individual who has anything to contribute to a solution of problems is given the opportunity to be heard. Weak, ignorant, and ineffective as we may be separately, we are capable of generating wisdom and power when we get together and pool our convictions, experiences, and capacities for constructive thinking.

Discussion presents itself to us in a variety of forms. When a conversation is consciously directed toward the definition and solution of a difficulty, it immediately begins to take on the character of what we call discussion. The discussions which occur in classrooms are rather informal in nature, and are not to be thought of as public, since there is no audience present, as distinct from the participants. Nevertheless, much of the activity in classes really is informal discussion. Usually the teacher leads the discussion, although at times he may appoint members of the class to take charge in his stead. The group is pooling its knowledge and its experience in this type of discussion just as truly as does any other group which has met to talk over common problems. Therefore in our classes we may learn much

NEW ENGLAND TOWN MEETING. *The New England town meeting has always been regarded as the very cradle of democracy in the New World. Here we really have " government of the people, by the people, and for the people." Matters of public concern are dealt with in these meetings through full and free discussion by the people themselves. Here a citizen in the rear of the assembly is rising to address the chairman on whom the eyes of the others are focused. The forms of parliamentary procedure are followed in such town meetings.* (Life Magazine, Black Star)

about the basic techniques and methods that will be extremely useful to us in other discussion groups all through our lives.

In the present chapter we are concerned with the more formal, planned, and public types of discussion, such as those we have in "forums of the air" and in legislative assemblies. These discussions are really purposeful conversations among the primary participants, in the presence of others who listen and are privileged to raise questions and state their own points of view.

THE PURPOSES OF DISCUSSION

The major function of discussion is to bring together the knowledge and the thoughts of a group of people and to focus them on some social, economic, or political problem which can be solved most satisfactorily through co-operative thinking and action. It has been said that the purposes of discussion are to "find the facts, focus the facts, filter the facts, face the facts, and follow the facts."

Finding the facts. In discussion, first of all we should undertake to find the facts. Suppose that the topic to be discussed is municipal finance. We probably would not be discussing the subject unless we had a feeling that something was wrong somewhere in the financial setup of our city or town. A discussion usually originates in an attitude of dissatisfaction and discontent with present conditions. However, before we begin to talk about remedies, we must discover the reasons for the existence of the problem. We begin by trying to find the facts. We cannot find the facts very well if we start out by being emotional; we must wait until later for emotion — if it has any proper place in our discussion at all. Therefore the preliminary stages of our discussion may well be centered upon such questions as: 1. What is the total cost of our city government? 2. What do the various city functions — such as police protection, fire protection, garbage collection, street department — cost? In other words, how is our tax money spent? 3. How does the city get its money? How much comes from taxes, and how much from licenses? 4. What have been the principal tendencies in recent years in expenditures, tax policies, and so on? We should not pass beyond this fact-finding stage until we have reached a maximum amount of agreement on the facts.

Focusing the facts. Then comes the second step, focusing the facts. By this we mean trying to figure out some of the more important implications of the facts we have found. What do they suggest? Have taxes been rising rapidly? Have government expenses been increasing sharply? Does it seem clear that some reform somewhere is called for? If so, what and where? In other words, in what major directions do the known facts seem to point?

Filtering the facts. Now we are ready to filter the facts. We have nothing else through which we can filter facts so well as through our own experiences. In the light of what we know, how shall we interpret our findings? If we carry out this filtering process satisfactorily, we shall begin to view the facts in terms of their impacts and effects upon the human beings who make up our discussion group. For example, we shall develop some basis for deciding how important the various municipal services are to the people who live in the community. Who would object most and who would object least if street improvements were to be curtailed? Who would approve and who would disapprove if certain types of government reorganization, such as the substitution of a city manager for a mayor, were to be instituted? Who thinks taxes are too high and who thinks they are not high enough? Thus, having put the facts through the highly complex filter of individual and group experience, we shall perhaps be able to strain out the less important and keep the more important.

Facing the facts. What do we mean by facing the facts? After we have discovered the facts, studied their implications, and evaluated them, we must now accept them and agree that whatever we ultimately decide to do should be undertaken in the light of them and kept in line with them. We must not permit anyone to disregard what we have all agreed to as facts. If we cannot all agree, perhaps at least we can be democratic enough to accept the judgment of the majority as to what the facts are, and govern ourselves accordingly. If we have found that property taxes have gone up 25 per cent in the past five years as a result of expansions in city services, we should not allow someone at a later stage in the discussion to pop up with the remark that after all our tax bill has not changed appreciably within a decade.

Following the facts. What does it mean to follow the facts? As

THE PURPOSES OF DISCUSSION 395

we have said, in the formulation of any program of group action we should be guided by what we have agreed upon as being the facts. When we have finished a discussion, we should find ourselves ready to debate available solutions. We end discussion by formulating these possible alternatives, and then we pass on to the weighing of the facts on the two sides, pro and con, with an honest purpose to act in accordance with the preponderance of the factual evidence. This procedure is the very essence of the democratic process.

COURTROOM SCENE FROM " EMILE ZOLA." *Paul Muni, playing the part of the novelist, makes his plea for the accused Dreyfus. " I may be condemned here. The day will come when France will thank me for having helped to save her honor." A motion picture conception of one of the greatest courtroom speeches of history. What can be learned from a study of the scene? (Culver Service)*

Here and there, throughout the nation, discussion groups of various kinds — agricultural, municipal, economic, and social — are studying public questions in accordance with the formula we have described, and are working out proposed solutions for the problems of a growing democracy. It behooves anyone who would be an effective citizen of his community, his state, and his nation to prepare himself for skilled participation in this process of discussion.

TYPES OF DISCUSSION

There are several possible organizational setups for public discussion. Among these are the panel, the symposium, and the forum. There are many other types and combinations of types listed in various textbooks, but all seem to be modifications of these three, which we shall now consider briefly.

The panel. In all varieties of public discussion, it is essential that someone be in general charge. For want of a better name we shall call this leader the chairman. Suppose the principal of your school desires to organize a panel discussion on the subject of interschool athletics. In choosing the participants he would want as many fundamentally different points of view as possible represented. In the practical working-out of a panel discussion, it is rarely advisable to have more than six speakers, although there is nothing particularly sacred and significant about that number. Usually more will present a confusing picture; fewer, an incomplete one.

The members of the panel on interschool athletics might be as follows:

1. A representative of those parents who oppose interschool sports
2. A representative of those parents who favor interschool sports
3. A representative of those students who oppose interschool sports
4. A representative of those students who favor interschool sports
5. A representative of those faculty members who oppose interschool sports
6. A representative of those faculty members who favor interschool sports

Each of the six speakers carefully prepares his topic. He presents his point of view, and lays before the others whatever factual material he considers especially significant. The principal may act as chairman. He and the six speakers rehearse the program in advance of its presentation in public. Following the rehearsal, each speaker revises his material in the light of what he has learned the others are planning to say, making an effort to reduce duplication, and to "point up" the discussion.

During the actual presentation of the panel discussion, the speakers sit on the platform, or at least in full view of the audience, and usually at the ends and the back of a table on which they can place their notes and printed materials. It is customary for the speakers in a panel discussion to remain seated while talking, unless the occasion is an extremely formal one, or the auditorium so large that they need to stand in order to be seen and heard by all members of the audience.

Following the exchange of ideas, the members of the panel question each other, offer rebuttals of what has been said by others whose views are contrary to their own, and furnish additional support for their opening statements. The function of the chairman is to keep things moving, to direct the conversation among the panel members as helpfully as possible, and finally, when the time has come to close the discussion, to summarize what has been said. In the concluding statement, the chairman should not overemphasize his own views, although a good chairman will not fail to introduce important items of information and evidence which have not been presented by the panel members.

A panel discussion differs from an ordinary conversation in the fact that it is prepared in advance and controlled and directed by a chairman. When time permits, the panel discussion should be followed by a period in which members of the audience may ask questions, add factual data, or present their own points of view. The chairman should see that all the ordinary rules of parliamentary procedure are strictly observed during the question-and-answer period, and that appropriate members of the panel are given opportunity to reply to each question as it arises.

It is of the utmost importance that only one member of the panel talk at one time. This rule is violated more often than one might think, even in panel discussions presented at great cost over radio chains. Sometimes a panel with six members will break up into two or three separate conversations simultaneously. Nothing could be more confusing to an audience, and the chairman should guard against such a condition rigorously.

The symposium. The principal differences between the symposium and the panel are: (1) symposium speakers usually deliver public addresses rather than conversational remarks to the other participants and (2) in the symposium each participant speaks but once (except as he may share in the discussion by the audience or answer questions in the question-and-answer period). The panel speakers discuss the subject *with each other* before the audience. The symposium speakers discuss the subject directly *with the audience.* " The Town Meeting of the Air," which is broadcast every week, is of the symposium type. Each of three or four distinguished authorities on a general subject delivers a ten-minute address. The chairman of the Town Meeting then solicits questions from the audience, to be answered by the several symposium speakers. Sometimes the speakers ask each other questions. In such a program no member of the audience is allowed to inject his own point of view or to make any use of the meeting time except to ask specific and definite questions. Sometimes in less formal symposiums conducted under more liberal time conditions, members of the audience are permitted to make statements from the floor, as in panel forums, the purpose being to give the largest possible number of participants a chance to speak. The larger the meeting, the greater the necessity of formality. Just as the chairman of the " Town Meeting of the Air " repeats questions asked by the audience when they are not clearly audible, so also should every chairman repeat questions before they are answered by the speakers. The chairman's main function is to see that time limits are observed, and that all other regulations which have been agreed upon before the meeting begins are enforced.

Lecture forums, and forums. When panel discussions and symposiums end with audience participation, they probably should be called panel forums and symposium forums. A lecture forum is simply a public speech followed by a period in which members of the audience question the lecturer, or make statements relating to the topic he has discussed. Sometimes the lecturer plays a double role, and acts as chairman too. At other times a chairman presides over the meeting, introduces the lecturer, and supervises the question-and-answer period. Sometimes a forum proceeds without the formal lecture. There are advantages in all of these systems. While the lecture forum is probably the most common of all public-discussion forms, in some ways it is the least satisfactory. It often emphasizes the particular point of view of the lecturer too much. And frequently it is extremely difficult to obtain any audience participation after a formal lecture. The lecture forum works best in smaller groups, where people feel free to speak their minds. It is less efficient in larger groups, where people are hesitant about getting up and raising questions or objections. Furthermore, although a member of the audience may feel a strong urge to take public exception to what a lecturer has said, he is reluctant to do so, lest the lecturer use his prestige to refute the questioner's point instead of considering it fairly.

It is to be noted that there are many possible combinations of the panel, the symposium, the lecture forum, and the forum; in any of them the essential features of public discussion should be preserved and made effective in coming to grips with the persistent problems of a democratic society. Training in these techniques will make better citizens of us all.

Tests of Comprehension and Application

PANEL DISCUSSIONS

1 Work out the following panel discussions and present them before the class.

    a Topic: Electric Utilities in the United States

Purpose: To decide what should be done to improve the manufacture and distribution of electric energy in the United States
Panel:
  Member 1. History and development of the utility industries
  Member 2. Importance of utilities to the public
  Member 3. Relation of the government to utilities
  Member 4. Experience with government ownership
b Topic: Medical Practice in the United States
  Purpose: To decide what can be done to improve the present system of medical practice
  Panel:
    Member 1. Cost of medical services
    Member 2. Distribution of medical services
    Member 3. The condition of the private physician
    Member 4. Experiments in group medicine
2 Prepare panel discussions on the following topics:
  a Government and Agriculture
  b The Good Neighbor Policy
  c Soil Conservation
  d Sales Taxes
  e Social Insurance
  f Public Health
  g The Community Union (Chest)
  h School Clubs
  i Assembly Programs
  j Homework
  k Examinations and Grades

SYMPOSIUMS

3 Take the topic "Political Parties in the United States." Organize and run off a symposium with speakers representing respectively: (a) the Republican party, (b) the Democratic party, (c) the Socialist party, and (d) any others which you think it wise to include.
4 Prepare and hold a symposium on "Advertising," with speakers representing: (a) the public, (b) the manufacturers, (c) the radio stations, (d) the magazine publishers.
5 Develop a symposium on some other topic of present and vital interest in your school.

COMPREHENSION AND APPLICATION TESTS 401

LECTURE FORUMS, AND FORUMS

6 Develop lecture forums or forums on the following topics:
- a Strikes and Lockouts
- b The Future of American Industry
- c Our Transportation Problem
- d Our Vanishing Natural Resources
- e Flood Control
- f Synthetic Rubber
- g Student Self-Government
- h Final Examinations under the Honor System
- i Secret Societies
- j The Relation of High-School Training to Success in Life
- k The Part-time Worker in High School
- l Compulsory Military Training
- m Physical Fitness
- n How to Spend a Vacation
- o What Your Teachers Can Learn from You

CHAPTER FIFTEEN *Debating*

IN THE preceding chapter the nature of the relationship between discussion and debate has been indicated. First we *discuss* a problem, and then we *debate* a possible solution. For example, we might discuss the problem of taxation. Having done that, we might proceed to debate " The State of _____ should adopt a general sales tax," or " The State of _____ should adopt a graduated income tax." Discussion is a preliminary stage, debate is the final stage, in the attempt to solve problems through the medium of speech.

DEBATE AS A METHOD OF DETERMINING POLICIES

Sometimes we make the mistake of supposing that debating is an activity in which we engage only occasionally, and that it is an artificial form of contest speaking that has little relevance to the business of daily living. When we stop to think that debating is essentially a process of trying to prove a statement or an assertion

LINCOLN–DOUGLAS DEBATE. *Seven joint debates between the "Rail Splitter" and the "Little Giant" clarified the national issues and set the stage for the terrible drama of civil war. Abraham Lincoln and Stephen Arnold Douglas were debaters of marvellous skill and power. A reading of what they said in their contests should be profitable for any student of speech. (Keystone View)*

through the use of evidence and reasoning, we realize that it is a speech activity in which we participate constantly. Let us think back over a period of two or three days and ask ourselves how often we have used speech for the purpose of supporting some proposition we wanted someone else to believe, or in attempting to convince someone that a particular course of action was proper and justifiable. Every time we have done these things, we have been debating.

We know what it is to want the use of the family car and to be denied it. Perhaps we accept the denial as one of the hardships of life and do not attempt to change it. However, under the pressure of special conditions we may decide that we will make an effort to modify the position our parents have taken on the problem. Therefore we approach Father and place before him the proposition "Resolved, That the children should be allowed to use the car tonight." Right then and there we are starting a debate, unless Father either unexpectedly concedes the point or flatly refuses to put down his newspaper while we present our "case." Assuming, however, that he is willing to give ear to our argument, one of us becomes the first speaker for the affirmative. Father is on the negative. If a proposition for debate is properly stated, it always is the duty and the privilege of the affirmative to speak first. Unless the affirmative starts something, conditions will remain unchanged; we simply will not be permitted to use the car. Therefore the first speaker for the affirmative opens the argument, stating some of the reasons for the request.

The first affirmative. Usually, the affirmative begins by pointing out what is wrong in the present situation; he argues that it is unjust, unfair, and extremely unsatisfactory not to be allowed to take the car. He draws attention to the obvious fact that the children are older now than they used to be, that they have driver's licenses, and that they are as good drivers as either Father or Mother. He says that other boys and girls have cars, and that they get along all right.

The first negative. Father may listen patiently, and after the first affirmative's arguments have been laid before him, either terminate the debate abruptly by announcing that nothing which has been said has changed his mind, or he may "open the case" for the negative. He tells us that he always got along without an automobile when he was a boy. He tells us how he often walked long distances, or rode on streetcars without complaint. "This is a soft and pampered generation," he says. "If you are going just around the block, you can't get there without an automobile!" He informs us that by denying us the use of the car, he is strengthening our characters, making us more resourceful and independent. He reminds us that we aren't as grown-up as we think we are. But there is no need of going on. We know the negative arguments perfectly well!

The second affirmative. Now let us suppose that the first speaker's sister makes the second speech for the affirmative. She repeats some of what already has been said, and then adds to it some other facts and reasoning. She tells Father that the boys and girls who are her friends all have the privilege of driving cars. She contends that we are being unnecessarily humiliated. She vouches for our need of the car, and our capability of handling it without getting into trouble.

The second negative. At the conclusion of Sister's remarks, Mother "goes to bat" for the negative. She summarizes the arguments Father has already made against the affirmative's proposition. She refutes some of the points the affirmative speakers have made, and then goes on to present further objections to the proposal. She talks about serious accidents which have happened recently. She reminds us that the family is not in a position to afford any more repair bills, and that even if we don't get into any accidents, there is a good deal of expense involved in driving the car, which is a drain on the family budget. She draws attention to the fact that automobile insurance is so costly that we have recently dropped our collision policy and that it would be dangerous to let us take the car without such coverage.

The burden of proof. By this time it begins to seem that the affirmative and the negative are pretty evenly matched, and that unless we can produce some very strong evidence or argument, we are not going to win the debate. If the contest were to stop at this point, and if there were judges present to render a decision, they would probably say that we, as affirmative speakers, have failed to carry our burden of proof — the responsibility of proving that the proposed action should be taken.

We do not need to be told that in such a family argument, numerous unimportant and irrelevant points are brought up. The ones who want the car may stress contentions which are totally disregarded by "the negative." Just so, the negative may cite objections which the affirmative speakers consider trivial and beside the point. Senator Beveridge once observed that this kind of debating is far more likely to generate heat than light! Everyone's interests will be best served if the debaters can keep calm, examine the problem thoughtfully and fairly, find out just where the real differences of opinion between the two sides are, and upon what assumptions, prejudices, and beliefs the two different points of view are based.

The issues. If we can succeed in doing this, we are formulating what are known as the issues. The issues are the vital points of disagreement between the affirmative and the negative. So long as these are present, the affirmative and the negative cannot hope to agree on the main proposition. In our imaginary family debate, the chances of agreement on the issues are directly proportional to the participants' fair-mindedness and their desire to understand each other's points of view. When a boy who argues with his parents begins with the generous and persuasive assumption that his elders have what seem to them excellent reasons for their attitude, the parents are likely to try to see his viewpoint also.

The rebuttals. After all the principal arguments for and against our taking the car have been stated, there may be a second series of shorter statements in which the various speakers point out, in the contentions of opposing speakers, inaccuracies, wrong conclusions, and weaknesses in reasoning. In a formal debate, these shorter speeches are called rebuttals. Rebuttals naturally start with the negative. This is so because it is felt that the affirmative speakers, who are obliged to begin the argument, are entitled to the final word, a result which is brought to pass by letting the negative open the rebuttal series of speeches. Why is the affirmative entitled to the last word? Because the affirmative speakers carry the burden of proof, they will lose if nothing is done, and we want to give them every opportunity to make good on their difficult task.

When the first negative speaker has had his turn at rebuttal, one of the affirmative speakers then tries to repair the damage the negative has done to the affirmative's arguments. Then he may go on to show up weaknesses in the negative arguments. If the debate is handled properly, there should be opportunity provided for each of the four speakers to make one constructive, and one rebuttal, speech.

The judges of debates. Of course, one unfortunate aspect of the debate about taking the automobile is that the speakers for the negative are also the judges, a situation which would not be permitted in a formal contest debate. In such a debate, judges are unprejudiced persons who understand the rules of debating.

The distinguishing characteristics of affirmative and negative. Those who advocate procedures and policies different from those which are in vogue are always on the affirmative. In this sense it is accurate to say that the affirmative speakers are the reformers or the radicals, while those on the negative are the conservatives, or the "stand-patters." Usually, in attempting to bring about any change it is necessary to start by showing specifically what is wrong with the existing situation. But the affirmative speakers must not stop at this point. They must show not only that *some* change is advisable, but also that the particular modification which they advocate is the right change to make.

THE PROPOSITION FOR DEBATE

As we have seen, the debate centers upon a proposition that something should, or should not, be done. There are a few rather simple rules which we should bear in mind when it comes to selecting propositions.

A declarative statement. Although we often speak about the "question for debate," we cannot very well argue for and against a question. What we debate is a positive statement which represents the affirmative position on a controversial question. Instead of attempting to debate a topic, a subject, a phrase, or a question, we should begin with a definite assertion. For example, we should not attempt to debate "Inflation," or "Will the government's wage-stabilization program help in the control of inflation?" Rather we should phrase the proposition, "Resolved, That the Congress should adopt a wage-stabilization program."

Clearness. The proposition should be precise, definite, and free of ambiguous terms. There should be a minimum of possibility that the affirmative and the negative will disagree as to the meaning of the proposition. Especially should we avoid terms which "slant" in favor of the affirmative or the negative. If we wish to place upon the affirmative speakers a clear and definite burden of proof, we should not ask them to support the proposition "Resolved, That interscholastic sports are harmful," but rather "Resolved, That this high school should abolish interscholastic athletics." Such a word as "harmful" may involve us in misunderstanding and bickering: harmful in what ways? harmful to whom? how harmful? and so on and so on. Worse still is the use of terms which give one side or the other an unfair advantage; for example, "Resolved, That the harmful effects of interschool sports should be condemned" or "Resolved, That the beneficial effects of the physical-education program justify making it compulsory." There always will be a sufficient amount of misunderstanding in debating without asking for it by using inaccurate, confusing, and question-begging terms.

Singleness. One thing at a time is a pretty good rule in life. Certainly one debate proposition at a time is a very important rule in debating. In a deliberative assembly, no one should make a motion which proposes two or more actions. If he does so, such a motion should be divided into parts and each part debated separately. For example, it is not proper to move that study hall, homework, and final examinations should be abolished. Neither would it be right to have such a triple proposition used in a formal contest debate. Each of the three proposals should be debated separately.

Affirmative statement. The proposition as phrased should represent the affirmative rather than the negative position. We must remember that the real affirmative is that side in the controversy which bears the burden of proof, the side which advocates a change and is prepared to present evidence to prove that the proposed change is wise. If we wish to debate the abolition of final examinations, we should not phrase the proposition "Resolved, That final examinations should be continued." They will be continued unless some affirmative speaker steps up and carries the burden of proof by showing that final examinations should be abandoned. In the lawcourt, the one who brings the suit, or initiates the action — the plaintiff or the prosecutor — is the affirmative and bears the burden of proof. The side which defends the suit, the defendant, is the negative. Thus we say that a man charged with a crime is presumed to be innocent until he has been proved guilty. The defendant against whom a damage suit is brought in the civil courts must be given the benefit of the doubt, if any doubt remains after both plaintiff and defendant have had their day in court.

Two-sidedness. It seems almost unnecessary to remark that the proposition must be debatable, and yet this apparently obvious fact is often overlooked. How futile it would be to debate "Resolved, That the segregation of persons with contagious diseases be discontinued in the United States," or "Resolved, That every United States citizen over eighteen years of age should pay an annual tax of $1000."

On many statements, for debate purposes there just are not two sides, at least so far as the vast majority of us are concerned. And it is unfair to debaters to assign them an impossible task. Usually there is not such an obvious lopsidedness to a debate proposition, but there still may be a wide difference in the amount of evidence and argument available to the affirmative and the negative respectively. What we want is an evenly balanced proposition which will not handicap either side.

Timeliness. It is always more interesting and worth while to debate a timely proposition than one which has been worn threadbare or is out of date. This demand for contemporaneous interest makes it very difficult to include in a book of this kind either good propositions for debate or even a list of topics from which good propositions may be phrased. A debate proposition which is timely today may be unfit for use next week. We should be on the alert for unsettled questions in the fields of economics and government. There will be no difficulty whatever in finding a large number of good propositions for debate available at any particular time.

CONTEST DEBATING

Formal contest debating is a game, just as football, tennis, and chess are games. It is a great mistake to treat debating as if it must always be designed to affect materially the settlement of important issues. The debates which occur in the City Council, in the State Legislature, and in the Congress of the United States are not to be considered as games. Contest debating is a school game that prepares us for debates which are not games. It is a kind of matched play. Two sides are chosen, rules are laid down to govern the players, and, usually, a referee is present to see that the rules are enforced. In addition to this referee (the chairman), there usually is a judge whose business is to decide which team plays the game more effectively. In a contest debate a vote for the affirmative should not mean that the affirmative has persuaded the judge that the proposition is correct and should be adopted. A vote for the negative should not mean that its position accords with the point of view of the judge. The basis for judgment should always be the relative quality of the arguing and the speaking which the two teams have done. The question the judge is attempting to answer simply is: Which of the two, affirmative or negative, has played the better game?

The problem of definition. In Chapter Five we have found advice which should be very helpful to us in approaching this problem of defining terms in a debate. We should note particularly that we can never be able to tell what a proposition means by simply considering the separate words of which it is composed. It is the combinations of words into terms which have to be considered. The dictionary may not be of much help in deciding what the terms of a debate proposition mean. The meanings are derived from common usage in the field of interest represented by the proposition. The way to find out what these terms mean is to study the origin and history of the controversy, and thus learn how the terms have been and are being used by those who talk and write about the proposition.

The rule of reasonableness must always govern in determining meanings. So long as the affirmative speakers can demonstrate that the meanings they are attaching to the terms are generally accepted by those who know most about the matter under discussion, they have a right to insist that the negative speakers accept these definitions. It is unfair to permit the negative speakers to insist upon different meanings. The affirmative speakers are making the proposal, and they have a right to say what the proposal means so long as they do not depart from the standard of reasonableness. If they do, the negative is of course duty-bound to point out this fact and show that the affirmative is failing to discuss the intended issues. All too frequently, debates are seriously damaged by quibbling over meanings.

Much of this difficulty can be avoided by careful phrasing of the proposition. If it contains ambiguous terms, more precise ones should be substituted before the actual preparation for the debate is begun. If it is not feasible to do this by actual rephrasing, then it should be done by advance agreement between the two teams. An affirmative team should never attempt to take unfair advantage in the definition of terms, and if they do not, a negative team has no business to object to the definitions the affirmative uses.

The affirmative case. In one form or another the affirmative case must always cover two main points, and must be organized closely about them. First, the affirmative must demonstrate that there is a need for action — that something in the present situation requires modification or change. Second, they must show that they have the right answer — that their proposal will remedy what is wrong. If the negative are willing to concede the first point, then the affirmative need say no more about that. The trouble is that the affirmative usually do not know just what stand the negative are going to take on either of the two points, and until it becomes clear that they have admitted the necessity for a change, the affirmative remain responsible for proving it.

The negative case. The negative's fundamental obligation is to block the affirmative from proving some point which they must prove in order to win the argument. There are various ways in which the negative may attempt to do this. In other words, there are a number of possible forms of strategy among which the negative may choose. We shall mention and explain four types of negative cases briefly.

The most conservative case for the negative is one of pure refutation. When the negative speakers adopt this strategy, they set themselves the task of pointing out weaknesses in the affirmative case without taking any definite stand themselves in favor of anything. In effect they are saying: "We object to what the affirmative propose on the ground that it would do no good, or that it would do more harm than good. Consequently, we will have none of it. We don't propose to commit ourselves as to whether or not any change should be made, or if it should, just what it ought to be. However, we feel sure of the unsatisfactory character of the affirmative's proposal."

The second stand that the negative can take is defense of the status quo. When the negative speakers undertake the defense-of-the-present type of case, they are endeavoring to stop the affirmative in their first step — the demonstration of the need for a change. They say: "Why adopt the affirmative proposal? Everything is substantially all right as it stands now." To illustrate, suppose the affirmative are arguing for the adoption of a sales tax. The negative take their stand on the contention that present taxes are fair and adequate and that there is no need for changing the system of taxation at this time.

The third position for the negative is one of patch and repair. In developing the repair or adjustment case, the negative are saying substantially: "We do not claim that everything in the present situation is perfect, but we do feel that the affirmative have exaggerated the need for change. The present system is not so bad as they have tried to make out. We suggest specific minor modifications which will make the present system work more satisfactorily and which will make the affirmative's plan unnecessary." Again, for example, the affirmative are arguing for the adoption of a sales tax. The negative say: "We do not contend that the present taxes are adequate to meet the expanding cost of government. The affirmative are right about this. However, before proceeding to adopt a sales tax, we think that it would be wise to lower the exemptions in the present income-tax law so as to produce the necessary additional revenue. Thus we would avoid all of the difficulties involved in setting up an entirely new tax. This plan is much more conservative and much simpler. Instead of buying a new car, let's try replacing the spark plugs in the present one."

The fourth plan for the negative is a counterproposition. When the negative speakers advocate a counterproposition, they begin by admitting that the present situation is unsatisfactory and that some major change must be made. But they take issue with the affirmative as to what the change ought to be. Suppose again that the affirmative are asking for a general sales tax. The negative say in effect: "We concede the necessity for a new tax in addition to those now in force. However, we think that a single-tax plan would be preferable to the further complication of a sales tax added to the hodgepodge of taxes which we now have."

A counterproposition must be fundamentally inconsistent with the proposition supported by the affirmative. If the affirmative can accept the counterproposal in addition to their own, it is not really counter at all. In the last example, it will be noted that, by definition, the single tax is always offered as the substitute for all other taxes. We cannot have a single tax with multiple taxes.

In a society meeting, someone moves that the organization hold a picnic on the coming Sunday afternoon. Another member rises and offers an amendment to the effect that instead of a picnic on Sunday afternoon a dance be arranged for Friday evening. This amendment is, in effect, a counterproposition; presumably the organization is committed to the idea of one function rather than two. Of course, if the society decides to do both, then the amendment was not really a counterproposition after all.

One point to be observed here is that the negative assume a burden of proof on their counterproposition. It is not enough merely to mention an alternative; the alternative must be presented more convincingly and more persuasively than the affirmative proposal if it is to be made effective.

In building the negative case, it is necessary to decide which plan is to be used, and then to stick to it. If we begin with a counterproposition, we cannot later fall back upon an adjustment or patch-and-repair type of argument, and vice versa. One weakness in negative cases is a failure to be clear as to what strategy is to be followed.

Concessions. One of Abraham Lincoln's contemporaries tells us that when Lincoln was practicing law in the courts of Illinois, he frequently upset the calculations of his opponents by his adroit use of the technique of concession. He raised very few objections to the case of the opposition as it was presented, going out of his way to indicate his willingness to concede the truth of arguments on the other side. Lulled into a false sense of security, opposing attorneys would find themselves brought up sharply when they advanced onto the ground where Lincoln was prepared to fight and intended to do so. He did not cavil over arguments he could not answer. He permitted the opposition to make what they could out of the truth which was on their side, and then he delivered sledge-hammer blows on those points where he thought that he could do the most damage. One of the common mistakes of debaters is to concede nothing; they charge head-on into a stone wall of facts the existence of which they do not even admit. It seems to hurt such debaters to admit that the other side can be right in anything. The sensible thing to do is to examine the situation, decide what in our opponents' case is not worth answering and what cannot be answered, and then meet the opposition squarely where we have a fighting chance. When we have decided what points are theirs and not ours, we should let the opposition have them. Facts are stubborn things — even more stubborn than a stubborn debater. Incidentally, by conceding what we cannot hope to refute we will gain a very real advantage by the resulting impression of generosity and fairness. One of the most unpersuasive techniques which can be followed in debate is to insist that black is white or that white is yellow!

Preparing material. Practically everything that is said in other sections of this book about the preparation and delivery of public speeches, particularly the advice in Chapter Thirteen, applies without any major modification to the preparation of debate speeches.

The debate speech should be close-knit and logical in structure. Rarely should a debater attempt to establish more than one main point. He should figure out carefully just how he can use his arguments and evidence to make this one point effective in the thinking of his audience. Seldom will we want to use more than two or three contentions to support a main point. Our job is to figure out the principal reasons for believing that our proposition is true. We make a statement, and then we ask ourselves, " How do we know that this is true? " If we answer this question properly, each answer will connect logically with our proposition by the conjunctions *because, since,* or *for.*

Let us be sure that we have arranged our points in the most effective possible order. Usually, the one which requires the most time for its adequate development should come first. That which can be handled satisfactorily in the shortest time should be presented last. Let us be sure to mark clearly the transitions from one point to the next. Statements such as " Having shown that the South American nations resent interference in their affairs by European Powers, I shall now demonstrate that they do not wish to be dominated by the United States either " will be very helpful as signposts to our audience, making it easier for them to follow the route we are taking. It is also advisable to summarize each argument before taking up the next. Frequently these summaries can be made to show relationships between what we have said and what our opponents have said on the same point. The old Negro preacher's rule — " First I tells 'em what I'm going to tell 'em; second I tells 'em; and third, I tells 'em what I'se told 'em " — may well be applied to the debate speech.

Important data, quotations from authorities, statistical information, and the like should always be prepared carefully in advance, *on cards*, and usually should be in the hand of the debater when he is making use of them in actual presentation. Most of us are inclined to feel just a touch suspicious of long and involved quotations or complex sets of figures when they are repeated from memory. It is reassuring to see that the speaker is checking his own accuracy in presenting such materials to us.

Delivery. While memorized speeches usually are ineffective in debate, because of the difficulty of adapting them to the debate as it progresses, nevertheless the phrasings of major points and summaries may well be worked out carefully in advance. There are important points a debater knows he is going to take up, and which he cannot afford to wait to phrase until the debate is in progress. Effective statements of these should be worded during the preparation stage. With the exception of such sections, the best debate speeches are extemporaneous.

Rebuttal techniques. The spice of the debate is always in the rebuttal speeches. The twofold function of rebuttal is to break down the opposition case and to strengthen one's own. Whenever we reply to an opponent, we should begin by stating his point accurately and fully, and then make our answer to it. We must be sure to show how the point being refuted is related to both cases. We should not merely peck at the separate arguments of our opponents. The least effective type of rebuttal is that in which we take up one by one all

AN AMATEUR STRATEGIST. *A high school student is explaining and defending a point of view with regard to military operations. He is utilizing a map which he has drawn on the blackboard to support his argument. He is exemplifying excellent technique in not letting the map or the paper in his hand distract his attention from his audience. (Library of Congress)*

of the arguments our opponents have made, important and unimportant, big and little, and answer each separately.

Mere answering back is not effective refutation. When we think we have destroyed an opposing argument, we should tell the audience what damage we believe we have done to our opponents' case. To illustrate: If an opponent has quoted an authority inaccurately, or if he has quoted only a part of a longer statement other parts of which may give an entirely different impression, it is not enough merely to point out the error. We should go on to examine the point our opponent originally used the quotation to establish, and show how the removal of its underpinnings wrecks that argument.

It should be perfectly clear that in a three- or five-minute rebuttal speech one cannot answer every point an opponent can make in a ten-minute main speech. Fortunately, it is not necessary to answer every point to be effective in rebuttal. What we should try to do is to weaken as much as we can the points in our opponents' argument which have had seriously adverse effects upon our case. If we are sure that an opposition shot has missed its intended mark, we should not bother to answer it. But, when our opponents have hit us, we cannot afford to overlook that fact.

If an opposition point is so good that we cannot answer it, we should have found that out before the debate began, and conceded it. However, if we are caught unexpectedly in this predicament, the best way out is to concede the point then and go on with what is left of our case. We must not run up a white flag the first time a hit is scored on us. As long as there is a gun which can be fired, a torpedo which can be released, or a motor which will chug along, a good fighter will be on the job doing what he can to sink the enemy.

The etiquette of debate. Wherever one goes, and whatever one does in life, it is an immense advantage to know and observe the conventions. This is especially true in contest debating, where the judge is likely to penalize the use of improper and unconventional methods.

When the presiding officer introduces the debater by saying, " The first speaker for the affirmative will be William Jenkins, of Wellington High School," William should take the platform, pause for a moment, with feet together, face the presiding officer, begin by saying " Mr. Chairman," and then address the audience. A salutation which is universally approved is, " Ladies and gentlemen." This may be varied according to situations. A debater may prefer to say, " Fellow students, and friends." In no event should we use the clumsy and outmoded form " Mr. Chairman, honorable judge, worthy opponents, and ladies and gentlemen." Let us assume that our opponents and the judge will be included in " Ladies and gentlemen "! The judge is simply one of the audience who has been given the responsibility of expressing a critical opinion on how well we play the game of contest debating. He will not enjoy being singled out for a special salutation.

Most important in the etiquette of debate is the treatment of opponents. Here the code of good sportsmanship should dictate what we should do and what we should refrain from doing. Seldom should we address our remarks directly to our opponents. They should be treated as part of the audience. As they speak, we should listen to them carefully, and not fiddle with our notes or confer with our colleagues in an impolite and distracting manner. If we are to avoid being guilty of the serious error of misquotation, we will need to pay careful attention to what our opponents actually say. If we do not, we may find ourselves answering arguments which the audience knows were not made in this particular debate. It is always a temptation to begin formulating our rebuttal of a point which is being made by the opposition before we have heard the whole of it. We may say to ourselves, " Here comes that argument on political corruption," and then we begin to get our answer ready without observing that the argument as presented this time is different from any that we have encountered before. The result is that our rebuttal argument does not fit. The audience and the judge, as well as our opponents, can see very plainly that we have slipped in one of the essential techniques of debating.

Observe the time limits strictly. If we have ten minutes for a constructive speech, we should stop with the completion of the sentence we are speaking when time expires. Continuing to talk beyond the fixed span is just as futile in debate as it is for a football player to make a couple of touchdowns after the gun has gone off; the spectators think him foolish, and the officials pay no attention to the scores thus made. Moreover, the debater who speaks overtime convicts himself of bad manners.

NEW TYPES OF DEBATE

In recent years, some modifications have been made in the traditional forms of debating. We mention them here to suggest that there is nothing particularly sacred about the usual arrangement. We may find it interesting to try out one of the two principal new procedures.

They are known as the cross-question debate, and the direct-clash debate.

The cross-question debate. This plan uses the same kind of proposition as does the traditional form. It begins with a speech by the affirmative, which is followed by a first negative speech. Then the second negative speaker cross-examines the first affirmative speaker by asking him questions for the same length of time that was used in the first speech. After this the second affirmative speaker cross-examines the first negative speaker, again for the same length of time. Then the second negative speaker has an opportunity to summarize the negative's case, and the second affirmative speaker concludes the debate with a summary of the affirmative's case.

In order to have this kind of debate work out well the chairman must enforce the rules rigorously. During the cross-examination periods, the questioners must limit themselves to asking questions, and the " witnesses " must answer the questions and not make additional constructive speeches. Furthermore, when a question has been asked, the person being questioned must be given full and free opportunity to answer it before he is bombarded with other questions.

The direct-clash debate. This requires a good deal of advance planning and conference between the participating teams. They must agree upon the issues which are to be taken up. The first affirmative speaker begins with any one of the issues he may desire to present. The first negative speaker deals with or answers the arguments which the first affirmative brings up. Following this negative rebuttal comes a further affirmative argument on the same issue, and this, in turn, is succeeded by another negative argument on the same issue. This procedure goes on until the chairman decides the particular issue in favor of one side or the other. After the judge has rendered his decision on the first issue, the process is repeated on the second issue, and so on until all vital points in the case have been considered. One advantage in this system is that the two teams are obliged to come to grips on certain major issues regardless of their desire to evade or "bypass" them in the presentation of their own case.

Tests of Comprehension and Application

TESTING THE PROPOSITION

1 Select a topic dealing with some phase of economics and phrase five propositions on it, making your statements as concise as possible. Work out a proper definition for each of the terms in each proposition.

2 Phrase one good proposition for debate on each of the following topics:

The Securities and Exchange Commission	The Next Presidential Election China
The Sales Tax	The Philippine Islands
War Debts	Automobile Insurance
Labor Unions	Methods of Nominating Political Candidates
Co-operatives	
War Veterans	Secret Societies in High School
The Western Hemisphere	The Presidential Term of Office
A World Organization	Trial by Jury
Foreign-Language Study	Federal Aid in Education
Physical Education	Motion Pictures
The Honor System	The United States Supreme Court
The Present Session of Congress	

TRADITIONAL FORMS OF DEBATE

3 Arrange for a week of classroom debating on propositions you have worked out. Try some debates with two members on each team, some with only one, and others with three. What you get out of this exercise will depend in very large measure on how much

time you spend studying the propositions and collecting worthwhile material.
4 Prepare and participate in interclass or inter-high-school debates.
5 Hold a class discussion on the benefits derived from debating.
6 Examine books devoted entirely to debating to see if there is additional material of interest and help to you.

NEW TYPES OF DEBATE

7 Try a cross-examination debate on one of the propositions you have formulated earlier. How do you like it? Does it seem to have advantages over the traditional form? Can you think of any way in which the two forms might be combined?
8 Hold a direct-clash debate on a proposition of interest to the class. Compare this method with those in exercises 3 and 7.

CHAPTER SIXTEEN *Parliamentary Procedure*

THERE ARE a great many mistaken notions about parliamentary procedure. Some people look upon its rules and principles as artificial and unnecessary. Others think that parliamentary practice is appropriate only in large legislative bodies, and that an attempt to use it in smaller and less formal organizations is likely to be harmful rather than helpful. Often those who do not understand correct procedure resent the knowledge of those who do; as in other situations, those who are not " up " on anything are likely to be " down " on it!

We approach our study of parliamentary law from the standpoint of those who believe that it is simply common sense made articulate. There is nothing whatever peculiar or unreasonable about the rules of parliamentary procedure. If all the books on the subject were burned, and if all knowledge of it were removed from the minds of men, we would inevitably be forced to build up some similar system before we could transact organizational business with any degree of effectiveness.

As the term " parliamentary law " implies, we are here dealing with principles and practices originally developed in the British Parliament. Similar rules are used in the Congress of the United States and in the various state legislatures. The larger the organization, and the more formal its transactions, the more comprehensive must be the rules which govern its procedures, and the more rigorously must they be observed. On the other hand, the smaller and the more informal the group, the simpler may be the procedures and the less strict the rules.

One reason for understanding and using the principles of parliamentary procedure is that they help us, as a group, to accomplish in an orderly and efficient manner whatever we want to do. Just as an individual, in order to do his work effectively, finds it desirable to go about it according to a prearranged plan, so an organization before proceeding to formal action first sets up a procedural code. The members must agree upon *ways* of doing things if they expect to do things efficiently.

Since a meeting which lasts an hour and is attended by one hundred people actually consumes one hundred hours of time, it is of great importance that business should be handled in an orderly and efficient manner. Any member of such a group who uses his knowledge of parliamentary law to obstruct business and waste time is abusing a system which is designed to make possible the dispatch of a maximum amount of business with the expenditure of a minimum of effort and time. In the use of parliamentary law it is a good rule to insist upon the observance of the code just so long as it will promote order and efficiency, and then to modify or disregard it when it leads to delay and confusion.

Majority rule is a basic democratic ideal. However, there is another principle of democracy which must not be overlooked — the protection of minorities. Many parliamentary rules are designed to make sure that we determine majority opinion fairly. Others arise from our desire to see to it that individuals and groups which do not agree with the majority are not overridden without what the American Constitution calls " due process of law." Among the duties which anyone assumes when he becomes a member of an organization is that of allowing the majority to have its way, providing that he is protected in the exercise of all the rights and privileges of membership as specified in the constitution and bylaws.

ORGANIZING A GROUP

Suppose people are meeting for the first time to organize a new society or club. They have come together at the call of those who are most interested in the project. This call may have been passed around by word of mouth, sent by written notices, or made by publication in a newspaper. This first meeting should proceed at once to form a temporary organization. One of those who have called the meeting should take the chair and make a brief statement as to why the meeting has been called, or ask someone else to make such a statement. Following this explanation, the person who has assumed the chair should ask for nominations of a temporary chairman. (It well may be that he himself will be nominated.) If it is a large group and there is more than one nominee, it may be desirable to appoint tellers and vote by written ballot. If it is a small group, or if there is but one nominee, the chairman may ask for a voiced vote, saying: " Mr. X has been nominated. All those in favor of Mr. X serving as temporary chairman will please say ' Aye.' All those opposed, ' No.' . . . I declare Mr. X elected and hereby turn the chair over to him." Ordinarily, the less fuss and feathers about the choice of a temporary chairman, the better. The most important consideration is to get the machinery set up for establishing a permanent organization.

When a temporary chairman has been chosen, he should appoint (or have elected) a temporary secretary, whose duty it will be to keep a careful record of every action taken until the permanent organization has been completed. When the temporary chairman and the temporary secretary have been selected, the major remaining item of business to be taken up at the first meeting is the appointment, or election, of a Committee on Constitution and Bylaws. Rarely should such a committee have more than three members. In small groups, there usually is no good reason why the temporary chairman should not choose the committee. Those who are most interested in the proposed organization should be put on the committee. After this committee has been constituted, it may be well to have some discussion of the most important matters that are to be covered by the constitution and bylaws, in order that the committee may do its work as effectively and as nearly in harmony with majority opinion as possible. Of course, there may be differences of opinion which cannot be settled until a first draft of the constitution and bylaws has been prepared and has been submitted to the group at the second meeting.

Drafting the constitution and bylaws. The Committee on Constitution and Bylaws should begin its work by obtaining copies of constitutions and bylaws of similar organizations. These may serve as guides. A constitution should contain only fundamental rules covering the following matters:

OUTLINE OF A CONSTITUTION

Preamble, or brief statement of aims and purposes
Article I. Name of the organization
Article II. Requirements for membership
Article III. Names of officers, with their respective duties and terms of office
Article IV. Provision for an Executive Committee which can take action on behalf of the organization in periods between meetings. Usually the Executive Committee is made up of the officers.
Article V. Stipulation for regular meetings, and provision for methods of calling special meetings. Usually special meetings can be called by the president, by the Executive Committee, or by a specified number of members.
Article VI. Statement of method by which the constitution may be amended

The following matters usually are dealt with in the bylaws:

OUTLINE OF BYLAWS

Section I. Methods of electing and admitting members
Section II. Dues

Section III. Methods of electing officers and committees
Section IV. Name of the parliamentary authority to be followed
Section V. Definition of a quorum (the number of members who must be present before business can be transacted legally)
Section VI. Method of amending the bylaws

The bylaws should contain everything necessary to ensure orderly procedure under the constitution. Particular attention should be given to the naming of the parliamentary authority. Robert, *Rules of Order*, Auer, *Essentials of Parliamentary Procedure*, or Hall and Sturgis, *Textbook on Parliamentary Law* are among the standard books on the subject.

Adopting a constitution and bylaws. The second meeting of the organization should be devoted to the adoption of the constitution and bylaws which have been prepared by the committee. After calling the meeting to order the temporary chairman asks for a report of the committee. The chairman of the committee reads the constitution and bylaws, article by article and section by section. After each article or section, the temporary chairman asks whether there are any amendments to be proposed. Proposed amendments are either incorporated by permission of the committee which has drafted the constitution and bylaws or are voted on as they are suggested. When the whole constitution has been read and each section has been voted on, the chairman of the committee moves the adoption of the constitution as a whole as it stands, with any amendments which may have been made. When the constitution has been adopted, the bylaws are taken up section by section, and adopted as a whole, in the same way. The constitution and bylaws usually go into effect as soon as they have been adopted.

Electing officers. The second major item of business to come before the meeting is the election of the officers provided for in the constitution, by the methods stipulated in the bylaws. Those elected usually take office at once. When a Committee on Nominations presents a " slate," additional nominations may be made from the " floor." If none is made, a member may move that the secretary be instructed to cast a ballot for the whole list.

Appointing standing committees. The final step in getting the organization under way is to elect, or to appoint, the standing committees which have been provided for in the constitution and bylaws. There usually are such standing committees as Program Committee, Membership Committee, and Finance Committee.

CONDUCTING BUSINESS

We shall here consider some of the simple but necessary principles to be observed in the orderly, efficient conduct of business.

Obtaining the floor. A member desiring to speak should rise in his place and address the presiding officer as follows: "Mr. Chairman," "Mr. President," "Mr. Moderator," "Madam President," or "Madame Chairman." Having addressed the chair, he should wait to be recognized by the chair before he continues to speak. The chairman recognizes him by name or by title: "Mr. Brown," or "The Representative from the Thirty-third." When the member has been recognized by the chair, he may enter upon a discussion of any motion which has been made, seconded, and put before the house, or he may himself offer a motion.

In case two members address the presiding officer simultaneously, the chair must use his judgment as to which he should recognize, keeping in mind such questions as: Has either spoken before on the question before the house? Is there any special reason why one or the other should be given preference? Ordinary consideration, tact, and courtesy should decide such an issue.

Making a motion. If a member desires to have a matter discussed by the group, he should always offer his proposal in the form of a resolution or a motion. If the proposal is complicated, it is best to present it in writing; a copy should be handed to the secretary. In making a motion the speaker should say, "I move that such and such action be taken," or " I desire to offer a motion to the effect that such and such a thing be done." The form " I move you " is wholly incorrect.

Putting a motion. When a motion has been made, the chairman should restate the motion and ask, " Is there a second? " If there is no second, the chair declares the motion lost for want of a second. A second may be offered by any member without rising and addressing the chair. When the motion has been seconded, the chairman should say: " It has been moved and seconded that (such and such action be taken). Is there any discussion? " The matter is then before the house.

Discussing a motion. No subject should be discussed by the assembly until it has been presented in the form of a motion, duly seconded, and restated by the chair. (Some motions, as is noted later, are undebatable and must be voted on without discussion.) In the discussion of a motion no member should be allowed to speak twice if anyone who has not had an opportunity to speak desires the floor.

Methods of voting. There are several methods of ascertaining the will of an assembly on a motion. The *viva-voce* method is the most usual. After everyone who desires to speak has done so, the chairman says, " If there is no further discussion, all those in favor will say ' Aye.' (Note that " Aye " is pronounced $\bar{i}$ and not $\bar{a}$.) . . . All those opposed will please say ' No.' . . . The motion is carried," or " The motion is lost," depending on the chairman's judgment as to how the vote has gone.

Any member is privileged to call for a *division* if he thinks the chairman has misinterpreted the viva-voce vote. A division means that the chairman must ask all those in favor of the motion to stand while the secretary counts them. After they have resumed their seats, all those opposed are asked to rise and be counted. Some assemblies take all votes by show of hands or by rising.

In deciding important issues on which it is desirable to allow each member to express his own opinion without being influenced by the voting of anyone else, the written *ballot* may be used.

Order of business. In most organizations the following order of business is the rule:

1. The chairman calls the meeting to order.

2. The chairman asks the secretary to read the minutes of the previous meeting, which are corrected if necessary and then approved.

3. The chairman calls for the reports of standing committees and the assembly acts on them.

4. The chairman calls for the reports of special committees and the assembly acts on them.

5. Any business which was left unfinished at the previous meeting is taken up.

6. New business is transacted.

7. The assembly adjourns.

Appointing or electing special committees. When in the opinion of any member a matter which has been brought up can be handled best by a committee, he may move that the chairman appoint a committee (or that a committee be elected) to consider it. The usual form of this motion will be found in the discussion of the motion to commit, page 432. Unless there is some good reason for doing otherwise, custom and courtesy suggest that the chair appoint as chairman of such a committee the member who made the motion.

Committee reports. When a committee brings in a report, the chairman of the committee usually reads it and then moves that it be adopted. If the report is complicated or long, it may be divided into sections and acted on, one section at a time. If the society does not care to act in accordance with the recommendations of the committee, but does desire to place the report on file, the proper procedure is to " receive " (rather than to " adopt " or " accept ") the report.

DUTIES OF MEMBERS

While we are all aware of the fact that officers have duties, we sometimes make the mistake of thinking that members have only privileges! Among your acquaintances there probably are boys and girls who do not want to play any game unless they can be leaders. These same people mistakenly suppose that they cannot be very helpful to a society or a club unless they are officers. We should realize that our school, our city, and our country need good citizens as well as good officials. As a matter of fact, competent officials can do their work satisfactorily only when citizens accept and live up to their obligations. As a member of an organization, you can do a great deal to promote its welfare by understanding and performing your functions. Every member should possess a knowledge of the principles of parliamentary procedure and practice them in every meeting he attends.

The members of most organizations are very quick to perceive special capabilities among their number and to choose competent people as officers. When one has been chosen as an officer of an organization, he should enter upon his duties realizing that he is now in a very special way responsible for its success and that upon his tact and technical knowledge depends much of the efficiency of the group.

Serving as president. The work of the presiding officer, whether we call him president, chairman, moderator, or speaker, is first of all to keep order and to see that every member has an equal chance to participate in discussion. His business is to apply rules and regulations in such a way as to protect the parliamentary rights of the minority while allowing the will of the majority, within certain prescribed limits, to express itself.

The presiding officer should be absolutely impartial in all that he does and says. He should not participate in the debate on any question. He does not vote except when his vote will be decisive or when the voting is by ballot. If for special reasons he desires to take part in the debate, he must call someone else to the chair while he takes the floor and speaks.

The presiding officer should always have at hand the constitution and bylaws of the organization and the recognized handbook of parliamentary procedure. As far as possible, he should know in advance what matters are to come before the meeting and be as helpful as possible to all of the members who desire to express themselves on the subjects under consideration. He should never parade his technical knowledge, and while he should always use the correct parliamentary forms, he should not do so in such a way as to embarrass members who may not be as expert as he. When a member does not use the correct form in offering a motion, the chairman should suggest the proper one as tactfully as he can. It is emphatically the chairman's business to be co-operative rather than superior, helpful rather than critical, and to follow the spirit of the law rather than the letter. H. M. Robert, in his justly famous *Rules of Order*, says, "Never be technical or any more strict than is absolutely necessary for the good of the meeting." However, we should not overlook the fact that in large and formal organizations the good of the meeting may require one to be very strict and technical.

Serving as secretary. The secretary, or clerk, of the organization should be chosen on the basis of his special fitness for recording accurately every item of business transacted. The importance of accurate and complete records can hardly be overemphasized. All resolutions and motions, whether passed or not, should be included in this record, which is commonly referred to as the "minutes." In addition to the resolutions and motions, the secretary should enter in the record all committee reports and other matters which in his judgment may be helpful in the future in indicating just what was done in a given meeting. Critical comments, the secretary's own private opinions as to the correctness or incorrectness of anything that is said, should never be put into the official report; it should be completely matter-of-fact. The minutes should always give the place and date of the meeting, and the names of members present. Ordinarily, they are typewritten and kept in a loose-leaf notebook. However, some organizations require the keeping of the minutes in longhand and in a bound notebook, in order to make unauthorized changes in the records more difficult.

Serving as treasurer. The treasurer has charge of the funds of the society. He keeps careful accounts and furnishes detailed statements or reports at regular intervals or on call. The treasurer should always remember that at any time he may be required to present documentary evidence concerning receipts and disbursements and therefore he should keep complete records. The treasurer is not supposed to pay out money without specific authorization, usually not without the written order of the president. When any considerable sums of money are being handled by the treasurer, he should ask for periodical official audits so that in case of future questions he may be protected. A treasurer who is not familiar with modern methods of accounting should consult with authorities in this field before undertaking the duties of his office. In a high-school organization, it may be desirable to choose as treasurer some student specializing in commercial subjects.

STUDENT LEGISLATORS. *Student " senators " and " assemblymen " learn about democracy in action by taking over the state legislature once a year. The young lawmakers work in committees to draw up bills, submit them to the model legislature, and debate them fully. This picture shows one of the committees engaged in drafting a bill. A member of the committee is arguing for the inclusion of an amendment in the report of the committee. Are his colleagues favorably disposed to his point of view? Has he won the complete attention of the other committee members? (Leigh, Pix)*

Serving as committee member. When the membership of a society is large, it is always desirable and often imperative to transact a good deal of the business in committee meetings. The advantages of the committee system are many. It saves the time of the whole organization, permits freer and fuller discussion, and makes possible the discovery and study of facts not ordinarily available to the whole society. Members are usually appointed on committees because of their special knowledge of, or interest in, the matters referred to the committees. Committee members should avoid the consideration of matters not referred to them, and try to contribute as much as they can to furthering the wishes of the society.

CLASSIFIED LIST OF MOTIONS
(Arranged so far as possible in order of precedence, from lowest to highest)

I. Miscellaneous motions (no order of precedence within this group)
1. Main motion (to initiate discussion of subject)
2. Reconsider
3. Rescind
4. Take from table
5. Make special order of business
6. Limit debate

II. Secondary, or subsidiary, motions (ways of disposing of other motions)
1. Postpone indefinitely
2. Amend
3. Commit
4. Postpone to a certain time
5. Previous question
6. Lay on table

III. Incidental motions (no order of precedence within this group)
1. Point of order
2. Appeal
3. Suspension of rules
4. Objection to consideration
5. Request for information
6. Withdrawal of motion

IV. Privileged motions
1. Call for orders of the day
2. Question of privilege
3. Adjourn
4. Fix time of next meeting

CONDENSED WORKING CODE

The following is an alphabetical list of the various motions. When we say that one motion "takes precedence over" another, we mean that it may be offered while the other is "before the house" and that it must be considered first. When we say that a motion "yields" to another, we mean that a second motion may be made while the first is before the house and that the second motion must be considered before the house can go on with the discussion of the one which "yields." Before we study this condensed working code we should memorize the list of motions on page 431.

Adjourn. Proper form: "I move that we adjourn." This motion is undebatable, and takes precedence over all other motions except the one to fix the time for the next meeting, to which it yields.

Amend. Proper form: "I move to amend the motion by striking out _____, (by inserting _____, by adding _____, or by substituting _____)." Usually only one of these proposals is made in one amendment. This motion takes precedence over nothing but the main motion and the motion to postpone indefinitely. It yields to all privileged, incidental, and secondary motions except the motion to postpone indefinitely. An amendment may be amended, but an amendment to an amendment cannot be amended. When an amendment is in order, someone may move to substitute an entirely new main motion for the one before the house. This proposed substitute motion is treated as an amendment.

One of the special forms of amendment is to divide the main question. When the main motion is complicated, this procedure may be desirable; it permits the assembly to vote on each of the several parts of a question separately.

Appeal from the decision of the chair. See *Point of order.*

Commit. Proper form: "I move that the subject be referred to the committee on _____ (designating the appropriate committee)," or, "I move that the chairman appoint (or that we elect) a special committee of three (or some other number) to consider the matter." If the reference is to be to a special committee, the member offering the motion should specify the size of the committee and the method by which it is to be selected. This motion takes precedence over main motions, motions to amend, and motions to postpone indefinitely. It yields to privileged motions; incidental motions; and to motions to lay on the table, for the previous question, and to postpone to a certain time. Debate is limited to the propriety of referring the matter to a committee; it does not open for debate the question to which it is applied.

Division of question. See *Amendment.*

Fix the time of the next meeting. Proper form: " I move that when we adjourn, we adjourn to meet at such and such a time." This motion takes precedence over all other motions, is undebatable, and can be amended only by changing the specified time. If this motion is made when no other motion is pending, it is simply a main motion, takes precedence over nothing, is debatable, and is treated in every way exactly as other main motions.

Lay on table. Proper form: " I move that the question be laid on the table." This motion takes precedence over main motions and all other secondary motions. It yields to privileged and incidental motions. It is debatable, cannot be amended, and if passed, cannot be reconsidered. Laying an amendment on the table results in laying the main question to which the amendment was proposed on the table also.

Limit debate. Proper form: " I move to limit debate on the preceding question to _____ (stating length of time)." This motion is made to expedite the transaction of business. It may be amended by changing the time limit, but it is undebatable. Since it restricts free discussion, it requires a two-thirds vote.

Make special order of business. Proper form: " I move that the subject of _____ be made a special order of business to be considered at _____ (stating time)." The purpose of this motion is to ensure consideration of a question at a particular time. It requires a two-thirds vote. If this motion is passed, the matter to which it refers must be taken up at the specified date or hour.

Objection to consideration of a question. Proper form: " I object to the consideration of this question." This motion can be made only before the debate on the motion to which it applies has begun. It requires no second. It is in order when another has the floor, and is undebatable. It cannot have any secondary motion applied to it.

When the objection is raised, the chairman should immediately say, "Shall the question be considered?" A two-thirds "No" vote is required to prevent consideration.

Orders of the day. Proper form: "I call for the orders of the day." See *Make special order of business,* above. The phrase "orders of the day" means the business scheduled to be taken up at a particular time. This call takes precedence over all other motions except the motions to fix the time for the next meeting, rights and privileges, and to adjourn. It is in order when another has the floor, is undebatable, and does not require a second. When anyone calls for the orders of the day, the chairman says: "Shall we proceed to the orders of the day? Those in favor say 'Aye'—opposed, 'No.'"

Point of order. Proper form: "I rise to a point of order." This action is open to any member who at any time feels that incorrect procedures are being followed. The chairman immediately says, "Please state your point." The member states his point and the chairman then says, "Your point is (or is not) well taken." No vote is required unless someone questions the chairman's ruling, in which event the proper form is "I appeal from the decision of the chair." The chairman then says, "Shall the decision of the chair stand? All those in favor say 'Aye.' . . . Those opposed, 'No.'" A majority or a tie vote sustains the decision. A point of order is undebatable. It cannot be amended. It does not require a second. It is in order when another has the floor. The object of the motion is to guarantee the observance of parliamentary principles. A member should rise to a point of order only when the departure from parliamentary procedure is likely to result in serious difficulties, such as denying to members their rights and privileges or obstructing the will of the majority.

Postpone indefinitely. Proper form: "I move that the question be postponed indefinitely." This motion takes precedence over the main motion and yields to all other motions. The effect of passing this motion is to kill the motion to which it is applied. It is frequently employed as a device to test the strength of the opposing sides on a motion before the house, in advance of a direct vote on it.

Postpone to certain time. Proper form: "I move the question be postponed until (naming a specific time)." This motion takes precedence over main motions, and the motions to commit, to amend, and to postpone indefinitely. It yields to the motions to lay on the table, to the previous question, and to privileged and incidental motions. It can be amended only by altering the time. Questions postponed to a certain time become orders of the day when that time arrives.

Previous question. Proper form: "I call for (or move) the previous question." This motion takes precedence over the main motion and all secondary motions except the motion to lay on the table. It yields to privileged and incidental motions and to the motion to lay on the table. It is undebatable. It requires a two-thirds vote. When a member moves the previous question, he is asking that the debate be terminated and that the assembly proceed at once to vote on the question under discussion. When the previous question is moved, the chairman should say: "Shall the previous question now be put? Those in favor rise. . . . Those opposed rise." If there is a two-thirds vote in favor, the assembly is then bound to vote on the motion which is pending, without further discussion.

Privilege. Proper form: "I rise to a question of privilege." The chairman should ask the member to explain what rights he thinks are being violated. The purpose in raising a question of privilege is to protect one's essential rights in a public meeting, to stop personal insults on the part of other members, or to deal with disorders which are limiting the freedom of debate. The chairman, having heard the member's complaint, may rule for or against his expressed point of view or may refer the issue to the assembly for decision by saying: "The chair is in doubt. Those who favor the point of view expressed by Mr. X, say 'Aye.' . . . Those opposed, 'No.' The decision is _____." The question of privilege needs no second and may not be amended or debated.

Reconsider. Proper form: "I move that we reconsider our vote on (naming the motion)." This motion must be made by a member who voted with the winning side in the vote for which reconsideration is proposed. The motion for reconsideration cannot be reconsidered. It must be made at the same meeting at which the original vote was taken, or at the following meeting. It is debatable only when the question to be reconsidered is debatable.

Request for information. Proper form: "I rise for information."

The chairman should ask the member to state his question and should proceed to supply the information desired by the inquirer. The purpose of the request for information is to guarantee that all members may know just what matter is before the assembly, what parliamentary forms may properly be used at the moment, and so on. The request requires no second and is not debatable.

Rescind. Proper form: "I move that the action taken (at such and such a time, on such and such a matter) be rescinded." This motion takes precedence over no other motion and is simply a special form of main motion. When the motion is made, the chairman should say: "It has been moved and seconded that the action taken (at such and such a time) be rescinded. All those in favor say 'Aye.' . . . Those opposed, 'No.'" The effect of an affirmative vote on the motion is to undo the effects of the previous action so far as that is possible. Sometimes it is moved that the previous action be rescinded and "expunged from the record."

Substitute motion. See *Amendment.*

Suspension of the rules. Proper form: "I move to suspend the rule (specifying)." This motion takes precedence over main and secondary motions and yields to privileged and incidental motions. It is undebatable, cannot be amended or reconsidered, and requires a two-thirds vote. The rules under which an assembly is operating may be suspended *by unanimous consent* at any time.

Take from the table. Proper form: "I move that the motion to (specifying) be taken from the table." This motion is neither amendable nor debatable. If it is passed, the motion from the table comes before the house immediately. To take from the table ranks as a special form of main motion.

Withdrawal of a motion. Proper form: "I ask leave to withdraw my motion." The chairman usually says, "Mr. ———— asks leave to withdraw his motion. Unless someone objects, permission is granted." If anyone objects, a vote by "Aye" and "No" is taken. This motion takes precedence over main motions, secondary motions, and a motion to suspend the rules; it yields to privileged motions, to a point of order, and to objection to consideration.

CONSTITUTION AND MINUTES OF A SCHOOL SOCIETY

To help in properly organizing and running a debating or literary society in your school, a model constitution, model bylaws, and specimen secretary's minutes follow. Examine them carefully.

MODEL CONSTITUTION

Preamble

In order to promote skill in public speaking and reading and to develop a more general interest in these accomplishments throughout the student body of this high school, this organization is established.

Article I: Name

This organization shall be called the Forest High School Speech Club.

Article II: Membership

Membership in this club shall be open to all regularly enrolled students of the Forest High School. The names of candidates for membership shall be presented by the Executive Committee and voted on at a regular meeting of the club. No candidate who shall receive less than a two-thirds vote of the members present at any regular meeting shall be admitted to membership.

Article III: Officers

The officers of this Club shall be: President; Vice-President; Secretary; Treasurer; Chairman of the Program Committee. These officers shall be elected at the last meeting of each school year.

Article IV: Executive Committee

The Executive Committee shall consist of the president, the secretary, and the treasurer.

Article V: Meetings

Section 1. Regular meetings of the club shall be held in the high-school assembly room on Friday of each week throughout the school year.

Section II. Special meetings shall be held at the call of the president or at the call of any ten members.

Article VI: Amendment

This constitution may be amended by a two-thirds vote of the members present at any regular meeting, provided that the proposed amendment has been submitted in writing at the preceding regular meeting.

MODEL BYLAWS

Section I

The Executive Committee shall hold tryouts at the beginning of each term for the examination of candidates for membership, and shall recommend only those who in their judgment would profit from membership in the organization and be a credit to it.

Section II

Dues of 25 cents per term shall be payable at the first meeting of each term. Any member whose dues have not been paid by the middle of the term shall be dropped from the roll.

Section III

The club may levy a special assessment on its members by a five-sixths vote of those present at any regular meeting.

Section IV

The officers shall be nominated from the floor and elected by ballot. A majority vote shall be necessary for election.

Section V

An officer shall be ineligible to succeed himself in office.

Section VI

The elected chairman of the Program Committee shall appoint two members to serve with him.

Section VII

When a quorum is not present at a regular meeting, the Executive Committee may transact necessary business, provided that no expenditure in excess of $10 is involved.

Section VIII

A majority of the members of the organization shall constitute a quorum.

Section IX

Robert's *Rules of Order* shall govern the parliamentary procedure of the club on all points not covered by the constitution and bylaws.

Section X

The bylaws may be amended by a two-thirds vote of the members present at a regular meeting.

Section XI

Any member who fails to perform a program assignment shall be fined $1 unless excused by the Executive Committee.

SPECIMEN SECRETARY'S MINUTES

The second regular meeting of the Forest High School Speech Club for the year 1945-46 was held in the assembly room of the high school on Friday evening, September 25, 1945, at 8:00 P.M. Those present were (insert names).

President Johnson called the meeting to order and asked the secretary to read the minutes of the previous meeting. The minutes were read and approved.

Reports of standing committees were called for. The chairman of the Program Committee announced that Mr. Dawson of the City Chamber of Commerce had consented to speak at the following meeting. The report of the Program Committee was accepted.

The treasurer, speaking for the Executive Committee, reported that six candidates for membership had been examined since the previous meeting and recommended that William James, Dan Williams, and Jean Kinney be admitted to regular membership in the club. On motion of Ralph Allen, seconded by Lucille Benson, it was voted that the secretary be instructed to cast a unanimous ballot for the three candidates.

Reports of special committees were then called for. Robert Jensen, chairman of the special committee appointed to arrange for a picnic, reported that the committee had investigated possibilities and recommended holding the picnic on the following Wednesday evening at Memorial Park. The committee had tentatively arranged for a special launch to leave the Wood Street pier at 5 P.M., and to return at 10:30. It was moved by Robert Jensen and seconded by Marcia Ashe that the committee report be adopted. The motion was carried.

The president then called for unfinished business. On motion of Patricia Spencer, seconded by Eugene Jones, it was voted that the resolution providing for musical numbers on the programs, laid on the table at the preceding meeting, should be taken from the table. After some discussion, on motion of Emily Greene, seconded by Richard Brown, the resolution was referred to a committee of three to be appointed by the chair. The president appointed on the committee: Emily Greene, chairman, Eugene Jones, and Richard Brown.

The president then called for new business. Stephen Jackson moved that Ruth Pierce be censured for her failure to appear on the program after she had been duly notified and had consented to appear. Arnold Christian seconded the motion. Alice Cummings objected to the consideration of the question. The objection was sustained. The chair announced that Ruth Pierce had paid the fine of $1 provided in Section XI of the bylaws.

Helen Prentiss moved that the club have a tag day on the following Monday afternoon. Dan Williams seconded the motion. After some discussion Patricia Spencer offered an amendment, which was seconded by Dorothy Lyle, to the effect that the boys should take complete charge of the sale of the tags. Robert Jensen offered an amendment to the amendment, providing that the word "girls" should be substituted for "boys." The amendment to the amendment was seconded by Frank Holt. Gertrude Joslin moved that the matter be referred to the Executive Committee with power to act. The motion to commit was seconded by Dan Williams and, after some discussion, was carried.

Wanda Lucas moved that the meeting adjourn. The motion was seconded by Robert Jensen. Eugene Jones moved that when we adjourn, we should adjourn to meet the following day at 5:15 P.M. The motion was seconded by Dick Hansen. The motion to fix the time for the next meeting was lost. The motion to adjourn was then carried.

The chairman declared the meeting adjourned at 9:10 P.M.

Respectfully submitted,
Mary Smith
Secretary

Tests of Comprehension and Application

WRITTEN PRACTICE

1 In order to aid in mastering the material of this chapter, it is suggested that each member of the class construct a chart showing five important facts about each motion. On horizontal lines at the left of the page, list the classification of motions exactly as it is given on page 431. Draw vertical lines half an inch apart to make squares with

COMPREHENSION AND APPLICATION TESTS

the horizontal lines. At the top of the page along the vertical lines write the following, one to each line:
  a Does it require a second?
  b Is it debatable?
  c Can it be amended?
  d What vote does it require to pass?

Now fill in the squares, answering these questions for each motion. This chart will help you learn these important details. It may be of service to you in the exercises below.

2 Write a letter to some other member of the class, inviting him to a meeting the purpose of which is the organization of a dramatic or a debating club.

3 Write a public notice of the meeting named in exercise 2.

ORAL PRACTICE

4 The class will meet at the call issued in the letter and notices mentioned in exercises 2 and 3 and proceed to effect a temporary organization. Appoint a committee to draft a constitution and bylaws, and spend whatever remains of the time in discussing the function and development of the club in the school.

5 The class will meet as the club, adopt a constitution and bylaws, and elect the officers provided for, in the prescribed manner.

6 At a meeting after the club is organized under exercise 5, let five members each present main motions and six members each present secondary motions.

7 Continuing exercise 6, let five members each present main motions and eight members each present one incidental or privileged motion.

8 Continuing exercise 6, let someone move to take from the table a motion laid on the table at a previous meeting. Let the organization hear a report on some matter referred to a committee at a previous meeting. Dispose of the committee report and let someone move to rescind some previous action. Let someone else move the reconsideration of the previous action. Carry each of the proposals out to a conclusion.

9 Correct the form of the following motions:
  a I move you that this club appropriate $5 from the treasury to pay all outstanding bills.

    b I move that the constitution be suspended and the proposed action taken.

    c I move that this motion be amended in any way the chairman sees fit.

10 Meeting as a club for the practice of parliamentary procedure under the constitution and bylaws adopted in exercise 5, let each student preside until someone rises to a point of order and shows that the chairman has made a mistake. When such a point of order is sustained by the chairman or by the club, let the chairman appoint someone to preside in his place. Let each student propose as many motions as he can in the time at his disposal.

11 After notice of a week let the club meet to discuss some debatable question. Let some member introduce the matter in the form of a main motion and then have each side of the question represented by three speakers who are expected to present separate aspects of the question in speeches of not less than five minutes. Make an effort to dispose of the motion in some way before the close of the hour. After someone has made a main motion, let someone else offer an amendment, and still another, an amendment to the amendment. Suppose someone now moves the previous question and the motion is lost. Let the chairman illustrate the correct procedure.

ORAL AND WRITTEN PRACTICE

12 Let five students each act as secretary of a meeting. Have each of them read the minutes as he has prepared them, and then let the class discuss the form in which each secretary has submitted the minutes.

13 The treasurer of the club will submit an annual report and the club will act on it. The treasurer may make a report dealing with imaginary funds. It is important to get the report into the correct form.

14 Let a committee bring in, and have adopted, a resolution on the death of a member.

15 Let a program of speeches, memorized and extempore, be arranged in advance of a meeting in such a way as to establish them as orders of the day, and then let these be taken up in due course at the appointed time.

16   Assign to each member of the club one of the following topics for a five-minute speech. Each speaker should illustrate the principles which he presents with as many specific cases as possible.
  a   The work of a committee
  b   Legitimate reasons for withdrawing a motion
  c   Legitimate reasons for objecting to the consideration of a motion
  d   Reasons for laying a motion on the table
  e   Reasons for postponing a matter indefinitely
  f   Reasons for suspending the rules
  g   Why some motions are undebatable
  h   Why the motion to reconsider must be made by someone who has voted on the winning side
  i   Why the chairman should be impartial

CHAPTER SEVENTEEN   *Radio Speaking*

THERE ARE approximately 50,000,000 radio receiving sets in the United States. There are not many of us who do not listen to the radio every day of our lives. We have come to depend upon it for news, entertainment, information, and inspiration. Radio tells us how to prepare our food, how to keep up with the styles, and for whom we should vote. It brings us commentators who report what is happening in Europe, Africa, Australia, and on the far-off islands of the Pacific. Radio speakers appeal to us for the support of civic causes and for our patronage of commercial products.

One of the leading executives of the radio industry recently drew attention to the fact that whereas for centuries we have been depending upon written language for mass communication, the radio has reversed this trend and has brought spoken language back into a central position in human affairs. It is an interesting fact that until printing was invented in the sixteenth century, speech was pre-eminently the means of communication among mankind. Then for five centuries the pendulum swung to the printed form. Now it has swung back again. Unquestionably radio has become and is destined to remain one of the most important forces in the life of mankind. With the new form of staticless radio (frequency modulation) and with television, we soon shall be able to converse with our friends anywhere in the world under conditions closely approximating those of face-to-face communication.

Unquestionably it is true that anyone who expects to do anything worth while in the world today will profit from the development of his ability to speak effectively on the air. In this book we are not greatly interested in special microphone training, — how far to stand from the " mike," how loud to speak, and so on. However, we are concerned with understanding the problems of radio speaking, knowing what makes it effective, and being prepared to do it reasonably well if we are called upon.

WHY RADIO SPEAKING IS DIFFERENT

Most radio speaking heard in living rooms. A United States Senator who is experienced enough to know better described his procedure in speaking over the radio as follows: " I imagine the largest audience I have ever seen, multiply it by a thousand, and then speak as I would if I were addressing such an immense gathering." It would be difficult to conceive of any less satisfactory mental approach to radio speaking. The Senator should give attention to the advice of a radio expert, who tells us that we should think of the radio audience not as acres of human beings crowded together but rather as individuals seated in their own homes in small family groups. We don't enjoy having anybody shout in our living rooms. If guests act that way, we probably are slow to invite them again. If the radio speaker is to sound appropriate and pleasant to us, he must behave quite differently from the way in which he conducts himself on the public platform. If the broadcaster is actually making a public speech to a real audience and permitting a radio audience to listen in at the same time, he will of course have to count on his radio listeners' indulgence toward his behavior. Radio listeners are not bothered by a type of speaking that they recognize as being necessary to meet the actual conditions under which the speaking is being done.

The audience cannot see the radio speaker. In a normal speech

"THERE SHALL BE NO NIGHT." *Lynn Fontanne and Alfred Lunt, foremost actors of the American theatre, in the opening scene of one of their most effective plays. The scientist is broadcasting a speech from his home in Greece to his fellow investigators in America while his wife sits quietly beside him. Can anything be learned about proper broadcasting technique from studying the picture? (Culver Service)*

situation, we appeal to both the ears and the eyes of our audience. In a radio speech, we must rely upon the ears alone. This fact has some important bearings upon the way in which we use our voices, especially with respect to our speaking rate. A good many people make the mistake of supposing that because the absence of visible signs reduces intelligibility, radio speaking requires a slower rate. On the contrary, it has been found that good radio speakers use the tempo of lively conversation, which is a good deal more rapid than that of platform address. When a speaker is visible to his audience, he makes very different use of pause from what he does when he is speaking over the radio. If we can see what a speaker is doing while he is pausing, we may understand the significance of the temporary halt in his vocal utterance. His gestures, facial expression, and other elements of the visible code continue to speak to us while his voice is silent. We know that he is intentionally and deliberately pausing. On the other hand, a pause on the radio may leave us wondering what in the world is happening. We do not know whether the speaker is unable to continue or whether we are about to hear the announcement " Conditions beyond our control make it impossible for us to continue this broadcast." Of course this does not imply that the good radio speaker rushes through his talk without any pauses whatever. He simply uses a quicker tempo with shorter pauses.

All of this discussion emphasizes the importance of a good radio voice, and skill in the control of it. If we are listening to a radio drama, we have a greater opportunity for the use of imagination than we have in looking at and listening to a movie or a stage play. The radio performers can stimulate us into picturing for ourselves just the characters we need in order to tell ourselves the story in the most acceptable terms.

Members of the radio audience do not affect each other as do those of other audiences. If a group of people are listening to a radio program, of course they are aware of each other's presence and do affect each other's behavior. When one of them expresses disapproval or dislike of the program, his reactions are bound to influence the attitude of his companions toward what is coming over the air. When one listener laughs, he contributes something to the enjoyment the other members of the group derive from the program. If one yawns or seems irritated, that behavior also has an effect on the others.

However, as we have already said, we usually listen to the radio either alone or in small family groups where we behave more as individuals than as members of a crowd. If we feel moved to do so, we can react enthusiastically without worrying about whether someone else will think that we are going to extremes. We can express violent disapproval without the fear of being thought impolite. In a public audience, the individual is restrained from doing anything he thinks may not be approved by the others about him. There is an almost complete absence of such social restraint as we listen to radio programs in our own homes.

The studio audience affects the radio audience. A good many of the popular radio programs are presented before studio audiences whose audible behavior comes to us with the voices of the performers. Thus the behavior of the studio audience, so far as it is audible, is integrated with the entire program. Those of us who have attended studio broadcasts know how puppetlike a studio audience is. Before the broadcast begins, the master of ceremonies instructs the audience concerning the rules and regulations to be observed in listening to the program. When the announcer wants applause, he asks for it in sign language which he has agreed upon with the audience, and when he wants the applause to cease, he stops it. The theory on which all this is done is that the radio audience is stimulated into enjoying the program more by hearing the evidences of the studio audience's enjoyment.

THOMAS E. DEWEY SPEAKS. *What emotional meanings are suggested by the speaker's physical attitude? What words appropriately might accompany such facial expression and hand and arm gestures? What principles of effective visible action are illustrated here? (Acme)*

Experimental studies have shown that the majority of radio listeners agree with this theory and think that the program is improved by the audible laughter and applause mixed with the rest of the performance. Some listeners do not agree with this point of view. They are annoyed by listening to evidences of the amusement of the studio audience when they are not always sure what is being laughed at. Frequently the merriment is caused by the visible speech of the performers, and since the radio audience cannot see this, they feel left out and cheated.

The speaker cannot hear and see his audience. Many people in speaking over the radio for the first time experience a lost feeling. The absence of any response from anybody gives them the impression of total ineffectiveness. The better they have been in dealing with audiences present before them, the more likely they are to feel this way; for they have become accustomed to observing their auditors carefully and adapting their procedures to the responses they are getting. If we are talking face to face with a friend, and we see that his attention is wavering or that he is acting bored, we have at least a fighting chance to regain his attention and interest. But when we are talking over the radio, we do not know how many dials are being turned, how many members of our audience are "walking out on us." If a member of a visible audience has failed to understand us, we may become aware of this fact and do something about it. We can repeat what we have said, perhaps restating it in other terms, but we have no way of knowing when our radio listener is puzzled and uncomprehending.

This difference in situation means that when we are speaking over the radio, we should do everything possible to be interesting and easily intelligible. Our language should be just as simple, clear, and informal as we can appropriately make it. We say "appropriately" because there are situations which demand greater formality than others. Simple sentences have great advantages over complicated ones in most speech situations. This is peculiarly true in radio speaking.

Radio speaking places stress on vocal elements. In radio speaking, there should be greater attention to the vocal tones and to the combinations of speech sounds. We ought to be as careful as we can about such matters in all speaking, but especially so in radio speaking, where there is no visible action to support and clarify the vocal sounds.

If we are going to be interesting as radio speakers, we must pay attention to vocal variety. We must recognize the special problem of using vocal variations over the radio because of the mechanical workings of microphones and loud-speakers. The range of force which can be transmitted efficiently over the air is somewhat limited; it is easy to "blast" and spoil otherwise good effects. Changes in vocal force, therefore, must be neither too great nor too abrupt.

THE RADIO PLAY. *A group of high school students present a radio drama. Timing is of great importance in radio acting. Note the director with index finger raised ready to give the signal to the actors. The girl to the right is watching intently for the signal. The man at the control board sees to it that the voices of the broadcasters are properly modulated and leveled out. (Charles Phelps Cushing)*

All speakers should form their sounds accurately. However, this consideration applies with special force to the radio speaker. Certain high-frequency sounds, such as *s*, *z*, and *sh*, have to be uttered with special care, because they are subject to unusual distortion in radio transmission.

Stricter time limitations. Again, the radio speaker needs to be especially careful that he is not " biting off more than he can chew," in the scope of his subject matter. It is much better to narrow the field and cover it effectively than it is to attempt too much and do it poorly. Time limits are rigorous in broadcasting. This means that the speaker must plan with great care, know just how much he can say effectively in the allotted time, and get set to do the job so as to finish right on the dot. An auditorium audience may remain to hear a very interesting speaker who runs over time, but when the radio speaker comes to the end of his allotted time, he is off the air!

Need for transitions. In proceeding from one point to the next, the radio speaker should put into words what he might say by visible action if his audience could see him. Thus instead of taking a step forward, he may have to say, "Now, to proceed another step in the argument," or instead of a gesture which might do the trick, he will find it helpful to remark, "But enough of that." It is recommended that the radio speaker should give special attention to brief summaries of what has been said and simple forecasts of what is coming. Thus he may say, "Now that we have seen the urgent need for taking this step, let us proceed to consider ways and means of doing it," or "My first point has been that some form of price control is necessary. Next I want to take up the various possible government agencies which may effect this necessary regulation."

RADIO DRAMA. *An exciting moment in a radio play presented by high school students. Note the generous use of visible action. How is this to be explained? What is the function of a director in the presentation of a radio play? (Keystone View)*

Reading manuscripts. Most radio programs come from manuscripts carefully prepared in advance, and usually submitted for approval by the authorities of the radio station. Although the reading of such manuscripts must have a definite extempore quality, nevertheless they do have to be read. Some people who can speak rather well have difficulty in reading equally well. The phrasing of their reading is wooden and unnatural. Before they can get far in the radio world they will have to learn to read. Obviously, we cannot take up the whole complicated subject of interpretative reading in this chapter. That was dealt with in Chapter Eleven, and we will want to review it before we do any radio speaking.

Freedom from regional dialects. In the matter of pronunciation the radio speaker, with an audience scattered over a wide area, faces a problem somewhat different from that of the platform speaker or the conversationalist. His speech may suffer seriously from regional pronunciation. He cannot conform to the pronunciation of one restricted area and avoid difficulty with people who use different pronunciations. The wise decision is to use as many widely acceptable pronunciations as possible and avoid localisms.

SCRIPT WRITING

If we are invited to speak over the radio, it is because we are authorities on some subject of interest or because there is available time on the radio station which the managers believe we can fill with profit to the listeners. In either case, we must make what we say worth while from the beginning to the end or the listeners will turn the dials and we will lose our audience. All the suggestions for finding appropriate topics and supporting materials considered in Chapter Thirteen should be recalled here, with especial emphasis on adapting the subject to the time limits.

A good radio script is well organized. The ideas follow one another clearly. At no time can there be any question about what the speaker is "driving at." The speech should be planned with the final objective becoming clearer at each step along the way.

In Chapter Five we considered the characteristics of good oral language. The successful script writer uses such phraseology. He employs familiar words which bring immediate responses. He varies his sentences in length and kind. He uses the first and second personal pronouns. He repeats. He pays attention to euphony. He realizes that good written language is not appropriate in a first-class radio script; it requires good oral language.

Almost without exception, the successful radio speaker prepares a manuscript and delivers it exactly as he has prepared it. He writes on cards or heavy paper to avoid rustling noises and to make sure that the pages can be shifted easily. The experienced radio speaker does not trust to luck!

Tests of Comprehension and Application

TRAINING IN BROADCASTING TECHNIQUE

1   A school public-address system furnishes all the equipment anyone needs for practice in radio speaking. Lacking this, about the best substitute is to have the radio program presented from behind a screen which separates the performers from the audience. This will at least draw attention to the part which visible action plays in normal communication, and will show what special burdens are placed on the audible code in radio speaking. A good preparation for radio speaking is to record the speech on a dictaphone or phonograph record, then to play the records over and over again so that people may study their special problems in vocalization.

2   Study your favorite program of radio entertainment. Tell the class what in your judgment makes it effective and, with the help of your classmates, try to present something equivalent to it.

3   Write to the program director of a radio station, asking him to send you whatever radio scripts he may have available for distribution, study these scripts for comparison with the actual broadcasts, and tell the class what conclusions you have reached.

4   Broadcast an imaginary athletic contest — baseball, football, or basketball — after the manner of your favorite sports announcer. Write out your script very carefully in advance and then try to do it with spontaneous enthusiasm over the school public-address system.

ACTUAL PROGRAM PARTICIPATION

5   Acting as a news commentator, make a five-minute broadcast of the events which have occurred within the last twenty-four hours. Model what you do on the performance of a favorite news commentator.

COMPREHENSION AND APPLICATION TESTS

6 Work out an interview with some prominent person, one of your classmates being the interviewer and you the "interviewee."

7 Prepare and produce a radio variety program in which one member of your group serves as master of ceremonies and each of the other members does an imitation of a favorite radio entertainer.

8 Working with a group of your classmates, give a radio presentation of a one-act play, or a scene from a longer play. One of you will have a special problem to solve in "setting the stage," indicating "changes of scene," and summarizing incidents which have been omitted from the actual dramatic presentation but which are essential to an understanding of the whole production. These must be worked out in advance with very great care.

9 Make an original dramatization after the manner of the "Cavalcade of America" program and present it as effectively as you can. Dramatize some important event in the history of the United States, rehearse it carefully, and present it. You will do well to limit the number of your characters to three or four. Perhaps the music department will be interested in working out incidental music for one of these programs. If so, they may be of great assistance to you.

10 As a climax to your study of radio, arrange with your local radio station for an actual broadcast of the best program you have worked up.

Part Four

SPEECH IN BUSINESS

GOOD SPEECH *is vital in our workaday world. It is the lubricant which keeps friction at a minimum in the economic machinery upon which we all must depend for our bread and butter. In the broad sense, every one of us is going to be a "businessman" and, as such, dependent upon speech for whatever measure of success he may be able to attain.*

18 Telephoning

19 Interviews and Conferences

20 Dictating Letters

21 Buying and Selling

22 Business Speeches

CHAPTER EIGHTEEN *Telephoning*

IN THE UNITED STATES there are 65,000,000 telephone conversations every day, 25,000,000,000 a year. The latter number is almost twice the yearly total of letters, post cards, and telegrams combined and sixteen times as many as the telephone calls for the rest of the world. The telephone is used in the United States more than any other form of communication except face-to-face speech. Any kind of speech employed so widely is worthy of careful consideration and study.

Most of us use a telephone at least once a day. Many of us use it a dozen times. By telephoning, we arrange meetings with our school friends; we converse with members of our families; we order food from the grocer's; we get information about train and bus schedules; we find out about class assignments; we make dates; we ask for help on our schoolwork; and we plan parties.

In spite of the fact that they use the telephone so frequently, many persons use it badly. They have never taken the trouble to examine the results of bad telephone technique; therefore they are not aware of the jobs that are lost because of inept or discourteous inquiries, the sales that are not completed because of careless answers, the mistakes in grocery orders due to slovenly speech, the dates that are turned down because of uncultured telephone voices, and the opportunities that are missed because of unintelligibility.

There is only one safe rule for telephoning: to make every conversation a success by being sure that we are not either discourteous or careless in the particular conversation we are engaged in.

Because of something that was happening when the telephone rang, all of us have, at one time or another, shown irritability in our voices when we answered it. Then when we discovered at the other end of the wire a person whom we did not want to offend, we were immediately ashamed of our poor manners. When a connection was bad, some of us have made a smart or a crude remark which we longed to recall when we discovered we had offended a person we were eager to please.

Beginning tomorrow morning, let us observe how the telephone is used in our own homes. Perhaps some member of the family will help make this survey by reporting on the number of calls made when we are at school. It will be interesting to find out: first, how many calls were made in all; second, how many calls were initiated in the home and how many were received; and third, how well each call accomplished its purpose. If we discuss with the members of our family the various telephone conversations of the day, we may discover why some calls were more successful than others. We can also try to judge whether our calls were more or less successful than those of other members of our family and why.

IMPROVING TELEPHONE TECHNIQUE

If in our examination of several telephone conversations we find one or two speakers whom we like especially, it will be a good idea to try to copy the good points of their conversational method. Since bodily action is not visible over the telephone, more emphasis must be placed on the voice. What we say, the words and sentences we use, and the voice in which we express our meaning — all these should be carefully considered in attempting to improve the way we speak over the telephone.

Telephone conversation usually differs from face-to-face conversation in that the aim is securing or passing on some information rather than pure enjoyment. True, there are individuals who carry on long social conversations over the telephone, but theirs is usually not a legitimate use of the instrument. We should keep in mind the fact that all the time we are talking on our telephones, others are unable to call either our co-converser or us. If we are on a party line, we are using time which also belongs to someone else. Therefore we should make sure that our reason for calling is a good one — that we have something worth saying, something important to the recipient of the call as well as to us. A pad and a pencil on the telephone stand will save time when something is said that we want to remember.

If we have a worth-while message, we should phrase it so that our hearer understands it exactly. In face-to-face conversation, it is unfortunate when a speaker stumbles over words, tries to express his idea first in one group of words and then in another without ever making his meaning clear. But groping for words is an even more serious fault in telephone conversation. In face-to-face conversation, facial expression, posture, movement, and gesture may help make the message clear. In telephone conversation, voice and language must convey the idea clearly without the aid of visible action. If we feel insecure about our language in telephone calls, it is helpful to select carefully ahead of time some particularly apt words and phrases to use when we telephone. This practice will help in developing a vocabulary which ultimately will meet every need extemporaneously.

A pleasant, communicative quality of voice is a tremendous asset in telephone conversations. To find out what impressions our voices make on others, it is well to begin by trying them on ourselves. If we record our voices on a dictaphone or a phonograph and then listen to them, imagining we have never heard them before and that they belong to persons whom we have never seen, we can decide objectively whether or not we like them. It is also a good idea to let someone who does not know us hear the recording. Without telling him whose voices they are, we can get frank reactions. If he is less favorably impressed by our voices than by us personally, there is something wrong with our voices. Our voices should tell the truth about us.

In speaking over the telephone, we should not shout as if we thought we had to bridge the distance between our friends and ourselves by sheer force. The telephone mechanism is built to transmit the volume of ordinary conversation. When the voice is louder than that, it is blurred in the ears of the listener; instead of hearing words and sentences, he hears only annoying, meaningless, and blaring sounds. We should speak as we would if the person with whom we are talking were face to face with us. We can prove the truth of this point of view by varying our vocal volume as we telephone to other members of the class. Their reactions to our voices as we speak with varying degrees of force may be invaluable to us in building better telephone techniques. There is one pitch of voice best suited to each individual's vocal mechanism. In Chapter Three, page 94, we learned how to find it. We should use this optimum pitch in our telephone conversations.

It is quite reasonable to speak a little more slowly over the telephone than we do in face-to-face conversation. Sometimes when making long-distance calls, we are very conscious of the fact that we are paying for every minute. In order to get everything said that we wish to say, we speak too rapidly. When we do, we usually are asked to repeat so frequently that instead of conserving time we waste it. A great deal can be said in one hundred and fifty words, and the average person can speak that many in a minute without hurrying. If we get some student in the commercial course to take down a conversation of ours in shorthand and keep a record of the length of time we have talked, we can find out whether we speak faster or slower than one hundred and fifty words per minute. We may discover that we should slow down if we are eager to be understood over the telephone.

AT THE TELEPHONE. *The right way to hold the cradle-type telephone. Observe the hand grip on the instrument and the position of the transmitter directly centered before the mouth of the speaker. A great many unnecessary words are spoken over the telephone because the instrument is held so that the words reach the receiver blurred and indistinct. (American Telephone & Telegraph Company)*

The most common cause of misunderstanding over the telephone is careless utterance. Speakers run their words together, slight final consonants, and omit vowels. The result is jumbled speech that is unintelligible. It is helpful to analyze our mode of utterance to see whether we enunciate, articulate, and pronounce clearly enough to guarantee intelligibility over the telephone.

In telephoning, many persons speak too near to, or too far away from, the mouthpiece. Also many persons rattle the receiver hook, or handle the instrument roughly and noisily. Telephone companies lay down these simple rules that should always be followed:

1. Speak directly into the mouthpiece.
2. Keep the lips about one-half inch from the mouthpiece.
3. Keep the receiver close to the ear.
4. Hang up the receiver quietly.
5. If central does not answer, move the receiver hook up and down *slowly*.

TELEPHONE ETIQUETTE

The person who is polite is more considerate of others than he is of himself. He looks out for others' comforts ahead of his own, he conserves time for others, and he tries to make others happy. If we keep in mind this principle of kindness to the other person, we can figure out what to do in most telephone situations.

When our telephone rings, we should assume that the person calling has a specific purpose in mind. Usually he wishes to accomplish this purpose as quickly as possible. If we wish to be considerate, we will help him. In the United States, a common salutation in answering the telephone is " Hello." This salutation may let the person calling us feel our friendship, but it does not conserve as much time as some other greetings. The caller then has to find out whether he has the right number, and whether he is talking to the right person, before he can explain his purpose. We can economize on time and effort by answering with our name, the number of our telephone, or both.

If we wish to be very courteous in calling someone else, we must think of his convenience before our own. This means that we will give him our name at once, and state our purpose. If we merely say " Hello " and state our purpose without giving our name, our listener, not knowing who is calling, is at a disadvantage. He does not know whether or not he wishes to grant our request until he finds out who is making it!

When the person we call is not in. We have all gone to the telephone when someone else in our family was wanted and have had the person who called " hang up " without a word. Such an incident has made us feel as if someone had slammed a door in our face. Certainly it would have been more considerate of our feelings if the caller had told us who he was, left his number, and thanked us for answering his questions. Such a courteous response is often neglected.

When someone else is wanted. When we answer and someone else is wanted, we have an opportunity to be of service to the person calling. Clearly, the best response is to summon the individual who is wanted, at once, or to tell the caller where he can be reached. If we are not able to do either, we can at least express regret at our inability to help. Sometimes we can suggest other sources of the desired information. We should always attempt to make the caller feel that we are willing and eager to be of service.

Ending a conversation. It is usually courteous to let the person who makes the call end the conversation. That is reasonable, for when an individual has a purpose in mind and telephones to accomplish that purpose, he knows better than anyone else when it is time to stop talking. In most telephoning, closing the conversation is no problem. When the information is secured we say " Good-by " or " Thank you," or " I'm glad to have talked to you."

But there are times when the person we call or the person who calls us continues to visit beyond the limits of good taste and consideration for others who may want to use the line. In such a situation, we must somehow contrive to break off the conversation without giving offense. False excuses are usually ineffective and smack of insincerity. Remembering that it is not so much what we say as how we say it that offends people, and that if we wish to stop talking, we must have some good reason for wanting to do so, we should be able to close the conversation without being discourteous. If we have an engagement, a guest, or work to do, we should say so. If our reason for wanting to stop talking is that we feel we are keeping the line too long, we should say that too.

Calling for information. Each one of us may have need to call a classmate to get the details of an assignment, a friend to find out about the arrangements for a picnic, the athletic coach for the price of football tickets, a store for the price of goods, or the railway station for train schedules and the price of tickets to various towns. If we follow a few simple suggestions we should make successful calls. Let us try to:

1. Decide exactly what information we want.
2. Make sure that we can phrase our request precisely.
3. Speak clearly and distinctly.
4. Ask for a repetition if we do not understand.
5. Use pencil and paper and record information at once.
6. Show our gratitude to the person who has helped us.
7. Stop talking when we have accomplished our purpose.

Extending an invitation. If we are going to invite a friend to come to our house for lunch, spend a week-end in our cabin, dance at a school party, attend a show, take an automobile trip, or tramp with us through the woods, we not only wish to give the necessary information concerning the occasion, but we wish to make the friend feel that it is to be a pleasant affair, and that we are eager to have his company. Therefore when we call him, let us make clear just what we are planning. Perhaps we will tell him who else is to be included, and let him know that we are anticipating the event. Such an opening has obvious advantages over the unfortunate " Are you going to be busy on Friday evening? " Our friend knows whether or not he wants to accept when he is invited and is not obliged to feel hesitant about committing himself until he finds out whether we are going to ask him to tend our baby sister or to go to a dance!

The steps in extending an invitation over the telephone are:

1. Call for the person we wish to invite.
2. Tell him about the occasion for which he is to be invited.
3. Be definite about the date, hour, and place.
4. Invite him.
5. If he accepts, show that we are pleased.
6. If he declines, show that we are sorry.

Accepting an invitation. When we are given an invitation over the telephone we should:

1. Make sure that we are clear about the occasion for which we are invited.
2. Make sure that we know the date and hour.
3. If possible, give a definite answer at once.
4. Ask for time to consider if we cannot give a definite answer at once.
5. Show that we appreciate the invitation, whether we decline, accept, or demur.

Buying over the telephone. Many of the principles of effective buying and selling can be put into practice over the telephone. There usually is a need to conserve time in buying over the telephone, and also to substitute careful word pictures for observations and demonstrations. If we wish to order over the telephone, we must know: (1) definitely what we want to buy; (2) approximately what we wish to pay; (3) the size, color, quality, and quantity; and (4) that our name and address have been given accurately. Grocers relate interesting stories of housewives who telephone half a dozen times in one forenoon concerning one order because they have not paid careful attention to these four items.

If we order over the phone, we should:
1. Make a list of the articles we wish to purchase.
2. Call the right number and the right department.
3. State clearly what we want — what size, color, quantity.
4. Get the exact price.
5. Give name and address for the delivery.

Making a complaint. Sometimes it is necessary to register a complaint over the telephone. An error has been made in a purchase, a taxi has not arrived as scheduled, we have not received the consideration at the club that we expected, our neighbor's dog has been disturbing us, or dozens of other matters require adjusting. The question is: How can we make our complaint yield the desired results?

The first step is to make sure we are talking to the person in authority, the one who can make an adjustment. The second step is to identify ourselves and make clear the nature of our interest in the affair. The third step is to explain clearly, briefly, and reasonably our cause for grievance. The fourth step is to listen politely to the response. Whether the outcome is favorable or unfavorable, we should remember that a cultured voice, effective language, and courteous behavior will always work in our favor.

Making an apology. When we feel that we should explain some injurious remark or act, it is a good idea to make use of the telephone. By using it we avoid delay, which may be important in attempting to make an adjustment. Directness is a good procedure in trying to right a wrong. We should talk to the person concerned. We should explain frankly and honestly and should not be afraid to say: "It was my fault. I was wrong." Then, of course, we must remember that accepting or rejecting our apology is up to the injured party.

Making an appointment. If we wish to make an appointment with the dentist, with a prospective employer, or with any other person to whose schedule we must adjust our time, we usually do so through telephoning to a secretary. The secretary answers the telephone by stating at once the name of the firm or individual for whom she is working. We must be ready to say who we are, and to explain why we desire an appointment. We must show that we consider her employer an important person, make clear that we will suit our schedule to his, and show our appreciation of the assignment of time to us.

Making a long-distance call. There are two kinds of long-distance calls. In one we ask to speak to a particular person, in the other we are willing to talk to anyone who answers the telephone at a given number. For the person-to-person call we pay slightly more than for the station-to-station call. There are also lower rates for certain hours when telephone lines are not so busy as at other times. When placing a call, we usually charge it to the phone from which we call. However, we may pay at a telephone booth, or reverse the charge and let the recipient bear the cost — if he is willing to do so. Because long-distance calls are expensive, it is especially important that we plan in advance pretty definitely what we wish to say. It is a wise idea to write out the important items we wish to cover and then make sure that we speak distinctly. It is easy to waste a large percentage of our time in repetition if we forget the techniques of good speech.

In making a long-distance call we should follow these steps:

1. Call central.

2. Ask for "long distance."

3. Give the place and name of the person, and/or the telephone number, we wish to call.

4. Give our own name and telephone number.

5. Ask central if she wishes us to hold the line. If so, wait for the call; if not, hang up until central calls us.

6. Speak distinctly and with appropriate volume.

7. Notify central if the connection is poor and communication is difficult.

8. Close the call.

9. Call the rate clerk and ask for the cost of the call.

For further helps in making long-distance calls it is well to consult a telephone directory.

Telephoning a telegram. If we are helping with the school annual or working on a debate team, the chances are that we will be asked to send telegrams before our work is completed. Usually telegrams are sent by means of the telephone. Because we pay by the word, it is important that a telegram be brief, and because it is seldom sent save on urgent business, it is important that it be clear. If we turn to Chapter Five, we may get some help on how to give a complete message in ten or twenty-five words. "Straight" wires are usually ten words. They are sent within the hour. Night letters are usually twenty-five or fifty words. They are sent at night and delivered in the morning. We pay as much for a "straight" wire as for a night letter. It is amazing how much meaning we can put into ten or twenty-five words if we plan carefully.

The procedure is this:

1. Call the central operator.

2. Give the number of the telegraph office. (In some sections of the country simply say "Western Union.")

3. Say that we wish to send a telegram (straight wire or night letter).

4. Give the name and address distinctly.

5. Read the message carefully.

6. Ask the operator to repeat the name, address, and message.

7. Give our name and telephone number.

Tests of Comprehension and Application

IMPROVING TELEPHONE TECHNIQUES AND CONVERSATION

1 Make a list of legitimate purposes for the use of the telephone. Make another list of purposes that you consider abuses of the telephone.

2 Classify the following. In one column put the purposes you consider legitimate; in another, the abuses. Support your opinions.

    a Calling a classmate and asking him to listen to and criticize a poem that you repeat from memory
    b Calling the bus station for a schedule of buses
    c Calling a classmate to get the assignment in geometry
    d Calling the principal of the high school to explain your absence from school
    e Calling a friend for a long visit because it is raining and you cannot go to his home as you had planned
    f Calling a friend and asking him to hear you spell a list of words for your English class
    g Listening while other persons on your line are talking
    h Calling a taxi company and asking for a car to take you to school
    i Calling a friend and inviting her to a luncheon at your home
    j Calling a friend to tell her you enjoyed a luncheon at her home
    k Calling a grocer to order food to be delivered
    l Calling your automobile dealer for information concerning the mechanics of your car
    m Making an appointment with your dentist
    n Dictating a telegram
    o Calling a friend just at meal time because you know he will be at home
    p Using a business telephone for a purely personal call

3 Work out exact wordings for the important parts of the following telephone conversations.

    a Tell a friend how to reach your home from the school.
    b Ask for an interview with an important person.

    c Break an appointment with your dentist and make a new appointment.
    d Make a Pullman reservation.
    e Order a book from a bookstore.
    f Invite a friend to a dinner party.
    g Find out whether a certain person has registered at a hotel.
    h Report an accident to the police.
    i Apply for a position.
    j Ask your music teacher to change the hour for your lesson.

4 Try some of the tongue twisters on page 117 over the telephone. Say them carefully and distinctly.

5 Make up some original tongue twisters.

6 Speak the following sentences in unison.
    a Say every word carefully.
    b Move your lips noticeably.
    c Try words that require agile tongue movements.
    d Exaggerate the pronunciation of words that require lip movements.
    e Correct enunciation means the clear utterance of vowels.
    f Correct articulation means the clear utterance of consonants.
    g Correct pronunciation means clear and accurate vowels and consonants with the accent in the right place.
    h Say words slowly and carefully. Then say them more rapidly but quite as carefully.

7 Read a paragraph from your text, giving full value to every sound.

8 Read a poem. First exaggerate each sound, and word, then read it clearly and distinctly without calling attention to your drill for careful speech.

9 Describe and analyze the best telephone conversations you have ever heard.

10 Take exercises for voice improvement from your text. Overdo and exaggerate careful and distinct enunciation of any paragraph. Move your lips noticeably in practicing speech. Open your mouth as you speak. Practice speaking very slowly, then increase the rate. With a dictaphone or other recording machine, practice until your voice makes the kind of impression on you that you wish to have it make on others.

11   Grade people whom you know on the way they make use of the telephone, the directory, the stand, paper and pencil. Grade yourself first. Allow 10 points for each answer in the affirmative. A perfect score is 100. How do you rate?
   a   When you do not get central at once do you move the receiver hook up and down slowly *without rattling* it? Yes____ No____
   b   Do you hold the mouthpiece directly in front of you and speak directly into it? Yes____ No____
   c   Do you keep your lips about one-half inch from the mouthpiece? Yes____ No____
   d   Do you keep the receiver close to your ear? Yes____ No____
   e   Do you hang the receiver up quietly? Yes____ No____
   f   Do you always make sure of the correct number before you call central? Yes____ No____
   g   Are you able to find a name in the alphabetized list quickly? Yes____ No____
   h   Are you able to use the classified directory when you do not know what person or firm to call? Yes____ No____
   i   Do you have a pad and pencil on your telephone stand? Yes____ No____
   j   Do you write messages and numbers as they are given to you? Yes____ No____

12   Try the foregoing test on each member of your family. Try it also on two of your classmates.

13   Which of the following greetings give the most information in the least possible time? Arrange them in three columns: (1) unsatisfactory, (2) fairly satisfactory, and (3) satisfactory.
   a   " Hello."
   b   " Alice Williams speaking."
   c   " Redding 8672."
   d   " Principal Read's office."
   e   " Bayview High School."
   f   " Ya? "
   g   " Editor of East High Weekly."
   h   " Superintendent Ewing speaking."
   i   " What do you want? "

j " Yes? "
k " City morgue."
l " This is Ray Brown speaking."
m " Whitfield's residence."
n " Uh-huh."
o " May I help you? "

14 Rate the following opening sentences for the person making the call. Which ones are unsatisfactory, which fairly satisfactory, and which satisfactory? Discuss your classifications in class.

a " Hello, who is this? "
b " This is Ralph Spears. May I speak with William? "
c " Is this the Daily Mirror? This is James Barnes of Central High School."
d " Sports Department? I want some clothes."
e " Hello, guess who this is."
f " We haven't had a long vacation for three years, so this year we may go to Yellowstone Park. Some members of my family have never been there, others have. Will you tell me what trains go out there? "
g " March's Bookshop? This is Alice Brown. May I speak to clerk 42 in the textbook department? "
h " I would like to have you for dinner on Saturday. Oh, Mrs. Weeks? I'm sorry. I thought it was Anne."
i " Oakwood 2882? May I speak to the head of the shoe department?
j " Gimme Professor Wilder."
k " This is Lida Trilling. May I speak to Superintendent Forsum? "
l " You say this is the Northwestern Station? Well, I want a ticket for Briggsville."
m " Julia Warner speaking. May I remind you of the community picnic on Saturday, August 4?
n " Hello, Alice. This is Betty."
o " You say this is Bering 6872? Is this the Wood residence? "

15 Write a short paper telling why you consider each of the following acceptable or unacceptable as responses when the one calling is informed that the person called is not in.

COMPREHENSION AND APPLICATION TESTS

    a   "May I leave a message?"
    b   "Will it be convenient for him to call Albert Heim at Curtis 888 if he comes in before ten?"
    c   Hang up.
    d   "Thank you. I will call again."
    e   "He will be in at nine? If it is convenient, I will call again at that time."
    f   "Where is he?"
    g   "Well, I don't want to talk to anyone else." (Hang up.)
    h   "This is Shirley Luce. Please tell her that I called."
    i   "That's strange. He told me to call at this time."
    j   "Thank you."

16 Work out some dramatizations of telephone conversations in which someone other than the person wanted answers. Get the class reaction to each of the following responses.
    a   "Robert is not here. He can be reached at Turmo 876."
    b   "Alice is not here."
    c   "William is in Canada on a two weeks' holiday."
    d   "Superintendent Brown is out at the moment. Would you like to speak to his secretary?"
    e   "I'm sorry, but Mother is not here. I have just come in from school. She seems not to have left a message. May I have her call you?"
    f   "My brother can't come. He's busy."
    g   "Mother is sleeping, and I'm not going to call her."
    h   "Mother is resting. Would it be convenient for you to have her call in an hour?"
    i   "Judith is not in. May I take a message?"
    j   "No, he's not here."

17 If you were in a telephone conversation and your friend closed it by any one of the following, would you consider him unkind?
    a   "I'm sorry, I have a caller." (When you are sure there is no caller)
    b   "I think we should stop talking, I am afraid we are keeping someone from using the line."
    c   "We must say good-by. I have a theme to finish for English." (When you believe that he does have a theme in preparation)

d "I must leave now. I'll call you back later." (You do not believe that he intends to do so.)
e "I'm so glad you called. We'll have to get together for a visit. We have so many interesting things to say." (You think he does plan to do this.)
f "I can't talk any longer. Good-by."
g "I'm sorry to stop, but the supper dishes are waiting for me."
h "I wonder if we aren't using the line too long?"

18 Listen to voices in five calls. Write a description of each. Rate each on the rating sheet for telephone conversation (page 473).

19 The next time you call your home, rate the person who answers on:

         Courtesy   Voice   Dispatch

20 Divide the class into pairs and work out dramatizations showing good and bad telephone techniques in each of the categories considered in this chapter.

21 Work out a dramatization demonstrating six "don'ts" for telephoning.

ACTUAL TELEPHONE CONVERSATIONS

22 Call for an interview about a job that interests you.
23 Call a restaurant and arrange for a class dinner.
24 Call to make an inquiry about the health of someone who is ill.
25 Call the railway station and arrange a trip to some city three hundred miles away.
26 Telephone to a lecturer (or a booking agency) to find out what arrangements could be made to have him speak before your high-school assembly.
27 Order three or four articles from some local store.
28 Call a bookstore and ask them to order for you a book not in stock.
29 Over the telephone, invite a friend to a formal party in your high school.
30 Over the telephone, invite your teacher to dinner at your home.
31 Telephone to the Automobile Association asking for help with your car.
32 Call a doctor for someone who is ill.

COMPREHENSION AND APPLICATION TESTS

33 Place a long-distance call.
34 Over the telephone, order supplies for a school party.
35 Telephone a complaint to your grocer or milkman.
36 Call a friend and introduce to him another friend who will be in his class the next day.
37 Rate yourself in telephone conversation. Place a check at that point which represents your ability.

Subject matter:		
Worth while	Average	Trite
Too much	Just enough	Too little
Language:		
Always finds precise words to express idea	Sometimes finds right word to express idea	Seldom finds right word to express idea
Too many words	Right number of words	Too few words
Voice:		
Excellent quality	Fair quality	Poor quality
Pitch too high	Good pitch	Pitch too low
Too much volume	Good volume	Too little volume
Too fast	Good rate	Too slow
Articulation too precise	Good	Slovenly
Enunciation exaggerated	Good	Slovenly
Words indistinct	Easily understood	Pronunciation too precise
Very courteous	Fairly polite	Very rude
Tactful	Sometimes tactful, sometimes tactless	Tactless

CHAPTER NINETEEN *Interviews and Conferences*

TWO AUTHORITIES on the technique of interviewing define an interview thus:

" A serious conversation directed to a definite purpose other than satisfaction in the conversation itself is an interview. This may serve as a working definition. There is give and take between interviewer and interviewee; and we must recognize that not only spoken words, but other means of face-to-face communication also, are used. Inflection, qualities of voice, facial expression, glint of the eye, posture, gestures, and general behavior supplement what is said. They all contribute to the purposeful exchange of meaning which is the interview." [1] Now that we are clear as to what an interview is, let us study some of the fundamental procedures and principles to be followed in interviewing.

THE INTERVIEW

Appointments for interviews. Most successful interviews result from careful preliminary planning. Usually the parties to an interview meet by appointment. Such appointments may be made orally or through correspondence. Very often all that is necessary is to telephone the office of the person to be interviewed and ask his private secretary or receptionist for a specific appointment. In some instances it may be desirable to secure an appointment by making an advance call at the " interviewee's " office or other place of business. In arranging an appointment, the interviewer should always consult the convenience of the " interviewee," making sure that the time and conditions are wholly satisfactory to him. It is surprising how many persons desiring an interview are thoughtless, and inconsiderate of

---

[1] Walter Van Dyke Bingham and Bruce Victor Moore, *How to Interview*, rev. ed., Harper & Bros., 1934, p. 15. Reprinted by permission.

the "interviewee's" preferences. Since the interview is being arranged in the interests of the interviewer, it is extremely unwise to arouse the hostility and prejudice of the "interviewee," the one from whom favors are to be sought. This principle of courtesy seems elementary enough, but it is often violated. It may be quite all right for the person seeking an interview to suggest possible places and dates, but he must not attempt to make the final decisions on these points.

Usually it is well for the interviewer to state the purpose of the interview clearly and frankly at the time the appointment is being made. There are real disadvantages in leaving the person to be interviewed wondering about the purpose of the interview. It is a rare occasion indeed when one wants to interview anybody on a subject the very mention of which will be irritating and annoying. The "interviewee" will appreciate knowing just what the interviewer wants to see him about and what his purpose is in coming; then he will have the opportunity to decline to see the interviewer if he wishes to, a privilege which should always be his. If the person whom we are planning to interview agrees to see us at some particular time and place, we should express our appreciation of his courtesy to us.

Types of interviews. It is a bit difficult to classify interviews, just as it is to classify other speech situations. Each interview is different from all others in its purposes, its participants, and its procedures. However, in general, there are three types: (1) information-seeking interviews, (2) information-giving interviews, and (3) action-getting interviews. Of course there may be all sorts of combinations of these three.

Information-seeking interviews. In this type of interview the object of the interviewer is to elicit items of fact and opinion from the one he interviews; for example, a reporter interviewing a celebrity. Sometimes the person to be interviewed is not co-operative; his attitude may result from a feeling on his part that he is not going to profit from the interview. He can easily perceive that the interviewer is getting something out of him, but quite naturally he is selfish enough to want to gain something for himself from the expenditure of his time and energy. When face to face with an unwilling or un-co-operative "interviewee," our first task must be to show him that some worthy end is going to be served by our taking his time and energy. For example, in the interview for which we are to make an appointment under project 4 at the end of the chapter, we will want to make clear to the manager how he can get something worth while out of providing us with the information for which we ask. We may find it advisable to tell him what we propose to do with the data when we have collected them. It may interest him to know that we are going to report on our experience to our class and transmit to them whatever information he may give us.

Information-giving interviews. Obviously, every time information is being obtained from an interview somebody is furnishing it. All of the exercises in interviewing which we will be asked to carry out involve at least one person in the problems of *giving* information clearly and helpfully. Sometimes the one who is the interviewer seeks a meeting for the purpose of giving information to the "interviewee." When this is the situation, it is of great importance that some common ground be found between the two parties to the interview. Before anyone can be very much interested in having information on any subject, he must understand and appreciate its significance to *him*. The world is filled with people who have the completely mistaken notion that there is nothing quite so easy as imparting information to others. This idea may be one reason for ineffective teaching!

We must remember that speech is not a device for transferring meanings; all that we can ever hope to do is to encourage someone else to develop out of the materials of his own experience the meanings we want him to have. Frequently an officer in a business organization fails utterly to give to one of his subordinates the precise information he wants him to have. Then when the subordinate fails to carry out the instructions, the officer is inclined to place all the blame on him for his failure to understand. In many such instances the major fault is the speaker's; he has not used the materials of the other man's experience skillfully enough to stimulate him into developing the proper meanings. We must use the vocabularies of others and build meanings out of their experiences if we are to employ the interview effectively for the purpose of giving information.

Action-getting interviews. When we get out of school, most of the interviews in which we will participate will be aimed at securing some specific action on the part of the persons we interview. We may want the "interviewee" to hire us, to buy a product we are selling, or to do something else which will contribute to our happiness or success. In this kind of interview it is important to utilize all that we know about the motivations of human beings. People will not do what we want them to do merely because we want them to do it. We must contrive ways and means of making them want to do what we ask. In other words, action-getting interviews are just a specialized form of persuasive speaking. Of course, all that we can possibly find out about the habits, attitudes, and actions of the people whom we try to persuade will help us to deal with them effectively.

Recently the president of a university was called on the telephone by a wealthy businessman who inquired as to whether or not a children's hospital might make a desirable and important addition to the university medical school. The president promptly replied that it would. The businessman then went on to say that he had been thinking of giving $1,000,000 to build a hospital as a memorial for his son, who had recently died. The university administrator could scarcely control his enthusiasm over the prospect of obtaining such a gift as seemed to be coming his way and, without waiting for the businessman to finish what he wanted to say, the president proceeded to outline his own plans for the development of the medical school. In the course of his remarks he named a surgeon on the staff of the institution as just the right man to head the proposed children's hospital. At the mention of the doctor's name the prospective donor changed his tone immediately, and terminated the telephone conversation quickly by saying: "Well, I was just thinking about the possibility of donating funds to the hospital. I may call you later." The trouble was that the wealthy man's son had died following an operation performed by this particular surgeon! That was the last the university president ever heard about the $1,000,000 which was hanging in the balance when he made his unfortunate reference to the doctor! If we think of this telephone conversation as an interview, we can see how important it is to have in advance as much information as possible about the "interviewee."

Preparing for the interview. As has been said often, what one gets out of any experience in life is directly proportional to the effectiveness of the preparation he makes for it. In preparing for an interview, we may well ask ourselves some or all of the following questions:

1. What is my purpose in this interview?
2. What important facts do I know about the person whom I am to interview?
3. If conditions were reversed and I were the "interviewee," how would I feel about the interview and the interviewer?
4. Just what points do I propose to cover in the interview? (A written memorandum may be helpful here.)
5. What in general do I know about human nature, the ways in which people react and so on, which will be helpful to me in approaching the "interviewee" properly?

Before we go to keep our appointment, we should consider our personal appearance. We must remember that this may be the first time the "interviewee" has ever seen us, and first impressions are often determining factors in interviews.

We should be prompt. We can scarcely make a more serious mistake than to arrive late in keeping a business appointment. It is much better for us to be on hand a few minutes early than it is to be one minute late. If anything delays the interview, do not let it be our tardiness.

When we go into an office for an interview, we should be careful not to slouch in and help ourselves to a seat before we are asked to sit down. It is important to wait until the "interviewee" takes the lead; we should conform to his suggestions.

We should be as brief as we possibly can and still get results. Businessmen are usually busy. Nothing is more annoying to them than calls from visitors who seem to have all the time in the world and assume that other people also have. Some people take forever in getting down to the point. The effective interviewer will behave in a businesslike manner, giving evidence of adequate and careful preparation; he will not waste that precious commodity, time. When he has obtained the information for which he has come, he will express his appreciation simply and directly and take his leave without unnecessarily prolonged and time-wasting formalities.

In an interview, as in less organized and formal types of conversation, we should beware of the temptation to monopolize the talking. Most of us do not enjoy a one-sided conversation, with ourselves on the short end! We want a fair chance to do our share of the talking. Many a man in an interview produces the same unfortunate effect as did the minister who preached too long. Mark Twain, who was in the congregation, said that after the sermon had been going on for fifteen minutes, he felt moved to contribute $50 to the cause the minister was presenting. After it had been going on for half an hour, he had decided to cut his contribution down to $5, and finally when the collection box came around at the end of the sermon, he thought that he could best express his sentiments by taking a $5 bill out of it!

We should not use an interview to get facts which we can obtain just as well or better in other ways. If we have a list of simple questions which we can ask in written form, many people would rather write us the answers in a letter than spend time in an interview. In either a written inquiry or an interview, we should phrase our questions just as carefully as possible. One of the great advantages of an interview over a letter is that misunderstandings can be clarified at once in face-to-face communication.

Frequently, we will want to take notes on what is said in an interview. When notes are taken, it is usually a good plan to read them to the "interviewee," and ask him whether or not we are quoting him correctly, before we make use of what he has said. Frequently there is a great deal more to an interview than just the language which has been spoken. We must take into account the manner of speaking, the tone, and the general attitude.

No matter what happens in an interview, we must not lose our tempers or become discourteous. Angry behavior may make a tragedy of what otherwise might be a wholly successful adventure in human relationships. We may be unfortunate enough to have an interview with someone who does not observe the rudimentary principles of civilized social intercourse. If such an unhappy experience comes to us, we must hang onto ourselves and not make a bad situation worse. Indeed, a soft answer from us may mollify the discourteous party to the interview and save the essential values of the whole transaction for both of us.

It is far better to be direct and frank in interviews than it is to be indirect and devious. To assure ourselves of this fact, all we need to do is to examine our own feelings and preferences. We do not like to talk freely with a person about whose motives we are not quite sure. When we talk with him, we put up our guard at once and become cautious and uncommunicative.

Frequently, in applying for a position, it will be found helpful to prepare in advance a typed statement of information about oneself. At the end of the interview, this data sheet can be left with the prospective employer. It will not only serve to keep the applicant's qualifications before him, but it will give him a tangible record to submit to others in his organization who may have something to say about who shall be put on the pay roll. Such a personal history should include name, address, telephone number, education, experience, previous positions, references, and a photograph. It should be observed that we should never give as a reference the name of any person without being sure that he will be willing to help us.

Among the qualifications employers look for in an applicant are those mentioned by Professors Bingham and Moore:

"Employment interviewers ordinarily make mental notes during the conversation which they record on the application form immediately afterwards. Some make use of the check list of traits or a rating sheet. One such form used in connection with the employing of professional and technical workers provides a graphic scale for recording impressions and space for remarks about each of the following points: (1) How does his appearance impress you, especially his facial expression, physique, carriage, and neatness? (2) How responsive is he toward the interviewer? (3) How intelligent and mentally alert do you think he is? (4) Does he appear to have good health? (5) Has he an analytical mind? Does he get to the root of matters quickly? (6) Is he frank and straightforward? What impression does he give you as to his character and integrity? (7) How well informed is he in his field of specialization? (8) Does he give evidence of initiative? Does he originate ideas? (9) Has he a good command of language? Does he speak good English? (10) Is he decisive? Does he know his own mind? (11) Does he understand the significance of our

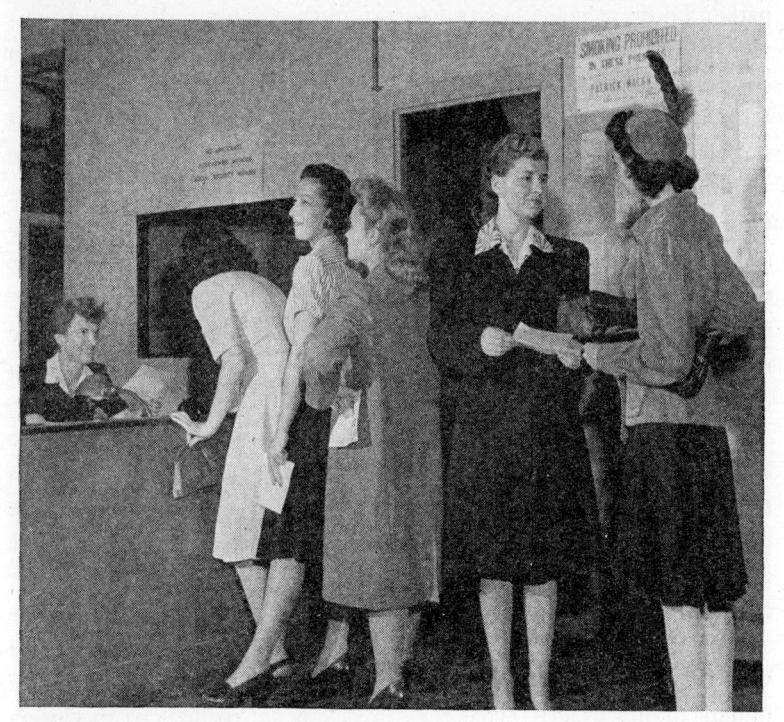

APPLICANTS FOR A JOB. *Five girls at the employment office of a department store. What do the facial expressions, postures, and costumes reveal? Which of the applicants look most promising and most likely to secure jobs?* (Dorothy Gale)

project and the social philosophy behind it? (12) Is he in sympathy with our objectives? Then in summary the interviewer jots down his answers to these questions: What are the applicant's outstanding strong points? Give most apparent weaknesses, general opinion of his characteristics and possibilities for development. For what position or kind of work does he seem best adapted? "[1]

A flexible plan. We have said that having planned an interview,

[1] *Op. cit.*, pp. 38-39. Reprinted by permission.

we should stick to our plan. This rule, however, must not be applied too strictly, for rigid adherence to a plan which does not seem to be succeeding is foolish. We must be ready to vary our procedures when those we had expected to use do not work out as we had anticipated. To do otherwise is to court complete disaster. We must control the interview, not allow an inflexible plan to control us. We can cover the ground we have planned to cover in many different ways. We can and should modify our procedures as we note the reactions of the person we are interviewing.

Time limits. Often employment interviews are extremely brief. One large firm in New York allows its personnel officers only one minute for a preliminary interview with each applicant and limits the time to five minutes for second interviews with those who have survived the first. If we are under such extreme pressure of time, we may find it necessary to formulate in advance what we are going to say.

We recall Emerson's oft-quoted observation, "What you *are* stands over you, and thunders so that I cannot hear what you say to the contrary." An authority on interviewing has emphasized the same principle by saying, "The one best way to gain a man's confidence is to deserve it." There is no substitute for sincerity, dependability, and character.

Closing the interview. Just as a public speech should usually end with the so-called action step made clear — that is, with the audience understanding exactly what they are expected to do — so the interview should end with some definite agreement upon what is to be done next. Sometimes interviews are extremely unsatisfactory because, although interviewer and "interviewee" have had a pleasant and wholly friendly talk, there is no clear understanding as to what is to follow. The applicant leaves not knowing whether he is going to be employed, and the prospective employer may not be quite sure either! Whereupon, the job seeker waits in vain for a call from the employer while the employer may be wondering why the applicant has never returned.

THE CONFERENCE

An interview is a purposeful two-party conversation; a conference is a conversation among a number of people for the purpose of securing unified decisions and actions. If a conference is to be successful, all important divergent points of view should be represented by those participating. This is an age of conferences in business, in government, in international affairs, and in the social order generally. One writer on the business conference has said: "Con-

WORKERS' COMMITTEE MEETING. *Seven workers gathered around a table in a factory discussing industrial problems. It is in just such meetings as this that churches, business organizations, and community groups arrive at decisions and plan co-operative action. (Library of Congress)*

ferences have multiplied phenomenally since the beginning of this century. They have come to stay, for they are now essential to an integrated nation. The sooner we can learn the new art of conferring, the quicker we can pass through the painful birth crisis of a new age of rational planning."

A conference differs from other less formal conversations in that it is usually aimed at some specific resultant action. The sales manager has a conference with the salesmen in order to utilize their separate and diverse experiences in the solution of common problems. When war strategy is being planned, when price-control policies are being established, when ways and means of settling labor disputes are being devised, conferences are indispensable. The object of such conferences is to pool group information for the purpose of developing co-operative action.

It is a great advantage to be able to hold a conference in a place and under conditions conducive to thoughtful and quiet consideration of problems. The participants in the conference should be separated from other people with other interests. Most large business organizations have attractive, pleasant conference rooms. An effective conference cannot be held on a street corner or in a public dining room. Just so far as is humanly possible everything irrelevant and disturbing should be shut out when a conference begins.

Direction of the conference. Usually, it is helpful to have one person serve as chairman of a conference. Most frequently, the one who acts in this capacity is the person who is primarily responsible for carrying out the policies which are developed in the conference. Thus the sales manager serves as the chairman of a conference of salesmen. The representative of the Department of Labor naturally would be chairman of a conference of labor leaders and managers. A good conference chairman is careful not to stifle the free expression of opinion by any of the participants. Indeed, it is his function to see to it that all of the different opinions are fully and fairly presented. In the last analysis, he may have to make his own opinion prevail, but he should not do so in an arbitrary, premature, and unreasonable fashion.

A meeting of the Cabinet of the President of the United States may follow the pattern established by Lincoln in considering the issuance of the Emancipation Proclamation. Tradition has it that the meeting began with the President reading his rough draft of the Proclamation. Then each member of the Cabinet was asked to express his opinion as to the advisability of announcing it. Although it appeared that a majority of the Cabinet members were opposed to the move, the President remarked that since he would have to take full responsibility for what was done, he might find it necessary to override their adverse opinions — and he did. Of course there are many conferences in which decisions are in a very real sense the products of compromise. Such meetings usually do not begin with a well-formulated plan of action but end with one, after full and free discussion. This type of conference is the very essence of the democratic process. Everybody makes his contribution, offers his criticisms and objections, and then agrees to co-operate in carrying out whatever plans may win majority support.

Tests of Comprehension and Application

TRAINING FOR INTERVIEWS AND CONFERENCES

1 Working in pairs, demonstrate before the class a preliminary meeting between interviewer and " interviewee " solely for the purpose of setting a time and place for an interview.
2 Using a dummy telephone, let a prospective interviewer call a prospective " interviewee " and make an appointment for a subsequent meeting.
3 Assume that you are a feature-article writer for a newspaper or a magazine. Let one of your classmates take the part of some well-known person who is much in the public eye, and conduct with him an interview designed to obtain a human-interest story about him. (In order to make this project interesting and successful, the person who takes the part of the celebrity must know enough about " himself " so that he can answer intelligent and pertinent questions interestingly and satisfactorily.)
4 Assume that you are sales manager of some manufacturing organization and that you are interviewing one of your subordinates for the purpose of giving him a background of information about a prospective customer for your line of goods. You want the salesman to know certain facts about his potential customer so that he may deal intelligently and effectively with him.
5 As business manager of the school annual you are to interview your assistant for the purpose of explaining the procedures you expect him to follow in soliciting advertising for the publication.
6 As program manager of your local radio station you are to inter-

view the president of a Parent-Teacher Association for the purpose of explaining what your station has to offer in the way of programs of special interest to elementary-school children.

7 What can you learn about skill in interviewing from study of the following? Consider both of the parties to this very interesting interview. Can you suggest improvements in what either says or does?

When Edward Bok stood before the home of Longfellow, he realized that he was to see the man around whose head the boy's youthful reading had cast a sort of halo. And when he saw the head itself he had a feeling that he could see the halo. No kindlier pair of eyes ever looked at a boy, as, with a smile, " the white Mr. Longfellow," as Mr. Howells had called him, held out his hand.

" I am very glad to see you, my boy," were his first words, and with them he won the boy. Edward smiled back at the poet, and immediately the two were friends.

" I have been taking a walk this beautiful morning," he said next, " and am a little late getting at my mail. Suppose you come in and sit at my desk with me, and we will see what the postman has brought. He brings me so many good things, you know.

" Now, here is a little girl," he said, as he sat down at the desk with the boy beside him, " who wants my autograph and a ' sentiment.' What sentiment, I wonder, shall I send her? "

" Why not send her ' Let us, then, be up and doing '? " suggested the boy. " That's what I should like if I were she."

" Should you, indeed? " said Longfellow. " That is a good suggestion. Now, suppose you recite it off to me, so that I shall not have to look it up in my books, and I will write as you recite. But slowly; you know I am an old man, and write slowly."

Edward thought it strange that Longfellow himself should not know his own great words without looking them up. But he recited the four lines, so familiar to every schoolboy, and when the poet had finished writing them, he said:

" Good! I see you have a memory. Now, suppose I copy these lines once more for the little girl, and give you this copy? Then you can say, you know, that you dictated my own poetry to me."

Of course Edward was delighted, and Longfellow gave him the sheet.

Then, as the fine head bent down to copy the lines once more, Edward ventured to say to him:

"I should think it would keep you busy if you did this for everyone who asked you."

"Well," said the poet, "you see, I am not so busy a man as I was some years ago, and I shouldn't like to disappoint a little girl; should you?"

As he took up his letters again, he discovered five more requests for his autograph. At each one he reached into a drawer in his desk, took a card, and wrote his name on it.

"There are a good many of these every day," said Longfellow, "but I always like to do this little favor. It is so little to do, to write your name on a card; and if I didn't do it some boy or girl might be looking, day by day, for the postman and be disappointed. I only wish I could write my name better for them. You see how I break my letters? That's because I never took pains with my writing when I was a boy. I don't think I should get a high mark for penmanship if I were at school, do you?"

"I see you get letters from Europe," said the boy, as Longfellow opened an envelope with a foreign stamp on it.

"Yes, from all over the world," said the poet. Then, looking at the boy quickly, he said: "Do you collect postage stamps?"

Edward said he did.

"Well, I have some right here, then," and going to a drawer in a desk he took out a bundle of letters, and cut out the postage stamps and gave them to the boy.

"There's one from the Netherlands. There's where I was born," Edward ventured to say.

"In the Netherlands? Then you are a real Dutchman. Well! Well!" he said, laying down his pen. "Can you read Dutch?"

The boy said he could.

"Then," said the poet, "you are just the boy I am looking for." And going to a bookcase behind him he brought out a book, and handing it to the boy, he said, his eyes laughing: "Can you read that?"

It was an edition of Longfellow's poems in Dutch.

"Yes, indeed," said Edward. "These are your poems in Dutch."

"That's right," he said. "Now, this is delightful. I am so glad you came. I received this book last week, and although I have been in the Netherlands, I cannot speak or read Dutch. I wonder whether you would read a poem to me and let me hear how it sounds."

So Edward took "The Old Clock on the Stairs," and read it to him.

The poet's face beamed with delight. "That's beautiful," he said, and then quickly added: "I mean the language, not the poem.

"Now," he went on, "I'll tell you what we'll do: we'll strike a bargain. We Yankees are great for bargains, you know. If you will read me 'The Village Blacksmith' you can sit in that chair there made out of the wood of the old spreading chestnut tree, and I'll take you out and show you where the old shop stood. Is that a bargain?"

Edward assured him it was. He sat in the chair of wood and leather, and read to the poet several of his own poems in a language in which, when he wrote them, he never dreamed they would ever be printed. He was very quiet. Finally he said: "It seems so odd, so very odd, to hear something you know so well sound so strange."

"It's a great compliment, though, isn't it, sir?" asked the boy.

"Ye-es," said the poet slowly. "Yes, yes," he added quickly. "It is, my boy, a very great compliment.

"Ah," he said, rousing himself, as a maid appeared, "that means luncheon, or rather," he added, "it means dinner, for we have dinner in the old New England fashion, in the middle of the day. I am all alone today, and you must keep me company; will you? Then afterward we'll go and take a walk, and I'll show you Cambridge. It is such a beautiful old town, even more beautiful, I sometimes think, when the leaves are off the trees.

"Come," he said, "I'll take you upstairs, and you can wash your hands in the room where George Washington slept. And comb your hair, too, if you want to," he added; "only it isn't the same comb that he used."

To the boyish mind it was a historic breaking of bread, that midday meal with Longfellow.

"Can you say grace in Dutch?" he asked, as they sat down; and the boy did.

"Well," the poet declared, "I never expected to hear that at my table. I like the sound of it."

Then while the boy told all that he knew about the Netherlands, the poet told the boy all about his poems. Edward said he liked *Hiawatha*.

"So do I," he said. "But I think I like *Evangeline* better. Still," he added, "neither one is as good as it should be. But those are the things you see afterward so much better than you do at the time."

It was a great event for Edward when, with the poet nodding and smiling to every boy and man he met, and lifting his hat to every woman and little girl, he walked through the fine old streets of Cambridge with Longfellow. At one point of the walk they came to a theatrical billboard announcing an attraction that evening at the Boston Theatre. Skilfully the old poet drew out from Edward that sometimes he went to the theater with his parents. As they returned to the gate of "Craigie House" Edward said he thought he would go back to Boston.

"And what have you on hand for this evening?" asked Longfellow.

Edward told him he was going to his hotel to think over the day's events.

The poet laughed and said:

"Now, listen to my plan. Boston is strange to you. Now we're going to the theater this evening, and my plan is that you come in now, have a little supper with us, and then go with us to see the play. It is a funny play, and a good laugh will do you more good than to sit in a hotel all by yourself. Now, what do you think?"

Of course the boy thought as Longfellow did, and it was a very happy boy that evening who, in full view of the large audience in the immense theater, sat in that box. It was, as Longfellow had said, a play of laughter, and just who laughed louder, the poet or the boy, neither ever knew.

Between the acts there came into the box a man of courtly presence, dignified and yet gently courteous.

"Ah! Phillips," said the poet, "how are you? You must know my young friend here. This is Wendell Phillips, my boy. Here is a young man who told me today that he was going to call on you and on Phillips Brooks tomorrow. Now you know him before he comes to you."

"I shall be glad to see you, my boy," said Mr. Phillips.

An hour later, when Longfellow dropped Edward at his hotel, he had not only a wonderful day to think over but another wonderful day to look forward to as well!

He had breakfasted with Oliver Wendell Holmes; dined, supped, and been to the theater with Longfellow; and tomorrow he was to spend with Phillips Brooks.[1]

ARRANGING AND HOLDING INTERVIEWS AND CONFERENCES

8   Write a letter to the secretary of some prominent man in your community requesting the privilege of an interview with the man.

9   Let each member of the class select some local store, factory, or professional office and, either over the telephone or by letter, arrange for an actual interview with the employment manager or head of the firm for the purpose of finding out what employment opportunities there are in that particular organization. Report to the class what you have learned in making these appointments.

10   Each member of the class should keep his appointment made under project 9 and report back to the class on the information he has obtained regarding some business or profession.

11   Interview some teacher in your school whose work you have not taken, aiming to secure important information as to what this teacher thinks about the relationship of his or her courses to the fundamental objectives of education.

12   Divide the class into groups of five or six and let each group work out a conference on some matter of vital and immediate interest to students of your school. A good deal of preliminary planning will be necessary if the conference is to be made real and significant.

13   Hold a conference of senior class officers on plans for commencement exercises.

[1] *The Americanization of Edward Bok; An Autobiography*, Student's Edition, Charles Scribner's Sons, New York, 1920, pp. 41-47. Reprinted by permission.

14 Hold a conference of the officers and the Program Committee of some school society to develop a program for the year. Other projects of a similar nature may be made the subject for conferences. Use your ingenuity in developing a number of them.

CHAPTER TWENTY *Dictating Letters*

TWO MILLION secretaries in the United States right at this moment are taking dictation or typing letters. About 40,000,000 such letters go through the United States mail every business day of the year. When we think of the time spent in preparing these letters, of the total salaries paid to stenographers, and of the huge postage bills, we realize the importance of making these communications just as effective as possible. Yet there is abundant evidence to indicate that a shockingly high percentage of business letters fail, wholly or partially, to accomplish the purposes for which they are written.

This is a textbook on speech and not on business-letter writing. Nevertheless, speaking and letter writing have so much in common that a student of speech properly may spend time and effort in learning how to dictate tactful, straightforward, convincing, and effective letters. Moreover, in a speech course, it is interesting and worth while to consider the special problems involved in the dictation of such letters.

Speech has a direct "person-to-person" quality which distinguishes it from other forms of communication. As we have said, when we desire to speak with others, a "station-to-station" call is not enough; we want the sense of dealing with someone in particular. When we write a novel or an essay, we realize that it may be read by all sorts and conditions of people and, in effect, we address it "to whom it may concern." Business letters should not be aimed so vaguely. A business letter is not a message to the world at large; like a speech, it is a personal communication to someone in particular. Therefore simple, direct, conversational language should be used in business letters. Says A. C. Benson: "The test of a good letter is a very simple one: If one seems to hear the person talking it is a good letter." While this is an exaggeration it is true that the business letter and speech have a great deal in common.

PLANNING THE LETTER

Just as there is a lot of planless talking, so also there is a great deal of planless letter writing. In fact, the quantity of letter writing needed for the completion of business transactions might be reduced substantially if careful planning invariably preceded dictation.

The one who is going to dictate a letter should realize that his fundamental problem is how to challenge and control the attention, the feelings, the beliefs, and the attitudes of the one to whom the letter is addressed. In letter writing, as in speaking, there is no substitute for intelligent purpose. Professor R. R. Aurner of the Department of Business Administration, University of Wisconsin, writes: "Competent judges hold the opinion that five per cent or about two million letters a day, on the average, are letters that the writers would not have had to write if the original situations had been properly handled. Thus wasted for postage alone is $18,000,000." The $18,000,000 figure is based upon the assumption that the first reply was wasted as well as the second inquiry, which means that five letters were used in the completion of each of the 2,000,000 transactions where two should have sufficed.

Marginal notes on letters to be answered. In preparing to answer a letter, it is a good plan to go through it carefully, underlining the points which are to be taken up in the reply. This procedure is a guarantee against omitting important points and wasting time on unimportant details.

Assembling necessary information. After we have decided just what we want to say in a letter, we should be sure that we have at hand the data we shall require to do the job well. A great deal of time may be wasted in attempting to dictate letters before we have assembled the materials we need. If we are going to cite figures, we should get the figures ready before we start to dictate. If we are going to employ other forms of specific information, we should be sure that we have them at our finger tips before we begin to dictate.

Thus we shall avoid making false starts and obliging ourselves to rush around looking up necessary facts and figures while our stenographer sits pencil in hand, with her notebook before her, waiting for us to do the job.

Making a working outline. No matter how short the letter is to be, if it deals with more than one point we have to face the problem of arrangement. Something has to come first and something else second. We should not leave this important choice to chance. It is a good policy to jot down the various ideas in what seems to be the most reasonable and effective sequence. We should always remember that it will pay us to clarify our own thinking in order to guarantee clearness in the mind of the one who is to read the letter. If our own thinking is disorderly and confused, how can we expect the reader to understand what we write?

The opening sentence. In our letters, we should try to avoid trite first sentences. We should never begin by informing our correspondent that his " favor of recent date has been received and contents noted "; he will assume that we have his letter if we are answering it! It is much better to open with a statement which implies that we have read his letter and understood it. We should try to start by hitting a high spot of interest, something which is really vital in the correspondence. A bad opening may spoil an otherwise good letter. It is well to begin with some statement which will get a favorable response from our correspondent and mold his attitude in such a way as to make it easier for us to get our message across to him. This principle is violated more frequently than any other in business-letter writing. If we are answering a letter requesting us to do something we are willing to do, why not open the reply by saying that we shall be glad to do it? Then, if we have any reservations to express, we can proceed to explain them tactfully. If our correspondent has asked us to do something which we are either unwilling or unable to do, we should not begin by suggesting that we are going to do it and then wind up by saying that we will not. Our first sentence should " slant " in the direction of refusal.

THE "SEVEN C QUALITIES" OF A GOOD BUSINESS LETTER

Professor Aurner says: " The aim of a good letter must be to help the person addressed. To the end, use the seven C's. There is nothing magic about them. They are simply the time-tested ways through which business writing has made itself economical, human, sympathetic, and forceful.

" We summarize them in outline thus:

1. Completeness   (Nothing left undone)
2. Courtesy   (Pleasant feeling tone)
3. Consideration   (Think of the reader first)
4. Clearness   (No misunderstanding)
5. Conciseness   (Every word counting)
6. Concreteness   (Details sharp, definite)
7. Correctness   (No stumbling blocks)

" Completeness is essential in order that the full picture may be laid before him who reads, so that further wasteful and needless inquiries may be avoided; courtesy, in order that the message may find a receptive hearing; consideration, in order that the reader may be truly helped and his wants truly understood; clearness, in order that the way shall not be clogged; conciseness, in order that every fact may be definite, informative, vivid, and interesting; and correctness, in order that costly delay and misunderstanding shall not be created, and that attention shall be neither diverted nor obstructed." [1]

Let us now proceed to examine these seven C qualities in further detail.

Completeness. The important consideration here is to include in the letter everything which really needs to be said. We should try to make it unnecessary for our correspondent to write us again asking for further information, or for additional data. Nothing essential should be omitted. Few considerations are more important in speaking or in letter writing than knowing how to evaluate materials so that we can leave out what will not help and put in everything which will contribute definitely to the accomplishment of our purpose. In

---

[1] R. R. Aurner, *Effective English and Business*, South-Western Publishing Co., Inc., p. 259. Reprinted by permission of the author.

deciding what to use and what not to use, we should employ the test: Will this particular bit of information appeal to, or be appreciated by, the person who is going to read the letter? It is always easy to fall into the error of assuming that what we ourselves consider significant the correspondent also is bound to think important. We should use the " you " test; evaluate everything through the interests of our correspondent. We aren't trying to influence ourselves, we are trying to influence him.

Courtesy. This second principle of successful letter writing arises naturally enough from what we have just been saying about completeness. Our letter is really complete only when it is complete in the mind of our correspondent. However, it is not enough to understand the one to whom we write; we must take also a friendly and courteous attitude toward him. Courtesy is more than formal politeness. Like beauty, it goes deeper than the surface of things. Suave or flowery language is not an adequate substitute for heartfelt and heart-warming friendliness. If we expect our correspondent to react with goodwill toward us, we must feel and express goodwill toward him. Ralph Waldo Emerson says: " Life is short, but there is always time for courtesy." This principle applies with special force to letter writing.

Consideration. It is difficult to distinguish between courtesy and consideration. A truly courteous letter writer must feel genuine consideration for his correspondent. Courtesy is the outward manifestation in manner and language of an inner consideration for others. All of us are prone to be concerned with our own interests to the exclusion of the interests of others. Consideration is practically synonymous with unselfishness. Someone has said that every letter writer crawls into the envelope with his letter, seals it, travels to its destination, comes out of the envelope with the message, and presents it to his correspondent. Unless we personally have this quality of consideration, we may not be very persuasive in this process. There is nothing we can say about any person much less complimentary than to remark that he is inconsiderate. Anyone who is inconsiderate in what he writes is likely to pay a high penalty in the unfavorable reception he stirs up for himself.

Clearness. Lord Chesterfield gives the letter writer excellent advice when he says: "Every paragraph should be so clear and unambiguous that the dullest fellow in the world will not be able to misstate it nor be obliged to read it twice in order to understand it." How hard it is to put this great principle into practice! When Abraham Lincoln was a boy, he was much annoyed by older people's using language he could not understand. He tried to remember what they had said, to find out the meaning of the long and difficult words, and then to put it into language so simple that no child could fail to comprehend it. It is not unlikely that, in this practice pursued over a long period of time, we may find the secret of Lincoln's power as a speaker and a writer. The Cooper Union Speech, the letter to Mrs. Bixby, the Gettysburg Address, and the Second Inaugural were the natural results of the discipline in simplicity and directness of expression which Lincoln had practiced. It is a good deal easier to speak and write vaguely and ambiguously than it is to be crystal-clear. Yet unless we achieve some measure of clarity, we shall find that we are misunderstood when misunderstanding is expensive, and even dangerous.

"An insurance man once wrote the following letter to a mountaineer in the eastern part of our country. As you read it, put yourself in the mountaineer's shoes:

"'Surrender of the policy is permissible only with the days attendant the grace period in compliance with citation, relevant options, accruing to the policy. We are stopped from acquiescing to a surrender prior to the policy's anniversary date. We are confident that an investigation relevant to the incorporation of this feature will substantiate that the policy is not at variance with policies of other companies.' Discussing this cloud of verbiage, L. E. Frailey, letter analyst, remarks; 'I suppose most of us in business are a little better equipped to understand the English language than that man of the hills, but tell me truthfully — did you understand the meaning of those sentences after the first reading? I think the insurance man should have been ashamed when he read the mountaineer's simple answer: "Dear Mister: I am sorry, but I do not understand your letter. If you will explain what you mean, I will try to do as you ask."'"[1]

[1] Quoted in R. R. Aurner, *op. cit.*, pp. 244-45. Reprinted by permission.

When we are in a hurry to get our correspondence out of the way, we may go through a meaningless, routine rigmarole of dictation and think that we have really *answered* our letters. A short time ago one of our popular magazines carried a delightful little sermon on this kind of letter writing, under the title " Jungle Tale ":

" A jungle of lushest verbiage crept over him. He panted, and hewed his way into language no white man had ever dared penetrate. A forward step, and the heavy foliage of ' inasmuchas ' snapped back into his face. He slashed at the underbrush of redundancy, and a coiled double negative sprang at him swiftly. A split infinitive flew up from the teeming path and stung him. A top-heavy adverbial clause lay in wait for him around the bend of the next semicolon; and the tom-tom of an unwieldy paragraph sounded sinisterly near. But on he fought, yet on — brave, stubborn, single-handed — till the foliage grew thinner, parted and, ' with the kindest of personal regards,' gave way to the blessed sunlight and safety of ' very truly yours '; and he brilliantly covered his tracks by saying casually, ' Just change that around, Miss Whiffleberry, anyway you see fit.' " [1]

If we are going to stay out of the jungle " of lushest verbiage " we must cling to a simple vocabulary which can be understood easily by the correspondents to whom we address our letters.

Conciseness. When we are writing business letters, we are not attempting to produce models of elegant and ornate literary composition. In such letters, we are trying to solve immediate and pressing problems. In doing this we should be as concise as we can be without sacrificing courtesy and consideration. Of course, it is possible to be too terse to accomplish our purpose effectively, but the temptation usually is to say too much rather than too little. We may well ponder the quaint observation of Lincoln, who when he was asked how long a man's legs ought to be, answered, " About long enough to reach to the ground." A study of Lincoln's letters, many of which are models of conciseness, will show that they were just long enough, and no longer than necessary, to reach to his objective.

When President Coolidge was a potential candidate for re-election he wrote, " I do not choose to run." When General Sherman was

[1] Edith Pellow, *Saturday Evening Post*, July 11, 1942, p. 32. Reprinted by permission.

asked to become a candidate for the Presidency he said, "I will not run if nominated, and I will not serve if elected." Probably the statements of the two men may be considered equally concise, but certainly Sherman's position was made clearer than Coolidge's was. Many of us use language in such profusion that our meanings get lost in unnecessary words. Often it is easier to make a long speech or write a long letter than it is to speak or write more concisely. Once when Woodrow Wilson was asked to deliver a speech, he remarked that if he could have an hour in which to speak he was ready immediately, but that if he was to speak for only ten minutes, it would take him two weeks to prepare. The letter writer who can say most in the fewest words is most likely to succeed.

Concreteness. The quality of vividness, much to be desired in all speaking and writing, can be achieved best through the use of the concrete. The parables of the New Testament and the homely anecdotes told by Lincoln are far more effective than abstract statements could be. If we would move the mind of our correspondent, we should write to him in figures of speech, comparisons, examples, and concrete illustrations. In business letters, facts and figures are more effective than wordy generalities.

A great many times our letters fail to get results because they do not tie in with the actual experiences of our correspondents. Those who read our letters are like the little boy in the first grade who failed an intelligence test in which his teacher asked him to button a series of buttonholes onto a string of buttons. He couldn't do it, or at least he said that he couldn't. The teacher reported his failure to his mother, who was greatly surprised and asked him why he had not done as he was told. She said, "You can dress yourself and button the buttons on your clothes." "Yes," he answered; "but you see those buttonholes and buttons *didn't button anything.*" If our language is going to button our reader's interests to our purposes, it must be clear that something more than abstract principles is involved. Most of the experiences in life which seem vividly real to us are very concrete. There is always something hazy and vague about abstractions.

Correctness. It was Mrs. Malaprop — of all people! — who remarked, "There is a decorum in these matters." We get along with others only as we observe the conventions of the social order in which we live. In letter writing, failures to conform to the code of correspondence can bring to naught the best of intentions. A mistake which in itself seems trifling may give offense out of all proportion to its intrinsic importance. Misspelling, ineffective paragraphing, the use of a wrong title, the addition of a cipher to a quoted price, the insertion of " not " where it does not belong, may utterly destroy an otherwise well-constructed letter.

No matter how nearly infallible a secretary may be, the careful letter writer reads his letters before he signs them. It is quite possible that misunderstandings may occur between the employer who dictates and the secretary who types a letter. Recently in dictating a letter, the phrase " articulation and enunciation " was used. In the transcribed letter, it appeared as " argumentation and denunciation." Just as a student finds it wise to read over his answers in an examination before he turns in his paper, so it pays for the one who has dictated a letter to check it through carefully before he sends it on its way. " Dictated, but not read," although a discourteous expression, may be useful in emergency situations; but it cannot absolve the letter writer of responsibility for serious errors. Even though the reader may be sure that the letter does not accurately express the writer's intended meaning, he may not be able to tell just what the writer did intend. This difficulty may produce unnecessary additional letters.

DICTATING DISTINCTLY

In dictating letters, we should speak distinctly and with properly placed pauses of sufficient length. When we use quotations, we should indicate clearly where the quoted matter begins and where it ends; we should say " Begin quote " and " End quote." If the punctuation is particularly important, we should include punctuation in our dictation. Similarly, paragraph beginnings, capitalization, underlining, and preferred spellings should all be dictated. Wordings which are considered especially important should be read back by the secretary from her stenographic notes before the letter is typed. Sometimes, letters should be typed in a preliminary form and reworked for the improvement of phrasing and organization before they are finally prepared for mailing. As has been noted, it is a good deal less costly in time and effort to make sure that a letter is written just as well as it possibly can be than it is to write two or three additional letters which might have been made unnecessary by taking pains with the earlier one.

We may find the following projects in dictation interesting if we approach them in the proper spirit and with the desire to learn everything we can from them. These activities may be undertaken jointly with classes in stenography and typing. While we ourselves are profiting in learning how to formulate and talk the letters, our fellow students in commercial subjects (they may be in our speech classes, too) will be having interesting and worth-while experiences in taking the letters in shorthand and in transcribing them according to the principles and rules they are studying. If our high school does not provide training in stenography and typing, we still may carry out these projects by working in pairs. " Stenographers " can take letters in longhand. Perhaps one of the secretaries in the school office may be willing to co-operate by giving some of the members of the speech class opportunity to dictate letters to her before the entire class, and by criticizing the dictation as well as the structure of the letters for the benefit of the entire group.

A number of the following projects are extremely complex, and adequate solutions of them might tax the ingenuity and the skill of a business executive of mature years and long experience. However, we may profit from studying these problems and doing our best to solve them in the light of what we now know.

Tests of Comprehension and Application

PRACTICE IN DICTATING LETTERS

1   Assume that you are salesmanager of the Free-Flowing Fountain Pen Company, Cleveland, Ohio. One of your customers, Mr. Nels Hanson of 227 Brown Street, Freeport, Illinois, has ordered one gross of Acme Model No. 73 pens, which are temporarily out of stock owing to heavy recent orders. You will be able to fill the order in about three weeks' time. Dictate an acknowledgment of the order designed to keep it open until you can fill it.

2   Assuming the situation in project 1, dictate an acknowledgment of the order designed to secure the customer's approval of the substitution of Streamlined Model No. 78 pens, at a price $6 per dozen higher than the price of the ones originally ordered.

3   You are a circulation manager of the *News Digest*. Acknowledge receipt of a $6 check from Mr. Wm. Carter, 171 Center Street, Brentwood, Ohio, for a two years' subscription, and try to enlist his co-operation in securing other subscriptions from Brentwood, which up to this time has not been represented on your list.

4   As credit manager of a leading department store in your community, dictate a letter to a woman who has been a customer of the store for a number of years past. This customer has been habitually slow in paying her bills. Your purpose is, *without losing her business*, to stimulate prompt settlement of accounts at the beginning of each month.

5   As manager of the gas company in your city, you have received a letter from the teacher of chemistry in your high school, requesting permission to bring his classes to your plant for a visit of inspection. Dictate a reply granting permission on condition that the group will come to your office at a specified hour on a certain date. Dictate another reply explaining that you are unable to grant the favor because of the laws relating to accident liability, and the shortage of competent guides. Try to make your refusal as tactful as possible, but do not leave the way open for a renewal of the request.

6   You have received a letter from the general chairman of the Community Chest Fund in your city asking you to serve as solicitor in your block. Dictate a letter declining on the ground that you have

too many other responsibilities at this time. Dictate a second letter accepting the appointment.

7   As manager of an insurance agency in your city, dictate a letter congratulating a young salesman who has written a very large amount of insurance during the past year. Your purpose is to keep him going at his record speed. Dictate a letter to another salesman who has made a disappointing showing, the purpose being to stimulate him to do better in the coming year.

8   Dictate a letter congratulating the captain of a football team on the completion of a successful season.

9   Dictate a letter of sympathy to some personal friend who has been obliged to give up his plan for attending summer camp.

10   As manager of a local typewriter agency, answer a letter of complaint about an allegedly defective machine which a customer has recently purchased from you. An examination of the typewriter has convinced you that the trouble is due to improper use rather than to structural defects. The customer has demanded a new machine, and you cannot fairly make any adjustment beyond " repairs at cost."

11   A friend tells you that he has applied to an airplane manufacturing company for a position as a mechanic, and asks you to write a letter of recommendation to the company for him. You do not feel very enthusiastic about the friend's qualifications, but you do consider yourself obliged to write a letter. Dictate the letter.

12   One of the prominent athletes in your school has applied for a position as counselor of younger boys at a summer camp, and has asked you to write the head counselor a general statement covering character and other qualifications. You think that your friend is fitted for the position. Dictate the letter.

13   Prepare a fifty-word night letter (telegram) as a substitute for one of the letters you have been asked to dictate. Dictate it to a classmate over the telephone. Report to the class on the difficulties you encountered in making the " telegraph clerk " understand your message.

14   Dictate the following, pronouncing each word only once. Compare your " secretary's " transcription with the original. What does your experience suggest as to stumbling blocks in dictating material?

Alexander Pope judiciously observed: "Men must be taught as though you taught them not, and things unknown proposed as things forgot." He also recommended: "Be silent always, when you doubt your sense; and speak, tho' sure, with seeming diffidence."

DICTATING LETTERS TO BE ACTUALLY MAILED

15 Dictate a letter to a summer resort, asking about rates, types of accommodations, and recreational facilities.

16 Select an editorial from a newspaper or a magazine expressing opinions with which you strongly disagree. Dictate a letter to the editor, asking him to furnish you with the evidence upon which his statements are based. Don't argue; make a tactful persuasive request designed to elicit information.

17 Dictate a letter to your Congressman or Senator, requesting specific information on some bill now before the Congress.

18 Dictate an answer to a newspaper advertisement for help wanted.

19 Dictate a letter ordering some article you see advertised for sale in a newspaper or a magazine. Specify preferred method of shipment, date of delivery, method of payment, and any other matters you think relevant and important.

20 Dictate a letter of introduction to some employer whom you know, presenting one of your personal friends who is going to make an application to him for employment.

21 Select some local firm for which you would like to work upon graduation from high school. Dictate a letter to the proper official in the organization, applying for a position.

22 Dictate a letter to a schoolmate, pointing out the advantage of reading regularly some magazine you especially enjoy and consider worth while. Your purpose is to get him to subscribe.

23 Dictate a letter to your alderman, censuring him for a statement which he has recently made expressing indifference to the wishes of his constituents. Your object is not to make him angry, but to modify his attitude.

24 Plan and dictate a letter to one of the printers or engravers in your locality, asking for price quotations on work for the school paper or annual.

25 Dictate a letter to the registrar of the college or university of

your choice, inquiring about enrollment dates, tuition costs, charges for board and room, and incidental expenses. Be sure to get the actual name of the registrar.

CHAPTER TWENTY-ONE *Buying and Selling*

MANY OF US do our own buying of the things that we need for daily living. We decide on the article we wish to buy, and we shop around until we find it at a price that we can afford to pay. Then we make the transaction. Some of us do much of our personal buying without the help of any member of our families. Few of us reach high school without doing some of it, and every one of us does more buying instead of less as time goes on.

Some of us have never stopped to think that we might get more for our money if we practiced effective methods of buying. We have not considered how to approach the person from whom we wish to make a purchase. We have never thought that the way we ask for information may determine the care a clerk will take in giving us the facts about the article we plan to buy.

If we wish to sell something, we have to think of the problem from another angle. The sale of cookies, candy, dairy products from the farm, fruit from the orchard, vegetables from the garden, second-hand books, tickets for plays, games, and benefits, lunches at the school cafeteria or restaurant, the school annual, and all types of papers and magazines — all these are carried on by high-school students. An understanding of methods of selling will increase our success in business transactions.

SUCCESSFUL BUYING

The first step in successful buying is to decide what we want to buy. Often this process is the most time-consuming in the entire transaction. When we go to a store "just to look around," thumb through a mail-order catalogue, examine purchases already in use by friends and acquaintances, have articles demonstrated, or gather information about anything we may later decide to purchase, we are engaged in the first step of the buying process. Whatever preliminary effort is necessary to reach a decision about buying is usually worth while. "I bought too hastily" is a more common source of regret than "I selected the article too carefully." It is easy to see that to decide on just what to purchase may require visits to stores, conferences with salesmen, interviews with friends and acquaintances, demonstrations, and receiving articles on approval. Many of the persons who give information and advice will not actually sell us anything, and since they do not profit financially, it is especially important that our contacts with them be pleasant.

Let us assume that we wish to buy some wearing apparel. We have a fixed sum of money to spend and we wish to get as much as we can for it. We may desire to visit several stores before deciding on the articles we intend to purchase. Let us be honest with the salesclerk about our mission. Let us not pretend that we are going to buy at once when we are sure that we shall not do so. Why not tell the salesperson why we have come? Let him understand that we value the help he can give us. He deserves courtesy and appreciation for displaying his wares. We should take what time is necessary to accomplish our purpose, but we should not waste one moment for other customers, the clerk, or ourselves. If our investigation is made with courtesy, frankness, and dispatch, unpleasant misunderstandings can be avoided. We will not be pressed to buy against our better judgment, we will have no need to manufacture an excuse for leaving without making a purchase, and the clerk, instead of feeling resentment because he expected to make a sale and did not, may feel pleased that we have expressed confidence in his advice.

Making the purchase. After we have decided what we want to buy, we should go where we can make the purchase. If we have met discourteous clerks, let us analyze ourselves to see whether we have treated them as we would like to be treated in similar situations. Sometimes customers approach salespeople as if they were unfeeling furnishings in an establishment rather than sensitive individuals. Naturally, in such circumstances a customer does not get the careful service given to the person who waits his turn courteously, greets the salesman in a friendly manner, calling him by name if he can, speaks clearly and distinctly, avoids unkind or critical comments, and takes only the time required to secure the specific articles he desires — in short, treats the salesman from whom he wishes to buy with as much consideration as he does the host or hostess in whose home he is a caller.

Effective speech essential. In finding out what we want to buy, it is necessary for us to speak effectively. And in buying it, it is important to speak effectively also. It is through speech that we make our first impression upon the salesman. It is through speech that we control his attitude. It is through speech that we make clear what we want. If our speech is ineffective, the entire transaction may be a failure. Before we go to make our purchase, we should be sure that we can talk so that our listeners will understand us, and that they will not be antagonized by our voice and attitude. Since we are doing the buying, it is incumbent upon us to take the initiative and make our desires clear. We must not expect the salesman to question us at length in order to learn what we want. It will save much time if we state clearly, accurately, and as briefly as possible the specifications for our proposed purchase.

Favorable and unfavorable observations. Following are comments about six students who were making purchases. It is not difficult to decide which ones probably received courteous treatment from the salesmen.

1. A boy enters a men's furnishing store. He says: " Say, you, do I have to wait all day? " He speaks with a loud raucous voice. He uses poor grammar. He criticizes the clerk because he does not have an abundance of information on a particular article. The boy walks away abruptly because he has not found what he wanted.

2. A girl wishes to purchase luggage in a department store. She taps on the counter for attention. She asks another customer where the luggage can be found. She pushes someone else out of her way to get close to the suitcases she wishes to examine. She mumbles her words so that the salesman does not understand her. She makes it obvious that she considers the salesman her servant. She uses time to tell an irrelevant story.

3. A girl goes to the millinery department to purchase a hat. She is chewing gum. Her dress is wrinkled. She speaks in a high, strained voice. She lets the saleswoman know that she has faith only in her own judgment. She handles hats — with soiled fingers. She visits with a friend as the saleswoman waits. She says she will return later, though that is not her intention.

4. A girl goes to the glove counter. She says: " Good morning, Miss Drew. Will you please show me some gloves for school wear? " She is wearing fresh, clean, well-pressed clothes. She has a pleasant and expressive voice. She shows respect for the saleswoman's judgment. She thanks the saleswoman for serving her.

5. A boy is selecting furniture for his room. He is neatly dressed. His hair is carefully combed. He has a friendly attitude. He asks the floorwalker to direct him to the right department. He uses words that express exactly what he wants to say. He offers to wait until someone else has been served.

6. A boy wishes to purchase golf clubs. He speaks clearly and distinctly. He tells the salesman at once exactly what he wants. He listens to the salesman's comments. He explains that the price is more than he expects to pay.

Testing buying skill. Let us rate ourselves as we go along. If we can answer the following queries in the affirmative, we are probably successful buyers.

1. Does our salutation make the salesman eager to serve us?
2. Does he understand every word we say without asking us to repeat?

3. Are we making the purchase without wasting our own time or that of the salesman?

4. Are we able to correct misunderstandings courteously and quickly?

5. Are we securing exactly what we want at the price we wish to pay?

SUCCESSFUL SELLING

Know the buyer. The first essential in successful selling is an understanding of the potential customers. If we have tried to dispose of tickets for a school benefit, we have discovered that we cannot approach the teachers in exactly the same way in which we approach our fellow students. A greeting which might offend a teacher might conceivably please a student, and vice versa. It is also true that not all teachers are the same, or all students either! The salesman who knows the special interests of his customers will find it easier to sell any article. If we know that our teacher likes to play golf and we too understand the game, we have a topic for conversation which may pave the way for a sale. The boy whose father is a doctor has had different experiences from the boy whose father is a building contractor. It is obvious that the girl who has given interpretative dances in public may respond favorably to a sales approach different from that which pleases the girl who is an inveterate reader and dislikes to appear before an audience. The successful salesman knows what his buyers like and dislike, where they have traveled, and in what business they have been engaged, and he uses this information as a means to the end — selling.

Many salesmen fail because they are too easy and informal with their customers. Others fail because they are too stiff and reserved. Some persons interpret informality as friendliness, and others as familiarity. What one person calls dignity and breeding, another calls coldness and unfriendliness. Some wish to be treated as equals, others as superiors. We should size up our prospective customer and decide by his looks, his actions, his responses, his voice, and his mannerisms what kind of person he is and what kind of treatment he responds to favorably. Then we should adapt our behavior to his likes and dislikes. While appearance, correct English, and a pleasing manner are assets to a salesman, some persons appreciate them much more than do others. Little irritations may become so important that they overshadow everything else in buying or selling. An unpleasant cough, a boastful manner, a high-pitched voice, a monotonous rhythm, an inquisitive nature, a disagreeable gesture, incorrect grammar — these, and other things like them, may become annoying enough to lose sales. We may label our lost customer " too fussy," but the point is that we wish to sell and he will not buy from us unless we change our ways!

Know how much time can be given to the transaction. Sometimes a customer likes to take his time in making a purchase. If we hurry him, he feels that we are not willing to give him all of the information he wants, and he is likely to become irritated and not wish to deal with us. Other customers want matters handled quickly. They resent the slightest irrelevancy because it is time-consuming. The average person is somewhere between these two extremes. He does not wish to waste time, but neither does he wish to be rushed. It is up to us to discover into which group our customer falls and to treat him accordingly. In salesmanship, as in all other speech activities, our behavior is to be determined by its effect on the " audience."

Learn how much this customer knows about the article to be sold. We should not try to sell the high-school newspaper to one of the contributors by explaining in detail the make-up and contents of the sheet. On the other hand, in soliciting a subscription from someone who has never examined a copy, we should not neglect a description of the paper. Sometimes a salesman is trained with a set speech about the merits of the goods he wishes to sell. He delivers this speech to informed and uninformed customers alike. Sales are lost because of such a lack of personal consideration. A few well-chosen questions will soon tell us what information will be welcomed by our prospect before a sale can be made.

Find out what price a customer wishes to pay. It is a waste of time and effort for a salesman to try to sell an article which is too expensive for the customer to buy. If we wish to sell a used history text to another high-school student, and we become convinced that he has no funds or goods to give in exchange, it is futile for us to go on trying to make the sale. Even if we show him that the text is the one in use, that it is well preserved and a bargain, we cannot complete the transaction and our efforts are to no avail. The wise salesman finds out whether or not his customer has something to give in return for the article to be sold.

Know the article to be sold. If we are trying to sell a newspaper and our customer asks why he should buy, it is not enough for us to say, " Well, because it's tops," or " It's the best of its kind " or " No newspaper can beat it." We must know *why* it is worth buying. If we are going to try to sell any article, it does not need to be the very best of its kind, but it does need to be good enough for us to sell. The quality must be such that if we tell the truth about it, we can honestly recommend its purchase. We should know all its good and bad qualities. In preparing to sell anything, we must anticipate every possible question that may be asked concerning it, and for each question we must have a satisfactory and adequate answer. We must know our customer, we must know our article, and we must know why that particular customer should be interested in that particular article.

Make a good impression in selling. As salesmen we should look to our personal appearance. If we dress appropriately, we are more likely to make a sale. It is axiomatic that whatever we wear should be clean, neat, and becoming. Our shoes should be polished, our hair combed, and our hands and nails clean. Let us see that our voice is expressive. A good voice does not call attention to itself; it calls attention to what we say. Our customers should not think of our voice as beautiful, clear, high, or loud. They should notice only that after we have spoken they have clear and definite ideas. Chapter Three should have helped us to improve our voices for use in salesmanship. Visible action should assist us in selling. What one sees is more definite and convincing than what one hears. We should use facial expression in helping our customers to know the good qualities of the articles we have to sell. Chapter Two contains suggestions as to making our bodies more expressive and communicative. We should use precisely the words that mean what we want to say. We may lose a sale if our language is misunderstood. Therefore it is im-

FARM AUCTION. *Bundled against the bitter winter cold, these Iowa farmers crowd about a truck which the auctioneer, the heavy-set man with outstretched index finger, is selling. The owner of the farm stands second to the auctioneer's left. How does he feel about what is going on? What meanings are to be read in the facial expression of the man with the stick in his hand?* (Press Association)

portant that we use words which express our exact meanings. Chapter Five tells us how to put proper words in proper places.

Examples of successful and unsuccessful selling. It will be interesting for us to consider some examples of successful and unsuccessful selling. These give us an opportunity to see the application of the principles considered in this chapter.

1. Harold Whitehead tells how Perkins sold a difficult prospect:
"It seems that he had been planning to sell insurance to a real-estate man for a long time. He knew the man was carrying only about $5,000 worth of insurance. Now if he approached Barnum (the real-estate man) and talked insurance, he knew he would fall through before he commenced, so he skirmished around for a month or more, studying his man.

"When Perkins was all ready he called on Barnum and said, ' Mr.

Barnum, I've called to see you about your business rating. I've discovered it isn't correct.'

"Can you guess what happened? You're right. Barnum blew up! He evidently thought Perkins was a credit reporter or something like that. He guessed his rating was right, and no one could say he padded his assets and got away with it.

"'You misunderstand me, Mr. Barnum,' said Perkins. 'You haven't padded your assets at all, but you've greatly underestimated one item of yours.'

"Of course Barnum cooled off at that and asked, 'What item?'

"'Let me ask you, Mr. Barnum,' parried Perkins, 'are you personally responsible for your remarkable success or do you owe it to a manager or someone?'

"'There's only one man responsible for Barnum's getting on in the world, and that's Barnum,' was his boastful reply.

"'It's as I thought,' came back Perkins, 'and yet in your assets you value the most important item you have at only $5,000. You give the world a false impression of yourself when you place such a paltry figure on yourself.'

"'Five thousand dollars? Important asset? Me?' Mr. Barnum hadn't tumbled. 'What do you mean, anyhow?'

"'Just this.' Perkins here hitched his chair a bit nearer Barnum. 'You carry only $5,000 worth of insurance, thus placing that sum as your estimate of your value. Five hundred thousand would be nearer the mark.'

"'Lordy!' said Barnum in admiration. 'You're a life-insurance agent, aren't you?'

"'Correct.' Perkins smiled.

"'Why didn't you say so at first?'

"'What would you have done if I had?'

"'Guess I'd have terminated the interview.'

"'Exactly, and by so doing you would have been deprived of knowing you were doing yourself an injustice, Mr. Barnum. You can't afford to put yourself in a poor light with the world any longer. Never mind the amounts now. Will you see the doctor in the morning?'

"Barnum looked at Perkins in open admiration.

"'A life-insurance agent! Say, you ought to be in the real-estate business; you're too good to be peddling insurance.'

"'Thanks. But how about the doctor for tomorrow?'

"'Bring him around, son. You've sold me, all right. I guess I ought to have more insurance and I can't dodge the logic of your sales talk.'

"'He isn't my biggest policyholder,' mused Perkins in conclusion, 'but I got him for $85,000.'"[1]

2-A. A well-dressed businesswoman, slim and somewhat above the average in height, was shopping in the coat department on the second floor of a department store which carried a complete line of medium-grade merchandise. The coat department was having a special mid-spring sale of $25 and $29.50 coats. The department was crowded both with merchandise and with customers. The values seemed to be good but were not exceptional. The customer appeared to be well able to afford coats at the prices of those on sale. The salesperson was a middle-aged woman who approached the customer slowly and with apparently no strong desire to serve her.

Customer. I want to see some of your blue or tan spring coats.

Salesperson. I suppose you wear a 36.

Customer. Yes, 36 or 38.

The saleswoman brought from a near-by case a blue coat. After the customer had removed her coat, the saleswoman assisted her in putting on the new one.

Salesperson. That's a good coat and a good value, too. We are selling it for $25, as this is a special sale.

Customer. May I see something without the fur collar?

The saleswoman took two coats from the rack. She did not assist the customer in trying either of them on except by merely holding the coat.

Salesperson. That coat looks good on you. It's a lovely coat.

Customer. But it is a little short for me and the sleeves are not right, either. What have you in a brown or tan plaid coat?

The saleswoman then disappeared and in a few minutes returned

[1] H. Whitehead, "The Business Career of Peter Flint," *New York Evening Sun*, June 18, 1918. Reprinted by permission.

with a plaid coat, which the customer did not want because of its similarity to the one she was wearing.

Salesperson. Well, that is all we have for $25, but I have some nice ones for $29.50.

The saleswoman brought out three or four more coats. In trying them on, she agreed that the coat did not fit when it was evident that the sleeves were too short; but if the coat was a poor fit in the shoulders or if it was too short, it made little difference in her comments to the customer. Again, she did not take into account the figure of the customer, for practically all the coats had long, straight lines. Her only selling arguments, which were practically the same for each coat, were to the effect that it was lovely, or looked well, or was a good value.

Salesperson (*as customer was trying on the last coat*). Well, these are all we have at those prices, but the coat you are trying on is a good buy. It is well made and the lining is of good material. I am sure you cannot do better anywhere else.

Customer. I don't believe these are what I want, but thank you very much for showing them to me.

Salesperson. You are welcome.

2-B. The customer then went to another department store, which carried a wide variety of coats in two departments, one department for coats over $37 and one for those less than $37; the customer went to the latter department. A middle-aged saleswoman approached her with a smile.

Salesperson. May I help you?
Customer. I want a spring coat for dress wear.
Salesperson. What color would you like?
Customer. Something in blue or tan at about $25.

The saleswoman helped the customer into a coat.

Salesperson. You have rather long arms, haven't you? Just a minute and I'll get a 38.

Customer (*as she tried on a tan coat*). I like this. The sleeves are so pretty.

Salesperson (*as she adjusted the coat*). This is a very fine coat; the collar is hand turned, and it is just the right length, just a little longer than your dress. I don't think you should wear a coat shorter than your dress. (*Smilingly*) I don't dictate style to anyone, because a person generally knows what looks best on herself; but the length of your skirt is just the right style.

The customer tried on several blue and tan coats, but was unable to find a satisfactory blue one.

Salesperson. I'm sorry I haven't what you want in blue. Why don't you try on that tan one again with the pretty sleeves? It is a very smart coat and it is easy to match up. It fits you very well in the shoulders, too.

The saleswoman aided the customer in trying on the tan coat again.

Customer. I had intended to pay only $25, and this is $35.

Salesperson. Yes; these days it is hard to shop and stay within limits, isn't it?

A minute or two passed while the customer looked at the coat in the mirror. The saleswoman made no further comment.

Customer. I think I'll take this coat anyway.

Salesperson. I am sure you'll like it.

The saleswoman adjusted the coat, put in a pin where the button should go, made out the sales slip, and had the coat wrapped.

Salesperson. Thank you so much.

Customer (*evidently pleased with both the service and the coat*). Thank you.[1]

HOW TO MAKE AND RECEIVE COMPLAINTS

Even though we make purchases with great care, there will be times when we will wish to obtain an adjustment. Here are some rules which have been recommended for such a contingency. Let us consider them carefully and try to justify each one. The dissatisfied customer should:

1. Assume that he is dealing with honest people.

2. Assume that satisfaction is the aim of both customer and salesman.

3. Make sure that his request for adjustment is reasonable.

[1] McNair, Gragg, and Teele, *Problems in Retailing*, McGraw-Hill Book Co., Inc., pp. 383–85. Reprinted by permission.

4. Go to the proper authority.
5. Be calm and courteous; not become angry or threatening.
6. State his case clearly and briefly.
7. Apply all of the principles of good speaking.

If we have sold an article that does not satisfy our customer, we must make every effort to rectify the mistake. The salesman should:
1. Listen courteously to the complaint.
2. Decide whether or not it is a reasonable complaint.
3. If it is reasonable, explain clearly what adjustment can be made.
4. If it is not reasonable, explain clearly why an adjustment cannot be made.
5. Not become angry or uncontrolled.
6. Be firm but courteous.

Tests of Comprehension and Application

PRACTICING BUYING AND SELLING

1 You have a definite sum of money to spend. It may go for clothes, room furnishings, school supplies, food, travel, necessities, or luxuries. Study the possibilities carefully, so that when you have decided you will be sure that you will not wish to change your mind. Decide to buy a specific article.

2 Decide on the make and the model of radio you wish to purchase. Consider whether you want a radio alone or a radio-phonograph-recording combination. Take into consideration the cost, tone, appearance, and performance of each model. If it is necessary, turn to the suggestions for conversation, conferences, interviews, and discussion, Chapters Fourteen and Nineteen, for help in getting your information.

3 Find the particular dog you want to buy. Prepare yourself on the important points to be considered in making a final purchase. Be able to talk to salesmen intelligently, so that they will have respect for you as a buyer and will willingly answer the inquiries you may wish to make. First decide on the breed, and then on the particular dog.

COMPREHENSION AND APPLICATION TESTS

4 You have $1 to spend for a book. What can you get that will not only be worth reading now but worth giving space to in your permanent library? Examine lists of worth-while books. Talk to authorities on novels, poetry, studies in science, biographies, or any type of literature of interest to you. Get lists of books selling for $1 or less. Visit secondhand stores and look through the books on their shelves. Talk to your friends about the literature they have enjoyed. Browse through books on bargain counters.

5 Write a pamphlet on "How to Buy and Sell." Illustrate it with original drawings or with pictures taken from magazines, newspapers, or books.

6 Prepare a five-minute talk on "How to Buy and Like What You Get."

7 Prepare a five-minute talk on "How to Sell Articles So That They Stay Sold."

8 Write a dramatization of a successful purchase, and act it.

9 Write a dramatization of an unsuccessful purchase, and act it.

10 Go to the library and supplement the suggestions given here by reading on buying and selling (salesmanship, merchandising, etc.).

PRACTICE ACTUAL BUYING AND SELLING

11 Get ready to buy a dress or a suit. Before examining garments in a store, study your needs. Decide whether you need the clothing for camp, for school, for evening, or for travel. Know what you can afford to pay. Look over the accessories you own to see which of them can be utilized if you buy a given color. Know what store is most likely to have what you want. Go there to examine the various styles and designs.

12 Prepare to buy an outfit for outdoor winter sports. First take into consideration the sports in which you participate. Get information on the best materials and styles for your particular needs. Model some to decide on the design most becoming to you. Examine only those within your price range. From those, decide which you will buy.

13 You need a briefcase for your books and papers. Get ready to go to the store to make the purchase. Decide whether you want to use the case for papers alone, books alone, or both books and pa-

pers. Consider size, color, and construction. Be sure to select one which will in every way fullfil your needs, not only today but in the future.

14 Ask your family to allow you to buy everything used in your home for one week. Follow the suggestions given in this chapter for successful buying.

15 Take charge of a selling project to raise funds for some worth-while cause. Write a report of your activities.

16 Arrange with several other students who live in your neighborhood to ride to school in your car. Persuade them to pay you a fixed sum. Then carry out the project. You will run the car and pay the cost of gasoline and upkeep.

TEST YOUR ABILITY IN BUYING AND SELLING

17 If you have a paper route, try out the suggestions in this chapter on your customers.

18 Look around your home and decide on some article that is needed. Investigate until you have come to a final decision as to what to buy and are ready to make the purchase. Write a report showing what steps you took in reaching your decision. Evaluate your procedure. Show wherein you were successful and wherein unsuccessful. Compare your experience with those of other members of the class who have chosen to do the same thing.

19 Using the helps in Chapter Nineteen, page 478, hold an interview with an expert salesman. Get his suggestions for successful buying and selling.

20 Do you consider the following to be good ways to get customers to buy? Write a paper showing which are effective and which ineffective. Support your opinions.

    a A young man will get a scholarship if he can sell a definite number of subscriptions to a magazine. In attempting to persuade a prospective customer that she should take a subscription, he explains all about the scholarship, points out that he needs only two more sales to get his reward, and gives facts concerning his financial need.

    b A boy is selling vegetables from door to door. His vegetables are fresh and arranged attractively. He shows them to his prospective customer, calls attention to the fine quality and the moderate price, and comments on new ways in which they can be used.

c A girl is selling candy in the hall at high school. A teacher is hurrying to her classroom to arrive before the final bell. The girl rushes after her, urging her to buy.

d A student is collecting contributions for a memorial to a former teacher. Another student has shown an interest and offers to give a small sum. The student collecting makes it clear that not the amount, but the thought, is more appreciated.

e A clerk in a store is serving you. You ask for a sweater at a given price. She says they have them at that price, but explains that with your income you will wish to buy a more expensive one.

f A boy is selling milk. The customer asks if the milk has been pasteurized. The boy does not know.

g Two boys are peddling apples from their orchard. The customers ask such questions as: Has this fruit been sprayed? Are the apples suitable for pies, jelly, or pickles? The boys know that the fruit has been sprayed and make that fact clear, but they also admit that they have no idea what uses can be made of the apples. They do not consider that their affair.

h The editor of the school annual is given time in the general high-school assembly to advertise the volume. He knows when the book will be on sale, the size, color, cover design, binding, kind of paper, type of print, and a great deal about the contents. He knows the cost, and the different ways in which payment can be made.

i A student is trying to sell a secondhand book. He urges you to buy at once, saying that there are no more copies on sale at the bookstore. He does not know whether the statement is true or not.

j A boy comes to collect for the daily newspaper. He has called five times in the last week and no one has been at home. The customer remarks about this and tells him he is sorry he has been inconvenienced. The boy makes light of the trouble and leaves the customer feeling that everything is all right.

k A girl is selling Girl Scout cookies and you know that if you buy, she will put the cookies in a bag with hands that are inky and nails that are black.

1 You go to a store to buy some writing paper. The clerk is inexperienced and does not know where to find it. The manager is on the mezzanine floor above her, and she calls for information in a raucous, high-pitched voice.

m A classmate is announcing in the morning assembly the sale of tickets for the all-school play. He alternately rises on his toes and settles back on his heels as he speaks.

n A clerk is selling a camera and showing the customer how it can be used in various lights. The customer asks many questions, but the clerk is never irritated.

21 Go to a store and observe some sales being made. Write a report showing wherein the techniques of buying and selling were acceptable and wherein unacceptable.

CHAPTER TWENTY-TWO *Business Speeches*

WHAT HAS public speaking to do with success in business? Why should the man who sits behind a desk in the executive office, or the man who is further down the line in the organization, take training in public speaking? If a man knows his line of business, is competent in talking over the telephone, in dictating effective business correspondence, and in handling interviews and conferences, is he not adequately equipped so far as speech is concerned? The answer must be an emphatic *No!* The fact of the matter is that anyone who achieves success in any line is bound to find himself called upon again and again to stand before others in public-speaking situations and do his best to influence them through the use of his voice, his language, and his visible action. Moreover, many times the question as to whether or not a man is to climb up the business ladder is settled by his competence — or his lack of it — in the techniques of public speaking. This is a day of co-operation and organization. As Elbert Hubbard, in his famous *Message to Garcia*, says, " No man succeeds unless he persuades others to assist him."

CONFERENCE SPEAKING

Ordinarily, speaking in conferences should not be thought of as public speaking, particularly when only a few people are involved. However, business conferences often are rather large affairs in which the speaking really does not differ from that which goes on in other public gatherings. Such conferences partake of the nature of public assemblies; very little actual "conferring" takes place in them. We are told that a conference of retail furniture dealers from Midwestern

DIRECTORS' MEETING. *A scene from the motion picture, "Employees' Entrance." Here we see the president of the company laying his plans before his board of directors. Do they seem interested? Which of them apparently are most favorable to the president's proposals? (Culver Service)*

states is to be held at one of the large hotels in Chicago. Obviously, when there are a thousand people present in the grand ballroom of the hotel, it can be called a "conference" only by stretching the term until it cracks. In such circumstances, people really do not "confer" with each other; they listen to public speeches by executives and by other authorities on various phases of their business. Perhaps a few of them participate by asking questions or mentioning pertinent facts which otherwise might be omitted. When the sales manager of a New York manufacturer calls in his five hundred salesmen from all parts of the country for a "conference," we recognize at once that what happens bears little resemblance to what goes on when three or four people meet in an office for a conference. The lesson of all this is that people who expect to be in positions of responsibility with large companies will inevitably be called upon for public speeches in the organizational gatherings that often are designated as conferences.

Of course, the line that separates private speaking from public speaking in conferences is shadowy, just as is the line which separates private speaking from public speaking anywhere else. When does private speaking become public speaking? Most of us will say that when one person speaks to a number of others, we have a public speech. The unsatisfactory word in such an explanation is "number." What number? If two or three people are listening to a speaker, we think of the talk as being a sort of one-sided conversation. But suppose the number of listeners increases to a dozen, or twenty-five, or one hundred. Somewhere along the way this one-sided conversation becomes a public speech, and all of the principles and techniques of public speaking then begin to apply.

PROMOTIONAL SPEAKING

A promotional speech is one in which the representative of a business firm attempts to sell services or goods to the members of an audience. Suppose the manager of an advertising agency, either by his own solicitation or by invitation, speaks before the United States Chamber of Commerce, the State Manufacturers Association, or some similar group. The purpose of his speech is to promote the use of advertising by those whom he addresses. He wants to persuade and convince them that their profits can be increased through more extensive and general use of advertising. He may talk little or not at all about his own advertising agency; he will stress the value of such service as organizations like his are prepared to render to business. Or to illustrate again, the president of a company which sells business stationery has an opportunity to appear before an audience of

A BUSINESS SPEECH. *The executive of a large manufacturing industry discusses employment problems with his staff. Is the arrangement of the table, the blackboard, and the speaker as effective as it can be made? What are the special problems involved in the presentation of figures like those shown here? What mistakes do speakers frequently make in business speeches in such situations as that depicted above? (Crane, Black Star)*

office managers. His purpose doubtless is to promote the use of the kind of letterheads and envelopes he is prepared to furnish. After all, both of these speakers are doing essentially what the individual salesman tries to do when he is face to face with his customer. Such differences as exist are due primarily to the fact that the treatment of an audience has to be somewhat different from the treatment of a single individual. Both the salesman and the promotional speaker have something to sell, and they are trying to sell it through the use of speech.

The principles and procedures of public speaking have been examined in considerable detail in Chapter Fourteen. The point we stress here is that promotional speaking in business is generally designed to secure definite action. Usually it is not enough for the promotional speaker to be entertaining, clear, impressive, or convincing, although the ability to be all of these is implied in the skillful adaptation of means to ends. The promotional speaker wants his audience to *do* something definite as the result of listening to his talk.

EXPOSITORY BUSINESS SPEAKING

As contrasted with the end which promotional speaking is expected to serve, the purpose of the expository speech is simply to explain a situation, a procedure, or an order. For example, a new filing system has been installed in the office of a mail-order merchandising firm. It becomes the duty of the office manager to make clear to all the filing clerks the differences between the new system and the old, and to show them precisely how they can master the new one with the least expenditure of time and effort. When preparing such a speech, he may safely assume that nobody needs to be convinced or persuaded. Members of the audience are in a wholly co-operative frame of mind, but they do not understand exactly what they are expected to do.

Obviously, before we can explain anything we must understand it ourselves. Elementary though this principle may seem, it is often overlooked by " explainers." Nothing could be more confusing than the explanation of a complicated filing system by an office manager who has never filed anything in his life, and who himself has no adequate conception of the process that he is to make clear to the members of his staff. Perhaps someone has done a good job in " selling " him on the new system without giving him a real grasp of its fundamental principles. He does not know where to start his explanation, what to take up second, what third, and where to end. He gets all tangled up, confuses everybody, including himself, and then winds up by charging the girls in the office with stupidity! It is perfectly true that often we can help ourselves to understand a situation by talking it over with others. What we need to remember is that we cannot afford to do that at the critical moment when we are trying to help someone else to understand. We should go through such preliminaries before we undertake the task of explaining to others. When we have the ideas crystal-clear in our own minds, we may have some chance of getting others to see them clearly also.

To be effective, explanations must be stated in language which can be understood by those who are listening. It is quite possible to comprehend a matter ourselves and yet to fail utterly in explaining it to others, simply because we use words which do not stir up the right meanings in their minds. We must be careful to couch explanations in language that will be meaningful to the listener. Only when we do so can we hope to make our meanings clear.

Expository business speeches should be courteous and tactful. Impatience at the " dumbness " of those to whom we are trying to explain is almost sure to handicap us hopelessly. We must put ourselves in the place of others, realize what they already know and do not know, avoid unnecessary brusqueness, and repeat essential statements, using a variety of phrasings, until those to whom we are speaking have been supplied with all of the essential information we have to give them. Sometimes, paradoxically, the people who know most are the poorest expository speakers; knowing so much themselves, they find it difficult to estimate the lesser knowledge of others, and they quickly become impatient and irritable when others are slow to develop the meanings they want them to get. We have had teachers like this! And all of us remember occasions in which our parents have done a poor job in explaining what they wanted us to do and then have held us accountable in a way that has seemed unreasonable to us. Perhaps, too, we can recall unhappy experiences when we have told our younger brothers and sisters just what they were to do if such and such an occasion arose and then have found that they have done exactly what we didn't want them to do because they misunderstood us. Life is filled with little tragedies like that when we do not know how to give directions effectively.

GOODWILL SPEECHES

One type of public speech which businessmen frequently are called upon to give is that in which the object is to develop a friendly feeling toward the speaker and his topic. This kind of speech is made upon a variety of occasions. If when a goodwill speech is finished, it has done something to build up a favorable attitude toward the speaker, the organization he represents, and the subject he has discussed, the effort must be considered successful. For example, a well-known business executive in our city is serving as Chairman of our Community Chest Fund. He is called upon to speak for twenty minutes before the local Rotary Club. At the moment of speaking no subscription drive is in progress; he wants nothing from anyone but a friendly attitude. He may hope to "cash in" on this attitude when the time comes for a more specific appeal. A good deal of the advertising which we see in periodicals and on billboards is like the goodwill speech. The advertiser does not expect us to read his copy and then rush out immediately to buy his product. He wants us to be favorably disposed toward the product, so that when we are in the market for such an item we naturally will think of his brand.

One of the most valuable assets any business can have is goodwill. Often when a merchandising concern is sold, more money is paid for the goodwill than for the physical property. In a small city in the Midwest there are a large number of mineral springs. The chemical composition of the water from all of them is practically identical. However, an extensive advertising campaign made one of the springs so popular that it was sold for over $2,000,000. Probably $100,000 would have been a large price for the building and land involved in the transaction. The other 95 per cent, or $1,900,000, was paid for the goodwill! Every businessman is eager to acquire and retain as much of this intangible asset as he can. This is why some companies adopt the seemingly unbusinesslike policy of assuming that the customer is always right. They apply this rule even when they know that the customer is dead-wrong, because they would rather incur the expense of making unreasonable adjustments than the greater expense of losing the customer's goodwill and patronage. Then too there is the ever present possibility that the dissatisfied customer will tell his friends and acquaintances about his "sad experience" in failing to secure what he considers fair treatment, and thus deprive the company of other people's goodwill.

In Chapter Fourteen, there is a discussion of the general end of impressiveness in public speaking. There we have learned something further about goodwill speeches. After-dinner speeches, talks before luncheon clubs, addresses at conventions, and speeches upon almost any occasion may be delivered for the purpose of developing goodwill. Therefore it would be superfluous to discuss this type of speech further in this chapter. It is important to note that almost every businessman will sooner or later be called upon to make goodwill speeches.

Tests of Comprehension and Application

PRACTICE IN BUSINESS SPEAKING

1 Let each member of the class work out the specific details of a business situation in which promotional speaking is called for. He will need to determine just what it is that he has to sell, just who will be present in the audience, and the time limits within which he must operate. Then, having made a preliminary statement covering these facts, and indicating the part which members of the class audience are expected to play, let us have a series of promotional talks.

2 Suppose you are the student business manager of the cafeteria in your school. Give a ten-minute promotional speech designed to increase the patronage.

3 Imagine yourself to be in some position of responsibility in the office of one of the large stores in your town. Make a speech to your class for the purpose of stimulating business for some department of the store.

4 Have you ever played the game in which you write out carefully directions on how something is to be done? The person who formulates the directions gives them orally to another person, who passes them along to a third, and so on down the line to the final one in the chain, who writes down what he has been told and then compares it with the original written directions. Try this with your speech

class, passing the directions along by calling each person out into the hall and letting him hear the directions from the one preceding him in the line. What do you learn from this experiment? On the basis of what you have learned, would you think it better for the manager of an office to give directions to all of the workers in the office simultaneously, or to call one in, tell her, and ask her to pass the information along to the others?

5 Work out carefully directions you could give to anyone who might ask how to find his way from the school to your home. Try to do it in words rather than in gestures.

6 Tell someone how to thread a needle. Make no use of your hands as you explain.

7 Do exercises 5 and 6 with gestures. What differences do you note?

8 Explain in as few words as you can the grading system in use at your school. (Please observe that becoming emotional about a subject is likely to injure your explanation rather than help it.)

9 Explain some action on the part of some older person toward you which you considered unfair. Make your point without showing any strong emotional attitude.

PRACTICE ACTUAL BUSINESS SPEAKING

10 As a member of the business staff of your school annual, prepare a ten-minute speech for delivery to the entire student body for the purpose of securing subscriptions. Practice this speech before the class, and if you are chosen as the most effective promotional speaker, try to get an opportunity to speak before the assembly.

11 As a representative of the circulation department of a national weekly or a monthly periodical, make a five-minute speech to the class for the purpose of securing subscriptions.

12 As a representative of the student body, make a speech to the Parent-Teacher's Association of your school for the purpose of getting additional equipment for your school cafeteria, your gymnasium, your library, or your science laboratories.

13 As a member of the class in typing, make a speech to the school board asking for the purchase of new typewriters.

14 Select some business practice which you yourself would like to understand better. Make a visit to some office where you can find

out what you want to know. Interview the proper person and then explain the matter to your classmates. What did you learn from both parts of this experiment?

15 Investigate some business which interests you particularly, with special reference to its social significance and value. Then plan and deliver to the class a five-minute talk for the purpose of developing an attitude of goodwill toward that business.

16 Make a speech on some school activity with which you are associated, not directly for the purpose of getting recruits, but rather to make nonmembers feel friendly toward the organization.

TESTING BUSINESS SPEAKING

17 Explain how to replace the ribbon on a typewriter. Make it your object to convey the necessary information in the fewest possible words, and with the least effort to everybody concerned. When you have finished, call on some member of the class to come up and actually change a ribbon. Can he do it properly? Or have your directions been inadequate?

18 Explain how to keep a simple expense account. Put the basic figures on the board and ask each member of the class to prepare an expense account in accordance with the system you have explained. How many of them understood you the first time without asking additional questions? Where do the difficulties lie, and what can you do to avoid them?

19 Pick out a magazine advertisement which seems to you particularly effective in its appeal for goodwill. Make a speech on the product with which the advertising deals, trying to accomplish the same result. What differences do you note between the way the advertiser approaches the problem and the way in which you approach it?

20 See if you can pick out a typical goodwill speech on the radio. When you have heard one, tell the class about it, explaining why you have chosen it, how the speaker accomplished what he was aiming at, where he fell short, and why.

Part Five

AFTER HIGH SCHOOL

WE NOW STAND *at the fork of the road. Some of us will take the trail that leads to college. The rest of us will turn toward our life vocations. All of us may profit from a brief look back over the highway of speech training which we have followed thus far. It will be well for us to plan some of the applications we intend to make of the principles and techniques we have learned to the new problems which lie ahead.*

23 Speech and Going to College

24 Speech and Life Vocations

CHAPTER TWENTY-THREE *Speech and Going to College*

NOW THAT we have come to the end of our high-school course in speech, it may be a good time to look back over what we have learned and to see what specific uses we are going to be able to make of it. Some of us are looking forward to at least four years more of education in a college or a university. Some of us are now finishing our schooling and will be embarking upon our life work. This chapter is particularly for those of us who are planning to go to college.

Those of us who are familiar with opera music know that the overture forecasts the melodies that are to come, and the finale recapitulates a good many of the arias which have been sung. In this book " A Preview " was the overture. Now we come to the finale.

The four fundamental purposes of education remain the same from kindergarten to graduate school. They are to help us: (1) to realize our full personal possibilities for intellectual and emotional living; (2) to fit ourselves efficiently into the social structure; (3) to accept and discharge the full responsibilities of citizenship in a democracy; and (4) to function satisfactorily in an economic order. This text is organized around these four major objectives, and should have continuing value for us wherever we may be.

Taking stock of our speech. Early in this book, we were asked to make an inventory of our abilities, to assess our own strong points and our shortcomings. Now it is time to repeat this process. It is to be hoped that as we go back over the questions we considered early in our speech course (see Chapter One), we will find it possible to make a more satisfactory score than we made then. Let us try it and see. College life is going to put a high premium on these precious speech capacities.

Action and voice. Our college associates and our instructors will form their estimates of our personalities through what they see when they look at us and what they hear when they listen to our voices. There should never be any letdown in the high standards we have set for our visible action and our voice. Let us be diligent to apply what we know about effectiveness in speaking to every experience that comes to us in college. We should check up on ourselves from time to time to guard against slipping back into bad habits of voice and visible action.

Language and pronunciation. If we could apply just one test to determine how well educated an individual really is, what would it be? Well, what is it usually? Almost invariably, we judge by listening to the person's conversation or to his talk in classroom or other discussion groups. If he seems to have a very limited vocabulary, if his language sounds inadequate, or if he mispronounces words, we are almost certain to regard him as not very well adjusted socially, and not very able mentally. As we do to others, they are simultaneously doing to us! If we have developed an interesting and effective style of oral language, if we know and use the generally accepted pronunciations of words, we can check these items as among those which will cause others to rate us as congenial and competent. If we are in difficulty on any of these points, it would be well for us to make a renewed effort to do better before we move into a college environment.

Meaning. A very large share of college education inevitably is tied up with the capacity to master and use the meanings of language. Think what would happen to high schools and colleges if there were no textbooks and no reference libraries! Even then we should have left on our hands a host of problems having to do with the meanings of the language used by instructors and professors in their lectures. As we prepare to enter college, it will repay us to check back over Chapter Five, paying special attention to the two different kinds of meanings which come to us from language. As we read books, we may very profitably stop and ask ourselves over and over again what meanings we are getting, how we are getting them, and how sure we are that they are the ones the authors intended us to get.

One of the aims of education in the field of self-development is training in the appreciation of literature. The kind of reading material a man really enjoys is a sure test of his education. Presumably, in this course we have done something to lay the foundations for literary appreciation. Now everything depends upon our willingness to use wisely what we have been taught.

Empathy and perception. Do we remember now what we have learned about the ways in which we get meanings from the behavior of others, and how we stir up meanings in the minds of others? It will pay us to consider carefully what sort of empathic responses we cause in others who look at us and listen to us. We want them to feel that we have attractive personal qualities. We want them to be comfortable and to feel well adjusted when we are with them. If we do, then we must look carefully to the ways in which we affect others unconsciously through their eyes and ears.

Creative listening. An American humorist once defined the college lecture system as a process by which information is transferred by the professor from the library to the notebook of the student without passing through the mind of anyone. Let it not be that for us! In our college lecture sections, we should recall and apply the techniques of creative listening. We should remember how to take notes effectively, and how to organize them into permanent form after we have taken them. It is necessary to react to what our instructor says — to make our contribution to the joint undertaking of the classroom — if we would really move on and up to the mental levels of which we are capable. It is wise for us to pick out some other student who is seriously interested in his work and make it our practice to discuss each lecture with him. Thus we will find it possible to supplement what we have derived from the lecture with what he has brought away with him, and vice versa. Nobody ever learns much by passive listening; the kind of listening that counts is active, dynamic, and creative.

Classroom discussion. Do we want to get good grades in our college courses? What a foolish question! Of course we do. We should not be among those who belittle a fine scholastic record. There is plenty of evidence to show that the people who do well in college succeed in later life, and that those who do poorly in college also do poorly out in the world. There are exceptions, of course, but this is the rule. More students get poor grades because they do not know how to speak and to listen in the classroom than for any other reason, except possibly failure to study. The person who can speak up in class and say clearly what he wants to say when he is called on certainly will get better grades than the mumblers, stumblers, and fumblers. Why shouldn't he? He is giving evidence of mastery of subject matter, in the form which counts most. He can make his intelligence negotiable and effective. We should remember always that the way to be sure that we have mastered any principle, theory, or fact is to put it into our own words clearly and succinctly. Classroom quiz sections are places in which we can do the kind of talking that will fix ideas and data in our minds and make them available for future use. Classroom discussion is not to be looked upon as a burdensome and uninteresting routine through which we must be forced. It is intended to be the heart of the educational process.

Storytelling. Storytelling — here is something which we certainly are not going to make any use of in college; storytelling is for children! Not so at all! If we stop a moment, we may think of a good many people who are popular in social circles because they are effective in narrating interesting incidents, in recounting unusual personal experiences, and in telling humorous anecdotes. Storytelling is an activity that has wide and varied uses, many of which properly fit into the worth-while experiences that college will make possible for us. It is a good idea to keep alive our mastery of the storytelling art. We need not be told that any good thing can be overdone. It is hard, however, to overdo the effective telling of appropriate stories.

Reading. It is all too rare to find a college student who can read aloud interpretively material that interests him and which he would like to make interesting to others. Many a time in college we shall find it extremely useful to be able to support a position we have taken in an argument, or to illustrate a point we have made, by the effective reading aloud of a few sentences or paragraphs from a newspaper, a magazine, or a book. This ability, which we have been developing in this course, should be kept on tap, ready for instant employment. It is appalling how often an interesting conversation or discussion breaks down into dullness when some college student attempts to read a few lines of prose or poetry.

Dramatics. A great many things we have learned from our experiences in formal and informal high-school dramatics should be useful to us in college. In college we shall find a varied program of theater activities. In some of these we may discover thrilling and worth-while experiences. One of the greatest values of dramatic work is that it brings us into happy co-operative relations with others who are like-minded. While it is true that we are not going to college primarily to participate in extracurricular activities, nevertheless we shall need the recreation, the refreshment, and the stimulus to better living which come from well-directed and inspiring dramatic activities. Many of us will want to put dramatics on our college " must " list.

Public speaking. The leaders of most college groups are people who have learned how to speak in public. False modesty should not prevent us from capitalizing on the skill and ability we have acquired in our high-school speech training. As occasions present themselves, whenever we appropriately can do so we should use our skill as public speakers. College life is filled with proper times and seasons for public speaking. We should watch for them and take advantage of them.

Discussion. There are too many " bull sessions " in college and too few serious, well-organized discussions. If any subject is worth talking about for long, it is worth talking about well. Instead of the aimless, wandering sort of talk which begins nowhere and ends at the same point, we should see if we can get the groups of which we are a part to engage in organized, purposeful discussions that will leave us with something more than a tired feeling when we have finished. It may be a rather ambitious dream for us to cherish, but if we will hold to it, we can raise the whole level of the college life about us. Instead of wasting precious time in hit-or-miss, unprepared discussions of matters on which it is not worth while to have informed opinions, we should resolve to cast our influence with those who are trying to make speech serve the higher and finer purposes of education. Why not a panel, a symposium, or a forum discussion occasionally on something really worth talking about, in place of endless gabfests in which everybody talks as much as possible without saying anything in particular?

Debate. Doubtless there will be intramural and intercollegiate debating in the college we attend. No extracurricular activity will yield larger dividends. Debating provides the opportunity for carrying on, in a more advanced form, our preparation for meeting our larger civic responsibilities. Through college debating, we may learn to sharpen our critical faculties and argue persuasively for those political principles and policies to which we give our voice and our vote.

Parliamentary procedure. Before we have spent many weeks in college, we probably will have been compelled to waste a considerable amount of time in meetings run by people who seem never to have heard of the principles of parliamentary procedure. There will be house meetings, class meetings, and club meetings presided over by people who do not know the rudiments of formal group activity. It may be disappointing to us to hear some of these inefficient, muddling chairmen express derogatory judgments of those who do understand parliamentary practice. What should we do when we find ourselves in such a situation? Of course we should not make the mistake of trying to show off our superior knowledge. Instead of constantly interrupting meetings with parliamentary questions and objections, we should make opportunities for the informal presentation of our belief that business could be handled more quickly and more pleasantly for everybody concerned if people would just agree to observe certain principles of parliamentary law. Above all, when chances come to us to preside over meetings, we should make a supreme effort to do the job so well that we will give the members a convincing demonstration of the right way to go at it.

Radio speaking. With the growth in educational broadcasting, campus radio stations and hookups with commercial stations have been developed. In connection with these, there are many chances for student participation in broadcasting programs. Even though we have no thought of going into commercial radio, we may want to acquire enough experience to guarantee our effectiveness as radio speakers. We should make it our business to familiarize ourselves with our university's radio program and take part in it as much as we can in fairness to our other responsibilities and obligations.

Telephoning. Among other things, the Second World War taught us that there isn't an unlimited amount of telephone service available — even in the United States of America! Under the stress of emergency, we found that telephone facilities can be wasted and cluttered up by unnecessary and unwise use. Think of telephone companies actually buying radio time and magazine space in order to make appeals for cutting down telephone service! Yet that is what they were obliged to do. What we should learn from this unusual situation is the desirability of using the telephone as efficiently as possible. We should always remember that when we are using circuits, they cannot be used by other people, and we should feel just as uncomfortable about depriving other people of telephone privileges as we would if we were blocking the way to a food counter in a cafeteria.

It is doubtful whether there is any place in the world where a larger amount of futile and unnecessary telephoning is done than in the college dormitory, rooming house, or fraternity. If we doubt this, we will find plenty of evidence in our own loss of time when we try to put through calls to our friends. As we have been told in Chapter Eighteen a telephone conversation is not a proper substitute for a social call. If we want to talk to a friend around the corner, we should go there and do it and save the telephone for important, brief conversations.

In the necessary and wise use of the telephone we shall have numberless chances to demonstrate that we know how to use the instrument properly, and thus create favorable impressions in the minds of others. In college life, as elsewhere, a good many of our contacts with other people will be by telephone. If we don't find ourselves able to do any better than we could have done before we studied

Chapter Eighteen, then clearly that part of our training has not been of any practical use to us.

Appointments, interviews, and conferences. Some of our very first experiences in college will be interviews and conferences. We will find that in the registration procedure a number of appointments have been made for us. We will be expected to see members of the enrollment committee and our faculty advisers, in order to get our program of studies worked out. We can save these people a lot of time, and get them to take into account our interests and points of view effectively, in proportion to the skill we have developed in the techniques of interviewing. We must not come to these important interviews unprepared. We should know what we want, why we want it, and the means which are open to us for getting it. We cannot hope to make a good start in college unless these interviews work out well.

AT THE TICKET WINDOW. *A railway ticket window is a poor place for a social conversation and even more so for wisecracks. The ticket-seller asks, " Where to, please? " The sailor replies jokingly, " Oh, no where in particular. Just give me five dollars worth of ticket." Many public speakers make the same mistake; they are not going anywhere but are just speaking for five minutes! In choosing a college or a vocation a definite sense of direction is of prime importance too. (Charles Phelps Cushing)*

We will participate in a good many conferences throughout our college years. There will be conferences in our rooming houses, there will be study-group conferences to which we are invited, and in many of our courses there will be formal conferences which are called laboratory or quiz sections. Ordinarily, we will get out of such meetings about as much as we bring to them.

Dictating business letters. While we are in college, we will encounter many occasions for writing business letters. As a matter of fact, there almost certainly will be a need for preliminary correspondence with college authorities before we get into college. We should handle it tactfully and efficiently. A review of the materials of Chapter Twenty may be helpful.

Buying and selling. As we look forward to our entrance into the college community we have selected, we will realize that a considerable part of our everyday life will be taken up with such prosaic but necessary matters as renting a room, arranging for our meals, buying clothing and textbooks, and similar transactions. We will be dealing with an environment which has in it many new elements. We can save ourselves a good deal of money, time, and effort if we remember to practice the principles we have studied in Chapter Twenty-one.

Expository speaking. We shall have a great deal of expository speaking to do, both in our college classes and in other groups of which we are a part. It may help us to practice what we have learned about such speaking in Chapter Twenty-two.

Goodwill speeches. Many will be our opportunities to promote friendliness and goodwill between the groups of which we are members and other campus groups. When our chances come to do so, we should be ready to stand up on our two feet and talk in such a manner as to gain the favorable attention of our associates. By so doing we can be sure of becoming real contributing members of our groups.

Tests of Comprehension and Application

Prepare for entering college life by doing the following:
1 Write a letter to the registrar of the college you expect to attend, asking for a copy of the catalogue and full information regarding entrance requirements, living costs, and so forth.
2 Interview one or more of the college representatives who visit your school this spring. Report to the class what you find out.
3 Take notes on assembly programs presented by representatives of various colleges for promotional purposes. Compare impressions in a classroom forum.

4 If possible, visit the college of your choice for the purpose of getting information or applying for admission. Report to the class on your experiences.

5 Interview someone who has some special connection with the college of your choice and see what you can find out beyond what you already know.

6 Arrange for the following:
 a A mock sorority rushing tea (some of you playing the part of "rushers" and some that of "rushees")
 b A sorority or fraternity tea or reception for faculty members

7 Demonstrate a college freshman's interview with his adviser in planning his course. (Let one student who is well informed about a college be the adviser.)

CHAPTER TWENTY-FOUR *Speech and Life Vocations*

SOME OF US PLAN to secure employment which will bring us income at once after graduation from high school. The training we have received in speech can function in the investigation of, the application for, and the carrying-on of our jobs. Careful planning may save us from the fate of the unhappy misfits we have known — persons who have not discovered the work for which they are best suited, who plod along year after year in jobs they detest, because early in their lives they failed to make the effort to investigate thoroughly the opportunities open to them.

The questions immediately arise: Where shall we begin? How shall we proceed? Is there any organized fashion by which speech can help us to study vocational opportunities, to secure employment, and to be successful on the job?

Let us take a bird's-eye view of the ground we have covered. We studied speech as an important contributor to happy and prosperous living. We did this first by examining our own speech abilities. We tried to realize individual potentialities by improving action for communication, by developing more expressive voices, by correcting pronunciation, by using meaningful language, and by listening actively. Next we turned to our human relationships and studied the techniques of getting and holding attention in various social situations. We practiced oral communication in conversation, classroom speaking, storytelling, reading, dramatics, and public speaking. Thence we moved on to our responsibilities as citizens in a democracy. We discovered how to solve problems by discussion, how to debate controversial issues, how to conduct meetings, and how to present and hear radio speeches. Finally, we considered the role of speech in business. We learned how to conduct interviews and conferences, how to telephone, dictate letters, prepare and deliver business speeches, and how to buy and sell. In short, our speech course has not swerved from its primary aim to open a better and fuller life to us.

SELECTING THE JOB

Students who plan to attend a college or a university before they select a life vocation have time after graduation from high school to consider the fields which interest them and to take the necessary training to equip them for the fields of their choice. But those who would like to go to a job immediately will be wise to explore vocational opportunities while still in high school. A survey of opportunities for high-school graduates will provide an excellent review for this course in speech, and at the same time help each person to find the work for which he is best fitted. The first step in such an investigation is to organize the group and delegate to each of its members some part in a program designed to give us the broad view of vocational opportunities. Such a co-operative venture will reveal a wealth of material on many vocations, and save each one of us the vast amount of work involved in collecting these data for himself. The first step will be carried on most fairly and efficiently if the rules of parliamentary procedure are recalled and used.

What are the responsibilities that are likely to be delegated to members of a class making a study of vocations? Clearly, they will vary from one school and community to another, but such a study always centers around getting information about vocations from people, from books, and from observation. Some classes will emphasize employment in factories; others, in mining; others, in dairy farming; others, in truck gardening; still others, in forestry. The vocations we study most effectively will be the ones we really plan to enter. With this objective in view, doubtless homemaking will interest a large majority of the girls.

We have had experiences in getting information from people. We have studied conversations, interviews, conferences, discussions, stories, oral readings, radio programs, debates, and public speeches. Now is the time for us to use them again in a big integrated project which may play an important part in making our futures more secure and happy.

The class might set aside one period for an exchange of ideas about vocations which the individual members gained from conversations with authorities in various fields. In preparation for it, each one of us could gather information about at least two types of work that have proved satisfactory to our acquaintances. We should try to anticipate questions which may come from our classmates. They will want to know many details about the jobs which interest them most. We will be most helpful, therefore, if we find out what kind of training is required for the jobs we investigate; where it can be obtained, how long it takes; and what abilities and skills make for success. We should find out, too, the average yearly income, and whether employment is scarce or plentiful. Interesting anecdotes about workers in these occupations will be a good way to make our project genuinely interesting.

A symposium. In the immediate community an alert class will find individuals who can be prevailed upon to present a symposium in which from four to six speakers appear — each prepared to explain a given vocation in which he is trained or about which he has detailed information. Such a performance will be successful only if it is carefully planned, and careful planning depends in a large measure on speech proficiency.

After we have decided on the speakers who will be most helpful to our class, we must persuade them to give the time and effort necessary for preparation of and participation in the discussion. Experts are not eager to do this unless they are convinced that the meeting is going to be worth while. Someone in our class must convince them, and this can be done by writing — in which case our training in dictating letters may serve us well — or by a telephone conversation, or by an interview. For any or all of them we will need to demonstrate our maximum skill in each of the elements of good speaking, for without them we shall be ineffective.

We will wish to devote more time to a consideration of some vocations than to others, especially when a number of us have identical interests and will profit by an intensive study of one type of employment. Such a study might be opened with a speech by an authority. A forum might follow. One whole period could be given to such a program with profit. Other meetings might be devoted to radio programs related to a particular vocation, including reading and storytelling. We should be on the lookout for entertaining ways of bringing together what we wish to know about a prospective field of employment. Such a project, including a variety of activities, could extend over a number of class meetings, and make use of committees and delegates as well as officers and members of the organization. Creative listening on the part of every one of us will help to make these meetings successful.

Not only can we inform ourselves on future vocational possibilities by bringing to our classes outside speakers, but we can continue to utilize every member of our group for assigned contributions. Let us assume that a survey is made of the available sources of information on possible vocations for students in our high school. Each student may be responsible for a certain number of investigations, after which reports will be made to the class. These reports may be presented as public speeches, readings, discussions, debates, or plays. The greater the variety in presentation, the more interesting the programs will be, and an interested audience profits more than an uninterested one.

Outside the classroom. One of the best ways to discover a liking for and success in a certain vocation is to watch experienced workers on the job. A visit to a mine, a factory, a farm, a radio station, a beauty parlor, or a home may be planned with profit. An interview with the supervisor of any work project will help us to decide what we wish

A FARMER SPEAKS. *A successful practical farmer explains his crop-rotation plan to a class of college students studying farm management. The qualities which make the farmer a good speaker also contribute to his success in his chosen vocation. Because he knows how to work with his head, he finds it unnecessary to work as hard with his back as do some of his less competent neighbors. Speech spells the difference in all vocations. (J. C. Allen, Ewing Galloway)*

to see and when a visit can be arranged. The usefulness of speech in getting such favors granted is clear to all of us.

Some of us would like to know ahead of time what chances of success we have in a number of different vocations. A guidance adviser, either in our high school or in the community, may be able to provide tests which will predict our success in various jobs. Such tests indicate ratings on the traits which are important in each type of work. Interviewing this expert, prevailing on him to give information, introducing him to our class, and leading our class in discussion are speech activities which logically follow the attempt to obtain such expert help. We should all be prepared to do our part in such a project.

If there is no one trained in vocational guidance in our school, interviews with teachers and fellow students will help. We should encourage our instructors and classmates to tell us frankly what they think about our aptitudes. Often such judgments are as valuable as vocational tests.

APPLYING FOR THE JOB

After having gathered information on various types of vocations, and having noted the opportunities in each, we will be wise to practice the special sorts of speech required in the occupations of our choice. For example, if we wish employment in a local dry-goods store, we will need to know how to get the job as well as how to hold it. In applying for the job, we may make use of a successful interview or a well-written letter of application. An interview between a "merchant" (someone playing his role) and a high-school student seeking employment will provide training for the real interview. Class criticisms and suggestions may prevent mistakes in similar actual situations later.

The procedure in applying for employment in a factory is much the same whether the plant is in New England or Chicago; therefore it will be profitable to practice in the same way in any classroom. Appointments must be made, interviews arranged for, and application blanks filled in correctly. There must be occasion for us to let the prospective employer know our abilities and interests, and for him to let us know the requirements of the job, and for the employer to learn whether or not we measure up to his standards. We should practice the interviews in mock situations and then actually make applications for jobs which we will accept after graduation. There are advantages in having jobs waiting for us when we get out of school.

We might begin with a visit to the factory where we hope to be employed. We can find out where men apply for work. We can learn something about the officers who are in charge of employment. We can get many pointers on how to make a favorable impression. And we can practice every speech activity which will make for success. This will help us to ask for a position with more confidence and with great likelihood of getting it.

ON THE JOB

Self-realization through speech. We have seen the importance of speech in choosing and securing our lifework. Now we are to see the importance of speech on the job. Let us look back over Part One of this text and try to think of a single vocation for which we are not better prepared because we have learned to make the most of our speech equipment. Will we be better farmers because our voices are distinct and pleasant? Will a command of good language be an asset to us as wives and mothers? Will the ability to listen creatively help us as storekeepers? Will acceptable pronunciation gain respect for us as beauty-salon operators? Will control of our visible action increase sales for us as insurance agents? Will the ability to get and hold attention make life easier for us as family breadwinners? We must answer all of these questions in the affirmative.

Speech in human relationships. As the years pass, the problem of getting along with others becomes increasingly vital. The early settlers of America had to adjust their lives to their fellow citizens in the local township. We have to learn to co-operate with the people of the whole world! This shows us how necessary and complicated is the process of "getting on" with our associates! We can all recall neighbors who are boring in conversation. We avoid them. The student who is inarticulate in class finds himself facing an inattentive audience. The Sunday-school teacher who does not understand how to prepare literary material for reading aloud sees his class dwindle in numbers. The foreman who reads directions badly finds work slowed up and materials wasted. The insurance supervisor who is unable to stimulate his salesmen and saleswomen is soon demoted. Any person who is unable to participate in and appreciate good drama misses one of the richest experiences of life. The dull storyteller loses friends and sales alike. In Part Two of this book, therefore, we have found that speech is essential to successful human relationships and have directed our attention to the importance of human relationships in earning a living.

Speech in civic living. If we were residents of a country ruled by a dictator, Part Three of this book would be less important. Voting and holding office would belong to the ruling class, and not to the people. But in the United States voting age means civic responsibilities, and all of us who work in a community must help to govern that community. In order to vote wisely we have to participate in discussion and debate. If we are elected to office, we must accept our responsibilities, conduct meetings, and become leaders of local, state, and national groups. We will all be authorities on some subjects, and if we are good citizens we must share our information with others in public gatherings or over the radio. We cannot expect a community to provide us a livelihood unless we do our part in governing this democratic nation.

BILL STERN BROADCASTING. *A noted sports announcer at work, broadcasting a football game. What makes him so successful? What techniques are peculiarly his? Note tensions in hand and jaw. Compare with pictures on pages 170, 445, and 447.* (Culver Service)

Speech in business. After we take our jobs, it will be worth while to review repeatedly the principles of good speech. Every person has business dealings, whether the life vocation is that of homemaker, storekeeper, farmer, forester, truck driver, miner, guide, mechanic, postman, or salesman. He increases his income in money and in pleasure if he knows how to talk over the telephone, how to hold interviews and conferences, how to dictate letters, how to make business speeches, and how to talk to salesmen and customers.

BETTER LIVING THROUGH BETTER SPEAKING

The main purpose of this course has been to make us more effective when we talk. This final chapter has tried to show how speech brings out latent personal possibilities in us, how it helps us to get along with our associates, how essential it is for all of us who would be good citizens, and how indispensable clear, communicative speech is in the business of earning our daily bread.

Tests of Comprehension and Application

1 Make a list of all the vocations for which you might qualify.
2 Rearrange the list made out in project 1 in the order of your preference.
3 What is the average income for each of the vocations you listed for 1?
4 Visit at least five establishments where work for which you might qualify is carried on. Write a brief account of your visits, including:
   a Attitude of workers
   b Age of workers
   c Information on whether opportunities are scarce or plentiful
   d Financial return
   e Time schedules
   f What you like particularly about each establishment
   g What you dislike particularly about each establishment
5 Read the story of the life of some famous person. Report on his selection of a vocation and his training for it. Try to profit by his experiences.
6 Arrange with the proper authorities of some plant where large numbers of men and women are employed to have the class visit the establishment.
7 Put on a debate on the pros and cons of college training versus apprentice training for a vocation.
   a Phrase the proposition.
   b Select speakers.

COMPREHENSION AND APPLICATION TESTS 551

    c Discover issues.
    d Gather material.
    e Organize material.
    f Practice delivery for main speeches and rebuttals.
    g Present the debate.
    h Have some members of the speech class act as judges and report their decisions.

8 Arrange an interview with a woman who is recognized as an expert homemaker. Discover what part speech plays in her success. Set up imaginary situations in which you can train yourself in speech for the homemaker.

9 Arrange to go with a successful automobile salesman when he visits a prospective customer. Tell the class about the experience.

10 Visit a stock buyer's yard and watch transactions between him and the farmers from whom he buys. Report to the class on the importance of speech in successful buying and selling of farm products.

11 Visit a farm when a buyer comes to purchase grain, fruit, calves, pigs, cattle, or horses. Notice how proficiency in speech helps the farmer to get a good price. Talk to the class on the importance of speech to a farmer.

12 Arrange for an interview with a dressmaker. Plan questions the answers to which will show how important speech is to a dressmaker.

13 Get permission to attend a meeting of insurance salesmen at which one of the managers attempts to motivate increased sales. Write a criticism of the talk, organized around the principles you have learned in this course.

14 Make a notebook showing the importance of speech in all vocations. Illustrate it with actual photographs or with pictures from magazines and newspapers. Devote a paragraph to the importance of speech in specified vocations.

15 Report to the class information on vocational guidance gained from a radio speech. Report also on the effectiveness of the voice and the language in delivery of the speech.

16 Give a talk to the class on:
    a Failure in speech results in failure in _____ (vocation)
    b Success in speech is a large factor in success in _____ (vocation)

Index

Page numbers in brackets refer to illustrations.

A Business Speech, [523]
A College Lecture Audience, [187]
A Contest Debate, [408]
A Cross Question Debate, [418]
A Discussion Panel, [397]
A Farmer Speaks, [546]
A Teacher Demonstrates, [225]
Accent, foreign, 106; shift of, 108
Accentuation, 106–107; variable, 108
Accepting an invitation by telephone, 463–464
Acting, amateurishness in, 332; entrances in, 336–337; gestures in, 333–334; illusion in, 333; memory in, 338; naturalness in, 333; principles of, 330–341; tempo in, 333, 335; unity in, 334; visible code in, 332–333; voice in, 330–332
Acting all in one piece, 332–333
Action, 534; appropriateness in, 38; power in, 36; stage, 337; unified, 36; visible, 13, 269
Action and meaning, 269
Action in conversation, 202
Action in storytelling, 246
Action-getting interviews, 477
Activity, co-ordination in, 36
Actors, height of, 327
Adam's apple, 58
Adaptation in conversation, 204
Adaptation to audience, 355–360
Adaptation to customer, 509
Addressing the chair, 425
Addressing the Chairman, [425]
Adenoids, 65
Adjourn, 432
Adjustments in business, 515–516
Admiral's Ghost, The, quoted, 298–302
Advertising manager, 329
Adviser, faculty, 540
Aesop's Fables, 241
Affirmative, first, 403
Affirmative case, 410
Affirmative statement of proposition, 407
After-dinner speeches, 368, 527

Alcott, Louisa, M., 218–221
Aldis, Dorothy, quoted, 287–289
Alertness, 35
Allusions, 264–265
Amateur Strategist, An, [415]
Amateurish acting, 332
Ambiguity in propositions, 410
Amend, 432
America Goes Abroad, quoted, 352–353
America Honors LaFayette, [142]
Americanization of Edward Bok, quoted, 486–490
An Amateur Strategist, [415]
An Interview, [476]
Analyses, individual, 8
Analyzing speech, 5
Ancient Mariner, quoted, 318
Andersen, Hans Christian, 245
Anecdotes, 238
Anecdotes and stories, 182–183
Animation, 35
Ankles, 40
Anodyne, quoted, 286
Another Audience, [358]
Antonyms in definition, 125
Aphonia, 32
Apologizing by telephone, 465
Appeal from decision, 432
Applause at plays, 336
Applicant, qualifications of, 480–481
Applicants for a Job, [481]
Application, letters of, 547
Appointments, 540; courtesy in making, 474; how to make by telephone, 465
Appointments for interviews, 474–475
Appreciation of literature, 535
Appropriateness, in action, 38; in gesture, 42; in storytelling, 246–247
Aptitudes, vocational, 546
Argument, 351–352
Arms, 43
Arnold, Ruth, 6
Around the Campfire, [247]
Articulation, poor, 67
Aspirate quality, 70

INDEX

Assimilation, 108
At His Brother's Grave, quoted, 283–284
At the Telephone, [460]
At the Ticket Window, [540]
Attack in voice, 65
Attention, 23; anecdotes and stories, 182–183; contests and struggles, 184–185; getting and holding, 548; irrelevant, 186–187; manner of speaking, 185; monotony, 185–186; novelty in, 184; personal interests, 183–184; problem of, 180–181, [184]; vigor, 185
Attention and movement, 39
Attention and Perception, 187–189
Attention and tension, 189
Attention-Getting, principles of, 181–187
Attitude, favorable, 355–357; hostile, 359–360; neutral, 357–359
Attitude and meaning, 74
Attitude and pitch, 93
Attitude in perception, 190–191
Attitudes, adaptation to audience, 355–360
Audibility, 21
Audience, comfort of, 37; favorable, 355–357; hostile, 359–360; neutral, 357–359; studio, 446–447
Audience in storytelling, 250
Auer, J. J., 424
Aunt Polly, 44
Aurner, R. R., quoted, 494, 496
Authority, 353
Awkward squad, 15
Awkwardness, 36, 42

Babcock, Stephen Moulton, 385
Baby learning to speak, 16–17
Baby talk, 16
Backgrounds, historical, 261
Back stage, organization, 329–330; rules, 330
Balance on stage, 338–339
Balfour, Arthur J., quoted, 135
Ballads, 241
Barnum, 511
Barry, Mary Ann, 263–264
Basic elements of speech, 13
Basic English, vocabulary of, 121–122
Benét, Stephen Vincent, quoted, 302–307

Bergen, Edgar, 20; *and McCarthy*, [55]
Better living and speech, 550
Beveridge, A. J., 404
Bible, quoted, 18
Biblical allusions, 321
Big scenes on stage, 339
Bill Stern Broadcasting, [549]
Bixby, Mrs., 496
Blackfeet of Montana, The, quoted, 257–258
Bliven, Bruce, quoted, 201–202
Body control, 45–47
Bok, Edward, 136; quoted, 486–490
Book, holding, 279
Bourdillon, Francis William, quoted, 89
Box office, 329
Boy and His Dog, [131]
Breath control, 59
Breathiness, 65
Breathing, correct, 59, 67; exercises to improve, 82–83; lower chest, 59
Brevity, 478
Broadcasting, dialects in, 451–452; manuscripts in, 450–451; time limits in, 449
Broadcasting techniques, exercises in, 452–453
Brook, The, quoted, 271, 318
Brothers Karamazov, The, quoted, 132
Brown, Charles Reynolds, quoted, 132–133
Building of the Ship, The, quoted, 291
Burden of proof, 404
Burroughs, John, quoted, 157
Business, order of, 426–427; stage, 333
Business Career of Peter Flint, The, quoted, 511–515
Business speaking, practice in, 527–529
Business Speech, A, [523]
Buying, 541; distinctness in speech, 506; effective speech in, 506; right and wrong ways, 506–507; successful, 504–508; tests of skill in, 507–508
Buying and selling, practice in, 516–520
Buying over the telephone, 464
Bylaws, adopting, 424; model, 438–439; outline of, 423–424
Byron, Lord, quoted, 90, 268

Cairns, W. B., quoted, 142
Caliban in the Coal Mines, quoted, 282
Campfire, Around the, [247]

INDEX

Canopus, quoted, 295
Cards, notes on, 372
Cards in debate, 414
Carryl, Charles Edward, quoted, 311–312
Case, affirmative, 410; counterproposition, 411–412; negative, 410–411; patch and repair, 411; pure refutation, 410–411; status quo, 411
Caskey, Margaret, quoted, 155–156
Casting the play, 327
Centipede, 46
Central idea, 265
Chairman, addressing the, 425, [425]; impartiality of, 428; temporary, 422
Chairman of conference, 484
Challenge, quoted, 282
Challenge to Explore, 209
Chapman, Allan, quoted, 214–216
Characterization, pantomime in, 47
Characters in dramatization, 322–323
Characters, Relative Heights of, [327]
Characters in stories, 246
Chase, Mary Ellen, 132
Chiang Kai-shek, Madame, quoted, 160–163
Choate, Rufus, quoted, 159
Choosing the play, 325–327
Christian Science Monitor, quoted, 152–153
Cicero, quoted, 2
Civic living, 548–549
Civic responsibility, 4
Civilization, depends on speech, 18
Classes, good speech in, 227
Classified list of motions, 431
Classroom, mispronunciation in the, 231–232
Classroom discussion, 536
Classroom speaking, weaknesses in, 229–233
Clearness, in debate proposition, 406–407; in letters, 494–495; of meaning, 73
Climax in storytelling, 245–246
Closing an interview, 482
Coat, sale of, 513–515
Code, the written, 257
Code of language, 17
Coherence, 260
Cold, head, 65
Coleman, Henry F., quoted, 351–352
Coleridge, 202; quoted, 318

College Campus, The, [533]
College Lecture Audience, A, [187]
Commit, 432–433
Committee members, duties of, 430–431
Committee on constitution, 422
Committee reports, 427
Committees, special, 427; standing, 425
Committing to memory, 33
Common mispronunciations, 111–114
Communicative quality of voice, 459
Comparison and contrast in definition, 125
Complaints, dealing with, 515–516; making, 515–516; over the telephone, 464–465
Completeness in letters, 494–495
Composite method of delivery, 371–372
Concessions in debate, 412–413
Conciseness in letters, 497–498
Concreteness in letters, 498
Condensed code of parliamentary law, 432–436
Conducting business, 425–427
Conference, chairman of, 484; defined, 483
Conference room, 484
Conference speaking, 521–522
Conferences, 540
Connected speech, 108–109
Connotation, 128–130
Connotations, [267]
Connotative meanings, 267
Consideration in letters, 494–495
Consonants, defined, 103
Consonants and vowels, 67
Constitution, adopting a, 424; committee on, 422; drafting of, 423; model, 437–438; outline of, 423–424
Contest Debate, A, [408]
Contest debating, 408–419
Contest orations, 368
Contests and interest, 184–185
Context, defined, 127; nonverbal, 127–128; situational, 128
Contexts and meanings, 127–128
Control of body, 45–47
Conversation, action in, 202; adaptation in, 204; courtesy in, 199; egotism in, 201; formality in, 204–205; how to improve, 198–205; interestingness in, 203; language in, 203; listening in, 168, 201–202; one-sided, 479; rating

chart for, 222–223; sincerity in, 199; tests of, 197–198; voice in, 54, 202–203
Conversation and conference, 483–484
Conversation at Sea, [22]
Conversation by telephone, 458
Conversationalist, the ideal, 196–197
Conversations on Contemporary Drama, quoted, 136
Coolidge, President, quoted, 497
Cooper, Shirley, 7
Cooper Union Address, 496
Co-ordination, 36; lack of, 230
Correctness in letters, 498–499
Corson, Hiram, quoted, 266
Counterproposition, 411–412
Courtesy, in conversation, 199; in letters, 494–495; in making appointments, 474; in telephoning, 461; speeches of, 364–368
Courtroom Scene from " Emile Zola," [395]
Creative listening, 535–536; activity in, 165–166
Creative Youth, 257–258
Crime and the Criminal Court, quoted, 353
Criticism, self, 46
Cromer, Lord, quoted, 98
Crossing in Acting, [335]
Crossing the Bar, quoted, 129
Cross-question debate, 418
Cross-question Debate, A, [418]
Crowding on stage, 323
Cues, memorizing, 328; timing, 335
Culture, depends on speech, 18
Curtain, management of, 340
Curtis, George William, quoted, 80, 91
Customer, always right, 526–527; knowing the, 508; knowledge of, 509

Daisy's Ball, quoted, 218–221
Data sheet, personal, 480
Deadness, 35
Debate, burden of proof in, 404; concessions in, 412–413; cross-question, 418; definition in, 409; delivery in, 414; etiquette of, 416–417; family, 402–405; first affirmative in, 403; first negative in, 404; issues in, 404–405; judges of, 405–406; logic in, 413; new types of, 417–419; reasonableness in, 409; rebuttal in, 405, 414–416; salutation in, 416; summary in, 414; use of cards in, 414
Debate and discussion, 395
Debate proposition, clearness of, 406–407
Debating, contest, 408–419; defined, 401–402; intercollegiate, 538; intramural, 538; related to discussion, 401
Definition, antonyms in, 125; comparison and contrast in, 125; defined, 124; description in, 125–126; diagrams and pictures in, 125; etymology in, 126; example in, 125; explanation in, 125–126; illustration in, 125; in debate, 409; methods of, 123–126; of words, 123–126; reactions in, 126; synonyms in, 125
Delivering speeches, methods of, 368–372
Delivery, composite method of, 371–372; extempore, 369–370; ideal method of, 372; impromptu, 368–369; memorized, 370; methods of, 368–372
Delivery in debate, 414
Democracy, speech in, 4
Demosthenes, 181–182; quoted, 149–150
Denotation, 128–130
Denotation and connotation, differentiated, 130
Denotative meanings, 267
Description, 350–351; accuracy of, 244
Description in definition, 125–126
Descriptive gestures, 45
Desk, reading from, 279
Devil and Daniel Webster, The [324]
Diacritical markings, 106–107
Diagram of Stage, [338]
Diagrams, in definition, 125
Dialect, 7; regional map of, [101]
Dialects, American, 101–102; in broadcasting, 451
Dialect Map of the United States, [101]
Dialogue in dramatization, 322–323
Dickens, Charles, quoted, 96
" Dictated but not read," 499
Dictating letters, 541
Dictation, distinctness in, 499–500; practice in, 501–504
Dictionary, how to use, 104–108; use of, 259; what is the, 103–104

Differences between spoken and written language, sources of, 138–140
Dinosaur, The, quoted, 295–296
Diphthongs, defined, 103
Direct-clash debate, 418–419
Direction, sense of, 540
Directness, in interviews, 480; in oral language, 143
Director's authority, 329
Directors' Meeting, [521]
Discussion, 537–538, 549; classroom, 536; formal, 391–393; forum, 399; panel, 396–398, [397]; public, 391–393; purposes of, 224–225, 393; related to debating, 401; symposium, 398–399; types of, 396–399
Discussion and debate, 395
Distinctness in dictating, 499–500
Distractions in speech, 140
Division, call for, 426; of question, 433
Dostoevski, quoted, 132
Dramatic preparation, 337
Dramatic production, kinds of, 321
Dramatic values, 340
Dramatics, 537; social values in, 319–320
Dramatization, characters in, 322–323; dialogue in, 322, 323; grouping in, 323–324; impersonation in, 322–323; movement in, 323; speech in, 320; stories for, 342–343; values in, 320–321; voice in, 320–321
Dramatizing a story, 321–325
Draper, Ruth, [275]
Dusk on the Roof, quoted, 263–264
Duties, of chairman, 428; of committee members, 430–431; of members, 427–428; of secretary, 429; of treasurer, 429

Ear and eye, 266
Ear and voice, 67
Ear-mindedness, 100
Earning a living, 5
Economic efficiency, 4
Education, four purposes of, 533; goals in, 1–5
Edwards, quoted, 86
Effective English and Business, quoted, 494, 496
Effeminate voice, 67
Egocentric speaking, 179
Egotism in conversation, 201

Elberfeld horses, 34
Election of officers, 424
Electrician, stage, 329
Elemental tones of voice, 79
Elements, basic, 13; importance of, 14
Elements of speech, 6
Elephant's Child, The, quoted, 248
Eliot, T. S., quoted, 126
Elizabeth the Queen, [326]
Emancipation Proclamation, 484
Embarrassment, 37, 39
Emerson, Ralph Waldo, quoted, 482
Emotional speeches, 169
Empathy, 41, 191–193, 535
Emphasis, 76, 260; time changes in, 80; types of, 76
Emphasis and parts of speech, 76
Emphasis and pitch changes, 80
Emphasis through inflection, 76
Emphatic gestures, 44
Encyclopedia, use of, 260
End of lines in reading, 272
Ending a telephone conversation, 462
English in selling, 509
English Journal, quoted, 118–119
Entrances in acting, 336–337
Enunciation, poor, 67
Etiquette, 199–200; in telephoning, 461–466; of debate, 416–417
Etymology in definition, 126
Euphony, 145
Euripides, quoted, 149
Evaluation, in listening, 166
Example in definition, 125
Exercises in broadcasting technique, 452–453
Experience, the basis of listening, 166; the source of style, 133–134
Explanation in definition, 125–126
Explanations in business, 524–525
Exposition, use of eyes and hands in, 226–228; in business, 524–525
Expository business speeches, 524–525
Expository speaking, [226], 524–525, 541
Extempore delivery, 369–370
Extending an invitation by telephone, 463
Extensional meaning, 128–130
Eye and ear, 266
Eye-contact, 44
Eyes, 43; use of, in exposition, 226–228

INDEX 557

Face, 43; lengthening of, 63
Facial expression, 35
Facing Front, [332]
Facing on stage, 335-336
Facing the facts, 394
Factors of voice, 58
Facts, facing the, 394; filtering the, 394; finding the, 393; focusing the, 394; following the, 394-395
Factual meaning, 73
Factual speeches, 169
Fairchild, Richard, 8
False excuses in telephoning, 462
Falsetto quality, 70
Family debate, 402-405
Farewell, speech of, 366
Farm Auction, [511]
Farmer Speaks, A, [546]
Fatigue, vocal, 54
Feeling and meaning, 74
Feet, 44; position of, 39
Ferguson, Adam, quoted, 293
Filtering the facts, 394
Finding the facts, 393
First meeting, call for, 422; conduct of, 422
Fix time of next meeting, 433
Flexibility in voice, 81-82
Floor, obtaining the, 425
Fluency, lack of, 232
Focusing the facts, 394
Folds, vocal, 58
Folk stories, 242
Following the facts, 394-395
Fool's Paradise, The, quoted, 290
Foot position, 39
Football Fans, [188]
Footnote to History, quoted, 293
For the Storyteller, quoted, 245-246
Force, vocal, 23
Formal play production, 325-341
Formality in conversation, 204-205
Forms, social, 199-200
Forums, 399; lecture, 399
Forward tones, 66
Frailey, L. E., quoted, 496
Frank, Glenn, quoted, 385-387
Franklin, Benjamin, quoted, 388-389
Frankness in interviews, 480
Free speech, 390
Freezing, 39
Funk and Wagnalls' pronunciation code, 110-111

Garland, Hamlin, 262
General Psychology, quoted, 190
Generator, vocal, 58
Geographical setting, 260-261
Georgha Da Wash, quoted, 294
Gesture, 41-45; appropriateness in, 42; arms in, 43; defined, 38; eyes in, 43; face, 43; feet in, 44; hands in, 43; head in, 43; instruments of, 43; integration in, 41; legs in, 44; literal, 278; reserve in, 42; shoulders in, 44; types of, 44-45; whole body in, 41
Gestures, awkwardness in, 42; descriptive, 45; emphatic, 44; gracefulness in, 42; on stage, 333-334; suggestive, 45; timing of, 42
Getting and giving meaning, 274
Gettysburg, 20
Gettysburg Address, 496
Ginn, Glenn, quoted, 351
Glottis defined, 58
Goals in education, 1-5
Good and Poor Posture, [230]
Good speech, defined, 20; tests of, 20-24
Good Techniques in Speaking, [37]
Goodwill as a business asset, 526
Goodwill speeches, 526-527, 541
Gracefulness, 42
Grandmother in Court, [277]
Green Pastures Speech, quoted, 362-364
Griffin, R. S., quoted, 351
Griffith, Margaret, quoted, 264
Grouping in dramatization, 323-324
Groupings on stage, 336
Guidance, vocational, 546-547
Guttural quality, 70

Habit, in learning, 46; in perception, 189-190
Habits, 15; routine, 24
Hall and Sturgis, 424
Hallowe'en, quoted, 290-291
Hamilton, Clayton, quoted, 136
Hamlet, 66; quoted, 43, 281, 319
Hand, The Upstage, [334]
Hands, 43; use of, in exposition, 226-228
Hay, John, quoted, 296-298
Hayakawa, S. I., quoted, 147-148
He Knew Lincoln, quoted, 307-311

INDEX

Head, 43
Hearing and voice, 62
Hearing our own voices, 57
Height of actors, 327, [327]
Helping Him Over, [192]
Henry, O., 264, 322
Henshaw, Sarah Edwards, quoted, 78–79
Hips, 40
Historical backgrounds, 261
Hodge, Frank S., quoted, 350
Holding book, 279
Hollowness, 66
Holman, William, 7
Homophones, defined, 116
Hood, Thomas, quoted, 87, 270
Hoover, Herbert, quoted, 353–355
Horatius at the Bridge, quoted, 265
Horses, Elberfeld, 34
How to Influence People, quoted, 195–196
Howes, Raymond F., quoted, 203
Hubbard, Elbert, 183; quoted, 520
Hudson, quoted, 273
Human nature, knowledge of, 199
Human relationships, 2, 548
Hunter and squirrel, 123–124
Huxley, Thomas Henry, quoted, 157–158
Hysteria, 70

I Like Words, quoted, 155–156
"*I Remember*," quoted, 270
Iconoclast, quoted, 153–154
Ideal method of delivery, 372
Illusion in acting, 333
Illustration, 351; in definition, 125
Imagination in storytelling, 239
Impersonation in dramatization, 322–323; in reading, 274–278
Impromptu delivery, 368–369
Inauguration, speech of, 367–368
Incidents in stories, 246
Indirectness, 229–230
Individual differences, 5
Individualism in oral language, 146
Inflection, 58; in emphasis, 76
Informal reading, 279
Informality in selling, 508
Information, calling for, 463
Information-getting interviews, 475–476
Information-giving interviews, 476

Ingersoll, Robert G., quoted, 159, 239–240, 283–284, 292
Instant intelligibility, 139–140
Instruction through storytelling, 239
Instructional Speech, An, [233]
Instructions, clarity in, 476–477
Integration in gesture, 41
Intelligibility, instant, 139–140; in radio speaking, 448
Intensional meaning, 128–130
Interestingness, 23; vocal, 81–82; in conversation, 203; in oral language, 146; in radio speaking, 448; in stories, 246, 249
Interests of others, 201
Interpretation, nature of, 255; purpose of, 255
Interpretation and impersonation, 247–248
Interpreter, function of, 255–256; *The*, [256]
Interview, An, [476]; closing the, 482; defined, 474; planning an, 481–482; preparing for, 478
Interview and letter, 479
Interviews, 540; appointments for, 474–475; types of, 475
Introduction, purposes of, 362; speech of, 364–365; to a speech, 362
Introductions, social, 199–200
Inventory of speech, 13, 25–30
Irrelevant attention, 186–187
Is America Safe, quoted, 350
Isolation, 3
Issues in debate, 404–405

James, William, 123
Jaw, freedom of, 62; looseness of, 62
Jayhawker, quoted, 290–291
Jim Bludso, quoted, 296–297
Job, applying for a, 547
Jody and Flag, quoted, 312–317
Johnson, E. E., quoted, 153
Johnson, Philander C., quoted, 154
Joke, how not to tell, 195–196
Jones, Daniel, 99
Judges of debate, 405–406; function of, 409
Judson, Lyman S., quoted, 353
Jungle Tale, quoted, 497

Kellogg, Elijah, quoted, 90
Key words, 107

INDEX

Keys to the mind, 193
Kipling, Rudyard, 2; quoted, 248
Klitz, Alfred A., quoted, 352-353
Kneeling on Stage, [334]
Knees, 40
Knowing the customer, 508
Knowledge, of article to be sold, 510; of human nature, 199
Knowles, James Sheridan, quoted, 75, 88

La Fontaine's *Fables,* 241
La Motte-Fouqué, quoted, 185
L'Allegro, quoted, 268-269
Lamb, Charles, 202
Language, 14, 534, 548; codes, 17; defined, 119; in conversation, 203; in telephoning, 459; learning of, 16; of stories, 249; spoken and written, differentiated, 141-146; weaknesses in, 8
Language and speech differentiated, 120
Language in Action, quoted, 147-148
Larynx, 61
Laughing Saint of Science, A, quoted, 385-387
Laughter at plays, 336
Lay on table, 433
Laziness, vocal, 62
Leadership, speech in, 4
Learning, conscious, 46
Learning to Speak, 16, [17]
Lecture forums, 399
Legs, 44
Length of stories, 245
Letter, outline for, 493; planning the, 492-493
Letter and interview, 479
Letter to Mrs. Bixby, quoted, 158
Letters and sounds, 97-100
Letters, "C qualities" of, 494; dictation of, 541; person-to-person quality in, 491
Life, success in, 1
Life insurance, sale of, 511-513
Lights on stage, 340
Limit debate, 433
Lincoln, Abraham, 20, 484, 496; quoted, 13, 130, 158, 159, 271
Lincoln-Douglas Debate, [402]
Linebooks, quoted, 287-291
Lines, interpretation of, 340; memorizing of, 328

Listener, good, 201
Listening, 548; evaluation in, 166; in conversation, 168, 201-202; notetaking, 166; selection in, 166; dependence upon experience, 166; to our own voices, 62
Listless Listener, A, [164]
Literature, appreciation of, 535; sounds in, 267; study of, 47; in stories, 243-244
Little Men, 218-221
Little, Richard Henry, quoted, 294
Liveliness, 23, 35
Logic in debate, 413
Long-distance telephoning, 465-466
Longfellow, Henry Wadsworth, 486-490; quoted, 86, 90, 94, 256, 291
Lord Chatham's Eloquence, quoted, 281
Loss of voice, 32
Lowell, James Russell, quoted, 89
Lungs, 61
Lutes, Della T., quoted, 150-151

Macaulay, Thomas Babington, quoted, 265, 281
Majority rule, 421-422
Making a motion, 425-426
Malaprop, Mrs., 498
Manner of speaking and interest, 185
Manners in conversation, 204
Manuscript, reading from, 370-371
Manuscripts Held in Hands, [370]; in broadcasting, 450-451; *on Desk,* [371]
Map of dialect regions, 101
Marginal notes, in letter writing, 492
Marjorie. F. W., quoted, 317-318
Mark Antony at Caesar's Funeral, [144]
Mark Twain, 33, 479; quoted, 17, 136-137
Marsh Morning, quoted, 285
Martini, Frank, 7
Mary Anne's Luncheon, quoted, 287-288
Mastery of body, 31
Material, poor, 229; recording of, 349; for speeches, 348-349
McCarthy and Bergen, [55]
McCarthy, Charlie, 19
Meaning, 534; attitude in, 74; clearness of, 73; connotative, 128-130;

denotative, 128–130; empathy in, 193; extensional, 128–130; factual, 73; feeling in, 74; intensional, 128–130; kinds of, 128–130; of sentences, 71–72; voice determines, 54
Meaning and action, 269
Meaning and pitch, 58
Meaning and vocal variety, 79–80
Meaning and voice, 71–81
Meaning of words, 123–130
Meanings and contexts, 127–128
Meanings and voice, 266
Mearns, Hughes, 257–258
Members, duties of, 427–428
Memorized delivery, 370
Memorizing, 33, 278; cues, 328; lines, 328
Memory in acting, 338
Mental processes, 14
Message to Garcia, A, quoted, 520
Meter versus rhythm, 269–270
Methods of delivery, 368–372
Microphone and reader, 56
Midsummer Night's Dream, A, quoted, 272–273
Milton, John, quoted, 268–269
Mind, keys to the, 193
Mind reading, 34
Minds, meeting of, 3
Minority rights, 421–422
Minstrels, 241
Minutes, secretary's, 429; specimen, 439–440
Mirror, use of, 26, 65; on stage, 340
Mispronunciation in classroom, 231–232
Mispronunciations, common, 111–114
Misunderstanding, risks of, 127
Monosyllables, 105
Monotony, 185–186; vocal, 231
Montana, [259]
Montgomery, Bernard Law, quoted, 18
Mood and pitch, 93
Mood and tone, 81
Moods, 71
Mother Goose, quoted, 269–270
Motion, making a, 425–426; putting a, 426
Motions, classified list of, 431
Motivation, 477
Motley Measures, quoted, 295–296
Mountain Whippoorwill, The, quoted, 302–307

Mouth cavity, 61
Movement, 39–40; defined, 38; forward and backward, 40; how much, 41; kinds of, 40; right or left, 40; sidestepping in, 40; stiffness in, 40; turning, 40
Movement and attention, 39
Movement as punctuation, 39
Movement in dramatization, 323
Muscle reading, 34
Muscles, control of, 32; use of, in visible signals, 34
Muscles and voice, 32
Muscular control, 31
Muscular co-ordination, 34
Musical instruments, 60–61
Musician, 329
Myths, 243

Narration, 350
Nasal quality, 69
Nasal resonance, 63–64
Nasal twang, 63
Nasality, 63–64; negative, 64; positive, 64–65
Naturalness, 36–37; seeming, 36–37; in acting, 333
Negative, first, 404
Negative case, 410–411
Negative nasality, 64
Nervous tension, 70
Nervousness, 38
New England Town Meeting, [392]
New Republic, quoted, 201–202
New Testament, parables of, 498
Newcomer, Ben, quoted, 262–263
Normal quality, 68
Note taking, 166, 171–174
Notes on cards, 372; rules for permanent, 172–174; running, 171–172; taking, 479
Novelty and interest, 184
Noyes, Alfred, quoted, 298–302

O Captain! My Captain, quoted, 270–271
Objection to consideration, 433–434
Obtaining the floor, 425
Occasion for speech, 346–347
Ocean, The, quoted, 268
Officers, election of, 424
On Leaving Wyoming, quoted, 262–263

Open throat, 67
Opening sentence in letter, 493
Optimum pitch, 93-94
Oral and written style, common characteristics of, 130-135; differentiated, 135-138
Oral language, directness in, 143; euphony in, 145; individualism in, 146; interestingness in, 146; repetition in, 143-145; sentence forms in, 143
Oral quality, 69
Oration, voice in, 69
Orations, contest, 368
Order of business, 426-427
Orders of day, 434
Organizing a group, 422-425
Orleans, Ilo, quoted, 153-154
Orotund quality, 68
Others, interests of, 201
Outline for letter, 493
Outlines, logical, 375-380
Outlining, 360-362; tests of, 375-380

Paget, Richard, quoted, 19
Panel discussion, 396-398
Pantomiming, 47
Parables, 498
Paraphrasing, 265
Parliament, defined, 391
Parliamentary law, authorities on, 424; condensed working code of, 432-436; source of, 420-421
Parliamentary procedure, 538; purpose of, 421
Partial tones, 60
Parts of speech and emphasis, 76
Patch and repair case, 411
Patrick Henry's "Call to Arms," [180]
Paul Bunyan, 242
Pausing, 80-81
Pectoral quality, 69
Pellow, Edith, quoted, 497
Perception, 535; attitude in, 190-191; empathy in, 191-193; habit in, 189-190; personality in, 191
Perception and Attention, 187-189
Perkins, 511
Personal appearance, 478, 510
Personal experience, 353-355
Personal interests and attention, 183-184
Personality, appearance in, 31; visible elements of, 31

Personality and perception, 191
Personality and speech, 19
Personality and voice, 53
Person-to-person quality in letters, 491
Phantom Lover, The, quoted, 290
Philosophy of the Race Problem, The, quoted, 351-352
Phrasing, 81, 272
Physical appearance, 31
Pictures, in definition, 125
Pierpont, quoted, 87
Pitch, best, 93-94
Pitch, optimum, 93-94
Pitch and attitude, 93
Pitch and meaning, 58
Pitch and mood, 93
Pitch changes, 58
Pitch changes and emphasis, 80
Pitch of voice in telephoning, 459-460
Placement, voice, 66
Plaint of the Camel, The, quoted, 311-312
Planning an interview, 481-482; the letter, 492-493
Plausibility in stories, 244
Play, choosing the, 325-327; reading the, 327-328; staging the, 338-341
Play production, formal, 325-341; informal, 321-325
Playground speech, 228
Playing Grown-up, [319]
Plays, applause at, 336; laughter at, 336
Plot, plausibility of, 244
Poe, Edgar Allan, quoted, 95
Poetry, reading of, 168; rhythm in, 271
Point of order, 434
Polysyllables, 105-106
Poor Techniques in Speaking, [36]
Poor voices, 63-67
Positive nasality, 64-65
Postpone indefinitely, 434
Postpone to certain time, 434-435
Posture, 38-39; defined, 38; *Good and Poor,* [230]; in reading, 81
Power, 36
Practice, need for, 37
Practice in dictation, 501-504
Precision and style, 135
Preparation, dramatic, 337
Preparing speeches, exercises in, 380-386

Presentation, speech of, 365-366
President, duties of, 428
Presiding officer's right to vote, 428
Previous question, 435
Prince and Pauper, The, 322
Private and public speaking, 522
Privileges of members, 435
Production personnel, 329
Projecting the Voice, [66], 332
Promotional speaking, 522-524
Prompter, 329
Pronunciation, 534, 548; assimilation in, 108; changes in, 104; common errors in, 111-114; defined, 97; ear-mindedness in, 100; exercises to improve, 83-85; Funk and Wagnalls' code, 110-111; importance of, 97; key words in, 107; respelling in, 107-108; strong forms in, 108; syllabication in, 104-106; weak forms in, 108; weaknesses in, 7; Webster's Code, 109-110
Pronunciation in acting, 102
Pronunciation of vowels, 63
Pronunciation on stage, 102
Pronunciations, dictionary, 103-104; different, 100
Properties, 329, 338
Property man, 329
Proposition, affirmative statement of, 407; singleness of, 407; timeliness of, 408; two-sidedness of, 407-408
Propositions, ambiguity in, 410
Propositions for debate, 406-408
Prose, rhythm in, 271
Ptah Hotep, quoted, 2
Public and private speaking, 522
Public speaker's best voice, 69
Public speaking, 537; purpose in, 346
Public speaking in business, 520-527
Public speaking in conferences, 521-522
Pulling, Anne, quoted, 212-214
Punctuation, 260, 272; bodily, 40-41
Purchase, making a, 504-508
Purpose in public speaking, 346
Purposefulness, 20
Putting a motion, 426
Pyramus and Thisbe, quoted, 272-273

Quality, aspirate, 70; falsetto, 70; guttural, 70; nasal, 69; normal, 68; oral, 69; orotund, 68; pectoral, 69; vocal, 61

Radio, 549; effects of, 443
Radio audience, 444; behavior of, 446
Radio Boys Trailing a Voice, The, quoted, 214-216
Radio Drama, [450]
Radio Play, The, [449]
Radio speaking, 538; intelligibility in, 448; interestingness in, 448; why different, 444-451
Radios, number of, 443
Ransom of Red Chief, The, 264, 322
Rate of speech in telephoning, 460
Rating chart, conversation, 222-223; telephoning, 473
Rating scale, 25-30
Rawlings, Marjorie Kinnan, quoted, 159-160, 312-317
Reactions in definition, 126
Reader, service of a, 256
Reader and Listener, [139]
Reader and Microphone, [56]
Reader and speaker, 257
Reader's Digest, quoted, 293
Reading, informal, 279; posture in, 81
Reading and Listening, [140]
Reading from desk, 279
Reading from manuscript, 370-371
Reading from memory, 278-279
Reading from printed page, 278-279
Reading the play, 327-328
Reasonableness in debate, 409
Rebuttal, techniques of, 414-416
Rebuttals, 405
Reconsider, 435
Recording voices, 56-57, 459
References, literary, 264-265
Refutation, pure, 410-411
Rehearsals, play, 328
Relaxation, 38; need for, 67
Repetition in oral language, 143-145
Repetition of stories, 244-245
Reports of committees, 427
Request for information, 435-436
Rescind, 436
Reserve in gesture, 42
Resonance, 59; back, 67; forward, 66; low, 67; mouth and nose, 64; nasal, 63-64; surface, 61
Resonation of vowels, 60
Resonators, vocal, 59
Respelling, 107-108
Response, speech of, 366-367
Rhymes and pronunciations, 98-99

Rhythm in poetry, 271
Rhythm in prose, 271
Rhythm in reading, 168
Rhythm in stories, 248
Rhythm versus meter, 269-270
Richardson, W. L., quoted, 157
Rigidity, 38
Robert, H. H., 424
Rogers, E. A., quoted, 195-196
Roosevelt, F. D., quoted, 362-364
Roosevelt, Theodore, in Action, [33]
Royalty, quoted, 264
Rules, back stage, 330
Rules for telephoning, 461
Rules of order, 424

S, z, and *sh* on radio, 449
St. Nicholas Magazine, 209
Salesman, personal appearance of, 510
Salesmanship, examples of, 511-515
Salutation in debate, 416
Salutation in telephoning, 461-462
Sargent, William, quoted, 257-258
Saturday Evening Post, quoted, 497
Scenes, planning the, 322
Scenes from Shakespeare, 344-345
Scenes in stories, 246, 249
Scott, Sir Walter, quoted, 94
Script writing for radio, 451-452
Sea, Conversation at, [22]
Second Inaugural, quoted, 271
Secretary, duties of, 429; temporary, 422
Selecting a job, speech in, 543-547
Selective listening, 166
Self-criticism, 46
Self-realization, 1, 12, 548
Selling, 541; English in, 509; informality in, 508; successful, 508-511; time in, 509
Selling techniques, examples of, 511-515
Sense and sound, 267-268
Sensitiveness and style, 135
Sentence, meaning of, 71-72; opening in letter, 493; topic, 347-348
Sentence forms, 143
Sentence length, variety in, 143
Sentence structure, 260
Sergent, Nellie B., 262
Setting, geographical, 260-261
"Seven C Qualities" in letters, 494
Shakespeare, 266

Shakespeare, Lecture on, quoted, 239-240
Shakespeare, quoted, 43, 66, 75, 76, 94, 95, 96, 272-273, 281, 318
Shakespeare, scenes from, 344-345
Shell-shock, 32
Shelley, quoted, 19, 96
Sherman, General, quoted, 498
Shoulders, 44
Shrillness, 67
Shurter, E. D., quoted, 145
Shylock, 75
Side-stepping, 40
Sidewalk Conversation, [205]
Signals, visible, 22
Simple Epicure, quoted, 150-151
Simple sentences, need for, 448
Sincerity in conversation, 199
Singleness of proposition, 407
Sizing up customer, 508
Slang, 20
Slouchiness, 38
Smith, S. and Guthrie, E. R., quoted, 190
Social ease, storytelling to develop, 240
Social forms, 199-200; introductions, 199-200; relationships, 548
Socrates, 266
Soft palate, 64-65
Solitary Confinement versus Fellowship, [3]
Son of the Middle Border, A, 262
Song of Hiawatha, The, 241
Sound and sense, 267-268
Sound in literature, 267
Sounds, difficult on radio, 449
Sounds and letters, 97-100
Speaker and reader, 257
Speaker with Microphone, [356]
Speaking, promotional, 522-524; thinking while, 32
Special committees, 427
Special order of business, 433
Speech, free, 390; good, 20-24; occasion for, 346-347; steps in preparing a, 346-364; two sides in, 17
Speech and better living, 550
Speech and language differentiated, 120
Speech and personality, 19
Speech and thinking, 19
Speech in a Mathematics Class, [228]
Speech in business, 549-550

564　INDEX

Speech inventory, 25–30
Speech of farewell, 366
Speech of inauguration, 367–368
Speech of introduction, 364–365
Speech of presentation, 365–366
Speech of response, 366–367
Speech situation, elements of, 179
Speech training, purposes in, 6
Speeches, after-dinner, 368; emotional, 169; exercises in preparation of, 380–386; factual, 169; goodwill, 526–527; kinds of, 169; types of, 364–368
Speeches of courtesy, 364–368
Spelling, 97–100
Spoken and written language differentiated, 141–146
Spoken and written language, sources of differences, 138–140
Spoken language, elements of, 102–103
Squirrel and hunter, 123–124
Stage, balance on, 338–339; crossing on, 335; diagram of, [338]; facing on, 335–336; lights on, 340; mirror on, 340
Stage business, 333
Stage carpenter, 329
Stage crew, 324
Stage diction, 102
Stage electrician, 329
Stage fright, 37–38, 232–233
Stage groupings, 336
Stage manager, 329
Stage whisper, 70
Staging a play, 338–341
Stance, 38
Statement of proposition, 406
Statistics, 352–353
Status quo, defense of, 411
Steamboat, 33
Stenography, 500
Steps in preparing a speech, 346–364
Stevenson, Robert Louis, quoted, 2, 74
Stiffness, 40
Stories, folk, 242; language in, 249; literature in, 243–244; plausibility of, 244; repeating, 244–245; sources of, 248
Stories and attention, 182–183
Stories for dramatization, 342–343
Story, choosing the, 243–248; dramatizing a, 321–325
Story-Reading Time, [238]
Storytelling, 536–537; action in, 246; aims in, 237–240; appropriateness in, 246–247; audience in, 250; final techniques, 250; history of, 241–243; imagination in, 239; instruction through, 239; vocabulary in, 240
Strange Drama, The, quoted, 351
Strong forms, 108
Strong Verbs, quoted, 154
Student Legislators, [430]
Studio audience, 446–447
Stuttering, 32
Style, common characteristics of oral and written, 130–135; oral and written differentiated, 135–138; related to experience, 133–134
Style and precision, 135
Style and sensitiveness, 135
Style and universality, 134–135
Styles, oral and written, 130–146
Subject matter for speeches, 348–349
Substitute motion, 436
Success in life, 1
Successful living, goals in, 1–5; speech in, 1
Suggestive gestures, 45
Summary in debate, 414
Suspension of rules, 436
Swing, Raymond Gram, at the Microphone, [170]
Syllabication, 104–106
Syllable, defined, 104–105
Symbols — Words, quoted, 153
Symposium, the, 398–399
Symposium on vocations, 544–545
Synonyms in definition, 125

Tableaux, stage, 339–340
Take from table, 436
Taking stock of speech, 534
Talking, purposes of, 179
Talking front, 332
Tarbell, Ida M., quoted, 307–311
Taylor, Bert Leston, quoted, 295–296
Teacher Demonstrates, A, [225]
Teacher, function of, 224
Telegrams, telephoning, 466
Telephone, At the, [460]
Telephone, how to hold the, 460; uses of, 457
Telephone conversation, 458
Telephone etiquette, 461–466
Telephone technique, improving, 458–461
Telephones, number of, 455

INDEX

Telephoning, 538; rules for, 461; tests for, 469
Telephoning telegrams, 466
Tempo in acting, 333, 335
Temporary chairman, 422
Temporary secretary, 422
Tennyson, Alfred Lord, quoted, 89-90, 129-271, 318
Tension, 38, 42
Tension and attention, 189
Tests for telephoning, 469
Tests of skill in buying, 507-508
Tests of speech, 25-30
The Audience, [357]
The Bridge, quoted, 285-286
The College Campus, [533]
The Interpreter, [256]
The Problem of Attention, [184]
The Upstage Hand, [334]
Theme, 265
"There Shall Be No Night," [445]
Thinking, 31; a muscular process, 32; efficiency in, 32; weaknesses in, 8
Thinking and speech, 19
Thinking while speaking, 32
Thinness of voice, 67
Thomas E. Dewey Speaks, [447]
Three Kinds of Dogs, [130]
Three Readers, [279]
Throat, open, 67
Ticket takers, 329
Ticket Window, At the, [540]
Time and emphasis, 80
Time limit on radio, 449
Time limits, 482
Time limits in debate, 417
Time limits in selling, 509
Timeliness of proposition, 408
Timing of gestures, 42
Tolstoy, Leo, quoted, 133
Tom Sawyer, 44
Tonality, 65
Tone and mood, 81
"*Tone of Voice*," quoted, 78-79
Tones, musical, 60
Tongue, positions of, 60
Topic sentence, developing, 350; in public speaking, 347-348
Topics, order of, 375-380
Town Meeting of the Air, 398
Training in Conversation, quoted, 203
Transitions, movement in, 40
Transitions on radio, 449-450

Travel in Central and South America, quoted, 212-214
Treasurer, duties of, 429
Trimming the stage, 339
Trojan Women, quoted, 149
Turner, Dorothy, quoted, 212-214
Turning, 40
Two-sidedness of proposition, 407-408
Two-sidedness of speech, 17
Types of gestures, 44-45
Types of interviews, 475
Typing, 500

Ugly Duckling, The, quoted, 245-246
Uncommunicativeness, 229-230
Understudies, 327
Unity, 260; in action, 36; in stage action, 334
Universality, the source of style, 134-135
Unplanned and Planned Shopping, [507]
Untermeyer, Louis, quoted, 282
Use of dictionary, 259
Ushers, 329

Variety, 23
Variety and meaning, 79-80
Variety in sentence length, 143
Variety in vocal force, exercises for, 87-88
Variety in vocal pitch, exercises for, 91-96
Variety in vocal quality, exercises for, 86
Variety in vocal rate, exercises for, 89-91
Variety in voice, 81-82
Variety of voice in radio, 448
Ventriloquist, 55
Verhaeren, Emile, quoted, 96
Vibrator, vocal, 58
Vigor, 36
Vigor and interest, 185
Visibility, 21
Visible action, 13, 548; mirror study of, 26; principles of, 35-38; weaknesses in, 6
Visible action in selling, 510
Visible code in acting, 332-333
Visible signals, 22, 34
Visible signs, absence of, in radio speaking, 444-446

Visible speech, 31
Vision of War, A, quoted, 292
Vocabulary, 534
Vocabulary building, 120-123
Vocabulary in storytelling, 240
Vocal elements in radio, 448
Vocal emphasis, 76
Vocal folds, 58
Vocal force, 23; exercises for variety in, 87-88
Vocal laziness, 62
Vocal pitch, exercises for variety in, 91-96
Vocal quality, exercises for variety in, 86
Vocal rate, exercises for variety in, 89
Vocal variety in radio, 448
Vocational aptitudes, 546
Vocational opportunities, 543-547
Vocations, studying, 543-547; symposium on, 544-545
Voice, 13, 534, 548; best for public speaking, 69; effeminate, 67; elemental tones of, 79; factors of, 58; fatigue of, 54; flexibility in, 81-82; generator of, 58; hearing one's own, 57; importance of, 53; loss of, 32; mechanism of, 54-61; placement of, 66; quality of, 61; recording of, 56-57; resonators of, 59; rules for improving, 62-63; the actor's, 330-32; thin, 67; useful qualities, of, 68-71; variety in, 81-82; vibrator of, 58; volume in telephoning, 459; weak, 230-231; weaknesses in, 7
Voice and action, 337
Voice and attitude, 75
Voice and ear, 67
Voice and hearing, 62
Voice and interestingness, 81-82
Voice and meaning, 54, 71-81, 266
Voice and moods, 71
Voice and muscles, 32
Voice and personality, 53
Voice and Spiritual Education, The, quoted, 266
Voice control, 31
Voice improvement, 63-67
Voice in conversation, 54, 202-203
Voice in selling, 509-510
Voice in storytelling, 246
Voice Qualities, Four, [68]; *Four Other*, [69]

Voice training in dramatics, 320-321
Voices, types of poor, 63-67
Volume of voice in telephoning, 459
Voting, methods of, 426; right of chairman in, 428
Vowel sounds, correct, 62
Vowels, back, 103; defined, 102; front, 102-103; pronunciation of, 63; resonators of, 60
Vowels and consonants, 67

Walking on, 333
Wanderer, The, quoted, 289-290
War and Peace, quoted, 133
Watson, John B., quoted, 19
Weak forms, 108
Weaknesses in language, 8
Weaknesses in pronunciation, 7
Weaknesses in thinking, 8
Weaknesses in visible action, 6
Weaknesses in voice, 7
Weaver, Bennett, quoted, 285-287
Webster's Collegiate Dictionary, quoted, 103-104
Webster's New International Dictionary, quoted, 104
Webster's pronunciation code, 109-110
Wee Little Verse, A, quoted, 317-318
Weeks, Ralph, 6
Weight, distribution of, 39
Whitehead, Harold, 511; quoted, 511-515
Whitman, Walt, quoted, 270-271
Whittier, John Greenleaf, quoted, 95
William Tell, 75
Wilson, Woodrow, 498; quoted, 3, 88
Withdrawal of motion, 436
Wood, James, quoted, 154-155
Word, A, quoted, 154-155
Word, defined, 120
Word, meanings of, 123-130
Word Study, quoted, 152-153
Wordsworth, William, quoted, 95, 159
Workers' Committee Meeting, [483]
Writer and Speaker, [138]
Writing and Speaking, [141]

Yearling, The, quoted, 159-160, 312-317
Yellow Peril, The, quoted, 351
Younger Poets, quoted, 262-264
Your Order Please, quoted, 152-153